Praise for Tom Clavin

"Clavin is one of the most p[...] authors writing about the [...] the story moving forward, [...] historical characters and e[...] read more on the topic after [finishing] the book."

—*True West* on *Follow Me to Hell*

"Clavin knows Western history. . . . He tells a good story."

—*Library Journal* on *Follow Me to Hell*

"*Lightning Down* has an overarching positivity and celebration of resilience."

—Associated Press

"*Lightning Down* is a wonderful testament to the human spirit, an incredible story of courage and resilience. Don't miss this nail-biter from a true master, Tom Clavin."

—Alex Kershaw, *New York Times* bestselling author of *Against All Odds*

"Clavin's latest, like his other histories, reads like a novel and it will keep readers turning the pages. . . . This is an engaging and captivating story capturing the courage and strength of humanity under extreme conditions. Highly recommended."

—*Library Journal* (starred review) on *Lightning Down*

"A heartrending tale of human endurance."

—*Booklist* on *Lightning Down*

"Breezy narrative style . . . fascinating lore."

—NPR on *Tombstone*

"With a former newsman's nose for the truth, Clavin has sifted the facts, myths, and lies to produce what might be as accurate an account as we will ever get of the Old West's most famous feud."

—Associated Press on *Tombstone*

"Rootin'-tootin' history . . . Updating the old notion that the Earp myth is the American *Iliad*, the author is at his best when he delineates those fraught spasms of violence. Buffs of the Old West will enjoy Clavin's careful research and vivid writing."

—*Kirkus Reviews* on *Tombstone*

"*Tombstone* is written in a distinctly American voice."

—T. J. Stiles, *The New York Times*

"Clavin tacks up the truth like wanted posters in every chapter." —*The New York Times Book Review* on *Wild Bill*

"A vigorous yarn . . . Clavin writes fluently and often entertainingly of a man shrouded in legend while being all too human." —*Kirkus Reviews* on *Wild Bill*

"Well written, full of vivid characters, and detailed. Fans of the Old West and the HBO show *Deadwood* will appreciate the wild ride." —*Booklist* on *Wild Bill*

"Rollicking . . . an entertaining tale of the man and the legend."
—*Publishers Weekly* on *Wild Bill*

"Absorbing . . . fun and revealing."
—*The Wall Street Journal* on *Dodge City*

"*Dodge City* cuts through popular mythology and offers both clarity and fine entertainment—in other words, it's a book that anyone interested in Western history needs to read."
—Jeff Guinn, *New York Times* bestselling author of *The Last Gunfight*

"An extraordinary account of the iconic Wild West town of Dodge City, KS . . . Clavin brings true personality to a severe Earp and the affable but steady-nerved Masterson during their roles in taming the wildest excesses of the Western frontier."
—*Library Journal* on *Dodge City*

"Tom Clavin has produced a sharp picture of the brief but vivid culture of the nineteenth-century cattle towns."
—Larry McMurtry, bestselling author of *Lonesome Dove* and *Comanche Moon* on *Dodge City*

Praise for the work of Tom Clavin and Bob Drury

"Drury and Clavin are to be commended for resurrecting with delicate poignancy the travails of men of the 2nd Ranger Battalion. . . . With its muscular prose and expert storytelling, *The Last Hill* deserves to stand beside Stephen Ambrose's *Band of Brothers* as one of the truly epic—and intimate—accounts of American heroism and sacrifice in World War II."   —*The Wall Street Journal*

"In this exhaustive history . . . Drury and Clavin pack the narrative with biographical details about the Rangers and skillfully toggle between battle scenes and big-picture analysis. WWII buffs will savor this deep dive."

—*Publishers Weekly* on *The Last Hill*

"For anyone who loves the adventurous side of American history, *Blood and Treasure* is a gem. It's full of action, thorough, and wide. Seek out this treasure and you won't be disappointed."

—Terri Schlichenmeyer, *Wyoming Tribune Eagle*

"Bob Drury and Tom Clavin challenge conventional wisdom about an American origin story and, in the process, weave a tale fit for the big screen."

—*The Washington Free Beacon* on *Blood and Treasure*

"Bob Drury and Tom Clavin together have given us a half dozen elegantly written narratives of exhilarating episodes in American history. [*Blood and Treasure*] may be the authors' finest work to date. Redolent of time and place, a raw and rugged tale."   —*The Wall Street Journal*

"Popular historians Drury and Clavin deliver a ripsnortin' tale of the early frontier and its first and most power-

ful legend. [*Blood and Treasure*] offers a vivid account of Boone's frontier years, one that may not be for the faint of heart."
—*Kirkus Reviews*

"Masterfully researched saga."
—*The Virginia Gazette* on *Blood and Treasure*

"*Blood and Treasure* tells the Boone story through the prism of the larger struggle for the frontier. It is a substantial and lively book by an accomplished history-writing duo."
—*National Review*

FOLLOW ME

TO

HELL

McNELLY'S
TEXAS RANGERS

AND THE RISE OF FRONTIER JUSTICE

TOM CLAVIN

ST. MARTIN'S GRIFFIN
NEW YORK

Published in the United States by St. Martin's Griffin, an imprint of St. Martin's
Publishing Group

www.stmartins.com

Title page fire filigree art © Igor Normann/Shutterstock.com

Frontispiece: Texas Rangers Gun Fight © Yogi Black/Alamy; Map of Texas (1863) ©
Niday Picture Library/Alamy

The Library of Congress has cataloged the hardcover edition as follows:

Names: Clavin, Tom, 1954– author.
Title: Follow me to hell : McNelly's Texas Rangers and the rise of frontier
   justice / Tom Clavin.
Description: First edition. | New York : St. Martin's Press, 2023. |
   Includes bibliographical references and index.
Identifiers: LCCN 2022051600 | ISBN 9781250214553 (hardcover) |
   ISBN 9781250214560 (ebook)
Subjects: LCSH: McNelly, Leander H., 1843 or 1844–1877. | Texas Rangers. |
   Police, State—Texas—Biography. | Frontier and pioneer life—Texas. | Texas—
   History—1846–1950.
Classification: LCC F391 .C624 2023 | DDC 363.209764—dc23/eng/20221214
LC record available at https://lccn.loc.gov/2022051600

ISBN 978-1-250-21457-7 (trade paperback)

First St. Martin's Griffin Edition: 2024

10 9 8 7 6 5 4 3 2

In memory of my son,
Brendan Clavin

CONTENTS

CONTENTS

ACT II: LONE STAR LAWMAN

ACT III: THEIR BACKS TO THE RIVER

Yellville
Huntsville
Athens
Smithville
N T E R.
Lebanon
Batesville
Clinton
North Fork
Ozark
Clarks-ville
Elizabeth
Bolivar
Van Buren
Dover
NOLES
Fort Gibson
FORT SMITH
ARKANSAS
Booneville
Danville
Waldron
Canadian River
Ouachita
Tarrant
Caddo L.
Jordan
Ft. Worth
Kaufman
Dallas
Buffalo
Port Caddo
SHREVEPORT
Marshall
Tyler
Mansfield
Henderson
Logansport
Fort Graham
Palestine
Rusk
Shelby
Nacogdoches
NATCHITOCHES
San Augustine
Springfield
Bucksport
Marion
Milam
Alabama
Burkville
Franklin
Wheelock
Booneville
Huntsville
Caldwell
Anderson
Washington
Montgomery
Bastrop
Belleville
Liberty
La Grange
Lynchburg
S. Felipe
Gonzales
Richmond
Cuero
Wharton
Columbia
Victoria
Brazoria
Texana
Lavacca
La Salle
G. OF M
Isla del Padre
Pt. Isabel
Brazos Santiago
19
15
Caldwell
Columbia
Harrisonburg
Monroe
Overton
Bellevue
Marksville
Providence
Princeton
Port Gibson
Raymond
NATCHEZ
Meadville
Washington
Woodville
Liberty
Clinton
Franklin
BATON ROUGE
NEW ORLEANS
Houma
Livingston
Carrollton
Greenville
O

AUTHOR'S NOTE

Some readers may be aware that I am the author or coauthor of a whole wagon train of books that are inhabited by a wide array of wonderful real-life characters. But writing about Leander McNelly was a special challenge. Let me amend that: Writing about the Texas Rangers was a special challenge and then there was McNelly on top of that.

This book is not intended to be a history of the Texas Rangers. However, to set the stage for the adventures of McNelly's Rangers in the mid-1870s, it seemed that including as much history of the Rangers as readers would tolerate was necessary. What made this additionally challenging was that one can consult, say, three sources of information on the Texas Rangers and be presented with three different versions of the same event. Just one example is the Texian-Karankawa fight at Skull Creek, which is said to have involved anywhere from eleven to twenty-five Texians and to have taken place in late 1822 or February 1823.

Such contradictions, I have often found, can be attributed to accounts provided by not the most reliable eyewitnesses on the frontier, whether that frontier is Kentucky, Kansas, Arizona, or Texas. But in the specific case of the Texas Rangers, many tales both tall and small have been spun during the last two centuries by a variety of tellers, and some previous writers have cherry-picked the most . . . let's say, useful ones. Some researchers and writers have made valiant efforts to separate facts—as best they could be determined—from fiction, and those are the sources I have tried to pay the most attention to.

Because this book is not necessarily a history of the Texas Rangers, not all events and participants leading up to the 1870s have been included. Using my judgment, for better or worse, I have presented an overview of the main events that had an impact on southeast Texas before the Civil War.

And then there is Leander McNelly. He is one of the more revered figures in the Texas Rangers' history. However, not only was he captain of a company for less than three years but also the men he commanded were not technically Rangers but members of the Washington County Volunteer Militia. And at least four of them wrote about their experiences, with each account differing significantly from the others. These discrepancies do not diminish the achievements of "McNelly's Rangers," but they do indicate that trying to write a true story about them can seem like a Sisyphean task.

But it was one worth undertaking. I am not contending that McNelly was the greatest of all Ranger captains. Very strong arguments have been made on behalf of John Coffee Hays, John "Rip" Ford, and John B. Jones, among others. But many Texas Rangers historians will agree that Leander McNelly was a transitional figure. He represented both the "old" Ranger ways and the new Rangers that evolved into the modern police force of today. McNelly was, without question, the most effective Ranger captain of the mid-1870s when this transition began. As Frederick Wilkins points out in his indispensable *The Law Comes to Texas*: "The Rangers of the 1870s and following decades were little changed from the men of the 1840s and 1850s. . . . In one basic improvement, for the first time a Ranger force was permanently established. This prospect of permanency corrected a defect in all of the earlier Ranger units; an experienced cadre of Rangers was maintained in service." Frontier justice had arrived.

One might think that McNelly, given his stature in the Texas Rangers' history, was a formidable figure whose very presence caused evildoers to surrender. This was not true physically: He was barely five foot five and 125 pounds, dressed almost like a dandy—brush jacket, duck pants, calfskin leggings, sometimes a beaver hat—and wore his long beard neatly trimmed. However, his men—occasionally referred to as "Little McNellys" in newspaper accounts—followed him because of the force of his personality, devotion to law and order (as he saw it), and undeniable courage. He was indeed one of a kind.

One more note about *Follow Me to Hell*: "Indian" was in common usage during the decades that I am writing about, but it is not nearly as common today. To this author, the word "Indian" is not by itself derogatory when used as a definition of America's aboriginal inhabitants. Still, I have endeavored to use as often as possible persons' names and/or tribal affiliations to keep usage of "Indian" to a minimum.

Okay, now that we got that out of the way, let's pretend we've gathered around the campfire and a tale of legendary people—especially Leander McNelly—is about to be told.

PROLOGUE

It was a bright, unusually mild late-autumn morning when the men known as McNelly's Rangers rode away from Richard King's ranch on fresh horses and, for those who needed them, new saddles. At a brisk pace, the riders searched for the vigilantes and bandits who had terrorized the Nueces Strip.

Their captain was Leander McNelly. Most descriptions of him echo that of Doug Swanson in his book *Cult of Glory*: "[He] was short, gaunt, thin of voice, and racked by tuberculosis. To a newspaper correspondent of his day, he appeared as 'the very reverse of robust.' One of his own men—an ardent admirer—described him as 'sick and puny . . . a little runt of a feller.' At the peak of his career, he was sometimes so weak he could barely stand."

But his company of Rangers would obey his every word and display as much bravery in action as he did. Now, in

November 1875, they were undertaking their most dangerous mission yet. To enforce the law, they might have to go south of the Rio Grande . . . even if an invasion of Mexico triggered a war.

As they neared the border, McNelly told his men to stop and rest—and double-check their pistols, rifles, and ammunition while they were at it. They did so, then drank from their canteens, mopped their weather-beaten faces, and readied themselves for arriving at the river.

Once the Rangers were rested enough and prepared to get on their new mounts, their captain addressed them: "Boys," McNelly began, "I may lead you into hell, but I'll get you out if you do exactly as I tell you to do. I'll never send you into a battle, I'll lead you. All I ask any man to do is follow me."

The forty men climbed up onto their saddles, formed a phalanx behind their captain, and headed south. Once in sight of the Rio Grande and the inhospitable terrain beyond, many of McNelly's Rangers wondered if this was only their first view of hell, and they inched their horses closer to the captain.

—— ACT I ——

COLONISTS
AND CAPTAINS

No man in the wrong can stand up against a fellow that's in the right and keeps on a-comin'.

—Ranger Captain Bill McDonald

CHAPTER I

"TEXIAN DEVILS!"

It is generally agreed that Stephen Austin created the Texas Rangers with a few strokes of his quill pen in August 1823. In this call to arms, he did indeed use the word "rangers," but before this missive there already were "rangers" in Texas. It would take two years before Austin's group were called the Texas Rangers.

When Anglo settlers first arrived in 1821 and began to put roots down in the fertile soil of the eastern section of Spanish Texas, the most serious threat they faced was the tribe known as the Karankawas. There were close to two thousand members of the tribe spread out between Galveston Bay and Corpus Christi Bay. They had a fearsome reputation—purportedly, they practiced cannibalism with captured and killed enemies—and an appearance few white men had encountered before. The Karankawa men were tall and muscular. During the summer they wore deerskin breechcloths or nothing at all, and in winter they donned buffalo and deer robes. Their bodies were painted and tattooed and pierced with small pieces of cane. They often smeared themselves with a mixture of mud and alligator or shark grease to ward off mosquitoes. The women also painted and tattooed their bodies and wore knee-length skirts of animal skin.

Anglo settlers suddenly appearing with ambitions to establish ranches and farms on traditional hunting grounds were not greeted warmly by the Karankawa. Immediately, there was conflict. One incident resulted in the death of two Anglos—or "Texians," as they began to be called. They were attacked and killed as they were transporting corn on a raft up the Colorado River.[1] Robert Kuykendall, a Kentuckian who was one of the original Anglo settlers, called upon two dozen other colonists to join him in a revenge ride. They knew the Karankawa had a camp on a tributary of the Colorado River known as Skull Creek, and that was where they rode.

The Karankawa were indeed there. The colonists stealthily approached, and after a quiet preparation of weapons, they attacked. Caught completely by surprise, the tribe's men, women, and children tried to flee. Many could not outrun the Texan long rifles. When the firing stopped, there were between nineteen and twenty-three Karankawa bodies left behind. This battle would turn out to be the first of many

---

1 The Karankawa contended that the two men—some accounts say three—were making off with stolen corn, but that point of view did not gain any traction among the colonists.

between Texans and the native inhabitants during the next six decades.

Having been so successful in their first foray, Kuykendall and another colonist leader, John Jackson Tumlinson, thought it a good idea to have a sort of militia always ready for future provocations. The Mexican government approved, and 1823 saw the establishment of a ten-man unit, to be led by Moses Morrison, who had served in the U.S. Army. They were not technically Rangers but pretty much served as such until Stephen Austin gave them a name. Their original purpose would expand to include battling interloping Mexicans, cattle rustlers, and others lumped together as bandits or "border ruffians." Many Mexicans soon came to calling them *Los diablos tejanos!*— "Texian devils!"

In August 1823, Stephen Austin resided at the colony he had established on the Colorado River in Spanish Texas. The colony contained a coastal prairie good for grazing and farming. He noted in his diary, "The country is the most beautiful & desirable to live in I ever saw."

But looking past the beauty, Austin could clearly see the dangers. He was becoming increasingly alarmed because, as he wrote to local authorities, "The roads are full of errant thieves united with Indians." With Mexican authorities apparently helpless to protect their own citizens, let alone the newcomer American settlers, Austin took matters into his own hands. He wrote and issued a plea for men with their own horses and guns to gather as a sort of militia. Austin vowed to pay fifteen dollars a month to each man. However, because he was strapped for cash, his offer really was that each month a volunteer would earn fifteen dollars' worth of land. At the time, the only thing Stephen Austin had a lot of, in addition to trouble, was land.

Most significant about this call to arms was Austin's writing that men were being sought "to act as rangers for the common defence." By 1823 in North America, a militia was a well-known entity. But for the first time in a Texas document the word "rangers" was used. To this day, it is one of the most familiar words associated with Texas.

CHAPTER 2

LUCKLESS LIBERATORS

One reason for the military impotence of Mexico on its northern border was that it had only recently wrested itself free from Spain and had plenty of political and financial housekeeping to do. Mexico had to worry much more about repelling an invasion by a spurned Spain than the safety of Texians.

Spain had not immediately joined France early in 1778 to enter the Revolutionary War on the side of the Americans. It was not quite as strong militarily as France and took more seriously than its neighbor the possible consequences of supporting insurgents against a monarch. Eventually, though, Spain provided some significant assistance to the rebelling Anglo colonists, much of it thanks to Bernardo de Gálvez.

The governor of Louisiana, barely in his thirties, eagerly embraced Spain's somewhat reluctant decision in June 1779 to recognize the United States as an independent nation. Gálvez used his soldiers to thwart British attempts to close the Mississippi River, which allowed for transported goods and raw materials to eventually find their way to the colonies along the East Coast, with some of its ports having been blockaded by the British. And Gálvez led a campaign east that threw the British out of West Florida, a satisfying revenge for the British having taken Florida from Spain two decades earlier.

But the biggest benefit Gálvez had for Texas was the creation of the cattle drive. To feed his troops as they pushed disheartened redcoats back from Baton Rouge to Natchez to Mobile, and on to Pensacola, Gálvez purchased two thousand head from ranchers in the San Antonio area who had vaqueros drive them north and east. The cattle drives continued until hostilities against the British ended in 1782. The effectiveness of these dusty treks demonstrated that ranching in Texas and moving thousands of tons of beef to available markets could work.

Suddenly, there was a rush of Spanish Mexicans wanting to become ranchers. The government made it easier to do so by granting a square league (4,428 acres) to every man who paid a fee and intended to raise stock. In the San Antonio region especially, that stock was cattle. With so much grazing land available for each owner and farming a more risky and low-return enterprise, after the war ranching looked like the way to prosper, and many men did.

Governor Gálvez, though only age forty, died in November 1786 and thus did not live to possibly regret the help he had given to the American cause. With the United States growing in productivity and confidence by leaps and bounds, Spanish authorities in Mexico began to wonder how expansionist the former colonists would become. The nascent nation's economy soon outpaced that of the New Spain territory, becoming twice as productive by 1800.

The population trend looked rather worrisome too. In 1790 the U.S. population was 3.7 million and that of Mexico was 4.8 million. But half of Mexico's population was composed of Indians who, unlike the Americans, were dwindling in numbers and did not contribute much to the economy. Inevitably, as the number of Americans grew, they would be spreading out to new territories, which included west and south of the Mississippi River.

The Spanish authorities were right to be nervous about northern intruders. A warning of what was to come for Mexico can be found in the brief but mercurial career of Philip Nolan.

He had been born in Belfast, Ireland, in 1771. By the late 1780s, the teenager was in New Orleans as a bookkeeper for the trader James Wilkinson, who did much of his business with Spanish merchants and lawmakers. Having learned to speak Spanish fluently by twenty, Nolan secured a trading passport from the Spanish governor of Louisiana and set out to trade with the Indian tribes across the Mississippi River. Nolan either overlooked or ignored that the passport was void in Spanish Texas, and soon his goods were confiscated by Spanish authorities. Before returning to New Orleans, he lived with the Indians for two years.

Thanks to trading with them, Nolan had at least fifty wild horses with him when he got back.

He made a second trip to Texas in 1794, with another passport from the Louisiana governor. He made acquaintance with Spanish Texas governor Manuel Muñoz and the commandant general of the Provincias Internas, Pedro de Nava. Though this offered more promise, Nolan was sent packing again, but this time he had two hundred and fifty horses trailing behind him.

Three years later, in the summer of 1797, Nolan left for Spanish Texas with a wagon train of trade goods, which he successfully brought to San Antonio, where he tried to insinuate himself in local society. He was instead given a one-way ticket out of Texas. Nolan arrived in Natchez with several hundred more horses.

He should have quit to enjoy the proceeds from selling the horses, especially after he was unable to obtain any more passports. Instead, Nolan persuaded some thirty frontiersmen to accompany him to Spanish Texas, where they would seize riches and land and create a kingdom for themselves. The expedition crossed the border in October 1800 and headed north of Nacogdoches to capture wild mustangs. The Spanish soon heard of their activities and created their own expedition.

The following March, a Spanish force of one hundred and twenty men left Nacogdoches. They encountered Nolan and his followers just upstream from where the current Nolan River flows into the larger Brazos River. Several of the Americans surrendered immediately to the Spaniards.

Nolan did not and was killed. His ears were cut off as evidence for the authorities back in Mexico City that he was dead.[2]

Even after Nolan was dead some of his followers continued to fight until they were promised safe passage to return to Louisiana. First, however, they were taken into Mexico, where authorities decreed one of the men must die for their resistance. After die were cast, the unlucky Ephraim Blackburn was hanged. The others were not sent to Louisiana but spent several years being rotated among several Mexican prisons.

The political landscape changed in 1803 with the Louisiana Purchase. President Thomas Jefferson's ambitious acquisition of 820,000 square miles meant even more far-ranging explorations. Texas was not part of that transaction, but that was only fine print to hunters, farmers, and others looking to hike and ride toward new horizons. In addition, a few Spanish authorities had the idea of encouraging Indian tribes to move south to Texas. They could roam freely to hunt, and their presence would deter white American adventurers. How long this might work became moot when Mexico began to catch the revolution fever. It had begun back in the homeland.

Because it really could not effectively do otherwise, Spain

---

2 It was unclear what happened to the rest of the Irishman's body. However, in 1949 Rev. Rhea Kuykendall (a descendant of Robert Kuykendall) and Joseph Pierce (who had settled on the "Dixon Grant" along Mustang Creek) found a flat, weathered stone, upon which was crudely carved "Sacred to the Memory of Nolan."

had gone along with Napoleon's quest to become the ruler of Europe. But in 1808, he determined that cooperation was not nearly as enjoyable as conquest and attacked Spain. It was not long before Charles IV and his son Ferdinand VII were removed from their thrones and replaced by Joseph Bonaparte, Napoleon's older brother. The subsequent war of resistance in Spain caused ripples in Mexico, where many of the political leaders, and those who wanted to be, were not fighting French occupiers but each other. In the process, they moved away from Spanish supervision altogether.

One would-be ruler of an independent Mexico was Miguel Hidalgo y Costilla. His defeat and execution in the summer of 1811 by forces loyal to Spain was one of several attempts to liberate Mexico. Another revolutionary leader was Juan Bautista de las Casas, whose demise that same year was more gruesome—he was shot, decapitated, and, as a warning to other rebels, his head was put on display in a plaza in San Antonio.

Such grisly conclusions to revolutionary efforts did not end the fighting among various factions. And what had spilled over into Mexico splashed on Spanish Texas too. A blacksmith with bigger ambitions than shoeing horses, Bernardo Gutiérrez de Lara believed he could succeed where others had failed. Displaying plenty of hubris, he traveled to Washington, D.C., and was not only granted a meeting with James Monroe but also encouraged by the secretary of state to stir things up back home.

This Gutiérrez did, recruiting an army that, on March 28, 1813, defeated royalist forces at the Battle of Salado. Four days later, Gutiérrez arrived in San Antonio and declared himself the head of a new government. And to be on the safe side, he had the dozen or so leaders of the army he defeated brought back to Salado Creek, where they were hacked to death. On April 6 Gutiérrez proclaimed Texas independent.

By August, Gutiérrez had vacated his command and was gone, and more fighting ensued.[3] Because of the dizzying array of leaders and atrocities committed by loyalists and insurgents, plus the deaths of a few Americans who had rashly fought for independence, the U.S. government washed its hands of Texas. Best to ignore it, especially given that there were millions of acres to the north to be explored, tamed, and settled once the native inhabitants were brushed aside.

To make things official, the secretary of state in the new Monroe administration, John Quincy Adams, and Luis de Onís, Spain's minister to the United States, negotiated a treaty in 1819 that ceded Florida to the United States and defined the Red and Sabine Rivers as the boundary between the United States and New Spain, which included Texas. That should calm things down, at least as far as American ambitions were concerned.

---

3 By living a quiet and unrevolutionary life, Gutiérrez de Lara escaped the stomach-churning deaths of other rebellious leaders, not passing away until May 1841, three months before his sixty-seventh birthday.

CHAPTER 3

THE LONG REPUBLIC

Hopes for a peaceful period during which Americans minded their own business were dashed by James Long. The Adams-Onís Treaty quickly proved unpopular with men outside Texas who were eager to do business and otherwise settle inside the territory.

One of them was the twenty-six-year-old Long. Born in Culpeper County, Virginia, he had become a U.S. Army surgeon and saw action at the end of the War of 1812 in the Battle of New Orleans. Afterward, he had settled in Natchez. Because of his army and combat experience, Long was voted to command an expedition that had the highfalutin goal of conquering Spanish Texas.

Among the two-hundred-man invasion force serving under Long that gathered in Natchez were José Félix Trespalacios, a Mexican who had escaped imprisonment for fomenting rebellion against Spanish rule in Mexico, and a twenty-three-year-old Jim Bowie, originally from Kentucky. Long also attempted to recruit the French pirate Jean Lafitte and his men, but Lafitte turned him down, having too much to do trying to hold on to the colony he had established at Galveston.[4] Several of Long's recruits were former French soldiers who had founded and quickly abandoned a settlement in Texas known as the Champ d'Asile in 1818 and were ready to try again.

By June, the Long expedition had arrived in Texas and captured Nacogdoches. Long was proclaimed the first president of the new "Republic of Texas," also called the "Long Republic." Despite this initial success, the surgeon-warrior's independent republic lasted just four months. His army eventually grew restless, and many men returned to the United States.

A Spanish force routed Long and his remaining nation builders in October. The deposed president escaped to Natchitoches, where he began raising money to equip a second expedition. He joined survivors of the first one on the Bolivar Peninsula in April 1820, confidently (or foolishly) bringing his pregnant wife, Jane, and three hundred troops. Though Long restored elements of the former government, the expedition stalled for more than a year as men deserted and were not replaced. On October 4, 1821,

---

4 In May 1821, Lafitte and his band of brigands, at the urging of the U.S. government, finally left the Galveston colony. They took immense amounts of treasure with them, and the forty-year-old Lafitte was accompanied by his young bride of a year, their infant son, and his biracial mistress.

Long and his troops seized Presidio La Bahía, but four days later Spanish troops forced them to surrender.

Surprisingly, given how exasperated Spanish authorities had become with American interlopers, James Long was not immediately executed. He was imprisoned for a time in San Antonio and across the border in Monterrey. In March 1822, he was transported to Mexico City to plead his case before the Mexican president at the time, Agustín de Iturbide. Alas, this was, at last, the end of Long, who was shot and killed by a guard on April 8. It is believed that the former ally Trespalacios, who conveniently had been freed, had bribed the guard to kill Long.[5]

The failure of the Long expedition might have demonstrated that white Americans could not successfully establish enclaves in Texas. But during this time the Spanish authorities had a much bigger worry—losing their colony altogether. Back in the home country, Ferdinand VII had become king after Napoleon had been defeated. His attempts to rule with an iron fist were resisted, enough so that in 1820 he was forced to acquiesce to a more liberal constitutional monarchy. An attempt to create a similar form of government in Mexico independent of Spain was successful.

Mexico's political fragility encouraged people of varying backgrounds who had found their way to Texas in less sensational ways than armed expeditions to change the

---

5 When her daughter, Mary, was born, Jane Long erroneously claimed this was the first child born in Texas of English descent. After her husband's death, Jane left Texas but later returned and stayed as a colonist.

complexion of the territory. As Randolph Campbell points out in his history *Gone to Texas,* "By the early 1820s the lure of Texas had brought a truly diverse population to its eastern woodlands. The Nacogdoches area had Hispanic ranchers and farmers, and the town proper had merchants of varied national origins. Anglo-Americans lived in small settlements and on isolated farms scattered from the Red River southward to the Neches. Finally, Indians, particularly the Alabamas, Coushattas, Caddos, Cherokees, Delawares, Shawnees, and Kickapoos, likely outnumbered settlers of European origin."

And then there was the man who would become the most prominent early American settler of Mexican Texas. By the time Mexico was establishing its independence, Stephen Austin's journey had begun.

CHAPTER 4

A CONNECTICUT YANKEE

Actually, the journey that would change Texas history had begun with the aptly named Moses Austin and his quest for a promised land. To understand Stephen, the man who some called the "Father of Texas," one should know about the father of the Father of Texas . . . who was a New Englander.

Moses was born to Elias and Eunice Phelps Austin in Durham, Connecticut, on October 4, 1761, representing the fifth generation of Austins in America. At twenty-one, Moses chose not to follow his father as a tailor, farmer, and tavern keeper and instead to enter the dry goods business in Middletown, also in Connecticut. Very soon, though, he moved to Philadelphia to join his brother, Stephen, who was in a similar occupation. There Moses met and married Mary Brown. The couple had five children, three of whom lived to maturity: Stephen, Emily, and James Elijah.

With entrepreneurial zeal, he moved to Richmond, Virginia, and established Moses Austin and Company. In 1789, he secured a contract to roof the new Virginia capitol building in lead. That the state promised to pay 5 percent above market price if the contractor used Virginia lead was a tip-off for Moses: He and his brother lost no time gaining control of Virginia's richest lead deposit and founded Austinville in Wythe County. They brought experienced miners and smelters from England. The brothers' expertise and energetic leadership went a long way toward establishing the American lead industry.

However, when they encountered problems in financing their enterprise, Moses looked to the rumored lead deposits in Spanish Upper Louisiana for relief. After visiting the mines there, he obtained a grant to partner in a mine in what is now Potosi, Missouri, and in 1798, he established an Anglo-American settlement there, west of the Mississippi River.

Imbued with the New England Calvinist belief that to those most able to manage assets should go the lion's share of them, Moses aggressively expanded his holdings. Using the efficient reverberatory furnace, he gained control of virtually all smelting in the region and amassed a bank account of $190,000, the equivalent then of being a multi-millionaire today.

In the frontier settlement, Moses constructed, in the style of a southern mansion, an imposing home that he called Durham Hall. Offering gracious hospitality was helpful in winning the friendship of men in prominent positions. The governor of the territory, the future president William

Henry Harrison, appointed Moses a justice on the Court of Common Pleas and Quarter Sessions for the Ste. Genevieve District. Moses joined others seeking to increase the money supply in circulation by founding the Bank of St. Louis. However, when it failed in 1819, the consequences for Austin's finances were severe.

With creditors beginning to hound him, Moses concocted a plan to create an American colony in Spanish Texas. Unlike the rather impetuous Nolan and Long, Moses was smart enough to realize an invasion was not the best way to go about it. In December 1820, accompanied by a slave named Richmond, Moses traveled to San Antonio to seek permission to bring colonists in. But the request was rejected by Governor Antonio María Martínez, who, like many other officials in Mexico, was smarting over the recent intrusions by Anglos, who were viewed as little more than vigilantes—or worse, usurpers. Martínez not only told his visitor no but also told him to get out.

Disappointed, and apparently with no plan B, Moses was disconsolately walking across Military Plaza when he happened to encounter the Baron de Bastrop. For the future of Texas, this would turn out to be a fortuitous chance meeting.

The real name of the "baron" was Philip Hendrik Nering Bögel, and he was born on November 23, 1759, in Suriname. Five years later, his parents and their children moved to the Netherlands, where, when he was old enough, Philip joined the cavalry. However, instead of continuing a military career, at twenty-two, he married Lady Georgine Wolffeline Françoise Lijcklama à Nyeholt in Oldeboorn Friesland, and they settled in Leeuwarden. Life was good for the charming young fellow—he had a noblewoman for a wife, was blessed with five children, and held a comfortable position as a tax collector.

That secure existence crumbled in 1793, when Philip was accused of using some of those taxes he collected for personal gain. He escaped arrest—bringing his stunned wife and children along—and the province put a reward of one thousand ducats on his head. The runaway family made their way to Hamburg, where Philip assumed the identity of the Baron de Bastrop, and they booked passage on a ship to Philadelphia. They found a place to live in Frederick County, Maryland, but after a few years of not adapting to uncouth American ways, Bastrop's wife and children returned to the Netherlands.

Where was a good place to start over? Texas, of course. After ventures in Louisiana that had him swaying between riches and poverty, the self-titled Baron de Bastrop was in San Antonio in 1806, introducing himself as having fled his home country because of its invasion by Napoleon's French forces. People believed his accounts of noble origins and enjoyed his charismatic cosmopolitan ways, offering him opportunities to participate in various ventures. He took advantage of them, but grand living led to empty pockets once more. Undaunted, Bastrop received permission to establish a colony near the Trinity River. It took root, and four years later he was appointed second alcalde (mayor or chief judicial official) of the colony.

It was in this capacity in December 1820 that Bastrop was in Mexico City. Serendipitously, he and Moses Austin had met years earlier while sharing the hospitality of a roadhouse in then Spanish Missouri. After Bastrop heard the enthusiasm with which Moses spoke of his own colonization plan and how unceremoniously he had been dismissed by the governor, the baron revealed that he and Martínez were well acquainted. Deciding that it made sense for them to team up on the settlement plan, Moses and Bastrop returned to the governor's office.

Coached by the more cultured baron, Moses offered several reasons why a settlement of Anglos in Texas would benefit Mexico, including that the Anglos' reputation as Indian fighters was well deserved. Spanish authorities had been hard-pressed to protect Mexican residents in the area, so if a bunch of Americans wanted to risk their necks and take on the problem, they could have it. This time Governor Martínez endorsed and forwarded the plan to a higher authority.[6]

The plan allowed for Moses to guide three hundred families—only Catholic ones, he assured Martínez—from Louisiana to the mouth of the Colorado River, where a settlement would be established. While Moses was enamored with the adventure of the entire enterprise, it was also his ticket back to financial health, since each

---

6 The Baron de Bastrop had only a few more years to enjoy the presence of the colony he helped establish. In 1823, he was elected to the provincial deputation of San Antonio, and the following year to the legislature of Coahuila y Tejas, where he served until his death on February 23, 1827, age sixty-seven. Because Bastrop did not leave enough money for his burial, the other legislators paid for it. In his will, he left land to his wife and children, who were somewhere in the Netherlands. It was not until well over a century later that the baron's true identity was ascertained.

family would have to pay him a fee to be members of this new settlement.

Sadly for Moses, his personal health gave out before his ambitions could be realized. Before the year had ended, he and Richmond were on their way home, but it was a nightmare of a journey—their horses and much of their supplies were stolen, and various ailments ganged up on the fifty-nine-year-old Moses, the worst of them pneumonia from being subjected to the wear and tear of the trek's wet and cold weather. Finally, in March 1821, he reached the home of his daughter, Emily Bryan, in Missouri. There would be no more Texas adventures for him.

In June, two days before he died, Moses called his wife to his bed. She reported in a letter, "After a considerable exertion to speak, he drew me down to him and with much distress and difficulty of speech, told me it was two [*sic*] late, that he was going." His dying request was that his son Stephen would lead those who would be dubbed the "Old Three Hundred" to their new home in Texas. On the tenth, Moses Austin died.[7]

---

7 Austin was buried in the Bryan family cemetery in Missouri. In 1831, the remains of both Moses and his wife were removed to a public cemetery in Potosi, on land they once owned. In 1938, the state of Texas tried to move the remains to the state cemetery in Austin, but the effort was rebuffed. To be on the safe side, Missourians had the grave covered in concrete to thwart future efforts by Texans to excavate it.

CHAPTER 5

THE EMPRESARIO

The problem with Moses Austin's last request was that he might not have actually discussed it with his son. And Stephen, at twenty-seven, had already embarked on a career as a lawyer, studying in New Orleans. He had served in the Missouri legislature, and with the territory soon to receive statehood, he contemplated returning to it. So Stephen may not have been thrilled at the prospect of assuming his father's place at the head of a herd of Anglos bound for what was still Spanish Texas.

But then he thought upon the opportunity some more. Thanks to his father's business failures and overly optimistic ventures, the Austin family was in debt. Stephen had debts of his own in Missouri that would not miraculously disappear overnight. Perhaps spending the next year or two holed up in mosquito-infested southern Louisiana ruining his eyes while poring over musty law books was not all that appealing. Why not give Texas a try?

When Stephen Austin arrived there in July 1821, he was better received by Governor Martínez than his father had first been. With the assistance of the enigmatic yet steadfast Baron de Bastrop, he developed and proposed a plan that would provide each family in his group with 640 acres of land for grazing or farming—340 acres if the parcel was riverfront—on the lower Brazos and Colorado Rivers. With plenty of land to provide and Martínez hoping the Anglos would assume much of the protection against Indian raids, the governor rubber-stamped the updated plan.

The settlers would focus their efforts on the prairies, woodlands, and coastal plain of East Texas intersected by the Brazos, Colorado, and Trinity Rivers. With most of them hailing from the Deep South states of Louisiana, Mississippi, and Alabama, cotton would be the primary crop. And the slaves they would no doubt bring with them would assist in the arduous labors.

In the space of a few months, Austin had gone from fledgling lawyer to being an "empresario" (at that time, being a colonization agent was the definition of this term). Even as lofty as this sounds, it had to still be beyond Austin's imagination that fifteen years later he would be one of the leaders of the independent Republic of Texas—that is, he would be if he lived long enough.

That September, as Austin and several companions rode alongside the Colorado River, they were halted by a band of Karankawa. There were fifteen men, each smeared with alligator grease and carrying a long cedar bow with a quiver of arrows hanging from his shoulder. Speaking Spanish, the lead man asked Austin what he was doing in Karankawa territory. This was disturbing information, because the Anglos had already heard about the tribe's penchant for cannibalism.

Austin managed a brief explanation, and in response the warrior, who called himself Coco, invited the Americans to the nearby Karankawa camp. Austin was not inclined to be so friendly. He held his flintlock rifle tight, and the handful of men with him did the same. The standoff might have escalated, but Coco put down his bow and quiver. Then, making the scene almost surreal to the Americans, five Karankawa women naked from the waist up stepped into view. Austin concluded his conversation with Coco, and he and his men went on their way.[8]

Now what the empresario needed most was colonists. This posed a challenge because Stephen did not have the leadership lure that Moses had had. As Noah Smithwick, who knew Austin as a young man and would later become a colonist and Texas Ranger, described Stephen: "Dark hair and eyes, sparely built, and unassuming in manner . . . there was little in Austin's outward appearance to indicate the tremendous energy of which he was possessed."

But the plan was bigger than the man. After Martínez gave the green light, Austin wrote letters to acquaintances

---

8 Though the encounter was peaceful, Austin came away from it convinced that Anglo settlers and the native population could not coexist. He would later state in his journal about Indians that "there will be no way of subduing [sic] them but extermination."

in Natchitoches and New Orleans about the migration of settlers. Returning from Texas, in Natchitoches Austin found dozens of letters from families ready to sign up. The response was even more robust in New Orleans. The plan he developed was to charge each of the three hundred families for participating, and calculations predicted Austin could clear close to $50,000 on the recruitment effort. Texas was indeed the promised land.

In New Orleans, Austin first went deeper into debt to purchase the *Lively,* a schooner that would sail the first batch of colonists and supplies to their new home. By March 1822, there were a hundred colonists who were either cotton farmers or trying their hands at raising stock on the new homesteads. Soon, the empresario would have his own compact empire in southeast Texas.

But the promising plan soon soured. Martínez revealed that there had been a glitch in the bureaucracy and the new nation's higher authorities in Mexico City had not approved Austin's settlement plan. The governor suggested the empresario go there to personally plead his case. On horseback, Austin set off on the thousand-mile trip and arrived at the end of April.

Now the problem was whom to plead his case to. The withdrawal of Spain's colonial government had left a power vacuum. In the process of trying to fill it was Agustín de Iturbide, who vied to create a monarchy headed by, of course, Emperor Agustín I. Austin would have to cool his heels while the political turmoil was resolved.

Months went by. Then more months. This seemingly endless delay by itself was very frustrating, but Austin had to also worry about the fate of the new colony in Texas. Was it carrying on? Expanding? Would the colonists agree to leave if the Mexican government told them to? The empresario was much relieved when, finally, in January 1823, the junta that served as the emperor's legislature approved a sweeping imperial colonization law, which covered Austin's venture.

The wait was worth it. What the Texas colonists had been promised previously was peanuts compared to what the new law allowed: each family received 4,428 acres for raising stock or 177 for farming, and Austin was granted over 97,000 acres. He was also to receive the windfall of 12.5 cents per acre granted to the colonists and a sixty-dollar fee from each family on top of that. The Austin family fortunes not only had been restored but also were likely to be exceeded.

The Mexican government was not being generous just to be generous. It simply did not have the money or other resources to prevent the Indian tribes in Texas from pillaging properties and killing Mexican citizens. The strategy was to let these new Texians become the prime targets. With luck, they would prove to be enthusiastic Indian fighters and establish a buffer zone to keep the tribes at bay. And if the Karankawa or other tribes massacred the Anglos, it would not be a Mexican tragedy, just a lost opportunity.

Stephen Austin could not wait to return to Texas . . . and then, Emperor Agustín I was overthrown.

CHAPTER 6

THE "MAGNA CARTA"

The Mexican congress, unimpressed with Iturbide's sudden royalty, refused to draw up a new Mexican constitution with a role for an emperor. Because of this and rumors of a conspiracy to kill him, Iturbide dismissed the congress and created the National Institutional Junta. It was directed to craft much-needed legislation in economic matters, enact a provisional set of laws for the empire, and issue a call for the new Constituent Congress, which would be responsible for drafting a new Mexican constitution. As if that was not enough, Iturbide had a score of former members of the old Constituent Congress tossed into prison.

As the colonists in Texas waited, wondering if they would be able to stay or be forced to go, in Mexico City some prominent politicians and military leaders, many of whom had initially supported Agustín I as emperor, turned against him. They included the well-known leaders Vicente Guerrero, Nicolás Bravo, and Guadalupe Victoria. Adding to Iturbide's difficulties, King Ferdinand of Spain expressed his intention to reconquer Mexico. One consequence was that no European nation was willing to recognize the former colony's independence. That its emperor was living extravagantly while his economic policies were draining resources did not sit well either.

When Iturbide was unable to pay his army, a significant portion of his power base became disgruntled. The days grew darker for Iturbide when, on December 22, 1822, the young and ambitious Antonio López de Santa Anna publicly opposed him.

Trying a different tack, Iturbide invited his new rival to Mexico City. Recognizing the danger of such an invitation, López de Santa Anna kept his distance and called for the reinstatement of the old Constituent Congress, which would then have the right to decide the form of government of the new nation. Rivals Guerrero and Bravo fled Mexico City and allied themselves with the growing legion of rebels demanding the reinstatement of the disintegrated congress.

Ironically, given later events, the fate of Texas hung on López de Santa Anna's success. The reinvigorated general led his army toward Mexico City, winning small victories along the way. The weakened Iturbide gathered and sent troops to combat the rebels, but most of them melted away when presented with López de Santa Anna's forces. Recognizing the wishes of the country, Iturbide reopened the same Constituent Congress that he had closed and presented his abdication to the members. The former Emperor Agustín I was allowed to go into exile.[9]

For a while, things settled down in Mexico City, which was finally good news for Stephen Austin. In early August 1823, having been away from the Anglo colony for over sixteen months, he returned. Realizing once more that the settlers were almost surrounded by Indians, who had not grown fonder of them, the empresario wrote on the back of a land document dated August 4 that he would pay for ten men "to act as rangers for the common defence" and that these rangers "will be subject to my orders."

The entire missive of 177 words, "though unsigned, would come to be considered the 'Magna Carta' of the Rangers," writes Mike Cox in his history *The Texas Rangers*. "While that may be an exaggeration, it represents the first known use of the word *ranger* in any Texas document."

9 Iturbide lived in Italy and England while composing his memoirs. Then he became alarmed by reports that Spain really would try to retake Mexico. In February 1824, he offered his services in defense of his country, but the new leadership ignored him. Instead of taking the hint, Iturbide returned to Mexico in July, accompanied by his wife, two children, and a chaplain. The latter would come in handy when Iturbide was arrested, tried, and sentenced to death. Upon being administered last rites, Iturbide said, "Mexicans! In the very act of my death, I recommend to you the love to the fatherland, and the observance to our religion, for it shall lead you to glory. I die having come here to help you, and I die merrily, for I die amongst you." Die he did, at the receiving end of a firing squad.

CHAPTER 7

AN INKLING OF INDEPENDENCE

Though the word "rangers" was new to Texas, it had been used in Europe for centuries to describe a militia-like group of men. In America, there had been a pretty famous and more recent usage.

A company known as Rogers' Rangers had been formed in 1755 by Robert Rogers in the colony of New Hampshire, the latest in a long line of New England ranger companies dating back to the 1670s. Fighting on behalf of the British, Rogers' Rangers undertook raids against French towns and forts. One prominent member was a Connecticut captain, Israel Putnam, whose early ranger service has tended to go overlooked because of the fame he achieved in the Revolutionary War, particularly at the Battle of Bunker Hill, as an officer in the Continental Army.

At the age of thirty-seven, Putnam was one of the oldest men to sign up to serve as a private in the militia in the

French and Indian War. Putnam, not lacking courage or initiative, had various exploits with Rogers, including saving Rogers's life. It was said that "Rogers always sent, but Putnam led his men to action."

"Old Put" was nothing if not resilient. In 1758, he was captured by Mohawk Indians during a military campaign near Crown Point in New York. He was saved from being ritually burned alive by a rainstorm and the last-minute intervention of a French officer. A lesser man might have decided that was enough service for one war, but the next year Putnam led a regiment in the attack on Fort Carillon on the shore of Lake Champlain, and the year after that he was with the British army when it marched on Montreal. In 1762, he survived a shipwreck during the British expedition against Cuba that led to the capture of Havana.

The usefulness of Rogers' Rangers during the war prompted the British to form a second company, which was soon followed by more. Eventually, there were fourteen ranger companies totaling more than twelve hundred men, with Rogers as the overall commander. This included three all-Indian units, two of Stockbridge Mohicans and one of Mohican and Pequot. When the Seven Years' War ended in 1763, the militiamen returned to their farms and villages.

When the American Revolution began in 1775, Robert Rogers offered his services to General George Washington. However, Washington turned him down, suspecting he might be a spy, since Rogers had just returned from a long stay in England. Infuriated by the rejection—or being found out—Rogers formed the Queen's Rangers and later the King's Rangers. Meanwhile, several of his former rangers served under General Benedict Arnold in the revolutionary forces around Lake Champlain. The rangers were reactivated during the War of 1812—without Rogers, who had died in London in 1795—but to fight for the British.

The "rangers" Stephen Austin was calling for were formed to take on Indians, with little consideration given to tribal affiliation. In addition to the Karankawa, nearby tribes included the Waco, Tonkawa, and Tawakoni. Such Indians were viewed as inherently hostile and ready to commit intolerable acts against white and brown settlers if given the chance. This was, of course, a misguided assumption, not to mention that Indians typically raided and fought only when provoked—for example, by the hundreds of Anglos who appeared in their homeland and competed for food and water.

A new militia company commanded by Moses Morrison became official on May 5, 1823, four months before Stephen Austin's message had mentioned "rangers." A few members of Morrison's team were immediately put to work—though, as it turned out, not against Indians.

That very same day, five Mexican vaqueros were killed at the suddenly dangerous Skull Creek campsite after their group had paused there while driving south a small herd of horses purchased in Louisiana. That night, five men showed up at the campsite and ambushed the seven vaqueros. Two of them escaped death, one of them staggering into the nearest settlement to tell the tale.

Without waiting for Morrison or any other men, Robert Kuykendall gathered six of the brand-new militia, and they set off while the trail was still warm. The killers appeared to be leading the remuda back toward Louisiana. The pursuers found three of the bandits as they crossed the Brazos. No quarter was given. The outlaws were not only killed but decapitated. Kuykendall had their heads plunged atop posts along the road as a vivid illustration of what would happen to other outlaws.

For a short time, this display had the intended effect of putting a damper on depredations. But on July 6, John Tumlinson and another colonist, Joseph Newman, were on their way to San Antonio to buy gunpowder for the militia when they encountered a group that included Wacos, who were considered to have a good relationship with the settlers. However, when Tumlinson reached down to shake hands, a warrior yanked him from his saddle and killed him with a lance. Newman instantly wheeled his horse around and took off. The Indians chased him, but Newman outdistanced them and was able to report the murder to Kuykendall, but it is not known if it was ever avenged.

Next on Stephen Austin's to-do list was to set up a local government. This included issuing a set of regulations, dispensing land titles, arbitrating disputes, and being the official head of the new special force he continued to refer to as rangers.

"Austin was one of the most complex and sophisticated men ever to influence the course of Texas," writes Charles Robinson III in *The Men Who Wear the Star*. "When his fortunes were at their height, he was devious and cynical. He dispensed land titles as though they were the largesse of a feudal lord, which, in effect, they were. As the sole administrator of the colonization laws and the only person authorized to deal with the government, he was suspected by many settlers of manipulating the laws to his own benefit and at their expense."

Whatever Austin's flaws, he had been the one who had finalized the deal that allowed the colonies to exist at all. A big step forward for the Anglos came in October 1824, when the government in Mexico City issued the Federal Constitution of the United Mexican States, providing more power to the individual states than to the central government. The colonists were still residents of Mexican Texas, but they were beginning to put more emphasis on Texas.

The pace of Anglo settlement there advanced further when the Colonization Act of 1825 was enacted. Boiled down to its basics, the government of Mexico would now charge newcomers a fee of only one hundred dollars—payment could be spread out over six years—in exchange for a league of land. Americans poured into the province. That a requirement was they become Mexican citizens and Catholics was taken seriously by some settlers but not so much by the majority.

One might wonder if the authorities grasped the significance of the Anglo land rush—that the territory was becoming more an extension of the United States and less of Mexico. But even those officials who did understand this went along with the colonization because it appeared that the Anglos had, in fact, become the target of the Karankawa and other hostiles and that the Anglos' militia was up to the challenge.

Another reason Mexico allowed the land rush was that

its government was occupied getting its house in order after many years of civil war and economic instability. In October 1824, thirty-eight-year-old Guadalupe Victoria, a veteran of the independence battles against Spain and Agustín I, was declared the first president of the United Mexican States. He was now in charge of rebuilding an economy devastated by the messy war of independence and the economic blockade Spain had imposed. Among the first president's positive achievements were the establishment of the National Treasury and the Military Academy, restoring Mexico City buildings and infrastructure, improving the education system, planning for a canal in the Isthmus of Tehuantepec, opening new ports for shipping, beginning construction of the National Museum, and unmasking a conspiracy led by a monk named Joaquín Arenas to restore Spanish rule.

A stable Mexico under Victoria was providing peace and the glowing promise of prosperity to its citizens. However, it was also during this time that there was a serious glitch in Mexican-Anglo relations—the first attempt by Anglo colonists to become independent was a precursor to what would indeed transpire in the next decade.

Haden Edwards followed in Austin's footsteps as an empresario, receiving a land grant from the Mexican government in 1825. To the west and north of this new colony were lands controlled by several Indian tribes who had recently been driven out of the United States. At the southern boundary were the settlements overseen by Stephen Austin. East of Edwards's grant was the former Sabine Free State, a neutral zone, which had been essentially lawless for years. The boundaries of the new colony and the municipality of Nacogdoches partially overlapped, leading to uncertainty over who had jurisdiction. The majority of the established settlers lived outside the eastern boundary of the Edwards colony.

This uncertainty somehow inspired Edwards and his colonists to declare independence from Mexican Texas and create the Republic of Fredonia near Nacogdoches.[10] The action and the increasing hostilities between Edwards's supporters and those settlers not eager for conflict led the government of President Victoria to revoke Edwards's contract.

In late December 1826, a group of Edwards's supporters took control of the region by arresting and removing from office several local officials. Going a step further, the insurgents declared their independence from Mexico. The nearby Cherokee tribe signed a treaty to support the new republic, but overtures from Mexican authorities and Austin convinced tribal leaders to repudiate the rebellion. On January 31, 1827, a force of over one hundred Mexican soldiers and 275 Texian militia marched into Nacogdoches to restore order. Haden Edwards and his brother Benjamin Edwards fled to the United States. An especially unfortunate local merchant was arrested and sentenced to death but was later paroled.

But damage to the relationship with the Anglo colonists had been done. The rebellion prompted Mexico to increase

10 Attention classic film buffs: This republic is not to be confused with Freedonia, the fake country headed by Rufus T. Firefly in the 1933 Marx Brothers movie *Duck Soup*.

its military presence in the area. Fearing that through rebellion the United States hoped to gain control of Texas,
the Mexican government severely curtailed immigration
to the region. A new, larger garrison was established in
Nacogdoches, and the Mexican government authorized
an extensive expedition, conducted by General Manuel de
Mier y Terán, to inspect the Texas settlements and to recommend a future course of action. Mier y Terán's reports
led to the Law of April 6, 1830, which further restricted
immigration into Texas.

Some historians do indeed regard the Fredonian Rebellion as the beginning of the Texas Revolution. Whether or
not their assertion is true, it is clear that the changing de-
mographics of Texas indicated that a revolt was inevitable.

CHAPTER 8

UNLEARNED LESSONS

By 1830 there were over ten thousand Anglo settlers in Texas. They were arriving not just from Louisiana and Mississippi but from Arkansas and Missouri as well as the southern states on the East Coast. That these settlers were supposed to be Catholics or vowed to convert was not a hurdle, thanks to Michael Muldoon, who is one of the more curious characters in Texas history.

He was born around 1780 in the Diocese of Kilmore, County Cavan, and ordained at the Irish College of Seville, Spain. Muldoon went to serve in the Diocese of Monterey, having arrived in Veracruz in 1821 in the company of Juan O'Donojú, the last Spanish viceroy of Mexico. A decade later, Stephen Austin selected Muldoon to provide for the spiritual needs of the Texian colonists. The priest became so proficient at converting Protestant colonists—the process took a miraculous fifteen minutes—that those men and women came to be known as Muldoon Catholics.

The government in Mexico City may not have fully comprehended that many of those ten thousand Anglo settlers had emigrated from states where independence and self-governing were important . . . as was the ability to own slaves.[11] There were differences, of course, but it was not surprising that more of these Texians were beginning to view Mexico similarly to the way American colonists over a half century earlier regarded Great Britain. Still, there were many men, like Austin, who preferred to focus on peace and prosperity in their beautiful and sometimes breathtaking surroundings.

Part of that focus on peace was to try to maintain it with their Indian neighbors. The series of regulations that Austin issued to govern his nascent colony in 1824 created a necessary criminal justice system, the first five regulations of which concerned the indigenous population, which, to some extent, was being displaced. If settlers were exposed to sufficient danger from attack or were actually attacked, one regulation was to "call out as many men as may be necessary to pursue and take said Indians prisoners."

However, extreme measures were to be avoided. Austin was not by nature a violent man, and he was smart enough to understand that deaths were more likely to escalate rather than resolve matters. But the somewhat lighter

---

11 Austin himself was a slave owner, and an 1825 count performed in his colony determined that as many as a quarter of the 1,800 people in it were slaves.

hand did not work. Two years later, Austin, claiming that the "frontier is menaced," continued in a message that the "whole colony is threatened—under these circumstances it became my duty to call the militia to the frontier to repel the threatened attacks and to teach our enemies to fear and respect us."

It was a lesson that had to be applied repeatedly. And that required plenty of available militia members. At around the time of Austin's recognition that the displaced residents were not going away quietly, there were over five hundred men who had signed up as ready to ride against the "savages."[12] One of them continued to be Moses Morrison. His adventure in 1831 is an example of the kind of conflict that had become routine in the area.

Aylett Buckner, a militia captain known to most by the nickname Strap, was alerted that a band of Indians had murdered two families who had settled in the Colorado district. This despicable act was made worse by the gruesome details and the fact that one of the families was a member of the "Old Three Hundred."

Charles Cavina was away from his property when it was invaded by a band of Karankawa. His wife and three of his daughters were killed. (A fourth daughter, though shot with an arrow, survived.) A female settler named Flowers who had been visiting Mrs. Cavina was also killed and her daughter wounded (she too survived). While the attackers

---

12 "Savages" was a term used frequently by white Americans and by the press to describe Native Americans. It was one way of dehumanizing them and justifying taking their hunting territory. This continued for decades and kept the national flames of bigotry stoked.

ransacked the house, Cavina returned but remained out of sight until the Indians rode away. After seeing the horror, Cavina rode off to sound the alarm.

Strap Buckner pulled together a posse of around sixty men, who set off in pursuit. Believing they were close to their quarry camped near the Colorado River, the Texans paused. One of them, Morrison, climbed quietly out on a ledge to survey the scene below. The ledge collapsed, sending Morrison tumbling forty feet downhill to the riverbank, where, after rubbing the dirt out of his eyes, he looked around and saw only perplexed Karankawa warriors. Before they could take any action, Morrison leaped behind the riverbank and began firing the rifle he had somehow managed to retain in his grasp.

Buckner had hesitated after Morrison disappeared, but upon hearing the gunshots he ordered his men to charge. They descended on the Karankawa, who were focused on trying to kill Morrison. By the time the battle was over, at least fifty Indians, including several women and children, lay dead on the ground and in the river, and the survivors had fled. To that point, it was the worst loss the Karankawa suffered at the hands of the colonists.

As Charles Robinson reports, "This was the last real engagement between the colonists and the Karankawa. Never a large tribe, they appear to have been devastated by their losses in this fight, and they gradually faded from history; within a generation they were extinct."

Still, by the early 1830s, the Anglos' fear of Indians and the Indians' anger at being invaded had not diminished, and "rangers" were called upon regularly. But a bigger conflict was looming on the horizon that would take up more of the Texians' time and energy: revolution.

The aforementioned General Manuel de Mier y Terán, while headquartered in Nacogdoches in 1828, had conducted a boundary survey on behalf of President Guadalupe Victoria's government. The general had become friends with Stephen Austin and was concerned about the growing friction between American settlers and Mexican citizens and officials.

Mier y Terán wrote President Victoria that the colonists appeared less interested in being Mexican citizens than they used to be—plus, they were not adhering to Catholicism and continued to own slaves. (Mexico would ban slavery the following year.) The population of Anglos in Texas had surpassed that of Mexicans, and that trend was only going to continue. He suggested that the governing of Texas be reorganized and that, in general, Mexico City should pay more attention to the territory.

The government did nothing about Mier y Terán's message until two years later, in 1830. Under President Bustamante, it cut Texas off from further American immigration. This affected trade too, and under the guise of combating Indians, new military garrisons were built. The Texians were unhappy, but they and the Mexicans coexisted, and the friendship of Austin and Mier y Terán endured. Then came the Battle of Velasco in 1832, which would prove a glimpse of the Texas Revolution to come.

CHAPTER 9

AUSTIN BEHIND BARS

Henry Smith and John Austin led a contingent of Texians who had gone to Brazoria to obtain a cannon.[13] Domingo de Ugartechea, commander of the Mexican fort at Velasco, was not willing to part with it. The battle between the Texians, as many as 150 of them, and the Mexicans, who numbered somewhere between 100 and 200, did not go well for the latter, who were forced to surrender when their ammunition gave out.

Most sources estimate that there were seven Texians killed and fourteen wounded, with three of the fourteen later dying from their wounds. The Mexicans had five killed and sixteen wounded. The formal surrender took

---

13 Stephen Austin and John Austin, who hailed from Connecticut and had been a member of the Long expedition, were good friends but were only distantly related.

place in camp at the mouth of the Brazos on June 29, and Ugartechea was allowed to return to Mexico on a ship the colonists furnished.

Had the dispute over a cannon been an isolated incident, the surrender could have marked the end of conflict. And there did not yet appear to be a strong desire for independence from Mexico. A more real and present danger that could not be ignored were raids by the various tribes, most prominently the remaining Karankawa. Resisting and retaliating for them required the ranger-like volunteers. As Austin had once written, such men were needed for the "defence of your firesides—of your wives and children, your friends—yourselves—your property"—and, of course, Texas.

"Anglo Texans held Indians in even greater contempt than Mexicans," explains Robert Utley in *Lone Star Justice*. "Anglos regarded any Indian within the line of settlements as bent on mischief and a fair target for their rifles . . . and no matter how vigorous their protests of peace and friendship, tribal leaders could not restrain their young men from an occasional plundering foray into the settlements. Thrust and counter thrust fed on themselves and, for whites and Indians alike, made the frontier a dangerous place."

However, the escalating enmity between the colonists and the Mexican government soon refused to take a back seat. Texian leaders decided following the Velasco incident to host a sort of convention in San Felipe de Austin to discuss recent events. Almost sixty "delegates," representing sixteen colonies, attended. A sinister outcome of the convention—to the Mexican authorities—was the creation of a new militia. It consisted of two battalions of six companies each. The militia was a stronger preparation for the inevitable conflicts with the various Indian tribes, but more than a few Mexican officials saw it as another step toward Texas independence, with the colonists planning to take advantage of the ongoing instability in Mexico City.

From March 1829, when Victoria's term as president peacefully ended, to May 1833, when the ambitions of Santa Anna were finally realized, Mexico tried to function under seven different heads of state: Vicente Guerrero, José María Bocanegra (who lasted all of six days), Pedro Vélez (eight days), Anastasio Bustamante, Melchor Múzquiz, Manuel Gómez Pedraza, and Valentín Gómez Farías. (For lawmakers and clergy, just attending all the swearing-in ceremonies must have been exhausting.) It made sense that a growing number of Anglos wondered, "If that's the best Mexico can do, why not try governing ourselves?"

Though he personally preferred that Texas remain part of Mexico, Stephen Austin agreed to take to Mexico City a "constitution" the colonists at the convention had created. Since Austin had the longest relationship with the Mexican government, it made sense to send him instead of strangers.

But this did not make sense to Santa Anna. None of it did. This looked to the president like an insurrection. Perceiving Austin as the leader of it, Santa Anna had him tossed into prison.

Being sent to jail was certainly not expected and may have hardened Austin's heart against the host country. At least he was not completely alone in the prison. As luck would have it, the well-traveled Father Muldoon was living in Mexico City when Austin was imprisoned there. For three months of that incarceration, Austin was allowed only one visitor, and it was the Catholic clergyman, who helped to preserve the Texan's sanity. Muldoon also kept petitioning for Austin's release, which finally occurred in the summer of 1835, when there was a general amnesty.[14]

After twenty-eight months of being away, Austin did not return to Texas full of zeal for independence. He had instead been encouraged by Santa Anna's presidency— first, that it had lasted more than a few months, and second, that he had granted the Texans more rights, including religious freedom and the ability to use English for official documents. If anything, Austin hoped for a territory content to remain the way it was and to focus on expanding settlements and prosperity, not friction. Anyone with a

---

14 Muldoon's own version of prison reform continued in 1837, when he helped William H. Wharton escape from a Mexican jail at Matamoros. Wharton, an early advocate of Texas independence who is credited with designing the Lone Star flag, left the prison disguised as a nun, proving that Muldoon's powers of quick conversion were undiminished. Two years later, Father Muldoon appeared in New Orleans, where he offered to serve as an interpreter for Colonel Barnard E. Bee Sr., who was preparing to embark on a diplomatic mission to Mexico. For his unofficial part in this mission—that of proceeding to Mexico City while the official envoys remained in Veracruz—and for his pro-Texan views, this time it was Muldoon who was imprisoned. Instead of being charged accordingly, however, he was accused of previously having left Mexico without the proper travel documents. The last sighting of the Irishman was in 1842, when he was again in Texas and received from Secretary of State Anson Jones a letter recognizing his service to the republic. Muldoon's ultimate fate is unknown.

taste for friction could sign up for the ad hoc "ranger" units that continued to fight the Indians.

But the scenario changed rapidly after the incident at Gonzales in October 1835. Many historians view it as the battle that began the Texas Revolution. And this time, rangers would be involved.

CHAPTER 10

"COME TO OUR AID"

Once again, the dispute was over a cannon. Gonzales citizens had obtained one four years earlier from Mexican authorities to help protect them from frequent Comanche raids. But in September 1835, with Anglo independence in the air, Colonel Domingo de Ugartechea, having failed upward to become the commander of all Mexican troops in Texas, felt it unwise to leave such a weapon in Gonzales and requested its return.

When the initial request was refused, Ugartechea sent one hundred dragoons to retrieve the weapon. The soldiers neared Gonzales on the twenty-ninth, but the colonists used a variety of excuses to keep them from the town while secretly sending messengers to request assistance from nearby communities. Within two days, up to 140 Texans gathered in Gonzales, determined not to give up the cannon. On October 1 they voted to initiate a fight. The next day, as a contingent of Texans approached their camp, Mexican soldiers opened fire. After several hours of desultory firing back and forth, the Mexican soldiers withdrew.

Although the skirmish had little military significance, it was evidence of a widening gap between the colonists and the Mexican government. News of the confrontation spread, even in the United States, where it was referred to as the "Lexington of Texas."[15]

Even so, both sides might have simply moved on, but then Martín Perfecto de Cos set foot in San Antonio. In addition to being a Mexican general, he was the brother-in-law of President Santa Anna.

He had arrived in Texas by sea at the port of Copano on September 20 with five hundred soldiers. On October 1 he proceeded to the town of Goliad, where he ordered the arrest of rebel leaders and garrisoned his men inside the nearby Presidio La Bahía. Even before his arrival, a group of Texans had plotted to kidnap Cos, but a rebellion committee rejected the idea. Texans saw the presence of this force as a further provocation and assaulted the Presidio La Bahía on October 10 . . . only to learn that Cos had already left for San Antonio.

Soon, Cos's men were besieged by a Texan army under the leadership of the now galvanized Stephen Austin. After a fifty-six-day siege of San Antonio and the Alamo mission, on December 9, Cos surrendered the town to the Texans. He

---

15 It is not certain what happened to the cannon at the center of the skirmish. One belief is that it was seized by Mexican troops after the Alamo battle. However, some claim that a cannon discovered in the area in 1936 was the contested weapon.

and his men were allowed to retreat across the Rio Grande with their muskets as well as one four-pound cannon. Mexican losses during the siege were about 150 troops. On his way south, the abashed brother-in-law met up with Santa Anna and his northbound forces. The president was no doubt regretting any courtesies he had previously bestowed on the Texans as his army marched to put down the rebellion.

It was thanks to the possibility of an armed conflict with Mexico that "Ranger" became an official position. At a convention of independence-minded Texans in mid-October, the Permanent Council was elected to act as a de facto government of the territory. It in turn called upon three colonists, Silas Parker, Garrison Greenwood, and D. B. Fryer, to create companies of men "whose business shall be to range and guard the frontiers"—Rangers. Every man in a company, in return for $1.25 a day in wages, would supply his own gun, ammunition, horse, and other necessities to be out on patrol.

Weeks of recruiting and organizing ensued. Then on November 28, 1835, the Permanent Council elected officers of the Ranger companies, though not the same three men who had formed those companies. Robert Williamson was appointed the major who would be in charge of the entire force of Rangers, and the designated captains of each company were John Tumlinson, Isaac Burton, and William Arrington.[16] In the case of Tumlinson, he hoped

---

16 Williamson's right leg had been disabled by polio. Because of the wooden peg that bolstered it, the new Ranger captain was known as "Three-Legged Willie."

for swift and serious action against Indians to avenge the killing of his father.

Because the reason for their existence was primarily for border security and to fight Indians who preyed upon settlers, the Rangers were not tasked with defending Texas against Santa Anna. By the third week in February 1836, the rebellion was centered on the Alamo in San Antonio. The Spanish mission now housed a Texan army commanded by Lieutenant Colonel William Travis in addition to Jim Bowie and Davy Crockett, who, only a few months earlier, had represented Tennessee in Congress. On the twenty-third, Mexican troops arrived in the city, and the president of Mexico observed the makeshift fort. After seeing what Santa Anna had arrayed against him, Travis dashed off a message asking for assistance. He noted that a "large force is in sight" and declared his 150 men "are determined to defend the Alamo to the last."

Major Williamson in Gonzales saw the note and sent out a call to arms. However, the members of the three official Ranger companies were not near enough to San Antonio to be of any use. But George Kimball, a lieutenant, had organized fellow volunteers into the imposingly titled Gonzales Ranging Company of Mounted Volunteers. Though composed of only twenty-two men, they planned to hurry to San Antonio and lend their rifles to the cause.

Their ranks swelled during the next forty-eight hours, thanks to the second missive composed and sent by Travis. Dated the twenty-fourth and addressed "To the People of Texas & all Americans in the world," the colonel reported that the Alamo had endured an artillery bombardment but that his men were more determined than ever to hold out . . . but help would be welcomed: "I call on you in the name of Liberty, of patriotism & everything dear to the American character, to come to our aid, with all dispatch."

That was good enough for Kimball. Joined by Captain Albert Martin, who had delivered Travis's message from the Alamo, he mustered his company and set off for San Antonio. By the time they arrived late in the daytime of the twenty-ninth, the Gonzales Ranging Company totaled thirty-two volunteers. Thus, there were Rangers among the 186 Texans who died on March 6, when Santa Anna's troops stormed and took the Alamo.

Gaining a measure of revenge for the loss of Kimball and his men was the Ranger company under Isaac Burton's command. They had joined up with the Texan army commanded by Major General Sam Houston. On April 21 their army turned on and attacked the pursuing army under Santa Anna at San Jacinto and soundly defeated it. Mexico was by no means out of armies and generals to lead them against the rebels, but the one who counted the most, the Mexican president himself, was among the prisoners taken by Houston's men. To secure his release, Santa Anna had to order all Mexican forces back across the Rio Grande and agree to negotiate Texas independence.

Before this was locked in, however, Burton's company played a crucial role. Given Mexico's recent history of instability at the top, General Thomas Jefferson Rusk, who replaced Sam Houston as commander of the Texan army while the latter recovered from a leg wound, sent the twenty Rangers on a scouting mission to make sure there was not another Mexican force on its way to San Jacinto.[17]

What Burton and his men found was the *Watchman,* a ship in Copano Bay waiting to unload supplies for the Mexican army. The Rangers rowed out and captured it. Soon, two other ships, the *Fanny Butler* and the *Camanche,* entered the bay for the same purpose. They too were taken. "Commander" Burton led his flotilla to Velasco, where $25,000 in prize money was paid out for it. These captures were enormously helpful to the basically broke Texan army and kept all those supplies from finding their way to the enemy.

Where was the "Father of Texas" in all this? Stephen Austin was in New Orleans. He had been advocating for Texas independence when he received word of Santa Anna's defeat at San Jacinto. With all hostilities on hold, now was the time to form a republic. Austin returned to Texas, and on August 4 he announced his candidacy for president of Texas. He looked to be a shoo-in . . . until August 20, when Sam Houston entered the race. Austin did not stand a chance against the recent hero of San Jacinto, who earned 5,119 votes to the former empresario's 587. Austin was not

---

17 Though he would not attain the fame of Houston, Rusk had a distinguished career in the early days of the Republic of Texas that included some controversy. In November 1838, he captured marauding Caddo Indians and risked an international incident when he crossed into U.S. territory to return them to the Indian agent in Shreveport, Louisiana. The following month, the Texas Congress elected Rusk as chief justice of the Supreme Court.

sidelined, however—he accepted Houston's offer to become the republic's first secretary of state.

It is likely that Austin would have had a long career of public service in the republic and later state of Texas, but he did not even survive the year. In December 1836, he was in the new capital of Columbia, where he caught a severe cold. Though only forty-three years old, as with his father, Moses, Austin's condition worsened. Doctors were called in but could not help him, and he died of pneumonia on December 27 at the home of George B. McKinstry. His last words were, "The independence of Texas is recognized! Don't you see it in the papers?"[18]

Upon hearing of Austin's death, Houston ordered an official statement proclaiming, "The Father of Texas is no more; the first pioneer of the wilderness has departed." Originally, Austin was buried at Gulf Prairie Cemetery in Brazoria County, but in 1910 his body was reinterred at the Texas State Cemetery in Austin. With no wife or children, Austin bequeathed all his land, titles, and possessions to his married sister, Emily Austin Perry, immediately making her one of the largest individual landholders and the wealthiest woman in the new Republic of Texas.[19]

---

18 One can speculate that spending twenty-eight months in a Mexican prison had not helped Austin's own constitution.

19 Among Mrs. Perry's activities until her death in 1851 (when she was buried next to her brother) was being a benefactor of charities and small businesses. An example of the latter is a loan to Gail Borden to buy his first herd of cows, and the company he subsequently formed was Borden Milk Products.

CHAPTER II

"HOW DO YOU LIKE THAT ANSWER?"

To understand the reputation that the Texas Rangers have to this day, it helps to know the story and adventures of those captains who were in command before the Civil War. The first of the truly great ones was John Coffee Hays. With him, the Rangers took a great leap forward.

Called "Jack" by his friends, Hays hailed from Wilson County in Tennessee, where he was born on January 28, 1817. His father, Harmon Hays, had served under General Andrew Jackson in battles against the British and against the Creek Indians and named his son after one of Old Hickory's top commanders, General John Coffee.

Jack Hays was sixteen when his father and mother died within a month of each other in the fall of 1833. The six Hays children (Jack was the oldest) were taken in by a maternal uncle who owned a plantation in Yazoo County,

Mississippi. That life did not suit the teenager, so he struck out on his own. His travels included learning how to be a surveyor. This was a pretty good occupation then as new lands—to white men, anyway—were being explored and purchased and it offered adventure.

In 1838, when he turned twenty-one, Jack, accompanied by one of his brothers, William, who was less than a year younger, arrived in Texas. They carried a letter of introduction to Sam Houston from one of their other uncles. It is not known how the president of the republic responded, but Jack Hays was soon working as a surveyor again, based in San Antonio. When he was appointed a deputy surveyor of the Bexar District, this was a step up but also put Hays in harm's way because the Comanches to the west were not happy about the increasing number of settlers showing up and the surveyors who figuratively helped pave their way.

The Comanche had replaced the Karankawa as the tribe most hostile to and active against the Anglo Texans. They frequently raided frontier settlements, and those whom they did not kill they kidnapped. What would become most famous example of the latter was the abduction of Cynthia Ann Parker.

Her story has been recounted numerous times, most notably in *Empire of the Summer Moon* by S. C. Gwynne, whose main character, Quanah Parker, was Cynthia's son. Thus, a much-abridged version: She was eight or nine in 1836 when she was kidnapped by a Comanche war band that had attacked her family's settlement. Parker was adopted by the Comanche and lived with them for twenty-four years, completely forgetting almost all of her childhood culture and identity. She married a Comanche chieftain, Peta Nocona, and had three children with him. (For how that turned out, see chapter 24.)

The number of Comanche killings and kidnappings like this one eventually provoked a military response, albeit not a very big one, in August 1838.[20] Hays would experience his first battle as one of twenty-one men led west by Colonel Henry Wax Karnes.[21] On the tenth of that month, the volunteer company paused at Arroyo Seco to rest their horses and were attacked by an estimated two hundred Comanche warriors. The disciplined and accurate fire of the volunteers beat back one charge after another until the Comanches retired, with twenty dead and wounded. Other than several horses killed, the only casualty the Texans suffered was that Colonel Karnes took an arrow in the hip.

During the rest of the year and the next, Hays would halt surveying to be a member of expeditions led by the recovered Colonel Karnes. However, it was under the combined command of Mathew "Old Paint" Caldwell (so nicknamed because of his spotted mustache), Ben McCulloch, and Felix Huston during what became known as the Great Comanche Raid in 1840 that the twenty-three-year-old Hays began to

---

20 Another grueling account of abduction and murder that spurred Texans into action was that of Sarah Hibbins. Comanche warriors killed her husband and kidnapped her and her two sons. One of them, an infant, was soon murdered by being smacked against a tree trunk.

21 Karnes, like Hays a native of Tennessee, had distinguished himself during the revolution as head of Sam Houston's spy ring.

build a reputation.[22] The catalyst for the climactic clash between the tribe and Texan volunteers was the Council House fight, one of the bloodiest events in Texas history.

That January, their ranks having been reduced by almost two decades of war and cholera and smallpox epidemics, Comanche leaders sent three emissaries to San Antonio. They were accompanied by a kidnapped white boy who was being returned as a peace offering. They met with Colonel Karnes, who told the emissaries that a lasting peace could be negotiated only when the Comanche gave up the other thirteen Anglo captives they held. Albert Sidney Johnston, the Texas secretary of war, had ordered San Antonio officials to take the Comanche delegates as hostages if they failed to deliver all captives.[23] Unaware of this, in March, Muguara, a powerful eastern head man, led sixty-five Comanches, including women and children, to San Antonio for peace talks.

When the Comanches arrived, they had only one white captive with them as well as several Mexican children who had been captured separately. This got the discussion off to a bad start. Muguara refused to deliver more captives, claiming that they were held in the *rancherías* of other head men over whom he had no authority. Worse, the lone white

---

22 A lawyer originally from Kentucky, Felix Huston was a general in the Texas State Militia. At one point, he was the head of the militia. After president of the republic Sam Houston promoted Albert Sidney Johnston over him, Huston reacted by wounding his new superior in a duel.

23 When the Kentucky-born Johnston was killed at the Battle of Shiloh on April 6, 1862, he became the highest-ranking officer, Union or Confederate, killed during the Civil War . . . and he retained that unhappy distinction through the end of the conflict.

captive was Matilda Lockhart, a sixteen-year-old girl who had been held prisoner for over eighteen months and had been beaten, raped, and suffered burns to her body. What the girl had endured did not put the Texans in a concilia-tory mood.

Asked about the more than a dozen abducted whites expected to be available for release, Matilda informed the Texans that she knew only about a Mrs. Webster and her two children (who, unknown to her, had just made their escape) and that the Comanche chiefs had decided to ransom them. The Texans believed this was against the conditions for the negotiations, which they insisted had specified that all abducted whites had to be released before the council.

Still, talks were held at the Council House, a one-story stone building adjoining the jail on the corner of Main Plaza and Calabosa Street. The Comanche warriors sat on the floor, as was their custom, while the Texans sat on chairs on a platform facing them. Matilda informed the Texans that she had seen fifteen other prisoners at the Co-manche camp several days before and claimed the captors had wanted to see how high a price they could get for her. Based on that information, they planned to bring in the remaining captives one at a time and barter for them.

When the Texans demanded to know where the other captives were, Muguara assured them that those captives would be able to be ransomed, but that it would be in exchange for a great deal of supplies, including ammuni-tion and blankets. He then asked, "How do you like that answer?"

The Texans did not like it at all. Militia entered the Council House and spread out against the walls. The chiefs were told they would be held hostage until the white captives were released.

Immediately, the Comanches attempted to fight their way out, using arrows and knives. The Texan militia opened fire at point-blank range, killing indiscriminately. The Comanche women and children waiting outdoors began shooting arrows at white people after hearing the commotion inside. At least one Texan spectator was killed. When a small number of warriors managed to escape from the Council House, all of the Comanche outside began to flee. The soldiers who pursued them again opened fire, killing and wounding both Comanche and Texans. Armed civilians also joined the battle, firing in all directions, and more women and children, white and Indian, were killed.

Once the gunfire ceased and some order was restored, it was determined that thirty-five Comanche were dead and twenty-nine were taken prisoner. Seven Texans died, including a judge, a sheriff, and an army lieutenant, with ten more wounded.[24]

The day after the Council House fight, a single Comanche woman was allowed to return to her camp and report

---

24 A German surgeon named Weidman helped treat the citizens who had been wounded in the fight. He was also a naturalist and had been assigned by the czar of Russia to make scientific observations about Texas and its inhabitants. Not only did he have this event to report, but when he left San Antonio to return to Russia he had the skeletons of two Comanche. To obtain them, he had boiled the bodies in water and dumped the resulting liquid into the San Antonio drinking water supply.

that the prisoners would be released if the Comanche produced within twelve days the Americans and Mexicans who were known to be captives. On March 26 Mrs. Webster, after nineteen months of captivity, staggered into San Antonio with her three-year-old, having left her twelve-year-old son with the Indians. Two days later, a band of Comanche showed up. Leaving the bulk of the warriors outside the city, a leader, Yellow Wolf, and one other man rode toward the fort and yelled insults. Citizens urged the soldiers to fight, but the garrison commander, Captain William Davis Redd, declared that he had to observe the twelve-day truce. Redd invited the Indians to come back in three days, but, fearing a trap, Yellow Wolf and his men rode away.[25]

The situation worsened: Of the sixteen white hostages the Texans were determined to recover, thirteen were tortured to death as soon as the news of the Council House fight reached the outraged Comanche. The captives, including Matilda Lockhart's six-year-old sister, suffered slow roasting, among other tortures. Only the three white captives who had been adopted, and thus by Comanche custom were truly part of the tribe, were spared. On April 3, when another band of Comanche appeared to bargain for an exchange, one of the three captives with them, Mrs. Webster's son Booker revealed the fate of the other hostages.

---

25 Another officer, Lysander Wells, accused Redd of cowardice for refusing to fight. His honor insulted, Redd insisted on a duel. During it, the two men killed each other.

While some of the Comanches held in San Antonio would eventually escape, Buffalo Hump was outraged at the deaths and what he saw as betrayal inflicted on the tribe. His vengeance that summer became known as the Great Comanche Raid—the largest Indian raid on white cities in U.S. history (though technically when it occurred it was in the Republic of Texas). Jack Hays would be in the thick of things.

CHAPTER 12

LOOTING AND SHOUTING

Beginning in that spring of 1840, Buffalo Hump and his deputies Yellow Wolf and Santa Anna (obviously, not a moonlighting president of Mexico) began to gather a raiding party. By mid-July, they commanded at least four hundred warriors, and with accompanying women and boys, almost a thousand Comanche set out from West Texas. As they rode east, they put homesteads and even towns to the torch.

The marauders attacked Victoria on August 6, arriving before the citizens could be warned. Residents hid in buildings, and the raiders, after killing a dozen or so towns-people and riding up and down the main street, departed when rifle fire from those buildings began to take its toll. Two days later, the Comanche attacked Linnville, which was the second largest port in the Republic of Texas at the time. They killed three men, including customs officer Hugh Oran Watts, and took his wife of only three weeks and a black woman and child captive. Other residents were saved by climbing into small boats and rowing out to a schooner anchored in the bay.

From that vantage point they witnessed the destruction and looting of their town, unable to do more than shout curses at the Comanche. The frustrated townsfolk observed the raiders burning buildings, draping themselves grandly in top hats and stolen linens, tying featherbeds and bolts of cloth to their horses and dragging them, and herding cattle into pens to be slaughtered.

One citizen, Judge John Hays (no relation to Jack), was so outraged that he grabbed a gun and waded ashore through the shallow water and challenged the Comanche to a fight. The bemused raiders simply jeered him, believing the white man to be insane. Judge Hays later discovered he had challenged hundreds of Indians with an unloaded pistol.

After loading loot onto pack mules, the Comanche finally began their retreat to the northwest late in the afternoon on August 8. A handful of Rangers had been trailing the war party, and the prolonged plundering in Linnville allowed them and militia to gather more men—including young Jack Hays. The combined force caught up with the Comanche, slowed by the plodding pack mules, on August 12 at Plum Creek, near the city of Lockhart. The Texans were led by General Felix Huston.

At first, what came to be known as the Battle of Plum Creek went poorly for the Texans. Unwisely, Huston had his men dismount, which allowed the Comanche to ride rings around them, shooting guns and arrows. Finally, after entreaties by McCulloch and Caldwell, Huston ordered the Rangers to get back on their horses and charge the Comanche.

What followed was a running gun battle, where Jack Hays and the other Texans attempted to kill the raiders and recover loot, and the Comanche simply attempted to get away. It ended only when the Texans' horses were too worn out to continue the pursuit. Fewer than two dozen bodies were recovered, but the Texans reported killing eighty Comanches. All told, at least twenty-five settlers were killed since the Great Raid had begun, with others taken prisoner.[26]

"Plum Creek represented a breakthrough for the Rangers," observes Doug Swanson in *Cult of Glory,* his history of the Rangers. "For the first time in a major battle, they had used Indian tactics—a moving attack on horseback—to fight Indians. In their own charitable assessment, they also prevented raids on other settlements." However, he adds, "Plum Creek was far from a smashing victory. Most of the Indians, along with hundreds of their stolen horses, were able to escape and return to their distant homes."

The Texans were not done avenging Buffalo Hump's deadly raid. Two months later, the administration of President Mirabeau Lamar selected Colonel John Moore to

26 One of the captives was Nancy Crosby, whose grandfather was Daniel Boone. Alas, the heroic pathfinder had died twenty years earlier and could be of no help. Both of her young children were killed as their mother watched. Mrs. Crosby was later murdered by her captors.

lead a raid of its own. The veteran of campaigns against the Karankawa had led a force of eager volunteers against the Comanche the year before and had suffered an embarrassing defeat at the San Saba River. He was back again in October 1840, this time assisted by Ben McCulloch, with an "army" of 107 men, including Lipan Apache warriors acting as scouts. When they left Austin, their destination was the Comanche homeland to the west.

Three weeks and two hundred and fifty miles later, Moore's company neared what the Apache scouts told the colonel was a Comanche village of sixty families. At dawn on October 24, the Rangers, having approached without being detected, attacked the village residents. The Comanche were slaughtered, both in the village itself and in the Colorado River, as they made a futile effort to escape the Texan firepower. The three dozen or so women and children who survived were later sold as slaves.

When word of Moore's stunning victory reached Austin, officials could allow themselves to believe that the attack so deep in Comanche territory would break the tribe's fighting spirit. This turned out not to be true. In any case, there would soon be a threat from another old foe.

CHAPTER 13

"HURRY ON!"

Jack Hays's bravery during the Battle of Plum Creek had been noted and appreciated by the older Rangers. While no one would doubt Hays's courage, he did not exactly look like he was one of the Texas frontier's early heroes. At five foot eight, he was a reasonable height for a man at the time, but he had a thin build and his voice was softer than typical for a commander of men. Still, Hays seemed a natural leader.

The following January, he was formally appointed captain of a Ranger company. From that point on, Hays was the epitome of a Texas Ranger in the 1840s. As Mike Cox put it in his *The Texas Rangers*: "The young Tennessean would shape the image of the early Texas Rangers as surely as a bullet mold turned hot lead into deadly rifle balls."

Hays actively dealt with Indians in 1841 because President Lamar had decreed an aggressive policy against them. But in December of that year, Houston was elected president again, succeeding his successor. In early 1842, he promoted a policy of peace, not only because he harbored no hatred for Indians (earlier in his life, Houston had lived with the Cherokee) but also because the Republic of Texas was close to being broke and could not afford an ongoing war with the tribes. His efforts were mostly effective, and it seemed that Texas would enjoy an unprecedented period of peace.

But Mexico had different ideas. The next three years saw a series of dramatic events that allowed the Texas Rangers—and especially leaders like John Coffee Hays—to demonstrate how necessary they were to the young republic.

The first of these events became known as the Vásquez Incursion. Almost six years after his surrender at San Jacinto, Santa Anna was still smarting over losing Texas as a territory of Mexico. By January 1842, he was sufficiently recovered in political power and manpower to instigate an effort to take Texas back. Almost immediately, rumors began to swirl through San Antonio that it might be 1836 all over again, as though Texas had never won its independence.

Those rumors were true: An army of approximately seven hundred men (including a contingent of Caddo Indians), commanded by General Ráfael Vásquez, would soon cross the Rio Grande and march to San Antonio. The city's leaders conferred and appointed Jack Hays to supervise the mounting of a defense.

By the first week in March, when General Vásquez arrived, there were few San Antonio citizens to greet him. Most of the population had skedaddled. Hays and the hundred or so men under his command found themselves in the untenable position of being vastly outnumbered and tasked to defend a virtually abandoned city. Hays's officers pointed out that nothing would be gained by another Alamo-like outcome. He was courageous but not foolish: Hays listened and ordered his men to retreat to Guadalupe. The Mexicans had San Antonio at their mercy.

For the next two days they occupied themselves by plundering the city. Meanwhile, while camped at Cibolo Creek, Hays sent out messages asking for reinforcements. Among those who responded was Juan Seguín and a band of Tejanos (Texans of Spanish/Mexican descent). The native of Mexico was one of the men under siege at the Alamo six years earlier but had not perished because he had carried one of William Travis's missives out of the mission and could not return in time. Seguín subsequently distinguished himself as an officer in the Texas army that had defeated Santa Anna. To him, it looked as if it was time to do that all over again.

But General Vásquez was not inclined to linger and risk retaliation for the sacking of San Antonio. His army, accompanied by wagons groaning under the weight of stolen goods, left the city, heading back to the Rio Grande. Captain Jack Hays and his somewhat upgraded special force followed the Mexicans, offering whatever harassment they could. Meanwhile, the Texas Congress wanted to declare war, but President Houston would not go along, explaining that if the republic did not have the financial resources to fight Indians, they certainly could not take on an entire country.

For the next few months Texans could only grind their teeth over the insult. Hays and his Rangers were occupied with responding to raids on settlements by Indians, especially the unrepentant Comanche. In July 1842, President Houston elevated Hays to the rank of major. But he was given the unenviable task of finding enough volunteers to guard the entire frontier against border ruffians and Indians. This might have proved too frustrating a mission for Hays, but only a few weeks later there was a more pressing matter.

In September, the Mexicans were back.

The previous invasion had proved easy and successful enough that Santa Anna decided to do it again. To add injury to insult, maybe this time the Mexican military force would remain as conquerors. The president dispatched the Second Division of the Mexican Army Corps of the North, commanded by Adrián Woll.

General Woll was not Mexican; he had been born in 1795 near Paris. He enlisted in the army that fought for Napoleon in the defense of that city in 1814. Once the emperor abdicated and went into exile, Woll exiled himself, emigrating to the United States, where he became an officer on the staff of General Winfield Scott. He eventually found his way to Texas and then Mexico, where he lived as a civilian. When Spain tried to retake Mexico in 1829, Woll was back in uniform, this time as the aide-de-camp to Santa Anna. The Frenchman took part in the assault on

Tampico and in the battle in Tamaulipas, and after being wounded, he was promoted to colonel.

By the summer of 1842, Woll was one of Santa Anna's most trusted and experienced generals. But he proved not to be quite as intrepid as Santa Anna had hoped, though he certainly had the manpower—there were fifteen hundred men, including cavalry, under his command. This army, more formidable than the last one, crossed the Rio Grande and lumbered toward San Antonio. Once more charged with defending the city, Jack Hays had posted lookouts south of it.

But on the night of September 11, the invaders left the main road and made a march through the hills. At dawn, with nonplussed residents still rubbing the sleep out of their eyes, Woll captured San Antonio. Even more out-numbered than the last time, the Rangers managed to escape, and the outfoxed Hays was left to send messages hither and yon pleading for reinforcements.

Instead of planting the Mexican flag as conquerors, General Woll, like Vásquez, mostly planned to humiliate San Antonio. He made the best use of his time by captur-ing the members of the district court, which happened to be in session, along with a number of other prominent Tex-ans. Because of the Mexican general's cleverness, there had not been enough advance warning to empty the city out.

While Woll was having his way, from all across central Texas small groups of men rode or walked to the relief of San Antonio. Hays's calls were being answered. Soon more than two hundred volunteers gathered at Seguin, every man eager to drive the Mexicans out of the republic. Juan

Seguín, by the way, had fled to Mexico after being falsely blamed for aiding the Vásquez Incursion, and he was now an officer in Woll's army. He would remain in the Mexican military, serving under Santa Anna in the Mexican-American War that began in 1846.[27]

Woll's biggest challenge was that there may not have been enough to steal in San Antonio after the city's sacking only months earlier. Another challenge was keeping in check the Cherokee who were part of his army. They were led by Vicente Córdova, who, several years earlier, had conspired with Mexican officials to launch a rebellion against the Texas government. He and his coconspirators had been defeated in a battle near Seguin by a group of militiamen and Rangers led by Edward Burleson and Mathew "Old Paint" Caldwell.

Jack Hays and his men were buoyed when the very same Caldwell galloped into town at the head of a strong detachment from Gonzales and the Guadalupe Valley. The well-known Indian fighter was immediately elected to the rank of colonel and given command of the small but expanding Texas army. Hays was selected to lead the forty-two-man mounted detachment, most of whom were already under his command.

---

27 By the end of 1848, the well-traveled Juan Seguín was back in Texas, where he became a rancher outside the town named for his family. He was elected to two terms as justice of the peace of Bexar County and became a founding father of the Democratic Party in the county. In 1858, he published a memoir of his life and adventures. In 1883, he returned to Mexico. He died there in August 1890, two months before his eighty-fourth birthday. Even while dead, Seguín continued to switch countries: On July 4, 1976, his remains were reinterred in his namesake town in Texas.

In 1808, at the age of ten, Caldwell moved from Kentucky to Missouri with his family. He found various ways to make a living and then sought a different edge of the frontier, arriving in Texas in February 1831 with his wife and children in a wagon. The family settled in Gonzales, and in time he was put in charge of minutemen there and in the surrounding area.

Actively recruiting before the Battle of Gonzales in October 1835, he rode from Gonzales to Mina informing colonists of the dire need of their support in the volunteer army. Because of this, some called him the "Paul Revere of Texas." His next mission would be more political. On February 1, 1836, Caldwell was elected a delegate to the Texas Independence Convention at Washington on the Brazos, and he was a signer of the Texas declaration of independence. The convention appointed a committee of three, of which Caldwell was a member, to assess the situation of the enemy on the frontier and the condition of the Texan army. What he saw persuaded Caldwell to recruit volunteers to become the Gonzales Ranging Company of Mounted Volunteers (most of whom died at the Alamo).

In September 1842, Caldwell was, at forty-four, older than most of the men gathered near the occupied San Antonio, and he was certainly one of the more experienced. After sizing up the situation, Caldwell issued his own Travis-like missive to appeal to volunteers: "Hurry on! Hurry on! And lose no time. We fear nothing but God and through him we fight our battles. Huzza! Huzza for Texas!"

He and the twenty-five-year-old Jack Hays knew that to stop these destructive forays by Santa Anna, his surrogate,

General Woll, would have to be given a good whipping. The time to do that was before the Mexican army went anywhere else for further plundering. What was needed was to find the best place for battle.

CHAPTER 14

"VICTORY PURCHASED WITH BLOOD"

By early morning on September 17, Caldwell and Hays, now with a total of 210 volunteers, were encamped on the east bank of Salado Creek, six miles northeast of San Antonio. Among the volunteers were men who would become well-known Rangers—William "Bigfoot" Wallace and Sam Walker. The Texans waited for the fifteen hundred Mexican troops to come and get them.

A natural earthen embankment on the east side of the creek and a good stretch of timber provided the volunteers with excellent cover. There was a clear field of fire into a wide grassy prairie that rose gently from the creek to a low ridge nearly eight hundred yards away. An army foolish enough to approach the creek across the prairie would be fair game for the accuracy of the Texans' long rifles. To the rear of the position, a steep, heavily thicketed ridge rose nearly vertical from the far bank of the creek, rendering an approach from the west practically impossible.

Now the challenge for Caldwell and Hays was to prevent their eager volunteers from giving up such good ground in favor of taking the fight to the Mexicans. They could never hope to drive General Woll and his army out of the location where he had set up their headquarters—as a further insult, the Alamo. The only answer was to somehow lure the experienced French commander into attacking the strong defensive position along Salado Creek.

The plan Caldwell concocted and put into action was to send Jack Hays and three dozen Rangers to the Alamo. Upon arrival, Hays and several of them rode along the mission's walls and shouted insults to the guards, challenging the Mexicans to a fight. Suddenly, bugles began to blare and a troop of lancers galloped out of the compound and toward their tormentors. Surprised by the Mexicans' alacrity and clearly outnumbered, Hays and his men bolted for Salado Creek, with a backup force led by Ben McCulloch providing some covering fire.

The Rangers reached the safety of the Texas lines well before the Mexican cavalry reined up on the low ridge to the east. After a brief rest, Hays led his Rangers in a series of skirmishes with the lancers. Putting their pistols and shotguns to good use, the Rangers managed to kill ten Mexican cavalrymen and wound twenty-three more before returning to the creek without suffering a single casualty. Once more, the other Texans took note of how calm and collected Hays was under fire.

By noon, General Woll and close to six hundred men plus two pieces of artillery were on the ridge east of Salado Creek. The guns were brought forward, and soon they were banging away at the Texas position. The barrage did little damage; even better, Woll had left most of his artillery at the Alamo. This was a serious mistake because a sustained bombardment from all of his guns may well have driven the Texans away from the protection of the creek bank.

Now it remained to be seen if the Texans could withstand another advantage the Mexican army had—many more men. As General Woll sat in a large white tent that shielded him and his staff from the harsh rays of the sun, his drummers began to beat out commands. Accordingly, the Mexican infantry formed up in four long lines of battle, with a thin line of skirmishers well to the front and the dragoons in the rear to act as a reserve. Cavalry served as a screen for each flank. The top commanders practically licked their lips in anticipation.

But for the next two hours there was no large-scale attack. Wisely, Woll waited for the Texans to come to him. But Caldwell was content to send out up to twenty skirmishers at a time to confuse and tease the Mexicans without revealing how few men he had under his command. As watches ticked away, it was a contest to see who had the most patience. "Old Paint" continued to bide his time, reassuring his men. The veteran Indian fighter's resolve was finally rewarded when Woll ordered his drummers to work again. The Mexican officers drew their swords and signaled their troops to advance across the open prairie.

This was exactly the scenario Caldwell and Hays had sought. The Mexicans marched forward to the beat of their drums with their bayonets glistening in the late afternoon sun. The Texans concealed behind the cover of the earthen embankment rose up, aimed their rifles, and issued one volley after another at the enemy's massed ranks. Mexican soldiers fell by the dozens, most of them hit in the head or center-punched in the chest.

During the battle, Vicente Córdova led close to fifty men, most of them Cherokees, in an attack on the Texans' right flank. Córdova had been a thorn in the Texans' side since independence and had fought before on behalf of Mexico. Now his men drew near enough that for a few minutes the fighting was hand-to-hand. Soon, eleven of the enemy lay dead. Córdova had remained almost a hundred yards away. His gestures exhorting the attack drew the attention of one of the Texans, who raised his rifle and shot him dead. Thorn removed.

Observing the carnage from his tent, Woll was horrified as the bodies piled up on the blood-soaked prairie after only twenty minutes. The Texan toll was one man killed and a dozen wounded. According to the eminent historian Robert Utley, "Once again, the Texan citizen soldier had demonstrated his courage and fighting prowess. He had also shown that led by a respected commander he could fight as a disciplined team and restrain his impulse to throw himself suicidally on the enemy. The battle of Salado testified to the Texan fighting potential when led by a man who knew how to harness it."

It was getting to be sunset when Woll couldn't stomach

it anymore. He ordered his battered troops to reassemble and begin a retreat to San Antonio. They left sixty bodies on the battlefield and filled their wagons with another forty-four dead and a staggering total of one hundred and fifty wounded. The following day, the Mexicans held a mass funeral in San Antonio rather than the grand victory fandango they had planned earlier.

Unfortunately for the Texans, another battle occurred on the same day, September 17, that took a lot of the pleasure out of the Salado Creek action. During it, unbeknownst to Caldwell, a company of fifty-four Texans, mostly from Fayette County and led by Nicholas Mosby Dawson (a veteran of the Texas Revolution), had hurried from LaGrange toward the Salado Creek battlefield. Suddenly, they found themselves between San Antonio and the retreating Mexican army. Woll, afraid of being surrounded, had a contingent of cavalry, possibly as many as four hundred men, and two cannons attack the newcomers.

The Texans were able to hold their own against the almost overwhelming rifle fire, but once the cannons got within range, their fatalities mounted quickly. Dawson realized the situation was hopeless and raised a white flag of surrender. However, both sides continued to fire. "Sell your lives as dearly as possible," Dawson called to his men. "Let victory be purchased with blood."

Moments later, Dawson was killed and the Mexicans advanced, overrunning the Texans' position. Most of them put down their arms and attempted to surrender, but the enemy troops bayonetted many of them. When the engagement was over, in little more than an hour, thirty-six of the

Texans were dead. The Mexicans took the rest prisoner, though two Texans did manage to escape.

Later that day, Caldwell's troops located the site of what became known as the Dawson Massacre and buried the dead Texans. They did not bury the dead Mexicans who had been left behind, leaving them to predators.

CHAPTER 15

TAKE THE FIGHT SOUTH

Fearing that more Texans might rally to the cause of re-pelling invaders, especially after reports of the Dawson Massacre, Woll wasted no time and had his army marching out of San Antonio the next day. The column included a herd of five hundred cattle and wagons bearing whatever plunder the city still had. Two hundred Mexican families seeking protection from the town's furious Anglo citizens also accompanied the column. "Old Paint" Caldwell called a council of war, and the Texans voted to pursue the Mexicans and attack them if possible.

Jack Hays was given the assignment of leading the pursuit. It began when he shouted "Charge!" and he rode ahead, followed by fifty men. He and his riders caught up with the Mexican rear guard near the Arroyo Hondo in midafternoon on September 22. By then, Woll's main column had crossed the river and assumed good defensive positions along the west bank. Only a company of infantry and a few cavalry remained on the east bank to protect two cannons and the Mexican families who had not yet crossed.

Caldwell gave Hays permission to assault the Mexican guns and promised to support the attack with his infantry. He and the Rangers made a valiant mounted charge into the face of the Mexican cannons, killing all five artillerymen as they galloped past.

But the attack was not a complete success, because Caldwell failed to support the effort as promised, and a determined advance by the Mexican infantry forced Hays and his men to spike the guns and withdraw. Hays was furious with Caldwell, who explained that the rest of the Texas volunteers had simply refused to advance on the strong position along the river with the cannons.

Woll led his tired and badly bloodied force away from the Arroyo Hondo during the night and reached the safety of the Rio Grande on October 1. Refusing Caldwell's order to withdraw, Hays and the Rangers had dogged Woll's column all the way back to the border, occasionally skirmishing with the Mexican cavalry.[28]

Though the combined volunteer force of militia and

---

28 Anguished that a bigger victory may have escaped him, Caldwell gave up his command, though he continued to command the respect of many Texans. Sadly, he did not have much life left to live, passing away that December at his home in Gonzales. He was buried with full military honors. Upon his return to Mexico City, Woll remained a strong ally of Santa Anna. Years later, after the takeover of Mexico by the French, Woll was sent to France on a special commission and never returned to Mexico. After the fall of the French Empire, he stayed in Montauban, where he died in 1875 at the age of eighty.

Rangers had ruined Santa Anna's plans to retake Texas, many people in and around San Antonio were not satisfied. Once more, their city had been ransacked and blood had been spilled. Many of the republic's citizens were furious. This time, they demanded, take the fight to Santa Anna.

Sam Houston preferred not to go this route, especially with the Texas treasury not any richer than it was before. However, the anger of his constituents grew, so on October 3, Houston elevated Alexander Somervell, the commander of the First Brigade of the Texas militia, to lead an army of volunteers in a reprisal mission. The canny president knew that the tentative and indecisive Somervell was exactly the wrong man for the job.

A native of Maryland, Somervell had arrived in Texas in 1833 as a thirty-seven-year-old merchant. Despite having almost no qualifications, three years later Somervell became a major in the First Regiment of Texas Volunteers and soon after was elected lieutenant colonel of that regiment. He participated in the San Jacinto victory and then chose politics as his next field of battle. In October 1836, he was elected to represent Colorado and Austin Counties in the First and Second Congresses of the new republic. The following year, Somervell was a general leading the First Brigade; thus, when the time came, he had the right rank to command an expedition against Mexico but not much of a commander's track record.

President Houston's instructions to Somervell were to raise an army and put it in good enough fighting shape to invade Mexico. Finding men was the easy part because once word got around that Texas wanted to do to Mexico what Mexico had been doing to Texas, volunteers poured into San Antonio. They were a mixture of men eager to defend the honor of the republic and those who cared more about the possibility of plunder.

Numbering approximately seven hundred men—including Jack Hays at the head of his company—the new army left San Antonio on November 25, 1842. It headed south, reaching the Rio Grande, and then, according to Robert Utley, "Somervell suddenly veered east into dense chaparral. Officers and men alike grumbled that he was feeling his way [and that] he himself probably did not know what he intended." In only a few days, "his horses were broken down, his provisions all but exhausted, and at any moment vulnerable to a concentration of Mexican forces that might destroy him."

Still, Somervell managed to lead his men to Laredo, and on December 8 they took possession of it. Soon, Texans flooded the town looking for loot. Stopping the stealing was thus far the toughest battle Somervell had. To his credit, he got his officers to put a halt to it and even managed to have some of the goods returned to their owners.

For close to two hundred Texans, Laredo was victory enough, and two days later they turned around to head home. The rest of the men voted to continue the expedition. With Hays and his Rangers scouting ahead of it, the diminished army's next stop was Guerrero, sixty miles southeast of Laredo, and it quickly surrendered. On the fourteenth, Hays and another Ranger captain, Samuel Bogart, and their companies found two canoes on the east bank of the Rio Grande. A half dozen men at a time, with their horses swimming alongside, the army crossed over, and the eagerly anticipated invasion of Mexico began.

And then it was over. Somervell got cold feet, and not only from the chilly downpour of rain mixed with sleet that fell upon him and his men. He had a nightmare that his entire army on the other side of the river was attacked by Mexican military and had to retreat the same laborious way they had arrived. Fearing disaster, the general ordered his men to disband and return home.

However, the Texans were so disappointed with the order that only 189 men and officers obeyed. The remainder, approximately 310 men, commanded by William Fisher, continued into Mexico.

One can debate whether Somervell's decision was reasonable. However, there is no doubt that the decision by his mutinous men was disastrous.[29] Their horrible adventure would become known as the Mier Expedition. While it marked a low point in Texas Ranger history, a subsequent event involving Jack Hays and his men at the Battle of Walker's Creek would be an indisputable high point.

---

29 The incompetent Somervell did not even have a dignified death. In February 1854, as a private businessman, he began a journey from Lavaca to Saluria in a small boat, carrying a considerable amount of money. When found, the boat was bottom-side up and Somervell was lashed to the timbers. Whether he was killed for money, which was never found, or the boat capsized was never determined.

CHAPTER 16

FROM BAD TO WORSE

William Fisher had served his adopted state with honor. However, in the last days of 1842 he was making the worst decision of his life in leading Texans further into Mexico instead of returning to San Antonio.

Born in Virginia, Fisher had emigrated to Texas in 1834 and settled in Gonzales. In March two years later, he reinforced Sam Houston's army with the company of volunteers he had raised, and they participated in the Battle of San Jacinto. Fisher served for eleven months as the secretary of war. Then, when Mirabeau Lamar took office, he appointed Fisher lieutenant colonel of a frontier cavalry regiment. He was in command of two companies of regulars in San Antonio at the time of the Council House fight.

In 1842, Fisher had been elected a captain in Somervell's

army. When that campaign ended, he was elected leader of those members of the expedition who continued into Mexico. But Jack Hays did not like the prospects of the invasion, and he and his men headed back to Texas—a decision that most likely saved their lives. President Houston, citing his "indomitable energy and generous perseverance, skill, and daring," appointed Hays to lead a company of mounted men to patrol the border. Meanwhile, Fisher's force moved on, approaching Ciudad Mier on December 20.

Another member of this expedition was William Alexander Anderson Wallace. Known as "Bigfoot," he was born and raised in Lexington, Virginia. Wallace was nineteen when he learned that one of his brothers had died in the Battle of Goliad in 1836. Pledging to avenge his brother's death, he headed for Texas. By the time he arrived, however, the war was over. Wallace found he liked the spirited independence of the new republic and decided to stay.

He cut quite a figure, even for Texas. Over six feet tall and weighing around 240 pounds, Wallace's physique made him an intimidating man, and his unusually large feet earned him the nickname. According to one description, he was "plenty tall and brawny. In his prime he had an arm spread of six feet six and he could swing his rifle as easily as a hoe. Black hair curled thick on his well-shaped head, and his eyes were so keen that he would never wear spectacles to the end of his long life."

Wallace was an experienced member of Jack Hays's company and a formidable fighter, but he chose to follow Fisher and risk his "long life." While there have been numerous accounts of this fatal foray into Mexico, a particularly colorful and detailed one of the Mier Expedition— albeit including a few grains of salt—can be found in John C. Duval's *The Adventures of Big-Foot Wallace,* published in 1870. Duval and Wallace were good friends, and in the account Wallace purportedly narrates the story of his life.

On the twentieth, the Texans, led by Fisher, approached Ciudad Mier, unaware that three thousand Mexican troops were in the area under the command of Generals Francisco Mejia and Pedro de Ampudia. Thus, the day after Christmas, when the Texans got around to launching an attack, they faced a ten-to-one disadvantage. Still, as Wallace recalled, "The fire from our rifles was so rapid and deadly that they at length fell back in confusion, leaving the streets and plaza strewed with their dead and wounded."

While they were able to inflict such impressive heavy casualties on the Mexicans—some estimates claim over six hundred dead—the outnumbered and outgunned Texans were finally forced to surrender. Close to 250 of them were taken prisoner.

The victorious Mexicans, according to Wallace, "fastened us up in some deserted stone buildings, like so many pigs, where we were kept for five or six days with nothing to eat except a little dried beef. To wash this down, we were furnished with a limited supply of muddy water from the Rio Grande." However, Wallace added, "There was no use to complain; we knew we were 'in for it' and principally through our own stupidity and folly, and we resolved to make the best of the worst situation in which we might be placed."

They could not have imagined how bad the "worst situation" was going to get.

Under heavy guard, the Texan prisoners were marched toward Mexico City. This seemingly endless trek took the rest of December, all of January, and into February. "Whenever a poor fellow lagged behind the column for an instant, they seemed to take an especial pleasure in accelerating his speed by the vigorous application of the bayonet," the Ranger Bigfoot Wallace reported.

Along the way, when they arrived in a town, "Our guards paraded us several times around the public square, to give the good people a chance to look at the 'wild Texans.' We were hooted at by the mob, that was sure to collect around us whenever we stopped for a few moments, who would call us by all sorts of hard names, and pelt us with stones and clods of earth, and stale eggs."

Miraculously, given their deteriorated condition, on February 11, 1843, 181 Texans managed to escape. But soon the lack of food and water to be found in the merciless surroundings had those men near death. Every morning, Wallace, one of the escapees, recalls, "We continued our course over the dreary-looking mountains that rose up before us, and their barren and desolate appearance disheartened even those who had been the warmest advocates for seeking the protection of their solitudes." He further recounts that "not a single drop of water had been seen on the whole route, and, thirsty and dispirited, we wrapped our scanty covering around us and lay down upon the cold ground, and endeavored to forget our troubles in sleep."

Men died during the night, while others, dazed by the relentless sun, wandered away from the staggering column of Texans, never to be seen again. Wallace was one of about sixty men who discovered a Mexican military encampment and promptly surrendered. "The Mexicans seized us at once, tied us in pairs together, and laid us on the ground. We begged and implored them, in the most piteous terms, to give us some water." Each prisoner was allowed a small cup. The next morning, they were back on their feet, finally reaching a water hole by early afternoon.

The prisoners were marched back to Saltillo, where they learned that an outraged Santa Anna had ordered all the escapees to be executed. When the document from Mexico City arrived and was about to be read aloud, Wallace and "some of the more sanguine among us fully thought that the paper contained an order for our release, and eagerly crowded around the interpreter to hear the joyful news." Instead, they were "stunned and confused" by the death sentence.

General Francisco Mejia thought the execution of men in such a piteous condition would be a dishonorable act and refused to follow the order. Instead, Colonel Domingo Huerta was selected to command the detail escorting the prisoners to El Rancho Salado. By this time, diplomatic efforts on behalf of the Texans by the foreign ministers of the United States and Great Britain led Santa Anna to compromise: Now only one in ten of the 176 prisoners had to be killed.[30]

---

30 Other escapees had either been caught or, defying heat and thirst, had managed to find their way back into Mexican custody.

To help determine who would die, Huerta had 159 white beans and 17 black beans placed in a pot. The Texan officers and enlisted men, in alphabetical order, were ordered to draw. The first man to draw a black bean was Major James Decatur Cocke. He held up the bean between his forefinger and thumb and, with a smile of contempt, said, "Boys, I told you so; I never failed in my life to draw a prize." He later told a fellow Texan, "They only rob me of forty years." Fearing that the Mexicans would strip his body after he was dead, Cocke removed his pants and gave them to a companion who had drawn a white bean and whose clothing was in worse shape.

As Wallace recalled about his comrades' courage, "Those who drew black beans seemed to care very little about it. Occasionally, one would remark, as he drew out the fatal color, 'Well, boys, the jig is up with me' or 'They have taken my sign in at last' or something of a similar character, and then give way to the next, apparently as unconcerned as if he had no interest whatever in what was going on around him." Bigfoot Wallace, of course, drew a white bean, or his recollections would never have been recorded.

The condemned men were allowed to write letters home. On the evening of March 25, 1843, they were shot in two groups, one of nine men and one of eight.[31] They were all buried in a freshly dug ditch.

------

31 James Shepherd survived the firing squad by pretending to be dead in the courtyard under the bodies, and he escaped in the night. Alas, several weeks later, he was recaptured and brought back to the same courtyard, where he was shot and this time stayed dead.

The survivors who picked white beans wound up in the horrid Perote Prison in the state of Veracruz, along with the fifteen survivors of the Dawson Massacre and as many as fifty other men captured by General Adrián Woll during his campaign. Some of the Texans escaped from Perote, and others died there. Many were prisoners until they were finally released by order of Santa Anna on September 16, 1844. One of those released was William Fisher. He had been wounded during the attack on Mier but survived that and the events that came to be known as the "Black Bean Episode." After his release, Fisher returned to Texas, where he died at his home in Jackson County less than a year later.

During the Mexican-American War, when the U.S. Army occupied northeastern Mexico, Captain John E. Dusenbury, a white bean survivor, returned to El Rancho Salado and exhumed the remains of his comrades. He traveled with them on a ship to Galveston and then by wagon to La Grange in Fayette County. By this time, the remains of the men killed in the Dawson Massacre had been removed from their burial site near Salado Creek in Bexar County. The remains of both groups of men were reinterred in a large common tomb in 1848, in a cement vault on a bluff one mile south of La Grange, with the ceremony attended by over a thousand people.

What of Bigfoot Wallace? While incarcerated in Perote, he fell ill with the one-size-fits-all "jail fever" and barely survived. He was released on August 22, 1843, and had to make his way back to Texas with several other men. En route, Wallace contracted yellow fever and again almost died. It was not until December—having sailed from Veracruz to New Orleans (arriving just as a hurricane hit the city) and then, on a steamer, to Texas, where he continued his journey by horse—that he finally arrived in San Antonio. He had been gone almost two years.

CHAPTER 17

THE FINEST COMPANY

As the sad story of the Mier Expedition survivors played out, Jack Hays and his company of between fifteen and twenty-five Rangers had been chasing bandits along the border with Mexico. Although he proved again to be an effective leader, in November 1843 he had to furlough his men for a familiar reason: money. Not only could Texas not provide the funds to pay them, but Hays had exhausted the four hundred dollars of his own money he had put up.

However, one too many bandits immediately took advantage of the border company's absence, and in January 1844 the Texas Congress authorized Hays to raise a new one "to act as Rangers, on the Western and South-Western Frontier." The top wage earner would be the captain, at seventy-five dollars a month, and his lieutenant, the veteran Ben McCulloch, would receive fifty-five dollars.

As his adventures resumed, Hays had the highest of support from none other than Sam Houston, who wrote, "The frontier of our country would be defenseless but for his gallantry and vigilance," adding that "no man on earth could be equally efficient on the frontier, particularly that of the Rio Grande."

Jack Hays's new company "was the finest he had ever commanded," writes Darren L. Ivey in the first volume of *The Ranger Ideal*. "The ranks were filled with experienced, well-mounted veterans who only needed one more tool to become a force with which to be reckoned." That "tool" turned out to be a particular kind of weapon, and it was obtained by Hays and his men just in time for what can be considered the pivotal pre–Civil War conflict for the Texas Rangers. The victory at the Battle of Walker's Creek can be attributed to Samuel Colt and Sam Walker as well as Capt. Hays.

The impact that this man had on the Republic of Texas cannot be overstated. Colt, born and raised in Connecticut as was Moses Austin, first greeted the world in Hartford in July 1814. An indication that his family life was not idyllic was that two of his siblings committed suicide—one of them, a brother, on the day before he was to be executed for murder.

As an adolescent he read about gunpowder, which would intrigue him throughout his life. During a Fourth of July event, he blew up a raft on Ware Pond. Onlookers were much impressed, but Colt's reward was being shipped off to boarding school. There he amused his classmates with pyrotechnics—until one of his demonstrations set the school on fire. He was then literally shipped off to sea, a voyage to Calcutta aboard the brig *Corvo*.

On the *Corvo,* inspired by the capstan, or windlass, which had a ratchet and pawl mechanism, Colt created a model of a revolver out of scrap wood. It differed from other revolvers in that it would allow the shooter to rotate the cylinder by the action of cocking the hammer with an attached pawl turning the cylinder. When Colt returned to the United States in 1832, his forgiving father financed the production of a rifle and a pistol. But when the pistol exploded, disillusioning his father, Colt had to find another underwriter.

He took a portable laboratory on tour and earned a living performing laughing gas demonstrations across the United States and Canada, billing himself as the "Celebrated Dr. Coult of New-York, London and Calcutta." He began giving lectures on street corners and then in lecture halls and museums, emphasizing the dramatic stories of salvation and redemption that his audiences craved. Colt constructed fireworks to complete the show. His stint as an itinerant pitchman was profitable.

Now having a nest egg and still wanting to be an inventor instead of a medicine man, Colt made arrangements to begin building guns. He designed a single fixed-barrel with a rotating cylinder. The action of the hammer would align the cylinder bores with the single barrel. During the next few years, the design improved, and Colt was ready to apply for a U.S. patent. He received one in 1836 for a revolving breech-loading, folding-trigger firearm named the Colt Paterson.

He formed a corporation of venture capitalists to bring his idea to market. The Patent Arms Manufacturing Company of Paterson was chartered by the New Jersey legislature. In its first year, Colt's company made more than a thousand weapons. But after the Panic of 1837, the company's underwriters were reluctant to fund the new machinery that Colt needed to make interchangeable parts, so he went back on the road to raise money. This sojourn included a demonstration for the military, but it passed on purchasing the weapon. Worse, Colt imperiled his own company by reckless spending, using corporate funds to buy an expensive wardrobe and lavish gifts for potential clients, including fancy dinners. Colt thought getting potential customers inebriated would generate more sales.

The company was briefly saved by the war against the Seminoles in Florida, which provided the first sale of Colt's weapons. But, ultimately, he proved to be a better inventor than businessman. In 1843, the Paterson plant closed and a public auction was held in New York City. Colt turned to selling underwater electrical detonators and waterproof cable of his own invention, teaming up with Samuel Morse (creator of the Morse code) to run telegraph lines under lakes, rivers, bays, and to attempt to do so under the Atlantic Ocean.

However, back in 1839, the Republic of Texas had purchased almost two hundred handguns for the Texas navy. When Samuel Houston disbanded the navy four years later, Captain Jack Hays armed his company of Texas Rangers with surplus stocks of the pistols. The repeating handguns became very popular with the Rangers, who believed that the sustained firepower would give them an advantage when fighting Indians. In addition to a rifle, each Ranger now had two five-shot Colt Patersons, allowing the shooter to take aim and fire ten shots in about forty seconds.

The Comanche could be efficient in delivering death too. Each warrior carried a lance and had a bow and arrow. Previously, he could send several arrows on their way while his opponent was trying to reload, and that, compared to strong horsemanship, had spelled doom for many Texans, including Rangers. But in June 1844, frontier combat changed.

CHAPTER 18

"MY MEN EVINCED NO DISMAY"

Walker's Creek is a tributary of the Guadalupe River, some fifty miles north of Seguin. On June 8, 1844, Jack Hays's company was on patrol. Two of the members were Robert Gillespie and Samuel Walker.

The latter was a twenty-seven-year-old Maryland native who had enlisted in the Washington City Volunteers in 1836 for the Creek Indian Campaign in Alabama. The following year he worked as a scout in Florida, and by 1842 he was a member of the Texas army that had repelled Gen. Woll. He survived the Mier Expedition and the Black Bean Episode but remained a prisoner until escaping. Apparently, his thirst for adventure had not been quenched, because as soon as Sam Walker got back to Texas, he joined Hays's company.

The Rangers were using the creek as a watering hole when

one of them guarding the rear caught site of approaching Comanches. There were ten of them, and Hays observed that after being spotted they did not retreat with any haste but instead ambled into a timber thicket. The captain's suspicion about an ambush was proved correct when, tired of waiting, as many as seventy Comanche emerged, led by Yellow Wolf. The Rangers were facing a formidable foe, one of whom Jack Hays had encountered in battle before.

Yellow Wolf and his close friend and cousin Buffalo Hump had earned status as warriors early when they led an expedition to raid the settlements in the Guadalupe Valley. Then in 1835, they led three hundred Comanche warriors in an attack against Parral, in the Sierra Madre Occidental. And there was the Great Raid in revenge for the Council House fight. Now, Yellow Wolf led his warriors in a charge.

Previously, Hays would have ordered his men to rush back to the creek and make a stand there, using whatever protection the bank offered. This time, though, the Rangers remained where they were, and the perplexed Comanche halted. Maybe *they* were the ones about to be trapped. Several long-range shots were exchanged. Then the warriors retreated up a hill and out of sight.

Captain Hays led his men forward. He had noted a steep base to the hill and believed that when the Rangers reached it they would not be visible to the Comanche. When they arrived at the hidden base, Hays spurred his horse and his men followed him around and up the hill. The Indians were startled when the Texans suddenly appeared on their flank. Rifle shots riddled their ranks until they recovered and rode down off the hill. The Rangers gave pursuit. Once on level ground the Comanche turned and attacked. They were confident because they clearly outnumbered their adversary.

"In the confusion of close combat, no man that day took the time to consider that the Rangers were altering tactics and history or that the West was being changed by a Yankee inventor and a band of frontiersmen," writes Frederick Wilkins in *The Legend Begins*. "Mounted combat was starting down a new path, but these Rangers were probably wondering if they had placed too much trust in the five-shooters."

They had not. The Comanches found themselves perplexed and startled again. They sensibly assumed that having fired their rifles, the white men had little left besides their one-shot pistols and knives and could not withstand an overwhelming foe. The warriors charged. The Rangers aimed their pistols and fired. After that first volley, they fired another . . . and another. Saddles emptied fast as warriors were jerked out of them. Now more angry than confused, the Indians rallied and charged again.

Sam Walker and Robert Gillespie had gotten too far out front and were surrounded by warriors with thrusting lances, but their repeating pistols helped them break free.[32] The other Rangers kept their horses anchored and fired their Colt Patersons, stopping the stunned Comanche. When the withering fire had taken enough of a toll, the

---

32 Some of the Rangers carried spare cylinders to replace empty ones in their pistols, further increasing their firepower.

warriors turned and hurried away. Hays shouted for his men to follow. They chased the war party for as far as three miles until their ammunition and horses were exhausted.

Several Rangers had been wounded, and one, Peter Fohr, who had come to Texas from Germany and served under Hays for three years, died. On the other side of the ledger, there were twenty-three dead and thirty wounded Comanches.[33] Not only had the tribe suffered a severe loss, but word spread along the frontier that the Rangers had new weapons. With them and the relentless population increase of the whites, the tribes would inevitably be at an even greater disadvantage in the fight for land and survival.

In his report of the Battle of Walker's Creek dated June 16, 1844, and written in San Antonio to Anson Jones, the Texas secretary of war, Hays gave a straightforward, just-the-facts account and concluded, "I will take occasion to say, that my men evinced no dismay; but, on the contrary, would dare them to come to the charge."

That attitude plus a deadlier weapon gave all enemies of the Texas Rangers more to fear.

---

33 The next day, four Comanche warriors returned to look for wounded comrades, unaware the Rangers were camped nearby. In the chase that followed, three more warriors were killed.

CHAPTER 19

"BOYS, FIGHT TO THE LAST!"

Very soon after it had been born, the Republic of Texas had requested annexation by the United States, but through the administrations of Martin Van Buren, William Henry Harrison, and John Tyler, that did not happen.[34] However, there was finally enough traction during the early days of the James Polk administration that Texas was granted statehood, which became official in February 1846. The already displeased government of Santa Anna became exponentially unhappy. There was also the question of what exactly Texas was.

The problem: Neither the U.S. Congress's joint resolution nor the ordinance of annexation contained language speci-

---

34 Okay, Harrison's term lasted only one month. On Inauguration Day 1841, the sixty-eight-year-old gave an 8,445-word speech in the rain and subsequently developed pneumonia and died on April 4. Harrison gave the longest inauguration speech in U.S. history and held office for the briefest time of any president.

fying the boundaries of the new state. They only refer in general terms to "the territory properly included within, and rightfully belonging to the Republic of Texas"—or, essentially, whatever the Texas government said it was. In addition, the new state was to be formed "subject to the adjustment by this [U.S.] government of all questions of boundary that may arise with other governments"—or, essentially, what the United States said it was, ignoring whatever Mexico desired.

Texas claimed the Rio Grande as its border, basing its claim on the Treaties of Velasco, while Mexico maintained that the border was the Nueces River farther north. Oh, and it had never recognized Texan independence in the first place. In November 1845, President James Polk had secretly sent John Slidell to Mexico City with a monetary offer for the disputed land and other Mexican territories. Mexico was neither inclined nor able to negotiate because of the persistent instability in Santa Anna's government and popular nationalistic sentiment against such a sale.

With Slidell unsuccessful, Polk ordered General Zachary Taylor to garrison the southern border of Texas—the Rio Grande. Taylor ignored Mexican demands to withdraw and began to build a fort near the river's mouth on the Gulf of Mexico. The Mexican government regarded this action as a violation of its sovereignty and immediately prepared for war. The United States beat it to the punch, declaring war on May 12, 1846.

During all the political jostling with Mexico, there had been no cessation of raids by Indians, even the depleted Comanche, and by those who fell into the "border ruffian" category. Texas Rangers captains still had to raise and find ways to pay for companies. But "war" was a siren call, especially when the fight would be for the honor and benefit not just of a republic but of the entire United States. When a call for troops was sent out, one new unit responding was the First Texas Mounted Rifle Regiment. The apparently tireless John Coffee Hays was elected colonel, and Sam Walker as lieutenant colonel. Familiar faces like Ben McCulloch, Bigfoot Wallace, Robert Gillespie, as well as others, signed up.

The regiment, mostly led by Rangers, cut quite a figure when it joined the regular U.S. Army units. They displayed eye-popping horsemanship, could knock a bird's eye out with a rifle shot, dressed with the casual practicality of frontiersmen, and sported plenty of beards as well as five-shot pistols. According to Frederick Wilkins, "To the United States Army, the Texans demonstrated the value of repeating firearms and, in the process, brought Sam Colt out of financial ruin and enabled him to reestablish his manufacture of firearms. The army also saw a new form of mounted combat which prepared it for the arduous years ahead fighting the Plains Indians."

The Texans' skills and experience were of great help to Gen. Taylor, who deployed the men as scouts and quick-strike units. Their adventures and effectiveness have been told in many tales, and the Rangers played an undeniable role in the outcome of the war. Walker, in particular, became a favorite scout leader of Gen. Taylor's, and he engaged in many colorful and successful missions.

Highlighting just one: Daybreak on September 24, 1846, found Walker and two hundred Texans under his command in a post office surrounded by the Mexican army during the Battle of Monterrey. No worries: Walker had his men regularly moving about and shouting, leading the enemy to believe they were the ones who were outnumbered. The ruse worked—later that morning, a Mexican officer carrying a white flag approached to say that General Pedro de Ampudia wanted to parley. Walker and a company commander, Tom Green, agreed to visit the general's headquarters.[35]

Ampudia was a tad insulted by their appearance—he had expected Zachary Taylor himself to show up. After some palaver between the general and Walker, it was decided that Ampudia would send a message directly to Taylor. That message turned out to be a request for the terms of surrender. On September 25 the Mexican army left Monterrey.

There followed a sort of victory lap for Jack Hays and Sam Walker, who traveled to New Orleans, Galveston, and then San Antonio, where the memory of Robert Gillespie was honored. The veteran Ranger—though still just thirty-one—had died on the twenty-third from wounds suffered the day before during the fighting in Monterrey. Then, in November, Walker made his way north. He had been summoned to Washington, D.C.—James Polk wanted to meet him. This get-together may have been the first time a sitting president met with a Texas Ranger.

Then there was business to attend to in New York,

---

35 As we'll soon see, this same Capt. Green will play a prominent role in Leander McNelly's life.

where Samuel Colt hoped to receive the Ranger's endorsement of the Paterson pistol. With firsthand knowledge of the weapon's effectiveness, Walker was glad to give it. And his support carried enough weight that Polk and William Marcy, the secretary of war, cut through the red tape and had the federal government purchase a thousand of the pistols. These revolvers became known as the Walker Colt.

The celebrated Ranger could not dally in New York and Washington, though, because there was still a war going on. On March 24, 1847, Walker was in Kentucky, having raised a hundred or so recruits along the way to serve under him. Six weeks later, he was back in Mexico, at Veracruz, with close to two hundred men. The rest of that spring and summer he was involved in various exploits as the armies under Generals Taylor and Winfield Scott drove deeper into enemy territory. Walker's toughest fight would happen that fall, on October 9.

His company was attached to a force of soldiers from Ohio, Indiana, and Louisiana serving under General Joseph Lane.[36] As the Americans neared Huamantla, spies reported that Santa Anna himself was in the town. Walker

---

36 After distinguished service in the Mexican-American War, Lane was appointed the first governor of Oregon Territory. When Oregon was admitted as a state in 1859, Lane was elected one of its first two U.S. senators. In the 1860 presidential election, Lane was nominated for vice president of the pro-slavery Southern wing of the Democratic Party, as John C. Breckinridge's running mate. Lane's views and subsequent sympathy for the Confederate States of America in the Civil War effectively ended his political career. However, one of his sons was later elected a U.S. representative, and a grandson became a U.S. senator, making Lane the patriarch of one of Oregon's most prominent political families.

and his men were ordered to enter the city and, possibly, capture the Mexican president and end the war, repeating what had happened at San Jacinto eleven years earlier.

Perhaps Lane's spies had forgotten to mention that, if indeed Santa Anna was there, he was far from alone. When Capt. Walker and his force of two hundred men neared Huamantla, they saw what could have been as many as a thousand Mexican troops there. Undaunted, with sabers held high, the Texans spurred their horses forward. The boldness as well as the ensuing butchery drove the Mexicans back. Soon Walker and his men occupied the town's central plaza and, with it, the three cannons the Mexicans had positioned there.

Word of the setback reached Santa Anna two miles away. He dispatched five hundred of his lancers to retake the plaza. Spotting their approach, Walker rallied his men—they had been distracted by pillaging—and they charged the oncoming lancers. As horses and men collided, sabers flashed in the sunlight and guns blazed. During one exchange, Walker was knocked out of his saddle. As a group of Texans surrounded him to prevent further harm, Walker called out, "Boys, fight to the last. Never surrender this place as long as one of you is living!"

The bulk of Lane's army arrived and entered the fray. The Mexicans, with as many as two hundred dead, withdrew. By then, Sam Walker too was dead. Furious, the victorious soldiers ransacked Huamantla, and it took until that night for Gen. Lane to restore order, which included putting out fires and treating injured civilians. Three days later, when the arrival of the Americans ended the siege of

Puebla and Gen. Scott had taken Mexico City, Santa Anna was finished once more.[37]

The Mexican leader's carriage was still of some use. It bore Walker's body to Perote, where burial took place. This was but a temporary rest, however, as his remains were soon unearthed, transported to San Antonio, and buried in the Old City Cemetery. The Ranger captain's remains were on the move again in April 1856, when, as part of celebrations marking the twentieth anniversary of the San Jacinto victory, he was reinterred once more, this time in the Odd Fellows Cemetery, sharing a grave with Robert Gillespie.

---

37 After the war officially ended in 1848, Santa Anna lived in exile in Kingston, Jamaica, and then in Turbaco, Colombia. Incredibly, despite his defeats, in March 1853, he was back as president of Mexico. Further, he declared himself dictator for life. That life was shorter than he anticipated, as he was overthrown two years later. He went again into exile, his travels including Cuba and Staten Island, where he introduced chewing gum to American consumers but failed to profit from it. In 1874, he was allowed to return to Mexico, where he died two years later, at age eighty-two. He was buried with full military honors.

CHAPTER 20

INVADING COMANCHERIA

With the Mexican-American War over, the primary role of the Texas Rangers returned to protecting the increasing number of settlements along the border. A population of thirty thousand in the territory in 1830 was now well over one hundred thousand in the still-new state of Texas. No tribe could withstand such a population surge, yet the Comanche and a few other holdouts continued to conduct raids. New Ranger leaders had to step up because of the deaths and retirements and absences of previous ones.

John Coffee Hays was an example of the latter. In 1849 he turned thirty-two, and though not quite yet middle-aged, he apparently had had enough of the rough life of a Texas Ranger. And he was a husband and father.[38] That year, Hays secured safer employment with the U.S. government as the Indian agent for the Gila River country in New Mexico and Arizona.

But Hays was not yet done with restlessness. He and his family joined the migration to California that was spurred by gold rushers. His wagon train pioneered a shortcut, later known as the Tucson Cutoff, which saved travelers from a long journey to the south. Soon after arriving, Hays was elected sheriff of San Francisco County and later became active in politics and was one of the earliest residents of the city of Oakland. Over the years, Hays amassed a considerable fortune through real estate and ranching enterprises. In 1860, while in Virginia City, Nevada, on business, he heard the news of the First Battle of Pyramid Lake, which was an opening salvo in the Paiute War. He commanded a force of volunteer soldiers at the Second Battle of Pyramid Lake. Hays sat out the Civil War, content to attend to family and business. In 1876, he was elected as a delegate to the Democratic Party national convention, which nominated Samuel J. Tilden for president (who lost to Rutherford B. Hayes). Jack Hays died in California in April 1883, age sixty-six, and his grave is in the Mountain View Cemetery in Oakland.[39]

---

38 Letting bygones be bygones, upon the birth of Hays's first son, Buffalo Hump sent him a gift, a golden spoon engraved with the chief's name.

39 A nephew, John Hays Hammond Jr., was an apprentice to both Thomas Edison and Nikola Tesla and was one of the founders of the RCA Corporation.

New leaders did emerge. The most well-known of them was John Salmon Ford, whose nickname was "Rip." He had been born in South Carolina but, like Hays, was raised in Tennessee. He first aimed to be a doctor, then spent some time as a surveyor and studied law. He had been elected to the Texas Congress in 1845 and had begun yet another career, as a newspaperman in Austin. The war with Mexico brought him into the Texas Ranger fold.

According to Mike Cox, "Ford filled Jack Hays's figurative boots as Texas's most notable Ranger captain of the 1850s. What Ford did as a Ranger leader, and the stories he told, kept his name—and the Ranger tradition—alive."

Despite the increasing population of white farmers and ranchers and the presence of U.S. Army forts—in the early 1850s, there were nineteen of them in the state—Indian raids continued to bedevil Texans. Not only were volunteer Ranger companies still welcomed by communities, but Jefferson Davis, the secretary of war under President Franklin Pierce, pointed out their absolute necessity in June 1854, when he wrote that the undermanned military would need mounted men to help "in repelling Indian invasions."

During the rest of the decade, Ranger companies were raised and disbanded—the latter because their missions ended or, no surprise, because the state treasury ran out of money to pay them. The climactic event of the 1850s in the ongoing fight with Indian tribes was known as the Battle of Antelope Hills.

"Comancheria" was a large swath of Texas into New Mexico where most of the Comanche remained. It was regarded as Comanche territory by Texans, but that recognition did not prevent Anglos from pushing farther west into it. Some members of the tribe melted away, seeking a hunting-and-habitat haven even farther west, but many responded to the repeated intrusions by violently striking back to protect the good grazing ground they already had.

The army proved wholly unable to stem the bloody raids, hampered by federal law and numerous treaties that barred the army from attacking tribes residing in the Indian Territories. In 1858, the Texas governor, Hardin R. Runnels, called out a fresh batch of Rangers. The leader he appointed was "Rip" Ford, who was ordered to lead his mounted men into the heart of Comancheria. Ford's outlook would be frowned upon by many today, but what made him an especially effective commander was his proclivity for ordering the wholesale slaughter of any Indians, men and women, he could find.

For this mission, Gov. Runnels seemed to give Ford a blank check: "I impress upon you the necessity of action and energy. Follow any trail and all trails of hostile or suspected hostile Indians you may discover and if possible, overtake and chastise them if unfriendly."

Ford recruited a force of about one hundred Texas Rangers and borrowed state militia. Realizing that even with repeating rifles, buffalo guns, and Colt revolvers he would need additional men, Ford also recruited ones he did not have to pay. Among the traditional enemies of the Comanche were the Tonkawa, and Ford went to their Brazos Reservation (near what today is Fort Worth). With the help of the Indian agent, Captain L. S. Ross, he called the head man of the Tonkawa, Placido, to a war council, where Ross stirred anger against their mutual enemy.[40] Ford succeeded in recruiting one hundred and twenty warriors, and Placido declared he was the "faithful and implicitly trusted friend of the whites." That would be put to the test in Comancheria.

Ford now had well over two hundred fighting men under his command. They adhered to the governor's orders to "follow any and all trails" of hostiles and inflict the most severe punishment, which was right up Ford's alley. Scouts were sent to locate Comanche camps north of the Red River. Ford and Placido were determined to follow the Comanche and Kiowa up to their strongholds amid the hills of the Canadian River and into the Wichita Mountains. If successful, their mission would not just kill warriors but decimate the Comanche food supply, destroy homes, and generally eliminate their ability to make war.

On April 15, 1858, Ford and his force crossed the Red River and advanced into the portion of Comancheria in Oklahoma. Ford knew full well he was violating federal laws and numerous treaties by moving into the Indian Territories but stated later that his job was to "find and fight

---

40 The agent was the father of Lawrence Sullivan "Sul" Ross, nineteen at the time, who would become a revered figure in Texas history (and who appears elsewhere in this book). As a soldier in the Confederate army, Sul Ross participated in 135 battles and skirmishes and became one of the youngest rebel generals. After serving as a sheriff and state lawmaker as well as being a rancher, in 1887 Ross became the nineteenth governor of Texas. During his two terms, he oversaw the dedication of the new Texas State Capitol. Afterward, he became president of the Agricultural and Mechanical College of Texas, now Texas A&M University.

Indians, not to learn geography." However, it was not until May 12 that the Rangers and their Indian allies saw their first action. That day, they attacked a small Comanche village in the Canadian River valley, which was flanked by the Antelope Hills. Later that day, they attacked a second village, which provided much stiffer resistance until its head man, Iron Jacket, was killed.

His son Peta Nocona—husband of Cynthia Ann Parker and father of Quanah Parker—arrived with reinforcements, and the battle was renewed. At day's end, Ford and his men were on their way back to Texas. There were four Ranger casualties and about a dozen Tonkawa killed or wounded. The Comanche side of the ledger was bloodier: as many as seventy-six warriors were killed or wounded, three hundred horses lost, and two villages burned to the ground.

Ford returned to Texas and requested that Governor Runnels immediately empower him to raise additional levies of Rangers to continue the campaign in the heart of Comancheria. But that same pesky problem arose—funds to underwrite Ranger actions had been exhausted and Ford's force was disbanded.

Still, the outcome of the battle in May was the beginning of the end for the Comanche and Kiowa. For the first time, a Texan force had penetrated Comancheria, attacked Indian villages with impunity, and successfully returned. The U.S. Army would adopt some of Ford's tactics, including attacking not just warriors but also women and children and destroying their main food supply, the buffalo.

Not long after the new decade began, the Texas Rangers had another battle to wage—this time, against the might of the Union. The state seceded on February 1, 1861, and with a new fight anticipated, men enlisted in companies and regiments to take on the Yankees instead of Indians. There were special forces raised to continue the fight against the occasional Indian campaign, but for the most part, during the war the Rangers were represented by the regiment known as "Terry's Texas Rangers."

In the months after secession, Benjamin Franklin Terry, a wealthy sugar planter, recruited and organized the regiment in Houston. Initially intended to serve in Virginia, the regiment instead was placed under the command of General Albert Sidney Johnston for service west of the Mississippi. They first saw action on December 17, 1861, near Woodsonville, Kentucky, when they engaged the Union and were supported by the Sixth Arkansas Infantry. The skirmish cost them Colonel Terry, who was killed.

Soon the Rangers regiment was part of the Army of Tennessee, led by General Braxton Bragg. The by now traditional riding and shooting skills often caused the Rangers to be used as shock troops. The first major action was at the Battle of Shiloh. The Rangers regiment also supported Nathan Bedford Forrest's cavalry during the Battle of Murfreesboro. After that, small units were sent behind Union lines to harass the enemy and break their lines of communication. The Rangers fought in the Battles of Chattanooga and Chickamauga, the Knoxville Campaign, and the Atlanta Campaign.

The Rangers' ability to harass the enemy was often called upon against William Tecumseh Sherman. By July 1864, Sherman's army had reached Atlanta. On the thirtieth, Terry's Texas Rangers met the troops of Union Colonel E. M. McCook and defeated them. Following the loss of Atlanta, the regiment pestered the flanks of Sherman's force as it marched through Georgia. Their last engagement was at the Battle of Bentonville, where they made their final charge. The Rangers regiment surrendered on April 26, 1865, with the rest of the Army of Tennessee.

But it was farther west where a lowly young soldier had survived a misbegotten campaign, subsequently rose through the ranks, and would go on to become one of the most famous Texas Rangers. And here, patient reader, with the stage sufficiently set, is where Leander McNelly enters the story.

—— ACT II ——

LONE STAR LAWMAN

The State Police had been organized, and McNelly had been placed on the force, so on consultation with friends, it was thought best that I should leave.

—John Wesley Hardin

CHAPTER 21

"WALKING WHISKEY KEG"

Both of Leander Harvey McNelly's parents were born in Ireland. Little is known about his mother, Katherine Killian, other than that she was fifteen when she married in 1830. Her husband, five years older, was Eoin McNelly of County Down. By 1833 the young couple had two children, Owen (the father's anglicized name) and Peter, and they were on the move, to America. One has to admire the pluck of Eoin McNelly, being all of twenty-three and uprooting his eighteen-year-old wife and two children, one an infant, and taking them across the Atlantic Ocean—or maybe it was a desperate gamble to escape starvation.

Of the twenty-four states in the United States in 1833, the McNellys wound up in Virginia, raising sheep in Brooke County, in the northwestern part of the state.[41]

---

41 The county is now in West Virginia.

Apparently, much effort was put into raising children too, because Eoin and Katherine had six more of them. The third one, born on March 12, 1844, was named Leander. Remarkably, for that time, all eight McNelly offspring survived childhood, though the fourth oldest, Thomas, died at sixteen years of age.

Less remarkable at a time of restlessness and exploration in America was that some of the children, when old enough, went seeking new places to live and to raise their own families. Peter, for example, after being married, trekked with his wife to Missouri, though after two years they returned, with their firstborn. The next trip Peter took would have an impact on his equally restless younger brother.

A Virginian the McNellys knew, Chauncey Shepard, was one of many men who, before the Civil War, was curious about the very large state of Texas. When he traveled there to find out about it for himself, Shepard was accompanied by Peter McNelly. Upon their return, they extolled the beauty of the land and its potential. Peter had been so convinced that he had purchased a parcel near Brenham, the seat of Washington County and ninety miles east of Austin.

Leander was at least twelve years old when Peter bought the property and began the process of moving family members to what the new owner deemed the McNelly plantation. There may have been another reason for Peter's keen interest in Texas—to save his younger brother's life. Leander, before even entering his teenage years, exhibited symptoms of tuberculosis. There was no cure for the so-called "white plague" in the 1850s, and physicians could only suggest a warm, dry climate—like the one available in Washington County.

As his health improved, "Lee" McNelly helped with the family sheep-raising business and tended the flock of a neighbor, Travis Burton. His father, John Burton, one of the first Anglos to settle in Texas, had helped found the city of Austin and was the namesake of a community being established near the McNelly plantation. It seemed likely that Lee would carve out his own farm, be married, and raise a family there. However, as the new decade took hold, talk of war against the northern states was prevalent.

When Confederate forces fired on Fort Sumter in April 1861, Lee McNelly had just turned seventeen. In August of that year, claiming to be eighteen, he enlisted in a company led by Captain George Washington Campbell in the Fifth Texas Cavalry. He also enlisted his horse and brought his own gun and ammunition. Before long, the young soldier would be marching in a Confederate army commanded by Henry Hopkins Sibley.

Born in Natchitoches in 1816, Sibley had some military pedigree, his grandfather having served as a surgeon in the Revolutionary War. At the age of seventeen, the younger Sibley was admitted to the U.S. Military Academy at West Point and, upon graduation, was commissioned a second lieutenant.

He saw quite a bit of action in the 1840s, first against the Seminoles in Florida, then on frontier duty in Texas, and then in the Mexican-American War. In 1850 Sibley was put back on frontier duty in Texas, where he would remain for five years. He apparently had enough time on his hands to be an inventor, creating what, not surprisingly, became known as the "Sibley tent," which was widely used by the Union army during the Civil War. (The design was also adopted by Great Britain's military.) He also invented the "Sibley tent stove," which the U.S. Army used into the early years of World War II.

From Texas, Sibley went from the frying pan into the fire: Kansas. In the mid-1850s, the territory was known as "Bleeding Kansas" because of the violence between pro- and anti-slavery supporters. Fortunately for Sibley, in 1857 he was sent out west, participating in the Utah War against the Mormons, and then in 1861 he saw service in New Mexico. After the outbreak of the Civil War, the native Southerner resigned from the army and joined the new Confederate States of America.

On the surface, it would seem that Sibley was a good officer for the Confederacy. However, his career had been troubled by a taste for spirits. The dependence was such an open secret that a nickname attached to him was "Walking Whiskey Keg." Still, he was otherwise a smart and experienced military man—with a plan. Sibley secured a sit-down with Jefferson Davis, now president of the Confederate States of America, and outlined his "Confederacy of the West" scheme. Davis was intrigued.

It was certainly an ambitious plan. And there had been some precedent for it: an expedition earlier in 1861 led by John Robert Baylor. A native of Kentucky, his résumé included having been an Indian fighter, rancher, member of the Texas State legislature, and cofounding

The White Man, a publication that stirred up ill feelings toward Indians.[42]

Following the secession of Texas in February 1861, Baylor, a lieutenant colonel leading a just-mustered Second Texas Mounted Rifles, was sent to occupy the series of forts along the western frontier that had been abandoned by the Union army. His orders further allowed him to advance into New Mexico to attack the Union forts along the Rio Grande. His first target was Fort Fillmore.

Leaving their camp on July 23, 1861, the Confederates arrived in the area the next night. The next day, Baylor led his battalion into Mesilla, to the cheers of the population. Two days later, leaving a small force behind to guard Fort Fillmore, its commander, Major Isaac Lynde, led three hundred and eighty Union troops to Mesilla. Once there, the Yankee officer demanded Baylor's surrender. When the Confederate colonel refused, Lynde deployed his men into a skirmish line and opened fire with his mountain howitzers. When an infantry advance stalled, Lynde ordered his three companies of mounted riflemen to charge the rebel line.

The cavalry was more brave than smart. The riders were picked off by Confederate riflemen and the Union assault was repulsed. Lynde re-formed his command but decided to return to the fort. The Confederate troops, joined by armed local citizens, gave pursuit. Lynde's troops

---

42 Baylor's uncle was R. E. B. Baylor, a judge on the Texas Supreme Court after whom Baylor University was named (although he did not found it).

picked up their pace and managed to reach the safety of the stockade walls.

At sunset the next day, Baylor ordered his artillery and cavalry to move into position to attack the fort. But when they were ready to do so, they found the fort abandoned. Lynde destroyed the ammunition and supplies, then retreated northeast toward Fort Stanton across the dry Organ Mountains via San Augustin Pass. Many Union troops apparently had filled their canteens with the fort's medicinal whiskey instead of water, hardly wise for a summertime march across desert country.

During the pursuit the following day, Lynde's dehydrated command, reduced to one hundred men by this time, was overtaken by the Confederates, some of whom used what became known as Baylor Pass to intercept them. Lynde was forced to surrender at San Augustin Spring on July 27. The parched prisoners were paroled, and Baylor was able to refit his command with new Springfield rifles and other captured equipment.

On August 1 Baylor declared the establishment of the Confederate Arizona Territory. He installed himself as the new territory's military governor and declared martial law.[43]

However, his reign did not last long, because of his virulent hatred of Indians. He exhorted his cavalry to attack

---

43 Perhaps Baylor believed that martial law meant he was beyond reproach. When the otherwise pro-Confederate *Mesilla Times* published articles critical of him, Baylor sought out the editor, Robert Kelley. Baylor beat him so badly the newspaperman died a few weeks later. The colonel was not charged with a crime.

Apaches without provocation, ordering them to "use all means to persuade the Apaches or any tribe to come in for the purpose of making peace, and when you get them together kill all the grown Indians and take the children prisoners and sell them to defray the expense of killing the adult Indians. Buy whiskey and such other goods as may be necessary for the Indians and I will order vouchers given to cover the amount expended. Leave nothing undone to insure success."

When news of this order reached Jefferson Davis, he relieved Baylor as governor and revoked his commission as colonel. Baylor returned to military service at the Battle of Galveston in January 1863 as a private. He was soon elected to the Confederate Congress.

Putting aside his demotion by Davis, Baylor had been on to something. Having taken note of this success, Gen. Sibley aimed to exceed it. During his meeting with Davis, Sibley proposed a force of about three thousand men, whom he would lead through the Rio Grande valley into New Mexico, where Fort Craig would be taken from the Yankees. Next to be captured would be Fort Union. With New Mexico then under Confederate control, Sibley would turn north and later west, bringing Colorado (and its silver and gold mines), Utah, Nevada, and eventually California into the Confederate fold.

And that was not all: Such success could be doubled by conquering the Mexican states of Sonora and Chihuahua. When all this was said and done, the Confederacy would be of such substantial size and possess enough appealing resources that Great Britain and France would be persuaded to recognize it. And there was the possibility that the Union would be so disheartened that it would sue for peace before the rebels could be even more successful.

One cannot blame Davis for being impressed. The plan glittered with audaciousness. The problem was that Henry Sibley would be carrying it out. Thus far, being a Confederate officer had not sobered him up any more than being a U.S. Army officer had. Unfortunately for members of the rank and file like Leander McNelly, as well as Sibley's superiors, his alcoholism would not become evident until the campaign was underway.

CHAPTER 22

GETTYSBURG OF THE WEST

In July 1861, the war barely three months old, Gen. Sibley was in San Antonio pulling together what would be known, sensibly, as the Sibley Brigade. Helping this effort was Colonel Thomas Green, who was as sober as he was capable. He was also trusted by the Texans under his command, like the young McNelly.

Also born in Virginia, Green was raised in Tennessee. He graduated from the University of Tennessee intending to have a law career. But when the Texas Revolution began, Green left to join the rebels. He arrived in Nacogdoches in December 1835 and enlisted in the army being formed by Sam Houston. During the Battle of San Jacinto, Green helped operate the famed "Twin Sisters" cannons, the only artillery present in Houston's army. A few days after the decisive victory, the wounded general rewarded Green with a commission as a lieutenant. He was soon promoted and assigned as the aide-de-camp to General Thomas Rusk. But soon after that, with Mexico defeated, Green resigned and returned to Tennessee to resume studying law.

Only a year later, he was back. The legislature of the new Republic of Texas granted large tracts of land to deserving veterans of the revolution, and Green laid claim to his in Fayette County. Over the years, he did double duty as a militiaman and a farmer. Green participated in John H. Moore's 1840 campaign against the Comanche up the Colorado River, and two years later, during the Vásquez Incursion, he organized the Travis County Volunteers and served as their captain. On the ill-fated Somervell Expedition, Green was its inspector general. In the Mexican-American War, he recruited a company of Texas Rangers from LaGrange and served as their captain during the U.S. capture of Monterrey.

So after Texas seceded in early 1861, Green was elected colonel of the Fifth Texas Cavalry, which became part of the Sibley Brigade. Colonel James Reily, a seasoned diplomat with military experience, commanded the Fourth Regiment, and Colonel William Steele headed the Seventh Regiment. By October 1861, the brigade's 3,200 soldiers were training for the ambitious campaign to conquer the West.

To impress the locals and boost morale, on the twenty-first the Sibley Brigade paraded through San Antonio, noting the shining eyes of young ladies waving white handkerchiefs. Leander McNelly and hundreds of other young men like him were finally marching off to war.

Alas, the campaign did not get off to an encouraging

start. After two months of tough traveling into an incessant north headwind and across rough, uneven terrain, the brigade arrived at Fort Bliss, where the deposed Lt. Col. Baylor's seasoned Second Regiment of Texas Mounted Rifles was incorporated into its ranks. When the new Confederate army of New Mexico marched up the Rio Grande and attempted to bypass the federal bastion of Fort Craig, the bloody Battle of Valverde began. Private McNelly, serving in Green's command, saw his first military action. Auspiciously, it was a successful one.

On the evening of February 13, 1862, Gen. Sibley halted the brigade's march fifteen miles south of Fort Craig. Judging the fort to be too strong to be taken by force, he deployed his troops in a line, and for the next three days he tried to entice the Union troops to attack. The fort's cautious commander, Colonel Edward Canby, refused to do so.[44]

In addition to underestimating Canby's common sense, Sibley was unaware that he was outnumbered. His command had been beset by disease, including smallpox and measles, as well as desertions, and now numbered about 2,600 men. By the time the rather distilled Confederate army of New Mexico approached his fort, Canby's

---

44 Though born and raised in Kentucky, Canby remained in the Union army when the war began. After it ended, he accepted the surrender of General Edmund Kirby Smith, which was not until June 2, 1865. As commander of the Pacific Northwest in 1873, Canby was assassinated during peace talks with the Modoc, who were refusing to move from their California homelands. He had the unwelcome distinction of being the only U.S. general to be killed during the Indian Wars.

command contained at least a thousand more troops than Sibley's. One of the units was the First New Mexico Volunteers, who were led by the fifty-two-year-old Christopher Houston Carson, known as Kit. He was now a lieutenant colonel having already established a national reputation as a legendary fur trapper, wilderness guide, and all-round explorer. Countless biographies and news articles, as well as exaggerated versions of his exploits in "dime novels," had been published about him. The First New Mexico unit he now led under Canby's overall command consisted of mostly Hispanic volunteers.

Already running low on rations, the Confederate army could not wait indefinitely. At a council of war held on the eighteenth, Sibley ordered the brigade to cross the Rio Grande and move up the eastern side of the river to a ford near Valverde six miles north of Fort Craig. The general believed that cutting off communications with Canby's superiors in Santa Fe would increase pressure on the Union commander. In addition, Col. Green began placing artillery on the heights overlooking the river and fort.

Canby decided not to remain idle. He had two mules loaded with barrels of fused gunpowder sent toward the Confederate lines. However, the hapless animals, having not fully understood their orders, instead wandered back toward the Union fort and exploded on the way. On the plus side, their loud demise stampeded a herd of Confederate beef cattle and horses into the Union's lines, depriving Sibley's soldiers of some much-needed food.

On the twenty-first, Sibley sent an advance party of four companies of the Second Texas Mounted Rifles under the command of Major Charles Pyron to the Valverde ford, with the Fourth Texas Mounted Rifles under Lieutenant Colonel William Scurry following close behind. When informed of this, Canby sent a mixed force of infantry, cavalry, and artillery to the ford under the command of Colonel Benjamin S. Roberts. Green's artillery slowed the column down, so Roberts sent Major Thomas Duncan ahead with the cavalry.

When the Confederates arrived at the eastern side of the Valverde ford, they found that Union forces were already there blocking their passage. Pyron sent for reinforcements while his men took cover in an old riverbed, which served as a solid defensive position. At first, despite having a numeric advantage, the Union cavalry did no more than deploy in a skirmish line.

During the rest of the morning and into the afternoon, the opposing forces maneuvered to gain advantage, with more men arriving on each side. The Confederates were at a disadvantage because they were mostly armed with short-range shotguns and pistols, which could not reach the Union positions three hundred yards away. Meanwhile, Canby ordered most of the remaining garrison at Fort Craig to join him.

The Confederates had another disadvantage—their commander. During the morning Sibley had remained with the wagons, where he had access to alcohol. However, he was conscientious enough to relinquish command of the brigade to Green. At 2 P.M., Green authorized a lancer company to attempt a charge on what they thought was an inexperienced New Mexico company on the Union extreme right. But those Union soldiers turned out to be a Colorado company that was able to defeat the charge without breaking. Twenty of the lancers were killed or wounded during the charge, with almost all of the horses disabled or killed as well. When it returned to the Confederate line, the lancer company rearmed itself with pistols and shotguns and continued fighting in the battle.[45]

Despite the setback, by four that afternoon Green's men appeared to have the advantage in the battle. Canby determined that a massive frontal assault would fail and instead decided to attack the Confederate left. Spotting troop movements and anticipating a Union attack, Green ordered an attack first. While this was underway, he had the Confederate right wing under the command of Scurry charge the Union center and the Union battery on its left. At this point in the day, the Confederates were also motivated by their desperate need for water, which could only be reached by dislodging the Union troops blocking their access to the Rio Grande. The result was a panic-stricken retreat by the Yankees.

Green was about to order another attack when Canby sent a white flag. A truce to remove the bodies of the dead and wounded was requested. After this was agreed to and done, the Union commander managed to reorganize his men for a retreat to Fort Craig. This left the road northward toward Santa Fe open to the Confederates.

Though victorious, Sibley's Brigade suffered thirty-six

---

45 Some historians contend that this was the first and last lancer charge of the Civil War.

killed, one hundred and fifty wounded, and one missing. But the battle was received well back in Texas, with *The Austin Gazette* proclaiming it a "glorious victory." In his report on the battle, Col. Green praised his men effusively. Private Leander McNelly's involvement has been the subject of debate for many years. Among the many disputed and disproven claims in N. A. Jennings's book *A Texas Ranger,* published in 1899, is that the seventeen-year-old McNelly was in the forefront of the battle, that he not only led the charge against a Union battery but escaped death when a bullet bound for his heart was stopped by a book kept inside his shirt. While this account might not be completely accurate, it is true that McNelly soon became a member of Col. Green's staff.[46]

A sobered-up Sibley ordered the brigade to continue north toward Albuquerque and Santa Fe, where he hoped to confiscate much-needed supplies. However, he was severely slowed by the losses in horses and mules from the battle, which forced him to convert the Fourth Texas from cavalry to infantry and, worse, to destroy some precious supplies laden on wagons that could not be pulled.

The Union forces had been hit hard too, with 68 men killed, 158 wounded, and 35 missing. Reasoning that he was outnumbered, Canby chose not to pursue the rebel army, instead sending mounted detachments against its rear for some token harassment. His remaining troops would remain at Fort Craig and try to cut off the Confederates'

---

46 Overall, in Jennings and elsewhere, there are several anecdotes about a well-placed book that takes a bullet for McNelly.

supply line. Canby could also attempt to intercept any reinforcements sent to join Sibley.

Meanwhile, the rebel brigade continued north and west. After taking Socorro on February 25 and Albuquerque on March 2, they marched on to Santa Fe, where they raised the Stars and Bars. Having thus seized the territorial capital, Sibley had his men move against Fort Union. It was urgent that the brigade take the fort, and fast, because on their way out, Union troops had removed or destroyed all the military and food supplies in Albuquerque. Every day, the Confederate army was becoming more thin and bedraggled.

Then fortune smiled on them. The Yankees had neglected to carry away supplies at a depot in Cubero, and they were gladly grabbed by the Confederates. Even better, a supply train consisting of forty wagons laden with goods for Union outposts was intercepted by the rebels. For the first time in weeks, there was plenty of food to go around—just in time for a battle that would later be called the "Gettysburg of the West."

Sibley sent some two hundred and fifty Texans under the command of Major Pyron on an expedition over the Glorieta Pass, a strategic location on the Santa Fe Trail southeast of Santa Fe itself. Control of the pass would allow the Confederates to advance onto the High Plains and make an assault on Fort Union. Sibley also sent six companies under the command of Colonel Tom Green to block the eastern end of the pass. The Confederate commander was unaware that Union reinforcements had marched from Denver, over Raton Pass, to Fort Union, and then on to Glorieta Pass, covering the distance of four hundred miles in fourteen days.

On the morning of March 26, 1862, the four hundred soldiers under the command of Major John Chivington captured the Confederate picket post in the pass, then found the main Confederate force behind it.[47] Chivington advanced, but rebel artillery fire threw him back. He regrouped, split his force to the two sides of the pass, and caught the Confederates in a cross fire, forcing them to retire.

Major Pyron's men retreated to a narrow section of the pass and formed a defensive line. But when Chivington's soldiers appeared, Pyron ordered another retreat. Chivington had a mounted company make a frontal charge, which succeeded in capturing several Confederates and scattering the rest. Not knowing if rebel reinforcements were on the way, Chivington had his men camp at the nearby Kozlowski's Ranch.

There was no fighting the next day, as reinforcements bolstered both sides. When Col. Scurry arrived, the Confederate force swelled to about eleven hundred men and five cannons. Expecting Green to arrive in the Union rear at any time, Scurry stayed put. On the Union side, Colonel John Slough arrived early in the morning of March 28 with about nine hundred more men, bringing the Union strength to thirteen hundred. He was not about to sit around waiting for something to happen.

---

47 If Chivington's name sounds familiar, it is because in November 1864 he would be the perpetrator of the Sand Creek Massacre, in which his Colorado troops killed 230 Cheyenne and Arapaho men, women, and children.

At dawn, Slough sent Chivington with two infantry battalions out in a circling movement with orders to strike the Southerners on one flank once Slough's main force had attacked their front. But Scurry must have anticipated this because his men suddenly advanced down the canyon. Startled, Slough immediately launched an attack. The Confederates dismounted and formed a line across the canyon as best they could given the terrain, then attacked.

The Union soldiers were initially successful in holding their ground, but by noon they had been outflanked. The battered Yankees were thrown back but Slough managed to re-form them. Not wanting to slow any momentum, Scurry launched attacks against the left, right, and center of the Union line, with the artillery firing in support. The assault on the Union left was beaten back, and when the attack on the center stalled, so did the overall assault.

The Confederates were not done. From a vantage point that would become known as "Sharpshooters Ridge," on the Union right, Confederate riflemen started picking off the artillerymen and infantry below them. Scurry again pressed the Union center, and this time Slough reluctantly ordered a retreat to a half mile east of Pigeon's Ranch, where skirmishing continued until dusk. There was a second trip to Kozlowski's Ranch, this one leaving the Confederates in possession of the battlefield.

If the situation had remained that way, the war in the West might well have a different history. But that afternoon, Major Chivington's scouts located the Confederate supply train at Johnson's Ranch. After observing it and listening to the sounds of battle for an hour, Chivington's force descended the slope and drove off the small guard with few casualties. They then looted and burned the eighty supply wagons and spiked the cannon and chased off about five hundred horses and mules before heading to the busy Kozlowski's Ranch.

That was the turning point in the turning-point battle of the West. With no supplies to sustain his advance, Scurry had to retreat to Santa Fe. Ultimately, the starving Confederates would keep retreating until they were back in San Antonio, meaning that they abandoned New Mexico Territory. This, in turn, meant that the Battle at Glorieta Pass foiled Sibley's hope to capture the major federal base at Fort Union, which would have compelled Union forces to retire north of Raton Pass and into Colorado Territory.

The long and exhausting retreat of the beleaguered Sibley Brigade included a disastrous trek across the eastern slopes of the San Mateo Mountains. A force of some six hundred men was left to guard the Mesilla Valley, part of Confederate Arizona, but it too retreated into Texas when General James H. Carleton's "California Column" approached.[48] When the campaign reached its ignominious end, it was found that almost a third of Sibley's 2,600

---

48 This contingent of soldiers had marched nine hundred miles east using the established route of the Butterfield Overland Mail, which had ceased operation the year before. They took advantage of the food and grain that remained at the mail stations.

men had been lost—they were dead, had been too badly wounded to travel, were taken prisoner, or had wandered off. Those who survived were hungry, thirsty, spent, and disillusioned.

CHAPTER 23

"COOLNESS AND COURAGE"

The Texans' commander had not served them well. According to Chuck Parsons and Marianne E. Hall Little in their biography of Leander McNelly, "For all practical purposes [Sibley] proved himself incapable of carrying out his own grand plan. His absence from the field of battle, either through legitimate illness or drunkenness, proved costly, not only in terms of the leadership he should have provided for his men but for the morale of his soldiers."

The rest of the career of Henry Hopkins Sibley was not a happy one, though it did take an exotic turn. After the failure of the New Mexico campaign, he was given minor duties in south Louisiana. He commanded the "Arizona Brigade" at the Battles of Irish Bend and Fort Bisland, where he committed several blunders. Struggling with alcoholism, he was court-martialed in 1863. Although not convicted of cowardice, he was censured.

After the war, Thaddeus P. Mott, a New Yorker who had served as a Union officer in the war, recruited former soldiers from both sides for employment in the Egyptian Army. Sibley was one of the first people to arrive in Egypt, and he served there from 1870 to 1873 as a brigadier general and military advisor to the Isma'il Pasha, khedive of Egypt, overseeing the construction of coastal fortifications. However, he fell back into problems with alcohol and was dismissed due to illness and disability. Back in the United States, Sibley lived with his daughter in Fredericksburg, Virginia, where he wrote articles and worked on military inventions. He died in poverty in 1886 at age seventy and was buried in the Fredericksburg Confederate Cemetery.[49]

The remnants of the Sibley Brigade were allowed to take leave to recover and replenish their ranks. Leander McNelly went home to Washington County, where he probably pitched in to help with late summer and early fall farm tasks. The brigade re-formed in October under the command of General Richard Taylor, whose father had been the twelfth president of the United States. McNelly and the other rebel soldiers were kept busy with drilling and other training exercises. This probably became wearisome as the weeks passed, and perhaps irritating too, as

---

49 Fans of the so-called spaghetti westerns will want to look for Sibley the next time they watch *The Good, the Bad and the Ugly,* directed by Sergio Leone. The general can be seen riding in the passenger seat of a carriage as his soldiers make their procession through a town.

reports arrived from elsewhere in the South about Union defeats.

Finally, the brigade was ordered to march toward Galveston. A plan had been developed by General John Bankhead Magruder to take it back from Union forces. "Prince Jack," as the general was known, was a West Point graduate who had distinguished himself under General Winfield Scott in the war with Mexico. He had soared to major general in the eastern theater of the Civil War . . . then came the Seven Days' Battle and subsequently the Battle of Malvern Hill in the summer of 1862. In both actions, General Robert E. Lee was angered by Magruder's lack of aggressiveness against the Union army, led by General George McClellan. In October he was sent to command the District of Texas, New Mexico, and Arizona.

To the embarrassment of Texans, Galveston had been one of the war's early losses in the Deep South. Several errors led to that outcome. Unwisely, most of the cannons in the city's defenses had been removed for use elsewhere. On October 4 five Union naval vessels approached Galveston, and a single ship, the *Harriet Lane,* was sent into Galveston Bay under a flag of truce. However, when a Confederate boat went out toward the *Harriet Lane,* it was regarded as an attack, and the Union ships opened fire. But before any damage could be done, a truce was arranged. It lasted four days, during which Galveston was evacuated. At the expiration of the truce, Union troops landed and soon raised the Stars and Stripes over the city.

More than two months later, Magruder put his own flotilla of four ships together. Two of them sailed toward

Galveston carrying units of the former Sibley Brigade—for obvious reasons, many of its members had stopped referring to it that way—now under the command of Tom Green. Other elements of the brigade were to attack by land. Curiously, on December 31, as Green stepped on one of the rebel ships (which also contained Leander McNelly), he handed his watch to another officer, saying he expected to die and asking that it be given to his wife.

The second Battle of Galveston was also determined by errors, but this time the Union side paid the higher price. Because of the cotton bales piled on the Confederate ships *Neptune* and *Bayou City,* the soldiers referred to them as "cottonclads." On New Year's Day, they lumbered into the harbor to take on the Union ships *Harriet Lane, Westfield, Owasco, Corypheus,* and *Sachem*. Outnumbered by the Northern ships, *Neptune* was severely damaged by gunfire and eventually sank, but the *Bayou City* succeeded in capturing the *Harriet Lane*.

Helping to even the odds, the *Westfield* was grounded on a sandbar. The Union fleet commander, William B. Renshaw, attempted to destroy the grounded vessel with explosives rather than let it fall into enemy hands. Apparently not a munitions expert, Renshaw was one of the Union troops killed when the explosives detonated too early. Somehow, this mishap persuaded Union troops on shore to believe that their ships were surrendering, and they therefore laid down their arms. The remaining U.S. ships did not surrender, but they did not linger either, leaving the harbor and retreating to Union-controlled New

Orleans. Magruder's somewhat harebrained scheme had actually worked.[50]

There are conflicting reports of McNelly's role in the attack. Almost certainly, he was a member of the boarding party who took the *Harriet Lane* as a prize. There are assertions that he was the first Confederate soldier to leap aboard, but other accounts—most importantly, Magruder's after-action report—gave that distinction to Captain Leon Smith of the Fifth Regiment.

McNelly's activities become less murky the next month, when his brigade was sent east. As Parsons and Little point out, "Although there is no contemporary record detailing McNelly's actions with the Sibley Brigade in New Mexico, nor records relevant to his specific actions at Galveston, his courage and bravery in the swamps and battlefields of Louisiana is well documented."

The first significant action for the brigade in Louisiana was in April. It was then attached to the Army of Western Louisiana with Gen. Taylor as the overall commander. The man who aimed to defeat him that spring was General Nathaniel Banks, who, the previous December, had been appointed commander of the Department of the Gulf. This was a political appointment more than a military one. Before the war, Banks rose through the state and then federal ranks rapidly, becoming speaker of the U.S. House of Representatives and governor of Massachusetts,

---

50 Perhaps even more remarkable, even though a Union blockade was imposed four days later, Galveston was the only major port that was still in Confederate hands at the end of the Civil War.

the first professional politician—meaning he had no other occupation—to hold that office. Because of the Massachusetts man's power and connections, President Lincoln appointed Banks a major general.

After suffering a series of inglorious setbacks in the Shenandoah River valley at the hands of Stonewall Jackson, Banks was transferred to New Orleans with the mandate to help gain control of the Mississippi River. The presence of the Confederate army under Taylor could confound that, so Banks came up with a plan: He would take his XIX Corps to Alexandria and secure the Bayou Teche region that was laden with natural forage and unused supplies. He would establish supply depots along the way and then move from Alexandria against Port Hudson.

But the quick movement necessary in Banks's plan was slowed by the rebels. When he departed New Orleans, he planned to capture Taylor's army in its entirety. On April 9, 1863, two Union divisions crossed Berwick Bay from Brashear City. Two days later, Banks began his advance in earnest. Taylor was well aware of the Union activities because of successful scouting by his cavalry under Tom Green. The scouts—one of whom was McNelly—shadowed Banks's army and reported back to Taylor every detail of the maneuvers.

On the twelfth, Banks sent a third division up the Atchafalaya River to land in the rear of Franklin. Taylor sent some of Green's cavalry to the front to ascertain the enemy's strength and slow his advance. Late in the day, more Union troops arrived and formed a battle line outside the Fort Bisland's defenses. An artillery barrage ensued between both sides until the federal troops fell back to camp for the night.

The next morning, Union forces again advanced on Fort Bisland. Banks had three brigades in position south of the Bayou Teche. Fighting began at eleven in the morning and continued until dusk. In addition to Confederate forces in the earthworks, the gunboat *Diana,* which had been captured and was now in Confederate hands, shelled the Union troops. Finally, U.S. gunboats arrived late in the afternoon.

In his camp that night, Taylor learned that the Union division that went up the Atchafalaya and landed in his rear would soon be able to cut off a Confederate retreat. He began evacuating supplies, men, and weapons, leaving a small force to slow any enemy movement. The next morning, Banks and his men found the fort abandoned and declared victory.[51]

Skirmishes and minor battles continued that month and into most of May. A significant change for the Texas brigade took place on the twentieth, when Tom Green was given command of it and promoted to brigadier general. Not long afterward, though still but eighteen years old, McNelly was also given a promotion, leapfrogging to captain.

An action that shined a light on McNelly's gumption took place on June 22. That evening, General Alfred

---

51 After the war, Banks returned to the Massachusetts political scene, serving in Congress, where he supported the concept of Manifest Destiny, influenced the Alaska Purchase legislation, and supported women's suffrage. In his later years, he served as a U.S. marshal.

Mouton led 325 men against Brashear City. They moved into position at night, and attacked early the next morning. The garrison soon fell, and as many as twelve hundred Union troops were taken prisoner. The men under Green's command were sent to prevent nearby bridges and locomotives from being destroyed, with McNelly in the lead. His advance horsemen arrived too late, but they did capture more federal troops and several cannons. Remarkable about this was that McNelly, who had maybe forty men, managed to corral four hundred or so Union soldiers.

He had employed a ruse. On the night of June 23, on a quarter-mile-long bridge that led to the Yankee encampment, McNelly had the scouts run across the bridge and back again repeatedly for an hour while he and several others shouted commands. To the spooked Union troops, it sounded like an entire Confederate army had arrived and was taking up a position to attack in the morning. Right after the sun rose, McNelly and his men approached the Union lines bearing a flag of truce and claiming to be only the advance guard. McNelly demanded to see the officer in charge, and when he appeared, he was told to surrender unconditionally or face an overwhelming attack. The officer, thoroughly unnerved by now, complied.

Despite seeing his share of action, McNelly—who in one dispatch Green praised for his "coolness and courage"—remained unscathed . . . until September 1863, during the Battle of Stirling's Plantation. General Mouton had become aware of a smaller federal force near this estate and hoped to remove them from the map. He ordered Green to plan an attack, and three days later, Green and the three thousand troops he commanded were at Centerpoint on the Atchafalaya River. They began crossing by ferry at 3 P.M., enduring a rainstorm. By the middle of the night, the entire of Mouton's command was across the river.

At eleven in the morning, the rebels engaged with federal cavalry pickets at the Fordoche Bridge. An hour later, Mouton initiated a full attack. The Union force consisted of about four hundred and fifty men who were pushed back from their position through the plantation's buildings. They took up a position on a levee that served as an excellent breastwork.

Still, the Confederates were in overwhelming force and found a gap in the levee. As they poured in, the Union commander, Joseph Leake, was wounded and captured, and no other officer assumed command. The heat of the day also took its toll on the beleaguered Yankees. In addition, Confederate cavalry had completely routed the federal cavalry to the south near the Norwood farm. The Union horsemen rode away toward Morganza with such rapidity that none of them were captured. With the flight of the Union cavalry, Green advanced his column up the road from the Norwood farm to the Stirling plantation. Vastly outnumbered, leaderless, and assailed from all sides, the Bluecoats surrendered piecemeal.

During the battle, McNelly was riding next to W. F. Spivey, a lieutenant in the Fifth Texas. There was a volley of shots that wounded McNelly and killed Spivey. Apparently, the wound was not too serious because McNelly remained in the regiment. Perhaps another book had borne the brunt of the bullet.

CHAPTER 24

FRONTIER FORCES

While many men had gone off to fight the Yankees, the Texas Rangers did not cease to exist during the Civil War. Some Indian tribes, especially the Comanche, had demonstrated right from the dawn of the decade that they were not about to stop their activities while white people were busy killing each other.

In 1860, Peta Nocona led the Comanches in a raid through Texas's Parker County—so named for the family of the girl he had kidnapped. Afterward, he returned with his band to what he believed was a safe retreat under the sandstone bluffs of the Pease River, near where Mule Creek flowed into it. The Comanche had long favored this site because it provided cover from the fierce blue northers that hit the plains, ample forage for their ponies, and placid buffalo herds. However, it might not protect against vengeful Texans. Sam Houston had commissioned Sul Ross, now a Ranger captain, to organize a company of forty Rangers and twenty militia to find the Comanche.

Ross and his Rangers began tracking the "Nokonis," who were considered the hardiest fighters in the tribe. They neared the Pease River at daybreak on December 18, 1860. Ross himself secretly surveyed the Comanche camp and confirmed what his scouts had reported the day before. Rather than risk the intervention of an early winter storm, Ross decided to attack.

He sent a detachment of twenty men to position themselves behind a chain of sand hills to cut off retreat to the northwest, while Ross led the remaining forty men down into the Indian camp. The band was indeed taken completely by surprise. In the book *Indian Depredations in Texas*—which is as one-sided as the title implies—Ross offers this report: "The attack was so sudden that a considerable number were killed before they could prepare for defense. They fled precipitately right into the presence of the sergeant and his men. Here they met with a warm reception, and finding themselves completely encompassed, every one fled his own way, and was hotly pursued and hard pressed."

What of Peta Nocona? Ross's account contends that he died trying to escape with his wife and baby daughter. According to the Ranger captain, seeing that the camp was hopelessly overrun, Nocona and Cynthia Ann Parker fled to the east up a creek bed. Reportedly, mounted behind Nocona was a fifteen-year-old Mexican girl, while Parker carried her two-year-old child, who had been named Topasannah ("Prairie Flower"). Ross and his lieutenant, Tom Killiheir, pursued the man they believed to be the

Comanche leader. After a chase of a mile or so, the Rangers closed in and began firing. The Mexican girl was killed instantly by the shots, and as she fell she pulled Nocona off the horse.

Immediately, he was up standing and firing arrows at the two Texans. One struck Ross's horse, but both Rangers kept shooting. One bullet broke Nocona's arm, while two other shots hit his body. Mortally wounded, Nocona managed to drag himself to a small tree, and bracing himself against it he began to chant the Comanche death song. His family captured—except for his son, Quanah, who had escaped the slaughter—and his warriors dead or dying, their families dead or prisoners, it may have been a mercy for Nocona to be killed by a shotgun while his wife screamed his name and wept.

Well, that is one version. Quanah Parker for years afterward insisted that his father had survived the attack and instead died three to four years later of complications from old war wounds suffered against the Apache. Parker maintained that he and his father, along with a few others, had left the camp late the night before to go hunting and thus were not present the morning of the attack. When they returned, virtually no adults were left alive to tell his father exactly what had taken place or what had become of his wife and two youngest children. Not knowing if they were alive, Nocona made the hard decision to flee in order to assure the safety of his remaining son.[52]

---

52 In a book published in 1890, *Carbine and Lance: The Story of Old Fort Sill,* Colonel W. S. Nye supported Quanah Parker's version of the story.

At first Ross believed the woman he had captured was an Indian. Some accounts say it was noted that she had blue eyes, a rare trait for a native Comanche, and as the woman was questioned, she pointed at herself and said, "Me Cynthia." When Ross returned to Fort Belknap, he sent for Isaac Parker, a brother of Silas Parker and uncle to Cynthia Ann. However, he was unable to positively identify this frail captive as his niece. But when she began to remember and utter more words in English, he became convinced.

Although Cynthia Ann was welcomed back into her white family, she was unhappy in her new surroundings. Topasannah died of influenza in 1864. Cynthia Ann, already in mourning for her sons when her daughter died, was left without a reason to live and starved herself to death. She apparently never learned that both of her sons had escaped the Battle of Pease River. Charles Goodnight, the famous scout and later rancher, found the sign of two horses who had gone at a normal trot out of the camp for about a mile, then taken off at a dead run to the nearest large Comanche camp. Goodnight trailed the horses fifty miles to that camp, but as it had more than a thousand Comanche in it, and he had less than a dozen men with him, he abandoned the chase. Years later, Quanah told Goodnight that he was one of those horsemen and that his brother was the other.

Nye wrote, "In the melee [Ross] pursued and shot Nawkohnee's Mexican slave, who was trying to save the fleeing Comanche women." Nye claimed that he encountered men who saw Nocona alive several years after the Pease River attack, when he was ill with an infected war wound.

At the end of his life, Parker would see his mother's and sister's remains disinterred and reburied next to the plot reserved for him at Fort Sill. Quanah died in February 1911, age sixty-five or sixty-six.

Once it became clear that the War for Southern Independence would not be short, the Texas legislature realized that neither Ross nor any other intrepid Ranger captain with only sixty men could adequately protect frontier settlements. Lawmakers in Austin created the Frontier Regiment for the protection of the northern and western frontier. By then, Comanche and Kiowa raiders had been killing settlers, slaughtering livestock, and stealing horses in communities along the entire frontier. These settlements faced the grim prospect of being raided out of existence, perhaps in only a few more months.

In January 1862 nine companies of approximately 115 to 125 men each were raised and then, throughout March and April, deployed. Many of the enrolling officers were elected captains of their companies. However, many of the men were indifferently armed and badly mounted, and sickness prevailed in all the camps. There was no medicine, and in the first year the camps were poorly supplied with food, feed for horses, and even ammunition. There were also discipline problems. Added to this, the distances between the camps, to be covered in one day, proved too great to allow for effective scouting, and the Ranger patrols were too small to engage larger bands of Indians. It was no surprise, then, that the attacks continued.

But only a year after the Frontier Regiment was founded, a financially frustrated Governor Francis Lubbock suspended it. Some Rangers went home while others reenlisted in a re-organized and renamed Mounted Regiment of Texas State Troops. Lubbock harbored the hope that the Confederacy would pay for it.

Colonel James McCord assumed command in February 1863. The "search and destroy" strategy he employed was meant to put the Indians on the defensive by locating and attacking their villages. Initially, the new Ranger missions proved successful . . . but small groups of Indian raiders remained active, creating panic in many settlements and jangling political nerves in Austin. Adding to McCord's miseries was that small violent bands of Union sympathiz-ers, called jayhawkers, were also conducting raids, which included murdering residents.

The final straw for the Mounted Regiment came in March 1864, when it was finally transferred into the Con-federate army, effectively putting it out of existence. The Indian war on the frontiers of Texas since 1861 had always been the unwanted stepchild of the Confederacy. Within weeks of the transfer, most of the Ranger companies had been stripped from the frontier and redeployed to other areas. Whipsawed by two simultaneous wars, the belea-guered settlers on the frontier might have fared worse had it not been for another state military initiative.

In December 1863 the next governor, Pendleton Mur-rah, and the legislature passed a law that established the Frontier Organization. By the following March, nearly four thousand men were on its rolls, and it provided pro-tection against Indian incursions and rounded up Confed-erate deserters too.

During 1864, things were finally looking up for the Rangers and the Texas frontier settlements. Then came the Battle of Dove Creek.

On December 9, 1864, Captain N. M. Gillintine and a militia scouting party of twenty-three men discovered a recently vacated Indian camp about thirty miles up the Clear Fork of the Brazos River. After receiving word of this, a militia force of about 325 men from Bosque, Comanche, Coryell, Erath, and Johnson Counties gathered under Captain S. S. Totten, and Confederate troops were dispatched under Captain Henry Fossett.

By the time they rendezvoused with Gillintine, the two forces had still not agreed upon a unified command. After waiting two days at Fort Chadbourne, Fossett impatiently set out on January 3, 1865, with 161 men and followed a broad trail to the North Concho River and beyond. Four days later, his scouts found the Indians encamped in timber along Dove Creek.

Operating on the frontier assumption that all Indians were dangerous, the commanders hastily formed a battle plan. The militia, on horses weary from a forced march, were to dismount and wade the creek for a frontal attack from the north. The Confederate troops were to circle southwestward, capture the grazing herd of Indian horses, and attack from the lower side, thus cutting off a retreat.

Turned out, there was no retreat to cut off. The battle went badly for the Texans. Fossett later estimated the Indian fighting force at between four hundred and six hundred. Totten said six hundred and insisted that Union jayhawkers were among them. The Indians' position in a heavy thicket gave them good cover, high ground, and an open field of fire. The militiamen were slowed by the creek, heavy briars, and brush. Capt. Gillintine and sixteen others were killed just in the opening minutes.[53] The militia was soon routed and out of the battle.

Meanwhile, Fossett's mounted force did capture the Indian horses. He dispatched seventy-five troops to enter the camp from the south, but they were repulsed by heavy fire that cost them twelve horses. The Confederate troops took positions in the timber and continued the fight, but they were caught in a cross fire and separated into three groups as the Indians closed in. An Indian counterattack early in the afternoon was repulsed, and the battle continued until almost dark before ending. During the afternoon, the Indians had recaptured their horses.

The battered white men spent a miserable night, drenched by chilling rain that turned to heavy snow. An added misery was they had left the dead behind and had to listen to the moans of the wounded.[54] The next day, cold and hungry, they were forced to eat some of the horses. A casualty count showed twenty-six dead and twenty-three wounded; Indian casualties were less certain. Only later did the Texans learn—to their further embarrassment—

---

53 To remove any doubt, after being hit, Gillintine turned to the closest Ranger and said, "I am a dead man."

54 To emphasize their contempt for their attackers, the victors had cut off the head of one Texan and it adorned the top of a pole. This grisly discovery was made later by Rangers who returned to the scene to retrieve bodies.

that the Indians they had attacked were not Comanche or Kiowa but Kickapoo, normally a peaceful tribe.

Crude litters strapped between pairs of horses carried the wounded as the Texans retreated eastward through the snow. The arduous journey ended at John Chisum's ranch near the confluence of the Concho and the Colorado Rivers.[55]

The battle motivated the Kickapoo to conduct vengeful border raids from the sanctuary given them by the Mexican government. White settlers along the Rio Grande bore the brunt of these attacks. Soon, though, there would be a welcome end to the Civil War and the return of Texans who had survived it.

---

55 Known as the "Cattle Baron on the Pecos," Chisum, originally from Tennessee, had moved longhorn herds from Texas into New Mexico in the mid-1800s. He would collaborate with Charles Goodnight and Oliver Loving on cattle drives, establish one of the largest ranches in the American West, and, with employee Billy the Kid, participate in the Lincoln County War. He would also be portrayed by John Wayne in the 1970 movie *Chisum*.

CHAPTER 25

"TRUE TO HIS COLORS"

Whatever the wound was he had suffered, the young Captain Leander McNelly was certainly well enough in November 1863 that Colonel Tom Green, referring to him in another dispatch as a "sagacious and daring scout," could recommend that he be given the authority to organize and lead a company of scouts. Several weeks later, this proposal was rubber-stamped by General Edmund Kirby Smith, who now commanded the Confederacy's Trans-Mississippi Department. Wasting no time, McNelly pulled a company together, culling the best men available, and he reported back to Green. They were fully operational in time for the Battle of Sabine Crossroads, on April 8, 1864.

General Banks was busy again, this time leading the Union's Army of the Gulf and supported by Admiral David Porter's fleet of gunboats, which ascended the Red

River. The plan was to defeat the Confederate forces in Louisiana and capture Shreveport. By April 1, the Yankees had occupied Grand Ecore and Natchitoches. While the accompanying gunboat fleet with a portion of the infantry continued up the river, the main force followed the road inland toward Mansfield, where Banks knew his opponent, Gen. Taylor, was positioned. The commander of the Confederate forces in Louisiana had retreated up the Red River in order to connect with reinforcements from Texas and Arkansas.

But now Taylor was through retreating. He selected a clearing a few miles south of Mansfield as the spot where he would make a stand. Sending his cavalry to harass the Union vanguard as it approached, Taylor called his infantry divisions forward. The cavalry found, on the morning of April 8, that Banks's army was on a single road through the woods between Natchitoches and Mansfield. Riding to the front, Banks decided that he would fight Taylor there and he ordered all his infantry to join him. A battle appeared inevitable. Taylor, believing correctly that he enjoyed a numeric advantage, gave the order, and at 4 P.M. his men surged forward. The attack began badly: almost immediately, Gen. Mouton was killed, several of his regimental commanders were wounded, and the charge of his division was repulsed.

However, a Texas division managed to wrap around the Union position, folding it in on itself. Hundreds of Union troops were captured, and the rest retreated in panic. As the first Union line collapsed, a division was arriving to form a second line, but it too was pushed back by the charging

Confederates. For several miles, the yelling rebels pursued the retreating Union troops until they encountered a third line formed by the Yankees. The Confederates launched several charges on the Union line but were beaten back, and nightfall ended the battle.

Between killed, wounded, and captured, Banks's army had suffered over two thousand casualties. Taylor had lost about half that. Captain McNelly was once again wounded . . . or maybe not. Some accounts have him being struck by a rifle ball—though, of course, not a fatal blow—during the Battle of Mansfield. However, others have him wounded four days later . . . when his mentor, Gen. Green, was killed.

On April 12 Green was leading an attack on Union gunboats on the Red River at Blair's Landing. A letter, published in *The Houston Telegraph* and written by a major on Green's staff, offers some details. During the attack, the general "was killed within forty yards of the gunboat that fired the fatal shot, and immediately on the bank of the river, on a bluff some forty feet high." The major, whose name was Hart, graphically continued: Green "died, as he wished, in front of the battle, with his face to the foe. He was struck by a grapeshot in the forehead, and the upper part of his head was carried away." Hart added that McNelly, "who was acting at the same time on the General's Staff, was wounded in the thigh."

The grieving captain was out of commission until later in May. After he rejoined his company of scouts, McNelly was kept busy. According to a variety of accounts written years later—meaning they may have been created or at least influenced by the Texas Rangers' fame—McNelly led his men on daring adventures and used more ruses to gain advantages on the Yankees.

An engagement in the first week in June 1864 near Plaquemine, Louisiana, is worth noting. McNelly's men had attacked a Union supply station and chased its defenders away. As the rebels were loading up mules with their takings, Texas troops arrived. These were not Confederate troops but ones known as the "First Texas Traitors" because they had sided with the Union. Their leader was Colonel Edmund Davis. As McNelly led his men on a merry escape back toward Confederate lines, he could not have imagined how he and Davis would cross paths a few years later.

Little is known about McNelly's activities for the rest of the war. Like other Confederate officers, his options became more and more limited as the Southern forces dwindled and the Yankees took larger swaths of territory. According to Parsons and Little, "When the war was nearing its end [McNelly] was given the responsibility of tracking down deserters."

The responsibility was a dangerous one and proved to be a useful experience for a future Texas Ranger. The men to be hunted down were not only deserters but thieves, and some were pretty hardened cutthroats. McNelly and the men under his command searched for them in outlying areas, where it was easier for men to hide. It is not known how many were arrested. No doubt, as the war wound down, it must have felt to the captain that his mission was also a lost cause, yet he persevered.

In April 1865 the armies of Lee and Johnston surrendered, followed by those of Richard Taylor in May and E. Kirby Smith in June. By that last surrender, McNelly, after four years of service in the Confederate army, was already home in Washington County. In a written testimonial, one of his superiors had written that McNelly "remained true to his colors to the very last" and that he had displayed "daring courage and consummate skill."

CHAPTER 26

FARMER AND FATHER

Leander McNelly was still only twenty-one when the war ended, but he was more interested in settling down than sowing wild oats. Apparently, his respiratory problems had not hampered his ability to wage war for four years, but enough was known about consumption then that he knew it was incurable. There was nothing else to do but try to make the most of however many years were coming to him.

The family farm in Washington County—which had escaped the ravages of the Yankees—welcomed McNelly back. He must have begun courting almost immediately, because only four months after his return, on October 17, 1865, he became a married man.

His bride had been born Carey Cheek in June 1848. She was seventeen on her wedding day. After her father had died, her mother married Richard Matson, who had two distinctions—possessing money and land and dying a hero during the Battle of Pine Bluff in Arkansas in October 1863. His body had been brought home and buried with honors at the Mount Zion Cemetery, and his estate, which included eleven hundred acres, passed down to Carey, as her mother had predeceased her second husband earlier in the year.

McNelly embraced being a farmer and, before long, a father. In 1866, Carey gave birth to a son, Leander Rebel McNelly, and two years later the couple had a daughter, Irene. In the five years following the end of the war, McNelly turned the former Matson property into a very productive farm. But evidence suggests that there was still restlessness in him: In July 1870, he accepted a commission in the Texas State Police.

This police force was organized by Edmund Davis—the man who had been labeled a traitor during the Civil War for leading Texans loyal to the Union. By 1870 he was, of all things, governor of the state.

Davis was a native-born Southerner, having greeted the world in Saint Augustine, Florida, in October 1827. His father, who came from South Carolina, was a land developer and attorney. The young Davis received his education in Florida and moved with his family to Galveston in 1848. There he worked as a clerk in the post office and studied law. The next year, he moved to Corpus Christi, where he was employed in a store. He was again studying the law and soon was admitted to the bar. He later became district attorney of the Twelfth Judicial District at Brownsville. Governor Elisha Pease named him judge of the same district, and Davis continued to serve as a state judge until 1861. He was a member of a Ranger company based in Brownsville and captained by William Tobin, who was involved in the Cortina affair at Brownsville in 1859 (more about that later).

Davis married well in April 1858, wedding Anne Elizabeth Britton, daughter of Forbes Britton, a state senator and friend of Sam Houston. By then, Davis was a member of the Democratic Party and, no surprise, a supporter of Houston. His political fortunes nosedived when he opposed secession in 1861, and he ran unsuccessfully to become a delegate to the Secession Convention. Choosing principles over politics, Davis refused to take the oath of loyalty to the Confederacy. After his judgeship was vacated, he fled the state.

He made his way north to Washington, D.C., where he was received by President Lincoln, who approved providing arms to the troops Davis and two colleagues wanted to raise. Accordingly, on October 26, Davis received a colonel's commission and began to recruit the regiment that became the First Texas Cavalry.

The unit saw extensive service during the war in addition to the action at Galveston. At one point, Davis became the center of an international incident. On March 15, 1863, Confederate citizens and off-duty soldiers crossed the border to Matamoros, where they seized Davis as he was attempting to take his family out of Texas. This event created diplomatic trouble between the Confederacy and Mexico that lasted until General Hamilton Bee released Davis to appease Mexican governor Albino Lopez.[56]

---

56 Hamilton Bee had served under Jack Hays in the First Regiment of Texas Mounted Volunteers during the war with Mexico.

Back in the saddle, Davis was in Texas as a part of Gen. Banks's unsuccessful Rio Grande campaign. The First Texas rode to Rio Grande City and seized cotton and slaves to help disrupt the border trade. In November 1864, Davis was promoted to brigadier general and was given command of the cavalry in the Division of Western Mississippi. The following June, he was among those who accompanied Gen. Canby to Gen. Smith's surrender of Confederate forces in Texas.

Showing more courage than sense, after the war Davis remained in Texas and became involved once more in state politics, this time as a pro-Reconstruction Republican. He ran unsuccessfully for the state senate but did become president of the Constitutional Convention of 1868–69. No wallflower, Davis championed political programs that would have restricted the political rights of secessionists and expanded rights for black residents of the state.

He believed he had enough supporters to run for governor in 1869. He was wrong, but that didn't matter. In a close and disputed election, Davis defeated Andrew Hamilton, another Republican. Well, that was the official story. On election day, General John Reynolds, the Reconstruction military commander in the state, simply told everyone Davis had won, and that was that.

One of the new governor's initiatives was a different way to spread law and order throughout Texas. And the state sure needed it after almost five years of Reconstruction enmity. In addition to pushing for a restored militia, public schools, internal improvements, bureaus of immigration and geology, and protection of the frontier, Davis wanted a statewide law enforcement agency. Accordingly, the Texas legislature authorized the formation of what it called the Frontier Force.

More important, the lawmakers funded the new entity. Company commanders would earn one hundred dollars a month, lieutenants eighty, and so on. The men had to provide their own horses and weapons. Enlistments were to be for twelve months. Notes Frederick Wilkins, "In such manner Rangers, by whatever name, returned to Texas."

Despite such a promising beginning, the Frontier Force lasted only until June 1871. It was the same old story: Texas was too strapped for cash to consistently underwrite frontier-protection efforts. By then, however, there was another option: Gov. Davis had managed to get approval for the state police. The distinction between it and the Frontier Force was that the state police would focus more on interior counties than the frontier. However, once the Frontier Force was no more, this separation of jurisdictions was mostly moot.

The agency had a rocky start . . . and never fully recovered. In one incident, after a contingent of state police searched the home of Colonel James Gathing, he had them arrested. The policemen sat in jail until James Davidson, the Texas adjutant general, arrived with a hundred men to arrest those who had arrested the policemen. Gathing and his associates were persuaded to surrender, and while they sat in jail, Davidson demanded five thousand dollars to release them and to not declare martial law. Officials managed to pony up almost three thousand of that, which was deemed by Davidson to be close enough.

There was another reason why the agency did not find favor. According to Doug Swanson, "The state police were widely reviled by white Texans, because many of them were black."

What was also not welcomed by many Texans was a speech made by Gov. Davis in which he pronounced, "We are the most lawless people on the face of the earth. There are more murders and assassinations in this state than there are in the same extent of population on the American continent or in the civilized world." With a governor like this, who needed enemies?

McNelly may not have realized the impact the new state police would have on Texans. He saw captain as a position of authority with a salary of $125 a month, and after five years of incessant hard work, farming may have lost its charm. So on July 3, 1870, when Davidson wrote McNelly to invite him to become a captain in the new force, the young man accepted. McNelly would be in charge of the Fourth Police District, consisting of thirty-four counties, including his home county of Washington.

Davidson seemed an unlikely selection by Davis to be both the adjutant general of Texas and the chief of the state police. An immigrant from Scotland, the twenty-six-year-old's sparse résumé included the claim that he had been a cavalryman in the British army and, not endearing himself to Texans, that he had served in the Union army with a Maine unit. But Texas had shown over and over again that it was where men could come to reinvent themselves, and Davidson was no exception. He managed to become military commissioner of Red River County and took a hard line against crime, which included the banning of carrying pistols and cracking down on those who attacked black citizens. Davis saw statewide potential.

Governor Davis ran for reelection in 1873 but was defeated by Richard Coke by a two-to-one margin. In the years that followed, Davis, often described as a "tall, gaunt, cold-eyed, rather commanding figure," stuck around as head of the Republican Party and chairman of the state executive committee. His subsequent campaigns for governor and congressman were failures, as were attempts to gain cabinet positions in the administrations of Presidents Rutherford Hayes and Chester Arthur. Davis would die in Austin on February 7, 1883, and was buried there in the state cemetery.

Davidson would have a longer tenure. And soon after the twenty-six-year-old McNelly's appointment as captain on July 13, 1870, the chief of police knew he had the right man.

CHAPTER 27

NO BOOK TO STOP THIS BULLET

The ink on his commission was not yet dry when Leander McNelly chased down two murder suspects.

One, Joe Barker, was accused of killing a man in Bastrop County. The new state policeman tracked Barker down and turned him over to that county's sheriff. Next up was John Watson, accused of murdering an Austin business-man. McNelly was on his trail and closing in, but before an arrest could be made another lawman had captured Wat-son and returned him to Austin to stand trial. McNelly, however, soon had an opportunity to use his six-gun for the first time as a civilian lawman.

Three men had broken out of the Travis County jail in Austin and eluded local lawmen. When word reached Davidson that the escapees were on their way to Bastrop County, he sent McNelly in pursuit. He caught up with the

outlaws on July 23, and when they initially refused to surrender, McNelly shot and killed one of them—or, as *The
Bastrop Advertiser* put it, the outlaw was "brought to grief"
and "was dispatched to that bourne from whence there is
no return." This persuaded the other two to change their
minds, and they were arrested. It appears that McNelly
saw efficiency as a virtue.

The next assignment was to track down John Pearce.
He and his brother Ed had been accused of various crimes
and had avoided arrest before there was a state police. Once
murder was added to the list of John Pearce's crimes, it
was time for a more serious pursuit. But this case got more
complicated quickly. In mid-August, McNelly and other
lawmen found where the Pearce brothers were holed up,
in Harrison County, but, as he telegraphed Davidson, there
were as many as fifty men with them. Then the likelihood
of an arrest became even more remote—McNelly, riding
by himself, was suddenly surrounded by Pearce men and
captured.

Such a tight spot tested whether the young lawman
could exhibit grace under pressure. As Chuck Parsons and
Marianne Little note, "McNelly was certainly aware that
the Pearce gang had committed murders, but he remained
calm in a dangerous situation which could easily have resulted in losing his life." Perhaps the gang thought it had
intimidated the state policeman or feared the repercussions
of killing one, because after less than a day of being a prisoner, McNelly was released.

John Pearce soon regretted this, because the very next
day, he was arrested by McNelly. (One has to assume the

lawman was somehow able to find the outlaw separated from his gang.) His brother and followers were believed to be near the coast. Davidson left Austin and joined up with McNelly in pursuit of the gang from Cedar Bayou to the Louisiana border, but it seems that Ed Pearce was able to make good his escape.

The effort was not a wasted one for McNelly, as it turned out his arrest of John Pearce earned him a five-hundred-dollar reward. Also, one newspaper, the *Daily State Journal* in Austin, bestowed credit on McNelly for dispersing the Pearce gang and relegating it to history.

It might seem that the state police would gain the support of the citizenry if officers like McNelly were arresting outlaws and causing others to flee. But to many Texans, McNelly was the exception, not the rule. There were too many members of the state police who abused their authority—some because they could and enjoyed it, others for personal profit. Citizens had been chafing under the yoke of Reconstruction, so they didn't need their own lawmen making life harder.

A poster boy for this sort of unsavory policeman was John Jackson Marshal Helm, whom everyone called Jack. He had fought in the Confederate infantry during the war and afterward worked as a cattleman for one of the more colorful characters in Texas history: Abel Head Pierce—a Rhode Island native with a massive build and a powerful, bell-like voice that, he claimed, could be heard a mile away. By the time of his arrival, he was known as "Shanghai" Pierce.

When the Civil War ended, he and his brother had established the Rancho Grande on Tres Palacios Creek in Matagorda County and were branding cattle over a territory more than fifty square miles. The bellow of "sea lions"—as he called cows—would be equaled only by Shanghai Pierce himself and was destined to be heard throughout the beef markets of the entire nation.

The biggest challenge for a cattleman after the war was to find a market for the rapidly expanding number of cows. But a simple formula was at work: People in the northern and eastern states needed beef, and Texas had the cattle. Pierce could foresee the possibilities that lay ahead for a man who could bring these two together. He became among the first to trail his herds north to meet the railroads that were beginning to push their way west across Kansas. Returning from these drives, Pierce brought back gold and silver, which he exchanged for other herds to drive north. To the men from whom he bought these herds, he was a savior, and soon he became a wealthy one.[57]

While working for Shanghai Pierce, Jack Helm was also the leader of the Goliad County Regulators, a group of vigilantes who attempted to restore order to the area without worrying about the technicalities of the law. To some, the Regulators were a necessary evil. To others, they were heroes.

At war's end, many Texans returned to find their farms and ranches neglected and their cattle running wild and unbranded. The federal troops sent to occupy Texas after

---

57 Readers of the book *Dodge City* may recall a chest-thumping confrontation Shanghai Pierce and his cowboys had with Wyatt Earp when the latter was a lawman in the "Wickedest City of the American West."

the final surrender in June 1865 could not control the widespread cattle thieving and general lawlessness that became the new normal. In this environment, Jack Helm and a few men like him could run rampant.

In June 1868 the Yankee military governor Gen. Reynolds appointed Helm a special marshal to the Goliad area. This allowed him to ride at the head of a band of fifty men, mostly local ranchers. They pursued criminals with vigor and often with cruelty. They ordered known and suspected lawbreakers to leave the state within ten days. Those who defied the warning were shot without benefit of trial. Essentially, Helm and the Regulators were a police department unto themselves.

By 1870 Helm's experience as a law enforcer—with emphasis on the "enforcer"—had caught the attention of Gov. Davis, who appointed him to the state police with the rank and authority of captain. His tenure did not last long.

On August 26 Helm and his men attempted to arrest Henry and William Kelly on a trivial charge. The brothers were killed, with Kelly family witnesses claiming they were outright murdered. Mainly due to his decidedly heavy-handed methods, and the public outrage following the deaths of the Kelly brothers, Helm was suspended in October. Two months after that, Governor Davis dismissed him from the state police. He was, however, legally cleared of any wrongdoing. Helm headed back to DeWitt County, where he had served as a lawman, and caused more mischief.

Officers like Helm were a major reason why many Texans feared and resented the state police. Yet on the other side of the ledger were men like Leander McNelly. His adherence to the rule of law almost cost him his life in December 1870.

On the fifth of that month, a sixty-eight-year-old freedman named Sam Jenkins was killed in Huntsville. He had taken the risk of testifying at the trial of four white men for having attacked him, and, it would appear, he was the victim of retribution. Davidson dispatched Captain McNelly and several men under his command to Walker County to investigate.

It did not take a Pinkerton detective to figure out what had happened, why, and by whom. On January 6, 1871, McNelly's team arrested John Parish, Fred Parks, John Wright, and the suitably named Nathaniel Outlaw for murder. The following week, a hearing was held before Judge James Burnett, when it was determined that Parks could be released but the other three men should stand trial. The judge instructed McNelly to return the accused to the county jail.

There was a slipup somewhere because Parish, Wright, and Outlaw had pistols hidden on them. They probably intended to use them to break out of the jail, but they did not get that far. McNelly and one of his men, Tom Keese, thought it prudent to search them first. When McNelly found the pistol on Outlaw, that set things off. Parish and Wright produced their guns and began firing. McNelly was shot in the leg, but by the time he hit the courtroom floor his pistol was out and it spit bullets. One of them found Wright. Meanwhile, Parish and Keese shot each other. Belying his ominous name, Outlaw threw himself on the floor and stayed there.

Despite the explosion of firepower—as many as thirty shots were fired—the wounded Parish and Wright were able to run outside. There they were met by armed allies who put them on horses and rode away.

As the two lawmen recovered (alas, McNelly did not carry a book in his pant leg), Gov. Davis declared martial law in the county. This included rounding up some of the men who had abetted the escape of Parish and Wright. As soon as he could ride a horse, McNelly was in pursuit of the two wounded men, but the trail had gone cold, and Walker County residents were not too cooperative. Outlaw was found guilty in the death of Sam Jenkins and given a five-year sentence, but he was almost immediately pardoned by the governor for not shooting anyone or trying to escape that violent day in the courthouse.

McNelly continued to undertake assignments given by Davidson . . . until the time came for the captain to try to arrest his own boss.

CHAPTER 28

FOLLOW THE MONEY

During his time as adjutant general and chief of police, James Davidson had embezzled close to $38,000 (equal to more than $900,000 today). No wonder the state police budget was routinely busted.

Ironically, it was during a trip to find money that Davidson's perfidy was discovered. In November 1872, Gov. Davis had his secretary of state, James Newcomb, travel to New York to market state bonds. He was accompanied by Davidson, who had recently resigned as adjutant general.[58] For him, this trip was an opportunity to disappear with the stolen cash. Davidson had become aware that an audit of the state police books was to be performed during his and

---

58 Newcomb had worked for and founded several newspapers before the Civil War. During the war, like Davis, he had fought for the Union, in his case as a member of Carleton's California Column.

Newcomb's absence. It did indeed reveal that funds were missing. A fuming Gov. Davis ordered Capt. McNelly to hunt Davidson down and bring him back to Austin.

Alas, by the time McNelly arrived in New York City, the fugitive had flown. Davidson had spent some of the missing money on a suite at the St. Nicholas Hotel, then checked out. No one, including Newcomb, knew of his whereabouts, though it was believed Davidson had fled to Canada.[59] After circulating the disgraced former state police chief's photograph and description to law enforcement agencies, including those in Canada, a well-traveled McNelly returned to Texas. While in Montreal, of all places, the Texas lawman sat for a portrait, done by the photographer James Inglis.

Because he did not record his impressions for Gov. Davis or anyone else, we can only speculate what the Washington County farmer and Confederate veteran thought of New York and the rest of the Northeast he traveled through.[60]

Only years later was it discovered that Davidson had gotten about as far away from the Lone Star State as he possibly could. The embezzler surfaced in New Plymouth, New Zealand, where he soon married Jane Ryan, in October 1874, and the couple had six children. We can assume

59 There were suspicions that Newcomb was in on the embezzlement. After he left office, Newcomb was charged with stealing nine thousand dollars of state funds. He was acquitted and became owner and editor of another newspaper, the *Daily State Journal*.
60 Modern-day audiences can picture the out-of-town frontier lawman as the title characters in the popular TV show *McCloud* with Dennis Weaver and the 1968 feature film *Coogan's Bluff* starring Clint Eastwood.

he did not reveal his previous law enforcement experience when he was hired as a member of the Armed Constabulatory Force in his adopted country.

By 1880 Davidson was a captain in the Taranaki Mounted Rifles headquartered in New Plymouth, and he served as mayor there from 1879 into the 1880s. He died by suicide on April 7, 1885, and was buried in New Plymouth. Ironically, his occupation at the time of his death was listed as accountant.

The reputation of the state police was further damaged as word spread that its own boss was a crook and had disappeared. McNelly had to wonder how long his job would last, especially once Governor Davis was replaced. Hedging his bets, McNelly accepted a commission as a deputy U.S. marshal, so he at least had federal pay coming in. And indeed, in 1873, the Texas legislature abolished the state police. With the exception of missions undertaken as marshal, McNelly's primary occupation was once again tilling soil and raising livestock.

Back in Burton, he may have anticipated doing this the rest of his life, however long that would be. While his health was generally good and he was still in his twenties, McNelly had a disease that was a known killer. Staying home with Carey and his children and tending to his crops was a good life coming after four years as a Confederate soldier and being away again as a state lawman.

His hiatus lasted less than a year.

While Leander McNelly and other lawmen were carrying out their state police duties, the Texas Rangers had not ceased to exist. However, they were diminished in both numbers and stature—and, especially, budget, with the funding priority having gone to the state police. Still, during the early years of the decade, there was plenty of Ranger action—and heroism—to be found.

In February 1871, Kiowa and Comanche had raided Clear Creek, after which they were hunted down and punished by a Ranger company led by Captain David Baker. That May, the Kiowa chief Satanta led a hundred warriors in an attack on a freight train, killing seven of twelve teamsters and just missing General William Tecumseh Sherman, who was traveling through the area.

There seemed to be no end to ongoing Indian "depredations" or the nefarious activities of cattle rustlers and border ruffians. And once the violence in DeWitt County got out of hand, it was time for the Rangers to intervene there. They would be led by the once and future lawman Leander McNelly.

CHAPTER 29

ANOTHER LONG AND BLOODY WAR

The first assignment for Leander McNelly as a newly minted Texas Ranger in 1874 was one that had bedeviled law enforcement for years—put a stop to the Sutton-Taylor feud in DeWitt County. The nasty series of events was well on its way to becoming the longest and bloodiest war between families in Texas history. And the participation of John Wesley Hardin in it was not helping.

As the historian Charles Robinson III notes, "The Mason County War was just one of the 'difficulties' that caused the decade of the 1870s to be known in Texas as 'the Terrible Seventies.' Most terrible of all was DeWitt County's notorious Sutton-Taylor Feud, which left scores of people dead and prompted the legislature to create a special unit of peace officers."

Technically, the company of men the new captain put together was the Washington County Volunteer Militia

Company A. Leander McNelly and his men had the full authority of and considered themselves to be Texas Rangers.

Robinson also notes somewhat gloomily about the unit's captain: "Physically, McNelly was thin and frail, his naturally slight build wasted by tuberculosis. When he took command of the new unit he already was a dying man, which makes his career all the more remarkable."

The above-referenced Mason County War was indeed another, and especially striking, example of the kind of conflicts that erupted in Texas during and especially after the Civil War. One would think that given the great expanses of open space in the state, people who rubbed each other the wrong way could just keep their distance. But the violent confrontations in Mason and DeWitt Counties testified otherwise. As it would turn out, McNelly was able to avoid the mess of things the Texas Rangers would make in Mason County.

The origin of the troubles was a combustible combination of land, cattle, and clans. Along the lines of John Chisum and Shanghai Pierce, in the early 1870s there were budding cattle barons who were building vast herds and driving some of that stock north. At the end of the trail in the rough-and-tumble "cow towns" in Kansas, they sold the "beeves" for good prices. Cattle were loaded onto waiting railroad cars and shipped off to slaughterhouses to the north and east. But complicating matters was that, with prices high, it was simply too tempting for a few trail bosses to include in their herds cattle that had wandered off other ranches or, worse, were stolen. Unbranded cattle, known as "mavericks," were swept along by the Kansas-bound drovers.

Increasingly irritated by rampant rustling was the German population that had emigrated to Mason County in the 1840s. To these immigrants, farming and ranching were hard enough occupations without the repeated raids by rustlers, but federal troops did not care. Finally, in 1872, the population in Mason County pooled together enough votes to elect John Clark as sheriff and Dan Hoerster as "cattle inspector," a benign title for the role of stopping rustling any way he could.

The duo had mixed results—some cattle-rustling operations were disrupted, but many were not. The truly serious trouble began when Sheriff Clark jailed nine men on charges of stealing cattle. Before a trial was held, four of them escaped. A mob of about forty men took the remaining five from the jail, led them to a place near Hick Springs, and hanged them. Lieutenant Daniel Webster Roberts of the Texas Rangers, a few of his men, and a group of citizens followed the mob but did not arrive in time to save the prisoners. Though a district court investigated the incident, nothing came of the inquiry.

The members of the mob, who had quickly dispersed, were thereafter referred to as a "vigilance committee" or "Hoodoos." Ignoring lawmen, they used ambushes and midnight hangings to get rid of the men they judged to be thieves and outlaws, who would otherwise have faced Mason County judges and juries.

Another arrest led to an explosion of violence in the county. Sheriff Clark sent the deputy sheriff John Worley to bring in Tim Williamson to be charged with cattle stealing. On the return trip, Worley and his prisoner were attacked by twelve men who had blackened their faces. The unarmed Williamson was killed, as was his horse for good measure. When no one was held accountable, Scott Cooley, a former Texas Ranger, swore revenge. When he was a child, his parents had been murdered during an Indian raid and he had been raised by the Williamson family.

Cooley collected the names of the men he thought responsible for Tim Williamson's death and gathered a posse of his own. It included John and Mose Beard, George Gladden, and John Ringgold. Cooley led them on a ruthless retaliation ride that resulted in the deaths of at least a dozen men. One of the posse's early victims was John Worley, who was shot on August 10 while working on his well. Cooley not only killed him, he took his scalp.

A string of incidents followed Worley's grisly death. The frightened citizens of Mason County sent a petition to Gov. Coke asking for the protection he had not adequately provided before. To emphasize the urgency of the petition, as Coke was contemplating it, Ringgold and several others burst into the kitchen of a man named John Cheney and shot him dead. Better late than never, the governor sent in a contingent of Texas Rangers with Major John B. Jones leading it.

On September 28, when the Rangers reached Cold Springs, they found Sheriff Clark with as many as twenty men. Clark reported that the Cooley faction was heading that way to "burn out the Dutch." Where was Dan Hoerster in all this? Unfortunately, it was his turn to be targeted. The same day that Jones arrived, and in broad daylight, Hoerster was shot off his horse and fell dead in the street in front of the Southern Hotel. Two friends with him were wounded.

Major Jones made an investigation at Cold Springs before he joined up with another squad of Texas Rangers led by Roberts, and they attempted to get to the source of the trouble. During a gunfight at Keller's store on the Llano River, Mose Beard and George Gladden were shot. After several more shootings and kidnappings, with even some of the perpetrators no longer sure what side they were on, Sheriff Clark hightailed it out of Mason County, leaving most of the law enforcement to the Texas Rangers.

Jones and his men focused much of their attention on the search for Cooley and his followers. They seemed to be getting little cooperation from the community, and it finally dawned on Jones that some of his Rangers had served with Cooley and had no desire to find him. The major fired them on the spot. But there were still more murders that did not involve Cooley, and now Jones was undermanned.

The Cooley conundrum took care of itself. With his supporters among the Rangers gone, he fled into Blanco County, where he was sheltered by friends. Cooley died a short time later, supposedly of brain fever.

Jones and his remaining Rangers had a calming effect, and a strained peace descended on Mason County in the fall of 1876. As a sort of coda, on the night of January 21,

1877, the Mason County courthouse burned, destroying all records relating to the feud.[61]

DeWitt County would outdo Mason County in convoluted alliances and violence. The feud between the Sutton and Taylor families began during the tough times for Texas immediately following the Civil War. The patriarch of the anti-Reconstruction Taylor clan was Josiah Taylor, a Virginian who had traveled to Texas in 1811. Soon after, he was serving under an adventurer named Augustus Magee—another one of the colorful characters who populate Texas history.

In 1810, Father Miguel Hidalgo y Costilla began a revolt against the royalist Spanish in Mexico. Not to be outshone by a priest revolutionary, a year later, as Josiah Taylor was getting his first taste of Texas, Juan Bautista de las Casas led a revolt against Spain at San Antonio, capturing the Spanish governor. But the Spanish struck back and crushed both revolts, with the governor, Manuel María de Salcedo, being restored to power. Father Hidalgo was executed in July, in Chihuahua, while Las Casas and his associates were given the same treatment in August.

The remaining rebels then turned to the United States for help. Bernardo Gutiérrez de Lara, a blacksmith from Nuevo Santander, traveled to Washington, D.C., but he received little more than an assurance that the United States

---

61 As some readers already know, John Ringgold was Johnny Ringo, who got out of Mason County when the going was good. As detailed in the book *Tombstone,* a few years later he would confront the Earp brothers before and after the gunfight at the O.K. Corral.

would not interfere with whatever escapade he had in mind. Frustrated, Gutiérrez, with a cousin, Guerro Caja de las Casas, a relative of the executed rebel, traveled to Louisiana to seek support for their next attempt at revolution. They met with Governor William C. C. Claiborne and William Shaler in New Orleans.[62] Even more promising—at least initially—the men recruited the services of Augustus Magee.

Born in Boston, in 1809 Magee graduated third in his class at West Point. Magee served as an artillery officer under Major General James Wilkinson in Baton Rouge and then at Fort Jesup under future president Zachary Taylor (whom Josiah Taylor claimed as a relative). He refused a promotion because he preferred the revolutionary duo's plan to support the push for Mexican independence via an invasion of Spanish Texas from American soil, even though this proposal defied the Neutrality Act. Magee resigned his army commission in June 1812 and recruited soldiers for a military expedition, installing himself as the colonel in command.

With just 130 men, he and Gutiérrez crossed into Spanish Texas and captured the town of Nacogdoches. Consequently, thanks to the early victory, their numbers increased to three hundred, and they marched on to take the town of Santísima Trinidad de Salcedo, on September 13. The expedition, thus far quite successful, carried on from there. The proactive Spanish governor Manuel María

---

62 Shaler was serving as a "confidential agent" for President James Madison and had a particular interest in revolutionary causes. Later, in calmer times, he would serve as a diplomat in the administrations of Madison and James Monroe.

de Salcedo, with about eight hundred men, went after the revolutionaries and found them occupying the Presidio La Bahía in Goliad. For four months, the fort was besieged. During this time, understandably, the fort's inhabitants lost confidence in Magee.

Before the situation could deteriorate further, he died, on February 6, 1813, following a long illness. (Rumors persisted that his own men had poisoned him.) He was replaced as commander by Samuel Kemper, a veteran of the successful revolt against the Spanish in West Florida in 1804. He proved much more popular, attracting the services of volunteers from Nacogdoches, Spanish army defectors, and a few Coushatta Indians.

Thus strengthened, Kemper led his men out of the fortress, and they defeated Salcedo, who retreated toward San Antonio. In March Kemper's army set off after the Spanish. Joining it were new volunteers consisting of Americans, Tejanos, former Spanish soldiers, and Lipan and Tonkawa Indians. On March 29 the Kemper and Gutiérrez coalition defeated Simón de Herrera's Spanish army of twelve hundred men at the Battle of Salado Creek. The disgraced Gov. Salcedo surrendered on April 1.

Gutiérrez suggested the prisoners be sent to the United States for safekeeping. This journey went very bad very quickly: As the prisoners were marched out of town, they were halted, tied to trees, and killed. On April 17 the army of the Republic of Texas drafted a declaration of independence for Texas and adopted a solid-green flag for a banner. Gutiérrez declared himself governor of the new state.

He fared little better than Magee had. Because of poor judgment, Gutiérrez would lose the confidence of Kemper and the other Americans. His proclamation and allowing the execution of the Spanish governor and other officials proved to be too much. Kemper ended up quitting, leading about one hundred Americans back to Louisiana and taking no further part in the campaign.[63]

Josiah Taylor reached Louisiana with the others and then returned to Virginia. But he could not get rid of thoughts of Texas, and by the late 1820s he was back. He settled near Cuero in DeWitt County with his family, which included five sons—Pitkin, Creed, Josiah Jr., William, and Rufus. After the patriarch's death, the family would keep expanding its ranks of in-laws, nephews and nieces, cousins, and various friends.

The other patriarch of what became a rival faction was William Sutton, a native of Fayette County who had recently moved to DeWitt County. Beginning in 1866, he and his kin killed both civilians and army soldiers and avoided arrest . . . but, eventually, not retribution—especially after members of the Taylor clan became victims.

In March 1868, William Sutton, now a deputy sheriff, led a posse in pursuit of a gang of horse thieves. They caught up with the outlaws and killed one of them, Charley Taylor. The other captured outlaw, James Sharp, was shot on the return journey as he was allegedly trying to

---

63 Kemper did not have long to enjoy postrevolutionary life. He contracted malaria and died in Louisiana in 1814.

escape.[64] However, the real beginning of the feud was the killing of Buck Taylor and Dick Chisholm at Clinton late that year, on Christmas Eve. In connection with the sale of some horses, Taylor accused William Sutton of dishonesty, and shots were exchanged.

This latest killing was one too many for Edmund Davis, who had recently become governor. Putting out this fire was the job given to the state police, and the man sent to do it was Jack Helm, whom we met earlier. The already notorious captain had amply demonstrated the brutality and prejudices that inspired people to detest the state police. According to the Southwest historian C. L. Sonnichsen, Helm was "an extremely ignorant man [yet] nevertheless convinced of his own wisdom and always able to explain why anything he did was the equivalent of an act of God." When he was recognized by or introduced to someone, he would often swell his chest and say, "I God, I'm the man, ain't I?"

In his latest crusade, Helm was assisted by Jim Cox; William Sutton; a familiar name, Joseph Tumlinson; and, if need be, the U.S. Army, units of which had been occupying Texas since the war ended. The threat of army assistance, especially, galvanized anti-Yankee sentiments. These became more intense when, using the excuse of pursuing horse and cattle thieves, the state police began terrorizing

---

64 The high number of Texan and Mexican prisoners who perished can be attributed to *la ley de fuga,* which translates to "the law of the fugitive," meaning captives were killed rather than having to feed, transport, or try them in court. This practice was not unknown to some Ranger captains, including Leander McNelly.

a large portion of southeast Texas, with members of the Taylor clan as the primary targets.

On August 23, 1869, a posse laid an ambush that resulted in the death of a Taylor relative named Hays. Then came the aforementioned assassination of Henry and William Kelly, who were related to Pitkin Taylor. There were four Kelly brothers in total, the other two being Wiley and Eugene. All were accused of a shooting incident in Lavaca County, though no one was reported killed. On August 25, 1870, a posse found and arrested Henry and William. Helm led the posse, which included William Sutton. It was reported that the two Kelly brothers were gunned down while—of course—attempting to escape. The Taylor faction insisted the deaths were cold-blooded murder.[65]

The feud between the families reignited in the summer of 1872. One night, a party of Sutton sympathizers lured Pitkin Taylor from his house by ringing a cowbell in his cornfield. Pitkin was shot and severely wounded, and he would die six months later. At his funeral, his son, Jim Taylor, and several of their relatives resolved to avenge his death.

Their first attempt to do so was made on April 1, 1873, when they caught William Sutton in a saloon in Cuero, fired through the door, and wounded him. They ambushed him again in June, but this time he escaped without injury. A few weeks later, the Taylor faction ambushed and killed

---

65 At another time and by a different posse, Wiley and Eugene Kelly were arrested. They stood trial for the Lavaca incident and were acquitted.

Jim Cox and a friend aligned with the Sutton family. And finally, it was Helm's turn to die.

In DeWitt County, the conflict was about to go from bad to very bad because the man determined to hunt Helm down was John Wesley Hardin.

CHAPTER 30

QUICK WITH A GUN

Hardin is near or at the top of any list of American West "man-killers." He was a homegrown Texan, born in Bonham in May 1853. The son of a Methodist preacher, Hardin was a precocious killer, his career of carnage beginning when he was only fourteen with the stabbing of another student during a schoolyard confrontation. The following year, he shot a man to death in Polk County.

Hardin was just getting started. After hiding out in his brother's house in Sumpter, he emerged to kill three U.S. Army soldiers who sought to arrest him. After soon adding another soldier to the tally, he correctly surmised that the army would step up efforts to nab him. Incredibly, Hardin laid low by briefly teaching school in Pisgah. His pistol did not cool off completely, though, because to win a bet and a bottle of whiskey, he shot a man's eye out. For Hardin, the school year ended early.

January 1870 found him in Hill County playing cards with a man named Benjamin Bradley. The gunslinger's winning streak angered Bradley, who threatened to cut out Hardin's liver if he won again. By now, being almost seventeen years old, Hardin was rather attached to his liver, so when Bradley drew a knife and a six-shooter, Hardin, who was unarmed, folded his cards and left.

That night, Bradley, instead of enjoying his winnings and being alive, went out looking for the young gambler. Finding him, Bradley fired a shot and missed. Hardin, now sporting two pistols, fired and did not miss, striking Bradley in the chest and head. Onlookers noted that Hardin had holsters sewn into his vest so that the butts of his pistols pointed across his chest and he crossed his arms to draw. Bradley did not live long enough to be impressed by such dexterity.

Later that month in Limestone County, Hardin was accompanying a woman home when they were accosted by her "sweetheart"—more likely, her pimp—who demanded money. Hardin threw some on the ground. "He stooped down to pick it up and as he was straightening up I pulled my pistol and fired," Hardin recalled in his autobiography, published in 1896. "The ball struck him between the eyes and he fell over, a dead robber."

Ironically, when Hardin finally was tossed in the calaboose, it was for a crime he claimed he did not commit. In early January 1871, he was arrested by the city marshal,

Laban John Hoffman, for a murder in Waco. Hardin was held temporarily in a log jail in the town of Marshall, awaiting trial back in Waco. Somehow, while locked up, he obtained a pistol from another prisoner.[66]

When the day came, two Texas state policemen, Captain Edward T. Stakes and an officer named Jim Smalley, were assigned to escort the accused. While making camp along the way, Stakes went to find fodder for the horses. Left alone with Smalley, Hardin produced the pistol, fatally shot him, and used the policeman's horse to escape. The fugitive found refuge with his cousins, the Clements, who were then living in Gonzales. They suggested he could make money by signing on to drive cattle to Kansas. This he did in February, and rustled cattle on the side. He did not kill anyone . . . but he came close. While the herd was being collected for the drive to Kansas, a freedman, Bob King, attempted to cut a beef cow out of the herd. When he refused to obey Hardin's demand to stop, Hardin hit him over the head with his pistol.

He must have completed the cattle drive, because Hardin next appeared in Abilene, which at that time was one of the more raucous Kansas cow towns. In 1871, Wild Bill

---

66 A Confederate army veteran with a wife and two young children, Hoffman did not have long to live. A few days later, at noon, he was in a Waco barbershop getting a shave. A man rode up on horseback, dismounted, and entered the shop from the rear. He examined the lathered face to make sure it was Hoffman then walked behind the barber chair and shot the marshal in the back of head, killing him instantly. The man remounted and fired two shots at approaching deputies. When the man arrived at the bridge, he tossed the toll collector a dollar and said, "Haven't time to wait for the change," and galloped away.

Hickok was the marshal there. The gunfighter turned lawman was aware of a Texas arrest warrant for Hardin but was not especially fond of Texans, so he ignored it. Instead, during a confrontation, he offered Hardin a haven in Abilene for as long as the young man did not kill anyone. This truce lasted until Hardin shot a man trying to break into his hotel room. As Hickok was responding to the gunshots, Hardin leaped out the window, stole a horse and wagon, and fled south, eventually returning to Texas.[67]

According to Hardin's own account, he kept busy while back in the Lone Star State. In September of that same year, he was involved in a gunfight with two Texas policemen who were also freedmen, Green Paramore and John Lackey, during which Paramore was killed and Lackey wounded. Soon a posse of black men from Austin pursued Hardin to avenge Paramore's death. They were not successful, with Hardin claiming they returned "sadder and wiser" after he ambushed and killed three of them.

Of all things, it was love that got Hardin involved in the Sutton-Taylor feud. That same year, he was in Gonzales County and married Jane Bowen. His new brother-in-law was Robert Bowen, a known rustler, and Hardin renewed his acquaintance with some of his cousins, who were allied with a local family, the Taylors. No doubt they brought Hardin up to speed on the feud with the Suttons that had

---

67 Yes, readers, this is a shameless plug: For more details of the relationship between Hickok and Hardin (and Hardin's dubious claim that he got the drop on Hickok), pick up a copy of *Wild Bill: The True Story of the American Frontier's First Gunfighter*.

been going on for years—mostly, they contended, to the Taylor faction's disadvantage.

However, for the rest of that year Hardin was so occupied with trying to stay out of jail plus stay alive that the Sutton-Taylor feud would have to wait. In August, he was wounded by a shotgun blast in a gambling dispute at the Gates Saloon in Trinity. Hardin responded by putting a bullet in the gambler's shoulder. But Hardin was wounded seriously enough—two buckshot pellets penetrated his kidney—that for a time it looked as if he would die.

He did not, but he had come close enough that he decided he wanted to settle down—presumably, with his bride.[68] He handed his guns over to Sheriff Dick Reagon of Cherokee County and asked to be tried for his past crimes in order to, as he put it, "clear the slate." However, when Hardin learned of how many murders Reagon was going to charge him with, he changed his mind. A relative smuggled in a hacksaw to Hardin, and it was also believed the guards were only too happy to look the other way.

During the first few months of 1873, Hardin stayed out of sight and recuperated from his wounds. In May, the Taylor faction killed Jim Cox and Jake Christman at Tumlinson Creek. It was reported that Hardin had decided to pitch in to help the Taylors and had been involved in these killings—and he did not deny that allegation. Then an event in July left no doubt.

---

68 The couple must have spent some time together because they produced a son and two daughters.

On the eighteenth, in Cuero, Hardin killed a DeWitt County officer, J. B. Morgan, who happened to be a deputy to Jack Helm. Because he was an avowed Sutton supporter, it was the county sheriff's turn next—that very same day.

In Albuquerque (Texas, not New Mexico), Hardin encountered Helm. The sheriff was with Sam McCracken, an acquaintance who claimed to be Albuquerque's first settler. They were at a blacksmith shop. The ousted state police captain also fashioned himself as an inventor, and he was in Albuquerque to demonstrate a cotton-worm destroyer that he had constructed. Not expecting trouble, Helm had left his boarding house without weapons. When approached by Hardin, Helm may have thought being unable to defend himself could actually save his life.

Such thinking was reasonable—Hardin, for all his faults, was not likely to gun down an unarmed man. But during the conversation, the more-motivated Jim Taylor crept up on Helm from behind, pointed a pistol at him, and pulled the trigger. The gun misfired. As the startled Helm turned, Taylor managed to get off a second shot, striking Helm in the chest. Helm rushed Taylor, but Hardin lifted up a shotgun and fired. The blast shattered Helm's arm. Even though badly wounded, Helm was able to flee into the blacksmith shop. While Hardin held the townspeople at gunpoint, Taylor chased Helm and unloaded the rest of his gun into Helm's head. "Thus did the leader of the vigilant committee, the sheriff of DeWitt, the terror of the country, whose name was a horror to all law-abiding citizens, meet his death," Hardin proclaimed.

As Hardin and Taylor mounted their horses and prepared to ride away, townspeople heard them boast that they had accomplished what they had set out to do.

Only a day after Helm's death, a strong force of Taylors moved on Joseph Tumlinson's stronghold near Yorktown. After a brief siege, a sheriff heading a posse appeared and talked both parties into signing a truce. But the peace lasted only until December of that year, when Wiley Pridgen, a Taylor sympathizer, was killed at Thomaston. Enraged by this murder, the Taylors attacked the Sutton faction, besieged them in Cuero for a day and night, and were besieged in turn when Joseph Tumlinson appeared with a larger band of Sutton supporters.

By this time the county was in an uproar. For residents, there was no neutral zone—if they wished to continue to live in the area, they had to take sides. There was constant pursuing and bushwhacking, and the body count rose. William Sutton, having had enough and believing his life span could be measured in hours, moved to Victoria in an adjoining county. Then he left altogether, the cover story being he was taking a herd of cattle to a northern market. In fact, on March 11, 1874, he boarded a steamer at Indianola, planning on getting as far away as he could.

Sutton did not manage to get far at all. Before the boat could leave, Jim and Bill Taylor rode up to the dock and killed him and his friend Gabriel Slaughter. It was believed—and Hardin claimed this to be true—that Hardin and his brother Joseph were also involved in the killings.

The response of the Sutton faction was to host a hanging party. The victims would be Kute Tuggle, Jim White, and Scrap Taylor. They were among a group of cowboys who had signed on to take a herd up the trail for Hardin. At Hamilton they were arrested, charged with cattle theft, and brought back to Clinton. Instead of being tried, though, one night they were taken out of the courthouse and hanged, because of being acquainted with Hardin.

On May 26, 1874, Hardin turned twenty-one, and he and several others were toasting that milestone in a saloon in Comanche. A county deputy sheriff, Charles Webb, walked in. Webb, a former Texas Ranger, was actually a peace officer in Brown County, but he was in Comanche as more of a bounty hunter, having heard of there being a price on Hardin's head. The gunfighter asked Webb if he had come to arrest him. When Webb replied he had not, Hardin invited him to have a drink. As Hardin led him to the bar, Webb drew his gun. One of Hardin's men yelled out a warning, and in the ensuing gunfight, Webb was shot dead.

Webb had been a well-liked man, and his death resulted immediately in the formation of a lynch mob. Hardin's parents were taken into protective custody, while his brother Joe and two cousins, brothers Bud and Tom Dixon, were arrested on outstanding warrants. A group of local men broke into the jail in July and hanged the prisoners. After this, Hardin and Jim Taylor parted ways for good.

There was another reason why Hardin decided to go while the going was good: He had heard that Leander McNelly was coming for him. He later wrote, "The State Police had been organized"—meaning the Washington County company—"and McNelly had been placed on the force, so on consultation with friends, it was thought best that I should leave."

By then, plenty of damage had been done, and with the likelihood that there would be more as long as there were members of the Sutton and Taylor factions still alive, Governor Coke was persuaded to take action. It was time for Captain Leander H. McNelly and the Texas Rangers to end the feud.

The Austin Daily Statesman bid the lawmen goodbye and good luck in its edition of July 25, 1874, concluding: "We trust that the boys may return home in due time to gladden the hearts of the girls who shed tears as the boys 'lit out' for the war in DeWitt County."

CHAPTER 31

"A PERFECT REIGN OF TERROR"

While Leander McNelly had been back in Burton tending to his farm and his family, the administration of Governor Richard Coke had concluded that a more permanent—and less despised—law enforcement agency than the state police was needed. Recent events had shown that there was still plenty of Indian fighting to do, but cattle rustling and other forms of banditry demonstrated there were too many Texas citizens not abiding by the laws of the state. And an exclamation point was the escalating violence of the Sutton-Taylor feud.

With the governor's support, the Frontier Protection Act had been passed in April 1874. Coke now had the authority to raise and pay companies and send them to counties plagued by violence. The size of a company could have a wide range, anywhere from twenty-five to seventy-five men, who could serve up to a year. There was a range of monthly wages too, from forty dollars for a private up to one hundred dollars for a captain. Each man brought his own horse and pistols, with the state supplying a rifle, ammunition, and provisions.

Collectively, this new force was known as the Frontier Battalion. It was, essentially, the latest version of the Texas Rangers. The turning point in the state's history, though, was that this time the police force was permanent—there would be continuity from the contingent of lawmen created in 1874 to the Texas Rangers of today.

Governor Coke selected the previously mentioned John B. Jones to be the "major," or superintendent, of the Frontier Battalion. He would turn out to be an excellent choice. Jones, born in South Carolina in 1834, moved with his family to Texas four years later. They settled first in Travis County and eventually wound up in Navarro County. A good student, Jones attended Rutersville College near La Grange and Mount Zion College back in South Carolina.

As with many young men at the time, the Civil War interrupted his studies. Jones enlisted as a private in Terry's Texas Rangers but left the regiment to join the Fifteenth Texas Infantry with the rank of captain. He later became assistant adjutant general of Polignac's Brigade and was promoted to major at the end of the war. Perhaps still wearing his uniform, Jones went to Mexico hoping to locate a suitable site for an expatriate Confederate colony. This was not a far-fetched notion.

In Reconstruction-era Texas some families, haunted by ruined farms and ranches, a wrecked economy, political persecution, and freedmen exercising their newly won rights sought to build new lives in foreign lands. Indeed, some estimates contend that as many as three million people would leave the vanquished Confederate States of America and emigrate west of the Missouri River, to northern cities, to Canada, to Egypt (like Sibley), and to Mexico and Latin America. The mission undertaken by Major Jones, however, failed, and he returned to Texas.

In 1868, he was elected to the state legislature but was denied his seat by pro-Reconstruction Republicans. Jones focused on making money instead. He became a successful stock farmer, founded a bank with several partners, and in 1872 he established John B. Jones & Company, a banking and mercantile firm.

After the legislature authorized the formation of the Frontier Battalion, Gov. Coke chose the former Confederate general William Steele to be the adjutant general to oversee it. Steele, in turn, hired Jones, whom he had known during the war, to command it. Within six months, Jones could report that, thanks to the Frontier Battalion, more than forty Indian raiding parties had been confronted and that fourteen of those encounters involved fighting.

Jones himself, not content to ride a desk in Austin, fought in one of those engagements. On July 12, 1874, he led a force of over thirty Rangers in an attack on a party of more than 125 Comanche, Kiowa, and Apache at Lost Valley in Young County. But "attack" can be misleading, because at first the Rangers rode into an ambush, one arranged by Lone Wolf and a Kiowa chief turned medicine man named Maman-ti, also known as Swan.

The latter had earned respect within his tribe from an incident that could have resulted in the death or at least capture of General William Tecumseh Sherman. Maman-ti and his Kiowa band had observed, without attacking, the passage of a small group of wagons and soldiers. They were unaware that this group was an inspection tour being taken by General Sherman. Thus, Maman-ti missed an opportunity to become the most famous Indian in America. He had held off because, the night before, he had envisioned that this small party would be followed by a larger one with more plunder for the taking. He turned out to be right, and the ten mule-drawn wagons filled with army corn and fodder was ambushed, with seven of the teamsters murdered and mutilated. The Kiowa lost three of their own but left with forty mules heavily laden with other supplies.

Five men managed to escape. One of them, Thomas Brazeale, walked to Fort Richardson, some twenty miles away. As soon as Colonel Ranald S. Mackenzie—who would find his own fame in the Red River War—learned of the attack, he dispatched cavalry to kill or capture the Kiowa. But in the ensuing roundup, Maman-ti escaped.

Now he had perpetrated another ambush. This time, though, his and Lone Wolf's warriors were up against members of the Frontier Battalion, not civilians. Major Jones rallied his men, and they launched an assault against their attackers. They broke through the encircling Kiowa and rode to a gully at the head of Lost Valley. Taking a defensive position there, the Rangers used their rifles to hold the warriors off. They were encouraged by Jones's defying of bullets and arrows as he strode back and forth beside the prone shooters.

Though as many as a dozen, if not more, of the Kiowa had been killed, by late afternoon the Rangers were still trapped, and they were hot and thirsty. Two volunteers, Mel Porter and David Bailey, slipped away with canteens to try to find water. Neither returned. In the latter's case, the Rangers reluctantly listened as the captured Bailey was tortured to death.

Despite this brutal death, another volunteer, John Holmes, snuck off to try to reach Fort Richardson. His timing was better, because the Kiowa, hauling their wounded, had moved on. This allowed the Rangers to make their way to a ranch owned by James Loving. That night, Holmes returned, bringing cavalry from the fort with him. Though Jones had led his men into an ambush, his cool demeanor under fire showed he was no bureaucrat.

Two days after the Lost Valley fight, Leander McNelly was commissioned captain of Company A of the Washington County Volunteer Militia. Jones, not distracted by his own adventures, recognized that DeWitt County urgently needed an intervention. It seemed like no resident was safe from being caught in the next cross fire. McNelly still carried with him an excellent war reputation and, unlike rogue lawmen like Jack Helm, had emerged unscathed from his state police experience.

Specifically, McNelly's orders were to aid existing law enforcement—such as it was—in DeWitt County, especially the outgunned and outmanned sheriff, William

Weisiger.[69] But McNelly's men were expected to be more than cheerleaders—when the thirty or so Rangers rode into Clinton, the county seat, on August 1, they carried with them, in addition to pistols and knives, fifty .50-caliber Sharps rifles and three thousand rounds of ammunition.

The residents of DeWitt County who encountered Leander McNelly saw a man much as he would soon be described in *The Houston Daily Telegraph*: "Of medium stature, and physically seems the very reverse of robust. He has a high forehead, and his head and face create the impression of great intellectuality. His hair and whiskers are brown, nose of medium size and somewhat curved, with steel gray glittering eyes under closely knit eyebrows." The columnist continued that "behind the quiet address and modest demeanor [are] the indications of inflexible determination and untiring activity that make him the terror of frontier outlaws."

Having McNelly as captain and being well armed reassured the populace, as well as the Rangers, who found the situation to be "a perfect reign of terror," as McNelly wrote to Steele. He reported that "armed bands of men were making predatory excursions through the country, while the civil authorities were unable or unwilling to enforce the laws." He further reported that "peaceful

69 Weisiger had served in the Confederate army, including the very last action, the Battle of Palmito Ranch, east of Brownsville on May 12–13, 1865. He was elected sheriff in 1873 and remained in that office until 1881.

citizens . . . were in jeopardy, as neutrals were considered obnoxious to both factions."

And now McNelly's Rangers, as the men had already begun to label themselves, had placed themselves between the two enemy camps.

CHAPTER 32

THE PEACEKEEPERS

They did not have to wait long to see action. Less than a week after the Rangers arrived in Clinton, they were attacked. On August 3 a grand jury had been convened and its no-doubt-nervous members were expected to hand down murder indictments. Three days later, McNelly dispatched one of his sergeants, Charles Middleton, and three privates to the ranch of John Taylor to bring him in as a witness. On the return trip, Middleton and his men were confronted by about two dozen members of the Sutton faction. Immediately, shots were exchanged.

The leader of the attackers was the cattle rancher and Sutton-Taylor feud veteran "Old Joe" Tumlinson. His father was the colonist who unaccountably was killed by an Indian in 1823. A member of McNelly's Rangers, known as "Pidge" (more about him soon), described Tumlinson as going about "with a gun on each shoulder and two Smith

& Wessons in his belt. He has the frosts of sixty winters on his head, and green spectacles on his nose, and, it is said, can see with his naked eye farther than any hawk on this side of the Rio Grande."[70] Where Old Joe led, supporters followed.

This time, however, he had led them the wrong way. Tumlinson had assumed the Rangers were allies of Taylor, not lawmen. The truth finally dawned on him after fifteen minutes of firing that wound up injuring one of the privates, a Ranger named Chalk, and three horses. As ornery as "Old Joe" was, he did not want to risk alienating the Washington County contingent, so instead of taking Taylor and stringing him up, the Sutton supporters backed off and allowed Middleton's group to proceed.

Still, upon hearing his sergeant's report, McNelly predicted that his company "will have hot work for awhile."

This does not mean they were going to withdraw from the feud. As McNelly would write to Steele, "Tumlinson could count on seventy-five well-armed men, and men who have no interest but in obeying his orders; he is a man who has always righted his own wrongs and he tells me that the only way for this county to have peace is to allow him to kill off the Taylor party."

The captain was not the least bit intimidated. He declared to the adjutant general, "I feel entirely able to whip Tumlinson with the men I have if it must be a fight but

---

70 About John Taylor, Pidge wrote that "when on foot [he] reminds one strongly of an old sundried bucket about to fall to pieces [but] when on horseback his powers of endurance are almost incredible."

will need more men, fifty cannot overawe these people." He added, "We cannot expect help from the citizens."

After considering Sergeant Middleton's report, McNelly realized he had to get out ahead of such incidents. Other Sutton partisans might not be so sensible. The captain harkened back to his Civil War adventures, which included recruiting spies and acting on the information they gleaned. McNelly began to do the same in DeWitt County. He found fertile ground for informants because many of the residents had ceased caring which side, Taylor or Sutton, was right or wrong and simply wanted the vigilante violence to stop. The captain was regularly informed of the activities of the two factions, vowing that there would be "no plot of which I will be ignorant."

In a separate report, McNelly told his boss, "The capture of Hardin and Taylor would go a long way to quiet things in this County and I feel quite sanguine of success in my contemplated effort."

However, *The San Antonio Express* had a different view. "We have just learned," it offered in the August 23, 1874, edition, "that Capt. McNelly, with his small company of Coke's State Police, finds himself powerless to quell the insurrection, or to give any relief to the county." The editorial went on at some length to continue bashing Gov. Coke.

For the most part, the Rangers could not force peace on the county, but the captain figured they could be persuasive simply by their presence. McNelly had patrols out constantly, letting the population know that the Washington County peacekeepers were not going away soon. They made a point of fraternizing with Taylor and Sutton family members, getting more results with the honey instead of vinegar approach. Going one step further, McNelly had one man each living with Joseph Tumlinson and Bolivar Pridgen, who had sworn revenge after two relatives had been murdered by Sutton supporters.

And when McNelly heard of any gathering of a sufficient amount of men to cause trouble, he sent Rangers to those locations. "When they hear of my men coming they scatter," he boasted to Steele.

By mid-November, McNelly, who had once again been appointed a deputy U.S. marshal, had brought the weight of the Rangers to bear, and the county enjoyed some peace. The patrols of the roads and main streets seemed to have nipped fights in the bud. It was getting to be time for McNelly and his men to move on from DeWitt County, though the captain would soon write Steele that he thought the troubles were "temporarily allayed." He would prove to be right, but at least it was not until 1876 that the feud flared up again.

But there was a loose end left to the Sutton-Taylor feud: John Wesley Hardin. Leander McNelly did not have the opportunity to confront him, which prevents the history of the American West from including what would certainly be one of its more riveting stories.

After the lynching of his brother and two cousins, Hardin had enough of riding with the Taylor clan. Further inspiration to get out of DeWitt County came when the Texas legislature authorized a four-thousand-dollar reward for his arrest. An enterprising Texas Ranger named Jack Duncan intercepted a letter sent to Hardin's father-in-law by Hardin's brother-in-law, Joshua Bowen, that mentioned the infamous outlaw was hiding out on the Alabama-Florida border using the name James W. Swain. He had adopted the alias from Brenham town marshal Henry Swain, who had married a cousin of Hardin's named Molly Parks.

Instead of laying low, in March 1876 Hardin wounded a man in Florida who had tried to mediate a quarrel between him and another fellow. That November, in Mobile, Alabama, Hardin was arrested for having marked cards, but apparently the alias held up because he was released right away. Some months later, in a rather bizarre gambit, two former slaves of his father's, Jake Menzel and Robert Borup, tried to capture Hardin, who was now residing in Gainesville, Florida. The young gunman killed one and blinded the other.

Texas, it seemed, was finally shut of John Wesley Hardin. Or so citizens assumed.

CHAPTER 33

REPORTERS AND RANGERS

Leander McNelly dutifully wrote reports about his company's activities. However, beyond these straightforward and somewhat terse accounts, there are ones that flesh out the adventures of McNelly's Rangers ... though one should keep a few grains of salt handy.

One of the young men serving in the company was "Pidge." True, this is not exactly a name that conjures up an image of a rough-and-ready Texas Ranger wearing dust-covered clothes and sporting untrimmed whiskers. Pidge did indeed share lawing adventures with McNelly's men, but he was as much a newspaper correspondent as a gunman. And there was a strange origin to his pseudonym. In any case, though his accounts at times strain credulity and tend to go off on tangents, it is thanks to Pidge that we have detailed and vivid reporting on at least some of the exploits of McNelly's Rangers.

According to what the western historian Chuck Parsons was able to piece together, in the early 1870s Thomas C. Robinson, born in 1847, was living with his father and younger sister in Campbell County, Virginia. Thomas Sr., a recent widower, had made a good living as a farmer. It can be assumed, based on evidence in his writings, that the younger Thomas had received the type of education that was available to a Virginia family of some means, which probably included study of classic literature, before the war upended everything. But the postwar Thomas Jr. had been in trouble with the law, having been tried (though acquitted) of assault. It was a new dispute with a neighbor, however, that truly changed the course of his life.

That neighbor was the decade-older Jesse Mitchell, who lived on an adjacent farm with his parents and a sister, Mary Elizabeth, who was called "Pidgie." In 1873, after an injury involving a saw, Jesse Mitchell was tended to at the Robinson farm, with nursing services provided by the twenty-three-year-old Lizzie May Robinson.

Apparently, some affection developed. Then, as Parsons puts it, "But in spite of the once warm neighborly relationship, something happened." One can only surmise that it was based on Thomas Sr. banishing Mitchell from his property, possibly because of inappropriate behavior.

Things became more complicated. Sometime along the way the younger Thomas had become enamored of Pidgie. But as a result of his exile, Jesse in turn banned Mary Elizabeth and Thomas Jr. from seeing each other. And the latter was arrested again, on an unknown charge. However, it must have been serious, and he was guilty enough that Thomas Jr. fled Virginia on New Year's Day, 1874. Where did many a young man go to escape and try to start over? Texas, of course.

By the end of January, Robinson was in Austin sporting the name T. Chanders. His first attempt to earn a living was as a cowboy on a cattle drive destined for Wichita. However, after only a few days, his cowboy career came to a quick end. It seemed that, in addition to horse-riding difficulties, a cowboy's hours were not to his liking. As he would later recall in an essay for the Austin-based *Daily Democratic Statesman*: "The next morning I was awakened by a rough shake. The sun was up and the herd was *en route* for the prairie. 'Young man, do you calculate that you can sleep this way on the trail?' I replied that I had no doubt of it, if I was not disturbed. 'Well, you'll be right apt to be disturbed, if you go with me,' replied the 'boss.' In vain I assured him that I could not sleep on as fast a schedule as the rest, and would be compelled to have more time. He was inexorable, and ordered me to rise and help brand a lot brought in that morning."

Things went from bad to worse for the inexperienced wrangler, and he determined the pen was mightier than the lasso. Aiming to be a newspaperman, Chanders first approached *The Statesman,* Austin's most-read publication, with a larger audience throughout Texas. The editor was John Cardwell, who turned out to be the right man to talk to.

The Georgia native was thirty-eight years old and had not started out hoping for a career in frontier journalism.

He had studied law at the University of Virginia in the mid-1850s but moved on to Texas before the war began, having inherited his father's plantation in Wharton County. He married Margaret Dunlap of Brazoria County on January 6, 1860, and they became the parents of one daughter. At the war's conclusion, Cardwell was another emissary sent south to investigate possible opportunities for the relocation of anti-Reconstruction Texans. In this case, Brazil was the target, but he returned with a negative report. Cardwell went back to plantation life.

Ink entered his veins in July 1871, when the Democratic Executive Committee offered Cardwell the position of editor of *The Austin Statesman,* a new newspaper. He accepted and became known for his vigorous attacks against Governor Edmund Davis and other public figures.[71] He was also known for giving young talent an opportunity. Thus, when a greenhorn calling himself "Pidge" showed up at his office with a few writing samples, Cardwell gave him a shot.

When Pidge went riding as a member of McNelly's Rangers, he brought his pen with him. In his essay titled "The Dull Season," which *The Statesman* published, he described how he came to be part of the company, having found Austin not as stimulating as he anticipated: "I went

---

71 In 1883, having had his fill of partisan politics, Cardwell resigned from the newspaper and once more retired to his Wharton County plantation. Apparently, he became restless because he lobbied the administration of President Grover Cleveland for a position and was appointed the U.S. consul general to Egypt, a post he held until 1889. Cardwell died at his home on April 17, 1893.

immediately to the captain of a frontier company who happened to be in town. I fell upon his neck. 'Let me,' I implored, 'join your command and lend my feeble assistance towards keeping back the copper-colored fiends from the sacred soil of this, my adopted State. Let me add my mite to help save our frontier citizens from the horrors of the scalping-knife. Allow me to devote my services toward saving our women and children from a fate worse than death. Let me strike a stroke under the Lone Star flag, for I am literally full and running over with martial ardor.'"

N. A. Jennings was another member of McNelly's Rangers who would detail many of their exploits. However, his accounts would not be written and published until decades later, when his memory was not the sharpest.

Napoleon Augustus Jennings was a big name for someone only eighteen years old in 1874. His Philadelphia merchant father had sent him off to a boarding school in New Hampshire, and while the teenager appreciated that he was receiving a good education, he explained in *A Texas Ranger,* "The reading of books of travel and adventure had roused in me a spirit of unrest, and I wanted to see the world." Further reading persuaded Jennings to downscale from seeing the world: "I was a callow youth at the time, however. After reading of the wild, free life of the Texas cowboy, I made up my mind that life would not be worth living outside of Texas."

He soon found that life might not be worth living inside Texas either. With few desirable skills, frontier living and survival were much more of a challenge than he had expected. As Jennings recalled, "I had been in a sad predicament in San Antonio, but now my situation was indeed desperate. I was not only penniless, but hungry and friendless." In his tenderfoot travels he had encountered "a good-natured, jolly set of fellows, but through my inexperienced young Eastern eyes I saw in them only a lot of rough, loud-talking, swearing ruffians."

Welcome to Texas indeed. More adventures did not result in life becoming easier for Jennings. He finally found himself stranded in Laredo . . . and that was where the possibility of salvation appeared. He was standing on a corner one morning when a troop of forty-two mounted men ambled toward him, led by Leander McNelly: "And at their head rode a man who was surely not a cowboy, whatever the others might be. This leader was rather under the average height and slimly built, but he sat so erect in the saddle and had such an air of command that he seemed like a cavalry officer at the head of a company of soldiers."

After ascertaining who the newcomers were, Jennings pondered, "Why shouldn't I join the Rangers? Here was a chance to get out of Laredo and to gratify my love for adventure at the same time. I resolved to apply at once." He presented himself at the hotel, where Jennings found the captain "sitting by the window, talking to his sweet-faced wife" and their two children. McNelly questioned the young and hungry adventurer and told him to return later.

When Jennings did, "I have decided to let you join" were McNelly's first words. The catch was that Jennings had to provide his own horse, saddle, bridle, blankets, and pistol. Miraculously, he found an acquaintance in Laredo who would advance him these necessities, and by that evening Jennings was also a member of the Washington County company.

A third young Ranger bore witness to the experiences of Leander McNelly and his men. William Crump Callicott was a native Texan born in November 1852. His unusual middle name was in honor of William E. Crump, who had been speaker of the Texas House of Representatives in 1846. William's mother and her first husband, Jacob Pevehouse, had come to Texas with Stephen Austin's first colony, settling near San Felipe de Austin. After Pevehouse died in an accident, his widow then married James Callicott. She died about 1854, leaving four children to be raised, with William the youngest. It had to be tough going for the family, yet when the Civil War began, James Callicott enlisted as a private.

After the war, Bill Callicott struck off on his own, working as a cowboy, then he saw the Texas Rangers as his ticket to adventure. He enlisted in Captain John R. Waller's Company A Frontier Battalion and served with it until August 31, 1874. During this period, Callicott was on detached service with Major John B. Jones as part of his expeditions. He then enlisted in the Washington County Volunteer Militia Company A. Callicott served with Capt. McNelly until he mustered out with an honorable discharge on November 30, 1875.

He did not write about his days with the Washington County company until many years later, beginning when he was in his late sixties, and he did so in a series of letters to Walter Prescott Webb, who was writing *The Texas*

Rangers, which would be published in 1935.[72] Despite the challenges posed by memory and approaching blindness, Callicott's accounts contain many instances of accurate reporting of events and of his fellow riders.

George Durham was the fourth man whose exploits riding with McNelly would be recorded, these accounts based on his participation while still only a teenager. He had grown up in Georgia, but his father had served under McNelly in Louisiana during the war. Having heard tales of the almost-mythical young Confederate officer, Durham was restless to chart his own course and yet at the same time wanted to follow in his father's footsteps.

"The way I heard it [about Texas], this was a fairy-land where beeves by the thousands ran loose and belonged to anybody with a rope and branding iron and able to hold his own," Durham reported. "I pulled out for Texas in the spring of 'seventy-five. I was nothing but a big hunk of farm boy straddling a plow horse, with a few victuals and a pistol."[73]

Sometimes, that was all a young man with dreams and ambition needed in Texas. And it did not take much time before he found his father's "old" commander. Durham had begun asking about Leander McNelly as soon as he

---

72 For many years, Webb's book was considered the definitive story of the Texas Rangers, but in the decades since publication the accuracy of many of Webb's accounts has been challenged. It still makes for riveting reading.

73 Durham's reminiscences are collected in *Taming the Nueces Strip.* Fifty years after the events Durham describes, he told them to the reporter Clyde Wantland. An imperfect memory explains the tale's shortcomings, but he seems more accurate than Jennings.

entered the Lone Star State. When he finally encountered him, Durham was not impressed: "I had pictured the Captain McNelly I came to see to be a picture-book sort of Texas fighter. Big and hairy, with his pistols gleaming. What I had just seen could have been a preacher. A puny one at that." It did not help that McNelly had just dismissed him for being too young and green.

But Durham was persistent, a quality McNelly admired. And that April, he caught up with the Washington County company in South Texas. This time the captain "half-circled me and sized me up from every angle." Finally, after consulting with one of his sergeants, McNelly told the teenager, "Your pay will be thirty-three dollars a month in state scrip and found. You furnish the gun; the state will furnish the shells. You want it?"

Durham could not accept fast enough. "I felt some chesty," he recalled. "Just a country boy, but I'd caught on fast. As time went on I learned that the most important lesson a man could learn on coming to Texas was to keep his mouth shut and not ask questions. I had learned that and just now passed that test."

One test, anyway. The bigger one for the captain and his entire company was their next assignment—to bring peace to what had long been a lawless area. In doing so, Robinson, Jennings, Durham, Callicott, and the rest would make use of as much ammunition as they could carry while taking on not just local bandits and border ruffians but an entire country.

THEIR BACKS
TO THE RIVER

All outlaws look good dead.

—Captain Leander McNelly

CHAPTER 34

PATROLLING THE NUECES STRIP

In the spring of 1875, called upon by Adjutant General William Steele to undertake a new mission, Captain Leander McNelly and his men regrouped, gathered sufficient supplies and ammunition, and rode out of Washington County. They arrived in Corpus Christi on April 24. A few days later, after consulting with local lawmen and officials, McNelly established his base camp at Las Rucias, which had been the site of an encounter between Confederate and Union forces in June 1864.

The new mission was to tame the turbulent section of Texas between the Rio Grande and the Nueces River. The latter river rises northwest of San Antonio in the Edwards Plateau, in Real County, roughly fifty miles north of Uvalde. It flows south through the Texas Hill Country, past Barksdale and Crystal City. At its narrowest, the river is within thirty-five miles of the Rio Grande. The in-between region is known as the Nueces Strip. Eventually, the Nueces River enters the Gulf of Mexico at Corpus Christi.

The river was named by Alonso de León, who was referring to the abundant pecan tree groves, or *nueces,* on either side. One of the first settlers to scout the area was the Spanish Captain Blas María de la Garza Falcón, in 1766. In the mid-1700s, two missions were established in the Nueces Strip, San Lorenzo de la Santa Cruz and Nuestra Senora de la Candelaria. The latter was located near the present-day ghost town of Montell. According to the narrative of Mexican missionary Juan Agustín Morfi, there were so many wild horses in the Nueces Strip in 1777 "that their trails make the country, utterly uninhabited by people, look as if it were the most populated in the world."

During the early decades of the 1800s, Texans and Mexicans and Indians took turns raiding in the Nueces Strip, and to some extent this continued even after the Treaty of Guadalupe Hidalgo ended the Mexican War. Before and during the Civil War, the strip was used by slaves fleeing on one of the lesser-known southern routes of the Underground Railroad.

The so-called Nueces Massacre occurred in the Nueces Strip. On August 10, 1862, German immigrants were ambushed and killed by Confederate soldiers. Many first-generation immigrants from Germany had settled not just in Mason County but in the region known as Hill Country. They tended to support the Union and were opposed to the institution of slavery. Because of these sentiments, the Confederate States of America imposed martial law on central Texas.

A group of Germans, fleeing from Hill Country to Mexico, intending to eventually make their way to Union-controlled New Orleans, was surprised by a company of Confederate soldiers on the banks of the Nueces River. The ensuing deaths represented an end to overt German resistance to Confederate governance in Texas and fueled outrage among the German-Texan population. As previously described, some of this spilled over to postwar Mason County.

For years afterward, the Nueces Strip "remained a no man's land," write Parsons and Little, "a dangerous area where every man had to be a law unto himself. The area was sparsely populated, and only the bravest of ranchers"—like Richard King—"attempted to establish themselves in this country."

Why was Leander McNelly needed in the Nueces Strip in the spring of 1875? The area seemed to have arrived at the point of having no law at all. One example occurred in December 1874, when the bandit Jose Maria Olguin, known as "the Needle," escaped from jail in Brownsville, rounded up a gang of other bandits, and made off with at least a hundred head of cattle belonging to James Browne, who also happened to be the sheriff of Cameron County.[74]

But the catalyzing event took place the following March, when another band of bandits carried out a bloody raid on a village unimaginatively named Nuecestown. This was by no means an out-of-nowhere event. As Darren L. Ivey

---

74 Olguin had earned the nickname because of the quiet way he had of slipping into houses and murdering the occupants.

points out, after the Civil War "endemic bloodshed in the Nueces Strip was once more on the rise. Well-organized bands of Indians, Mexican, and American cattle and horse thieves were prowling every range between the Nueces River and the Rio Grande and driving stolen stock to eager buyers in Mexico." While they were at it, "the most vicious looted stores and ranch houses, burned them, and murdered the occupants, as well as innocent travelers. From 1865 to 1873, an estimated 100,000 head of stolen cattle were driven across the Rio Grande."

On the other side of the river, Mexican stockmen were happy to add more American cattle to their herds, and butchers quickly turned the animals into beef products. After a good score, the bandits slipped back across the border into Texas to look for the next one. There was little doubt the Mexican military and civilian authorities knew about and ignored such activities. On the northern side of the Rio Grande, there were not nearly enough U.S. Army troops garrisoned along the border and, especially during the Reconstruction years, the Bluebellies were not inclined to work up a sweat protecting Texan property and lives.

The brazen stealing escalated that March, when a force of one hundred and fifty Mexican bandits rode across the Rio Grande near Eagle Pass.[75] Once in Texas, they split into four groups, each going its own way to find cattle

---

75 In March 1849, the U.S. Army had established Fort Duncan a few miles upstream from Eagle Pass to protect the legal flow of trade through it. During the Civil War it had been a Confederate stronghold. On July 4, 1865, General Joseph O. Shelby, en route to offer his troops' service to the French emperor Maximilian in Mexico, stopped at Fort Duncan and

and other plunder. Three of these groups were spotted by U.S. cavalry contingents and fled back into Mexico. The fourth group of some thirty Mexican marauders reached and caused some mischief where they could before turning toward Nuecestown.

On the way, the band raided a ranch near Tule Lake, stealing horses. Next, the bandits robbed a home and took its owner hostage. On the twenty-sixth, as many as two dozen raiders arrived at a structure known only as Frank's store on the Juan Saenz ranch, demanding and taking all valuables as well as supplying themselves with fresh horses and new saddles. They killed a Hispanic man who worked for Frank after he refused to join the marauders, and eleven men, women, and children were taken captive. The raiders then left and rode to Nuecestown, having created as much havoc as they could.

But there was more: Chancing upon the store owned by Thomas Noakes, they found it closed. A bandit managed to get the door open and received a bullet from the owner for his trouble. Immediately afterward, a man known as "Lying" Smith rushed out of the store and was shot and killed. The building was set on fire, but Noakes escaped through a door in the floor to a trench that had been dug for this very purpose. He looked on as all he owned was destroyed.[76] Before moving on, the raiders released their

---

then buried the last Confederate flag to have flown over his men in the Rio Grande.

76 After Noakes died some years later, his sons filed a claim for fifty thousand dollars against the Mexican government. The lawsuit languished until 1945, when Mexico paid $7,125 to Noakes's heirs.

female captives, probably less out of compassion than irritation that the women and youngest children were slowing them down.

A postscript to this particular event was that the bandit Noakes shot was not killed but wounded and was taken to Corpus Christi. He survived several attempts to lynch him—at first, locals could not find anything to use as gallows. Then, when they thought a church steeple was appropriate, no one could tie a noose correctly. Finally, outside the city, the mob found a gatepost that would suffice. They had the hapless rustler stand in a cart, tied a rope around his neck as best they could, and then had the horse and cart lurch forward. The bandit was left hanging, and was dead for sure by the next day, when a priest cut him down.

In Corpus Christi, two companies were formed to go after the Mexican raiders, who had moved on. One was led by the veteran sheriff of Nueces County, John McClane, and the other by Pat Whelan. The latter had emigrated from County Wexford, Ireland, with his three brothers. Listed as a bricklayer in the 1870 census, he had been appointed to the state police created by Gov. Davis and then was elected the city marshal in Corpus Christi. Whelan would latter succeed McClane as the county sheriff and serve nine terms, until 1896.

It was Whelan's group who found the bandits first, and though the group was outnumbered ten to thirty-five, they attacked. In the gun battle, one of Whelan's men, John Swanks, was killed. The Texans retreated when they ran low on ammunition, but the bandits had been bloodied enough that they released their remaining captives.

A statue dedicated to Moses Austin, whose goal was to establish an Anglo colony in Texas, can be found in San Antonio. *Courtesy of the Library of Congress*

Stephen F. Austin carried on after his father's untimely death, and in August 1823 made an appeal for "rangers" to protect the expanding frontier. *Courtesy of the Texas State Library and Archives Commission*

The painting *The Settlement of Austin's Colony*, by Henry Arthur McArdle, depicts Stephen F. Austin in 1824 rallying colonists against the Karankawa Indians, with an unnamed scout at the cabin door sounding the alarm. *Courtesy of the Library of Congress*

Many consider John Coffee Hays the first great Texas Rangers captain. *Courtesy of the Library of Congress*

Among the adventures of William "Bigfoot" Wallace (seen here as an older man) was barely surviving the Mier Expedition. *Courtesy of the Texas State Library and Archives Commission*

Samuel Walker was another man who became a Texas Ranger legend. *Courtesy of the Library of Congress*

Santa Anna was unsuccessful in 1836 in keeping Texas as part of Mexico and in later efforts to take it back. *Courtesy of the Library of Congress*

During the Battle of Huamantla in 1847, Samuel Walker died a hero's death. *Courtesy of the Library of Congress*

The Kiowa warrior Lone Wolf, seen here with his wife, Etla, was a frequent frontier antagonist of the Texas Rangers. *Courtesy of the Library of Congress*

John "Rip" Ford was a Texas Ranger captain who led several campaigns in the 1850s. *Courtesy of the Texas State Library and Archives Commission*

Sam Houston was the hero of San Jacinto and served as the president of the Republic of Texas and governor of the State of Texas. *Courtesy of the Library of Congress*

Gen. Thomas Green was a mentor to Leander McNelly during the Civil War. *Courtesy of the Texas State Library and Archives Commission*

Edmund Davis was a Union officer who after the Civil War became the governor of Texas. *Courtesy of the Texas State Library and Archives Commission*

A fanciful portrait of Leander McNelly, a heroic and transitional figure in Texas Ranger history. *Courtesy of the Texas State Library and Archives Commission*

The outlaw John Wesley Hardin claimed he fled Texas rather than go up against Leander McNelly. *Courtesy of the Wild West History Association—Robert G. McCubbin Collection*

The powerful Juan Nepomuceno Cortina waged war on both sides of the Rio Grande. *Courtesy of the Library of Congress*

It was during the administration of Governor Richard Coke that the Washington County Volunteer Militia was formed, with McNelly as captain. *Courtesy of the Library of Congress*

Richard King was the owner of a large ranch in southern Texas and a strong supporter of McNelly's Rangers. *Courtesy of the Texas State Library and Archives Commission*

Historians are divided over whether the man on the left is Thomas "Pidge" Robinson, a lieutenant in McNelly's Rangers, who chronicled their exploits. *Courtesy of the Walter Prescott Webb Papers, Dolph Briscoe Center for American History, University of Texas at Austin*

George Durham was another of McNelly's men who wrote about their exploits. *Courtesy of the Western History Collections, University of Oklahoma Libraries*

John King Fisher proved to be quite the worthy adversary in the Nueces Strip. *Courtesy of the Wild West History Association*

McNelly's Rangers in camp in 1877, awaiting their next assignment. *Courtesy of the Walter Prescott Webb Collection, University of Texas*

John B. Armstrong (seated center, bottom row), seen here with five of his Texas Ranger colleagues, was one of Leander McNelly's most loyal sergeants. *Courtesy of the Texas State Library and Archives Commission*

Jesse Lee Hall was appointed to take over as captain when McNelly could no longer ride with his Rangers. *Courtesy of the Texas Ranger Hall of Fame and Museum*

Managing to keep some of their plunder, the raiders pressed on and passed through Piedras Pintas, along the way shooting and killing a man for his horse.

On April 2 the bandits surrounded the town of Roma in Starr County with the intent to rob the customhouse but were stopped by U.S. Army troops in the area. It appears also that several people were killed by the same bandits in Hidalgo County and Laredo. Once back in Mexico, some of the raiders were identified, and Mexican authorities arrested them, but the intervention of Juan Cortina (more on him soon) enabled them to avoid a trial.

Many residents in the Nueces Strip retaliated against the vigilante-like invasion with a vengeance. Bands of volunteers organized "minute companies" in every county. They proceeded to hunt down Mexican outlaws, but they were indiscriminate, also arresting peaceful rancheros and merchants, looting property, and burning homes. Since saddles were among the goods stolen by the raiders, any Mexicans seen with new saddles were killed instead of questioned.

Retaliation extended outside the immediate geographic area. In La Parra, the *jacales* (thatched huts) of squatter Mexicans were burned. The avengers also killed all the adult males at the Mexican-owned La Atravesada ranch. Similar incidents resulted in the murders of farmers and stock raisers. Stores were also burned down.

After the devastation, Mexican rancheros in the area fled in fear for their lives. Some stayed because they were afraid to travel. The region was descending into chaos, and Sheriff McClane, unable to quell the violence and destruction, turned to Austin for assistance. Gov. Coke and his adjutant general responded swiftly. Steele told McNelly that his job was to subdue or, if necessary, destroy "the armed bands of Mexican marauders infesting the region between the Nueces and the Mexican Boundary."

As soon as the Rangers arrived, they were ready to get to work.

CHAPTER 35

"YOU MUST BE THE JUDGE"

Leander McNelly began the work of subduing the marauders by ordering all self-appointed armed defense groups to fall out and go home. Some of these men had banded together purely for the protection of their homes and families, but others were using violent methods to settle scores or take out their anger against any Mexicans found north of the Rio Grande, even longtime Tejano workers and property owners.

To start this effort, the captain published what some readers soon referred to rather loftily as the "McNelly Pronunciamento." It included this warning: "In consequence of the recent outrages committed in this portion of the country by armed bandits of men acting without authority of law, I find it necessary to notify all such organizations that after the publication of this order I will arrest all such bands and turn them over to the civil authorities of the counties where they are arrested."

Next, going with the tried and true, McNelly weaved together a network of spies. He did not have much trouble finding men, including Tejanos, to join his spy ring. Some legal cover had been provided by William Steele. He had written the Ranger captain, "Your object will be to get as early information as possible . . . and to destroy any and every such band of freebooters," meaning rustlers. However, don't go too far: "At the same time be careful not to disturb innocent people, who speak the same language with robbers." Ultimately, the adjutant general instructed McNelly that "you must be the judge; recollecting that the best way to protect all is to find the robbers and make them harmless."

Essentially, Leander McNelly had been designated the chief law enforcement officer in the Nueces Strip.

Soon, as bandits and their sympathizers were tracked down, the Ranger captain took advantage of another way to obtain information—the interrogation of prisoners. His principal weapon was Jesus Sandoval, or as the other Rangers pronounced his name, "Old Casuse." As Parsons and Little note with some understatement, "Jesus Sandoval certainly lived a full life filled with danger and excitement." The emphasis was on "danger."

It was believed that Sandoval was born in Mexico in the last half of the 1820s, emigrated across the border, and, as he claimed, served in the U.S. Army in some capacity during the Mexican-American War. Afterward, he lived in Cameron County, as he appeared there on the 1850 census.

His household included a wife named Maria and four sons. Sandoval and his wife subsequently had a daughter.

Sometime in the early 1870s, the Sandoval family had a small ranch. It was attacked by Mexican bandits. They stole his cattle and horses and burned his house and barn. Sandoval himself was not home at the time. At the ranch, the raiders found only Sandoval's wife and fourteen-year-old daughter, who were beaten and raped. This outrage, according to Parsons and Little, "transformed Sandoval from a peaceful rancher into a man obsessed with the idea of revenge. Estimates vary as to the number of men he killed, whether by gun or by a noose around the neck of a suspected raider, but accounts by contemporaries place the figure at several dozen."

He was at this time a lone wolf, having placed his traumatized wife and daughter in a convent run by the Sisters of Mercy.

Sandoval was a merciless avenger, and the Mexican bandits—and even men on the U.S. side of the river who cooperated with them—came to fear him. He killed men by ambush, burned their homes, drove off their livestock, and poisoned their water holes. His identity was unknown for months, and large rewards offered for the capture of the violent vigilante went uncollected. N. A. Jennings reported—with maybe only some exaggeration—that Sandoval's vendetta rampage continued for eight months, during which scores of ranches were burned, as many as forty men murdered, and hundreds of horses and cattle destroyed. Sandoval remained an elusive man, staying in the wild and emerging to visit Brownsville only for provisions and ammunition.

It is not certain how he and Leander McNelly met. Upon discovering a frontier force who wanted to hunt Mexican bandits almost as much as he did, and to do it legally, Sandoval may have simply showed up at the Rangers' camp and offered his services as an interpreter and, very soon, interrogator. Officially, once accepted, he was no more than a private in the company, but "Old Casuse" became a valuable asset to the captain.

As Jennings recalled of Sandoval: "In appearance he did not differ from hundreds of other Mexicans on that border, except that he was rather taller than the majority of them, and he was also remarkably thin and angular. His eyes were as black as jet and singularly piercing. He was very sinewy and strong and as active as any man I ever saw. He could mount a pony without putting his hand on him at all. He would simply run alongside of the horse for a little way and spring into the saddle with a bound."

Though Sandoval was Mexico-born, "There was no fear that he would ever betray any of the Rangers to his countrymen. He had no country, in fact. He had renounced all allegiance to Mexico, and he hated the Mexicans with such a bitter, consuming hatred that his life was devoted to doing them all the injury possible."

A further impression Sandoval made on the Rangers was that he held himself aloof, believed he had a superior education, and had a haughty bearing with an air of condescension. On the other hand, the impression of the men he interrogated was that Sandoval was a stone-cold killer.

McNelly and his new enforcer apparently had an understanding about the necessity of information and methods used to obtain it. Few men taken prisoner by McNelly's Rangers during their patrols wound up in the local jails and standing for trials—which they would have much preferred compared to Sandoval's techniques of persuasion. His favorite was to drop a noose around a prisoner's neck and toss the rest of the rope over a tree limb. Sandoval tugged on the rope to briefly lift the captive off the ground. The desperate man usually offered what he knew about bandit activity. Some men were then released; with others, Sandoval pulled on the rope, tied it to the trunk of the tree, and left the poor devil dangling as he sauntered away.

While there was certainly an unsavory aspect to how McNelly's Rangers conducted their business of catching bandits, they received the support of many local lawmen, who had found a big burden lifted from their shoulders, and of the citizenry, who began to feel safe for the first time in years. Officially, the U.S. Army did not acknowledge the captain's intelligence-gathering strategies, but General Edward Ord, the top officer in Texas, later acknowledged that McNelly gleaned vital information "by means by which I could not legally resort to, but which were the only means of getting at the actual facts."

Important too was the support of the former riverman, steamboat entrepreneur, and livestock czar Richard King, who was only too happy to welcome McNelly's Rangers to his ranch. The captain struck up an immediate rapport with King, another of the larger-than-life figures synonymous with success in nineteenth-century Texas.

King was a New York City native, born in July 1824 to poor Irish parents (which in New York at that time was pretty much a given). He was indentured to a jeweler in Manhattan when only nine years old. Two years later, he stowed away on a ship bound for Mobile, Alabama. When he was discovered, King was taken in as a "cabin cub" and schooled in the art of navigation. Thus began a life of travel and adventure.

Between 1835 and 1841, King pursued steamboating on Alabama rivers, which included becoming a pilot by age sixteen. In 1842, he enlisted under Captain Henry Penny for service in the Seminole War in Florida, where he met Mifflin Kenedy, who would become a lifelong friend and business mentor.[77] King plied the muddy waters of the Apalachicola and Chattahoochee Rivers until 1847, when he joined Kenedy on the Rio Grande for Mexican War service. King served for the war's duration as commander of a ship transporting troops and supplies.

Like many men given a taste of Texas, King could not leave the new Lone Star State. He remained on the border and became a principal partner in the steamboat firms of M. Kenedy and Company, which evolved into King, Kenedy, and Company. These firms dominated the waters of the Rio Grande during the next two decades. By all accounts, the experienced riverboat man was a hardy risk-taker who thought that he could take a boat anywhere "a dry creek flows," as King put it. He was also an innova-

---

77 Kenedy also qualifies as a legendary figure in Texas history, as a wealthy and powerful rancher. However, readers of *Dodge City* might recall the sad duty he had to perform of bailing out his son "Spike," who murdered the actress Dora Hand and was chased and caught by a posse led by Wyatt Earp and Bat Masterson.

tor, designing specialty boats for the narrow bends and fast currents of the Rio Grande.

He proved to be an even more accomplished speculator and diversified businessman, his fingers in many pies with a variety of associates. Eventually, most of King's attention was devoted to undeveloped land. He began speculating in Cameron County and in vacant lots in Brownsville.

As King's cash flow increased, his investments included property in the Nueces Strip. In several partnerships, he first bought land there in 1853, acquiring the 15,500-acre Rincón de Santa Gertrudis. The next year he purchased the 53,000-acre Santa Gertrudis de la Garza grant. These were combined to form the regal King ranch. By the time of his death in 1885, King would make over sixty major purchases of land and amass some 614,000 acres.

During the Civil War, he entered into several contracts with the Confederate government to supply European buyers with cotton; in return, they supplied the Confederates with beef, horses, imported munitions, medical supplies, clothing, and shoes. By placing their steamboat interests under Mexican registry and moving their operations into Matamoros, King and Kenedy for the most part successfully avoided the Union blockade and earned a considerable fortune. In an attempt to dampen this trade, Union forces captured Brownsville in late 1863 and raided the King ranch, looting and destroying most of it. King, however, escaped before the raid and resumed business after the Confederates under the former Ranger John "Rip" Ford reclaimed South Texas in 1864. King went to

Mexico at the war's end and returned after securing a pardon from President Andrew Johnson in late 1865.

Though remaining fast friends, King and Kenedy dissolved their partnership in 1868 and became individual proprietors, King ranching at Santa Gertrudis, and Kenedy at Los Laureles, near Corpus Christi. Flush with war profits, they advanced the economics of South Texas ranching with the introduction of fencing; cattle drives to northern markets; large-scale cattle, sheep, mule, and horse raising; and the scientific breeding of livestock.

When McNelly's Rangers arrived at his Santa Gertrudis spread, King did not offer full support to them for purely altruistic reasons. His cattle empire was, inevitably, a frequent target of the Mexican bandits, who saw the Rio Grande as a turnstile. King estimated that in the past decade he and other prominent ranchers had lost tens of thousands of beeves to Mexico-based thieves.[78]

That had to stop, and immediately King believed McNelly was the man to do it.

---

78 George Durham reported that King and other cattlemen in the area had lost close to nine hundred thousand beeves combined to Mexican rustlers, but that figure does not seem reliable.

CHAPTER 36

EMPEROR McNELLY

Though he was more formidable than most ranchers in southeast Texas, even Richard King and his crew could not keep up with the cattle and horse thieves, though not for lack of trying. George Durham noted that the main house of the King ranch alone contained eighty stands of Henry repeating rifles and at least a hundred boxes of shells, and there were plenty of men ready to spring into action. To watch for rustlers, there were two men up in a lookout tower day and night. However, Durham lamented, "That did not stop the raiders."

No, that was now Leander McNelly's job. To help, King provided more than hospitality. He gave each man in the company a fresh horse. "Most of the rascals are mounted on my stock," King said of the bandits, "and I at least want to do as good by you."

There was an important task McNelly had to complete

before moving on toward Mexico—call off the vigilantes, as his "pronunciamento" had promised he would do. *The San Antonio Express* disapproved, fuming that it was "an extra-ordinary proclamation emanating from a Captain of a Corporal's guard sent by the so-called Governor of the State." The editor continued, "This high-handed way of ordering citizens to disband by a Captain of Police, exceeds anything that ever happened under the Davis police; martial law had some semblance of authority, but McNelly issues his order like an Emperor."

The most visible of the bunch of vigilantes was the band of a hundred or so men under the leadership of Martin Culver and T. Hynes Clark. Both were in their late thirties and had been born in Louisiana but had lived and ranched in Texas since before the Civil War.

Though outnumbered, the Ranger company tracked down and confronted the ad hoc posse. According to Durham, McNelly told the two leaders, "You damn fellows have been doing more mischief than the bandits themselves." He ordered the vigilantes to go back to their homes and jobs and stay there. For a few tense moments, it appeared that the biggest impediment to trying to tame the Nueces Strip was Texans killing Texans, with McNelly ready to give the order to fire. But Culver and Clark backed down.

A reporter for *The Valley Times* later contended that the confrontation was not that dangerous and that Culver and Clark offered to cooperate with McNelly. However, the Ranger captain was not looking for allies and wanted no interference in Ranger business.

Yet another view of what happened was provided by N. A. Jennings. He reported that the company of men led by Culver and Clark rode into the Rangers' camp one night and offered their assistance. "We need no one to cooperate with us," McNelly responded. "I have heard that some of you men are the very ones accused of a number of outrages committed on Mexican citizens of this State, and you must disband at once and not reassemble. If you don't do what I say, you will have us to fight."

And according to an account published in *The Galveston Daily News,* McNelly told the heads of vigilantes "to take their men home and disperse them, or else he would have them arrested . . . even if it cost him the life of every man in his company."

According to Jennings, "The Texans didn't like this high-handed way of talking . . . but the Captain showed them very quickly that he meant business and they disbanded."

In any case, with growing admiration, Durham wrote that the confrontation confirmed that "from that moment on, Captain McNelly was the law west of the Nueces."

This was the time, then, to take on the law south of the Rio Grande: Juan Cortina. As the Rangers prepared to get on their new mounts and head farther south, McNelly told them, "Boys, I may lead you into hell, but I'll get you out if you do exactly as I tell you to do. I'll never send you into a battle, I'll lead you. All I ask any man to do is follow me."

George Durham represented the younger and more impressionable men of the company: "After that only death could prevent my following Captain McNelly."

The man McNelly was about to go up against had been a nemesis of Texas since the war with Mexico had ended almost thirty years earlier. Juan Nepomuceno Cortina had been born on May 16, 1824, in Camargo. He had the good fortune of having a mother, Estefana, who was one of the heirs of a large land grant in the lower Rio Grande valley, including the area that surrounded Brownsville. The family moved to that land when Cortina was still young.

During the war against the United States, Cortina served as a member of an irregular cavalry. He fought in the Battles of Resaca de la Palma and Palo Alto under General Mariano Arista of the Tamaulipas Brigade. At the war's conclusion, he returned to the northern side of the Rio Grande, where he was indicted at least twice by Cameron County grand juries for stealing cattle. By this time, though, his political influence among Mexicans in the county and beyond, including being a war hero to them, persuaded the local Anglo authorities not to arrest him. And he kept the cattle.

In the decade following the war, Cortina came to hate a clique of judges and Brownsville attorneys, whom he accused of expropriating land from Mexican Texans unfamiliar with the American judicial system. He became a leader to many of the poorer Mexicans who lived along the banks of the Rio Grande. The incident that ignited the first so-called Cortina War occurred on July 13, 1859, when Cortina saw the Brownsville city marshal, Robert Shears, brutally arrest a Mexican American who had once been employed by Cortina. He confronted Shears and shot him. No one interfered as Cortina and the prisoner rode out of town.

For over two months, there were no sightings of Juan Cortina. Then, on the morning of September 28, he rode into town again, this time at the head of some seventy-five of his own militia. They shot five men, including the city jailer, as they rampaged through the streets shouting, "Death to the Americans!" and "Viva Mexico!" Some of the other men who believed they were on Cortina's retribution list managed to escape or go into hiding as the bullets flew.

The U.S. Army was either unavailable or, with Southern secession brewing, uninterested in protecting Brownsville. Instead, Texans took the extraordinary step of appealing to Mexican authorities in Matamoros. Preferring peace over an escalating conflict, they dispatched José María Jesús Carbajal to Brownsville. He was known to many, including Cortina, on both sides of the border.

As a teenager in San Antonio, Carbajal was mentored by Stephen Austin. He then attended school in Virginia. He was a surveyor by trade and married well, into the influential De Leon family of Victoria, Texas. But Carbajal called himself "a true Mexican," and his allegiance lay with the people of Mexico—especially when the new Republic of Texas took his land as well as the lands of many other Tejanos. Carbajal moved to Mexico, where, instead of making new friends, he conducted guerrilla warfare against Mexican military forces of Santa Anna. Readers may recall that he was active in the establishment of the Republic of the Rio Grande and made an unsuccessful attempt at establishing the breakaway Republic of Sierra Madre. He was an early supporter of Benito Juárez, and soon after the twenty-sixth president of Mexico took office in January 1858, Carbajal was appointed the military governor of Tamaulipas.

Juan Cortina was certainly not going to dismiss the persuasions of Carbajal and, in fact, agreed to evacuate Brownsville. His ego was not diminished one iota, though: He retreated to the family ranch at Santa Rita in Cameron County, where, on September 30, the supposed illiterate issued a proclamation asserting the rights of Mexican Texans and demanding the punishment of anyone violating those rights.

The conflict could have ended right there, but tensions remained high in Brownsville. A match was struck when a local posse captured Tomás Cabrera, one of Cortina's men. The posse expanded to twenty men, who dubbed themselves the Brownsville Tigers. Assisted by a militia company from Matamoros, they went after Cortina himself, who was reported to be at his mother's ranch some six miles upriver. With two cannons, the Brownsville-Matamoros force launched an attack. Cortina and his men not only repulsed the attack but also took the cannons as the embarrassed militia force fled.

Such a decisive and insulting victory for Cortina made quite an impression on many of the poorer Mexicans on both sides of the river. As a result, his small army grew as recruits joined his ranks. He demanded that Cabrera be released and threatened to burn Brownsville to the ground.

While Cortina awaited a response, in early November, William Tobin arrived commanding a company of Texas Rangers from San Antonio. The captain rejected Cortina's demand and put an exclamation point on it by hanging Cabrera. Then he and his men attacked Cortina but were routed like the last force.[79] Trying a different tactic, Cortina issued a proclamation asking Governor Sam Houston to defend the legal interests of Mexican residents in Texas.

Instead, Houston upped the ante in early December by sending a second company of Rangers commanded by the familiar Rip Ford. They were joined in Brownsville by Major Samuel Heintzelman with 165 U.S. Army troops. Cortina and his four hundred or so followers retreated upriver, laying waste to much of the lower valley as they went. On December 27, 1859, Heintzelman caught up with Cortina, and the Battle of Rio Grande City ensued. Cortina was decisively defeated, losing as many as sixty men and much of his equipment.

But he wasn't done, nor was the so-called Cortina War. He next appeared at La Bolsa, a large bend on the river below Rio Grande City, where he attempted to capture the steamboat *Ranchero,* owned and operated by two of his antagonists, Richard King and Mifflin Kenedy. With the approach of the steamboat, Ford and his Rangers crossed into Mexico, secured the south bank, and forced Cortina to retreat. Colonel Robert E. Lee, now in command of the

---

79 Tobin had better luck in later endeavors. He served as a captain again, this time in the Confederate army, and after the war he converted a former Confederate headquarters in San Antonio into the Vance House. Tobin was an early advocate of Texas-type Mexican foods and in 1881 negotiated with the U.S. government to sell canned chili con carne to the army and navy. A few years later, he operated a large factory for the canning of chili con carne and other Mexican specialties.

Eighth Military District, arrived in the lower valley determined to restore peace and threatening to invade Mexico if necessary. Cortina, however, had retreated into the Burgos Mountains, where he remained for more than a year.

With the secession of Texas from the Union, he appeared on the border again. In May 1861, Cortina invaded Zapata County and attacked the county seat, Carrizo. He was defeated by a force led by the Confederate captain Santos Benavides. The victor hoped he had sent a message by hanging or shooting the eleven Cortina followers taken prisoner.

Cortina remained in Mexico, and a year later, during the period of French intervention, he helped defend San Lorenzo at Puebla and saw action at Matamoros. In 1863, Cortina proclaimed himself governor of Tamaulipas. Icing on the cake was being promoted to general of the Mexican Army of the North by President Benito Juárez.

Hoping that a post–Civil War America would be more welcoming, especially to a general, Cortina returned to the border in 1870. Forty-one residents of the area, including a former mayor of Brownsville, signed a petition asking that he be pardoned for his crimes given his service to the Union during the Civil War. Puzzled by what that service actually was, and not being fans of the Union anyway, the Texas legislature rejected the petition. Rebuffed, Cortina devoted himself in the first half of the 1870s to operating an extensive cattle-rustling operation throughout the Nueces Strip. By 1875 he had one of the largest ranches in northern Mexico, with eighteen hundred head of cattle and as many as two thousand men in his personal army.

Testily, William Steele told Gov. Coke that Juan Cortina "is the recognized head and protector of all the cattle thieves and murderers, from Camargo to the mouth of the Rio Grande. It is impossible to conceive . . . of the extent of the power of this great robber chief." As far as help from Mexican police forces, Steele offered this example: "The police of Matamoros is composed entirely of ruffians, ready at any moment to commit murder or any other crime, at his bidding."

Most of the cattle Cortina had accumulated had been stolen from ranchers in Texas. The "robber chief" simply kept getting away with it . . . until Leander McNelly and his forty Rangers arrived.

CHAPTER 37

"GOT YOU NOW!"

Obviously outnumbered, McNelly could not hope to defeat Cortina in an open battle. One way to reduce the odds was to try an old trick: plant a spy. The captain turned to one of his trusted sergeants, George Hall, who managed to infiltrate the Cortina camp. Soon, he was secretly providing information to McNelly. The intelligence would lead to what some historians have called the Second Battle of Palo Alto.

Of course, this indicates there was a first battle in the same general neighborhood. The Battle of Palo Alto was significant in that it was the first major engagement in the Mexican-American War and also introduced the "flying artillery" tactic. When the war began in April 1846, Mexico claimed it would be in a defensive posture and portrayed the United States as the aggressor. However, President

Santa Anna undercut his own position by proclaiming that he had annexed Texas, and he sent an army commanded by General Mariano Arista across the Rio Grande. That Battle of Palo Alto was fought on May 8, 1846.

It was not an auspicious beginning for Mexico's military ambitions in Texas. The fighting began at 2 p.m. against an American force led by General Zachary Taylor and lasted until dark, with both armies bedding down on the battlefield. Of 3,461 troops that formed the Mexican Army of the North, Arista's commissary reported 102 killed, 129 wounded, and 26 missing. Lieutenant George Meade, who interrogated captured Mexican officers, concluded that Mexican casualties were closer to four hundred men.[80] The American army, which totaled over 2,200 soldiers, reported only forty-eight casualties.

During the battle, Gen. Taylor deployed the "flying artillery" developed by Major Samuel Ringgold, who was mortally wounded that day.[81] Guns were mounted on light carriages drawn by specially trained teams of horses and could be moved quickly for tactical advantage. Soldiers on both sides expected the traditional bayonet charge across

---

80 Meade would find enduring fame seventeen years later. On June 28, 1863, Gen. Meade was handed command of the Army of the Potomac, and only three days later he and General Robert E. Lee began their clash at Gettysburg.

81 No relation to Johnny Ringo, Major Ringgold has been called the "father of modern artillery" because of his innovations. During the war, to honor his sacrifice, Fort Ringgold was constructed at Rio Grande City. A reporter for *The Baltimore Democrat,* Robert D'Unger, claimed he was the first person to use the telegraph to report breaking news—the death of Ringgold, caused by Mexican artillery.

the field, but the artillery duel dominated the action. There was a desperate Mexican charge at sunset, but after it failed, all was quiet.

The Mexican army moved southward at dawn the following day to Resaca de la Palma. Taylor's army caught up and attacked. The Americans captured Matamoros, and Gen. Arista retreated farther south, toward Monterrey. Other American participants in the two related battles included notables Lieutenant Ulysses S. Grant and the Texas Rangers captain Samuel H. Walker.

On June 5, 1875, McNelly received a message from Sgt. Hall that Mexican rustlers had crossed the Rio Grande below Brownsville. The captain sent Lieutenant Pidge Robinson (he had dropped the Chanders alias) and eighteen men to find the intruders. One consequence of this sudden activity was speculation that the "special force," as it was often referred to, under McNelly was about to lead an attack on Mexico, possibly setting off a new war.

"The appearance of State Troops on the Rio Grande has produced great excitement among the people on the Mexican side," *The Galveston Daily News* reported, based on a telegram from Brownsville. "The residents of the ranches above Matamoros have organized to resist invasion. They have sentinels at the crossings of the river and the roads. In some ranches the women and children do not sleep in the houses at night."

When a Ranger patrol spotted and captured one of the alleged rustlers three days later, "Casuse" Sandoval applied his persuasive methods. They prompted the prisoner to reveal that Juan Cortina had dispatched eighteen to twenty men to rustle cattle—and not just a few of the beeves but as many as eighteen hundred heads. Cortina, the Rangers were told, already had a buyer in Cuba waiting for them.

That certainly caught McNelly's attention, and he cast a net for more information. On June 11 Sandoval was able to provide it, thanks to what a second prisoner had revealed: That very night, a band of bandits with three hundred cattle would be crossing the Arroyo Colorado en route to the Mexican border. Stopping this excursion could disrupt Cortina's entire brazen plan.

The Rangers almost missed that opportunity. Soon after midnight, McNelly's men were in position, waiting for the cattle and their thieving escorts to appear. A scout arrived to inform the captain that they had actually passed four miles to the east, on the other side of the Palo Alto Prairie from the Rangers' position. Leaping onto their horses, the lawmen set off. At 7 A.M., they found the rustlers.

Seeing the Rangers, Cortina's men spurred their horses and goaded the cattle into a run. As Frederick Wilkins notes, the outlaws "were not accustomed to a determined pursuit." Out in front of that pursuit was McNelly. The horse Richard King had provided him was a fine animal and was such a strong runner that the captain was leaving his Rangers in the dust.

Three miles later, the bandits and beeves reached an island in the Laguna Madre salt marsh. They would make a stand there. Seeing this, McNelly wisely halted and waited for the rest of his men to catch up.

During this interval, he observed that the rustlers had formed a line on the south side of the salt marsh and behind a four-foot-high bank. When his men arrived, McNelly formed them into a skirmish line. "Boys, the only way we can get at those thieves is to cross through the mud of the swamp and ride them down," McNelly said, according to Jennings's recollection. "I don't think they can shoot well enough to hit any of us, but we'll have to risk that. Don't fire at them until you're sure of killing every time."

At his command, the Rangers advanced into the marsh "at a walk," the captain later reported, "and not firing a shot or speaking a word, our line well dressed."

The rustlers fired their rifles, but their aim was indeed poor, and the wayward bullets did not halt the Ranger advance through the salt marsh. Very soon, intimidated, the bandits bolted. As best they could while glancing behind them, the rustlers climbed on their horses and tried to escape. Now it was the Rangers' turn to fire rifles, and their aim was much better. Bandits began to fall off their mounts. Clearing the marsh, some of McNelly's men dismounted and, taking more careful aim, continued to fire. Others gave chase and used their pistols to punish the thieves.[82]

The captain came close to being a casualty. As usual, McNelly was out in front. One of the outlaws tried to hide himself in a thicket and, his gun empty, drew a knife. McNelly knew he had just one bullet left in his six-shooter. Time for another ruse: He called out loudly that he was out of ammunition and someone had to bring him more. Hearing this, the hidden man jumped out of the thicket at

---

82 One of the bandits wounded was Jose Maria "the Needle" Olguin. He later died in jail.

McNelly, shouting, "Got you now!" As the bandit began to shout again, the captain aimed carefully and shot him in the mouth.

The rest of the battle involved small groups and individual Rangers and rustlers having at each other across the prairie. The Rangers killed sixteen bandits and, thinking all the rustlers were dead, began to regroup. Then two of the Rangers, Spencer Adams and L. B. "Berry" Smith, spotted at least one more rustler running into tall grass. Smith volunteered to dismount and go into the grass after him. He had enlisted with his father in the Washington County Volunteer Militia on July 25, 1874, and he was also called "Sonny" because at seventeen he was the youngest in the company.

Adams stayed on his horse to see over the grass and prevent an escape. What Adams saw was Smith shot dead. The "fury in our hearts," reported Jennings, "boded ill for the men in front of us." The other Rangers surrounded the tall grass and shot into it, killing the last bandit.[83]

The day was far from over for the grieving Rangers. They had bodies to transport and a statement to make to Juan Cortina.

---

83 To this day, Smith is the youngest Texas Ranger killed in the line of duty, and the youngest recorded line of duty death in the state of Texas.

CHAPTER 38

"MASTER OF THE SITUATION"

The bodies of the dead bandits were retrieved and piled onto their remaining horses. Sonny Smith's body was draped over his horse. In Brownsville, he was transported to the city's cemetery, escorted by most of his fellow Rangers and several army cavalrymen who were in town.

On June 16 Smith was given a full military funeral, with Rip Ford serving as one of the marshals. With McNelly's Rangers in the lead, two horses drew the wagon containing Smith's coffin. The funeral procession also included marching bands. The first stop was a church, where a service was performed, and then the mourners regrouped for the journey to the cemetery. A line of army troopers stood next to the grave and fired shots in the air as the coffin was lowered. The young man's anguished father, D. R. Smith, would complete his service in Capt. McNelly's company for a total of twenty-nine months, mustering out in November 1876.

It had been a very different delivery of the bodies of the Mexican rustlers: They were dumped in the town square. McNelly's intention was that word of this gruesome tableau would speed across the border to Juan Cortina. The display also sent the message that there had been a severe loss of life among the Mexican leader's men, but only one Ranger had been killed. (Two Ranger horses were wounded, including Pidge Robinson's.)

About the solemn event, Parsons and Little comment, "The funeral of Ranger Smith was an opportunity for McNelly to make a statement to all rustlers: he was promising no quarter, and death would be the result if caught in the act. Clearly, the death of a McNelly ranger was the political equivalent to the assassination of a king."

That same afternoon as the battle, an exhausted McNelly had sent a telegram to Gov. Coke. "It was a running fight," was how the captain described the action. The rustlers "fought desperately." He added, "My men are all trumps."[84]

Word did indeed spread on both sides of the Rio Grande of the actions of McNelly's Rangers. According to Jennings, "Nearly the entire population came to see their dead countryman. The Mexicans were very angry. And we heard many threats that Cortina would come across with

---

84 A second telegram with a terse description of the fight was sent two days later to William Steele, and it ended with a cheeky "Wish you were here."

TOM CLAVIN

his men and kill us all." McNelly sent back word to Cortina that he was waiting for him.

General Philip Sheridan telegraphed his superiors in Washington, D.C., about a "well-founded fear that Cortina may retaliate for the punishment administered on the band of Mexican robbers."

But an army of avengers commanded by the "robber chief" never materialized. Before their bodies could decompose too much, McNelly had the bandits buried in one long trench. In addition, most of the stolen cattle, which had scattered during the running battle, had been rounded up and brought to Brownsville. In total, they displayed thirty-six different brands.

For a time, cattle rustling along the border decreased considerably. *The San Antonio Express* lauded McNelly as "master of the situation." But he and his Rangers could not take all the credit for calmer times. That summer, word reached the American side of the Rio Grande that Juan Cortina had become a resident of the Prison Militar de Santiago Tlatelolco in Mexico City. Perhaps for having become too powerful, he had run afoul of Sebastián Lerdo de Tejada, who had succeeded Benito Juárez. The new president had not been a fan of Cortina in the first place. Among the charges against the border chieftain were smuggling and theft of government property.

This was certainly good news in Texas. Not coincidentally, for the most part, the Nueces Strip was quiet through the summer and into early autumn of 1875. That McNelly's Rangers remained on duty there, camped near

Santa Maria, had much to do with the relative tranquility. Their numbers increased in mid-July, when twenty-five more volunteers from Washington County arrived. A scribe for *The Daily Democratic Statesman* characterized the newcomers as "splendid-looking scalp hunters."

Even better, McNelly's ultimate boss, Governor Richard Coke, weighed in favorably. "The conduct of yourself and the officers and men under your commanding discharge of the arduous duty of defending the Rio Grande border, and especially the skill and gallantry displayed by all in the signal blow struck the freebooters on the 12th day of June last, merit and receive the highest praise from the authorities and people of the State."

The governor added: "The pride of true Texans in the historic fame of the Texas ranger, is fully gratified in the record your command is making and the people of the State are confidently expecting that your combined efforts will contribute greatly towards the restoration of peace, and a sense of security to our long-suffering border."

Perhaps Coke's words were of some comfort to the captain as he suffered from a recurrence of the symptoms of consumption. McNelly checked into the Brown Hotel, and there he remained, visited by his wife, Carey, and their son, Leander Rebel. By now, the boy was old enough to have a pretty good idea of how ill his frail father was.

"Most people had a fear of any consumptive and hesitated to go near them," notes Frederick Wilkins. "The medical staff at Fort Brown did everything possible to make McNelly comfortable, sending him goat milk each day. Few of his men ever saw him."

Then none of his men saw him when McNelly left Brownsville, being brought home to Burton, in Washington County. There was nervous concern among the Rangers that their captain would never be in command again—or worse, that he might die any day.

"McNelly could dispatch bandits with celerity, but the captain had no jurisdiction over the killer microbes lurking in his lungs," writes Mike Cox about what was often called "galloping consumption." McNelly "had been ill when he accepted his commission from Coke, and life in the field had not helped."

In the captain's absence, Pidge Robinson, as lieutenant, took on the supervision of the men and coordinated the patrolling activities they had that summer. Meanwhile, thanks to home cooking and Carey's nursing, McNelly slowly regained his strength. He also had kept in touch with his spy network—and, of course, his company of Rangers.

With Lt. Robinson in charge, they had been busy. As they had done in DeWitt County, they actively roamed the Nueces Strip, knowing their presence alone was curbing cattle thievery. As Pidge put it in *The Austin Gazette* (which was now publishing his missives), "I would have written you long before now, but we have kept so constantly on the move that it was impossible." He added that "there is not a ranch, no Mexican or American in four counties who does not know every man in this company as well as his own brother."

In November, Capt. McNelly received intelligence that led him to believe that the "peace" and "security" Gov. Coke had desired was about to end. Physically ready or not, Leander McNelly was about to embark on his most challenging campaign.

CHAPTER 39

"THE JAWS OF DEATH"

For the consumptive captain, the prospect of mixing it up again with Mexican rustlers was energizing. He also believed, as he wrote in a letter to Mifflin Kenedy, that whatever came next "will forever stop our border troubles." McNelly, for all his intelligence, could not have envisioned how much this would entail.

He had received a report of the theft of between two hundred and two hundred and fifty head of cattle. The herd, stolen in Cameron County, had been brought across the Rio Grande to Monterrey. This time, however, they were not bound for the pens of Juan Cortina. While the bandit king—or champion of poor Mexicans, depending on one's point of view—had managed to escape the first prison he was in, his freedom was short-lived. Cortina was captured again and detained because of his ongoing political power feud with President Lerdo de Tejada. His prospects would brighten the following year, when Mexico's leader was overthrown by General Porfirio Díaz ... but that relationship would soon sour too. In autumn 1875, the new boss of the rustlers was the rancher Juan Flores Salinas.[85]

Other than being informed that Salinas was also a general of a force of "rurales"—ironically, a police force formed in 1861 by the Mexican government to hunt down and punish bandits—not much was known about him. McNelly would later learn that the Mexican rancher had signed a lucrative contract to deliver eighteen thousand head of cattle. The Monterrey herd was just one part of the collection effort.

To this point the rustlers had been a wily bunch, grabbing herds of only a few dozen head here and there and spiriting them to Mexico. Thus far, they always seemed to be one step ahead of the Rangers. Even when the persistent persuasions of "Casuse" gleaned information, it was acted upon too late to catch the thieves before they splashed across the Rio Grande.

Then, finally, there was a solid tip that a larger theft had occurred. The information was that as many as two dozen

---

85 Juan Cortina never regained the power he had wielded, yet he did have the good fortune not to be murdered. President Díaz had decreed that Cortina be executed, but the man dispatched to do it, General Jose Canales, feared there would be an uprising. Plus, requesting mercy for his former enemy was, of all people, the Ranger Rip Ford. Díaz relented enough to toss Cortina into prison without a trial. He remained behind bars until 1890, when he was allowed to be under house arrest at his home near Mexico City. Juan Cortina died four years later.

rustlers were driving the stolen herd to the river crossing at Las Cuevas. The size of it implied either that Salinas needed to accelerate his cattle gathering or that he was just being more brazen because he believed he could get away with it.

Here was the kind of situation that made McNelly feel even healthier. Right after rejoining his men, the captain ordered some two dozen of them to get ready as fast as they could and follow him. He himself could not wait— McNelly jumped on his horse and took off. The captain vowed to get to Las Cuevas before the stolen cattle did.

But when a sleep-deprived McNelly arrived atop a wet horse at the Rio Grande on November 18, there was no sign of the bandits or the beeves. Once again, he was too late and the cattle had emigrated to Mexico. That evening, after covering fifty-five miles in six hours, the Rangers joined their frustrated captain at the crossing opposite Las Cuevas. The men were also pretty worn out because much of the ride had been into the wind while being battered by "sizzling rain pellets [that] fairly singed your beard," as Durham wrote.

What none of them anticipated was that some two hundred troopers from the Eighth Cavalry would be there too. They were led by the Massachusetts-born Captain James Randlett. His orders had vaguely allowed for the possibility that he and his troopers could cross the river and chase thieves into Mexico, but he had not done so. Randlett and his command had, however, engaged with the bandits the day before. The troopers had arrived late in the afternoon to find the last cows in the herd crossing the river, with as many as three dozen men tugging the beeves out of mud.

Randlett had his men open fire. At least two rustlers were killed, and the rest retreated, leaving the remaining cows to drown. Fearing that his troopers' horses could also be trapped by mud and with the sun low in the sky, Randlett decided not to try crossing the river. Another consideration had to be provoking a war with Mexico.

Further roiling the waters, the next day Randlett's force was joined by another contingent of cavalry, this one commanded by Major David Clendenin, a former teacher from Pennsylvania whose military résumé included serving on the commission that had tried and convicted the Lincoln assassination conspirators. Now, Clendenin, like Randlett, was averse to risking war with Mexico. Upon learning that Randlett had sent a message across the river demanding the return of the herd that had crossed hours earlier, Clendenin decided that was good enough.

When McNelly arrived—about noon on the eighteenth— the major advised him to stand down and wait for negotiations to resolve the matter peacefully. Clendenin informed him of the message Randlett had sent and said that the prudent thing to do was wait for a response.

To the fired-up Ranger captain, this was a ridiculous waste of time. The rustlers were not going to cross the river and turn over the cattle with a few muttered apologies. The matter had to be taken to them.

But what about inciting a war with Mexico? McNelly was not troubled. Given how the last war had gone for the

Mexicans, they were probably not so keen on another one. And more specifically, McNelly's Rangers did not represent the government of the United States. They were Texans, and that was a different story.

The Ranger captain declared that, as soon as his men arrived, he was going to find the stolen herd and return it to American soil. All the army officers could do was wish him luck. They were not about to risk their careers for a bunch of cows.[86]

With this lack of support, another commander might have hesitated. But McNelly's blood was up. When his weather-beaten Rangers did arrive, he collected them around him. They could not help noting that their captain was dressed more for a formal dinner than a battle. Despite the hard ride, his breeches appeared clean and pressed, he wore a small necktie, and his beard was trimmed.

"Boys, you have followed me as far as I can ask you to unless you are willing to go with me," McNelly told them in a speech that must have taxed his ailing lungs. "It is like going into the jaws of death with only twenty-six men in a foreign country where we have no right according to law. But as I have gone this far I am going to finish with it. Some of us may get back or part of us or maybe all of you or maybe none of us will get back. I don't want you unless you are willing to go as a volunteer. Understand there is no surrender in this. We ask no quarter nor give any."

---

86 Clendenin's career would include being a lieutenant colonel in the Third U.S. Cavalry Regiment in 1882 and colonel of the Second U.S. Cavalry Regiment six years later. After a solid career, he retired from the army in April 1891.

He concluded: "If any of you don't want to go, step aside."

No one did. Callicott recalls one of the Rangers saying to the captain, "If you can risk your life we can certainly risk ours."

"All right, that's the way to talk," McNelly said. "We will learn them a Texas lesson they have forgotten since the old Mexican War." He added, "Well, boys, all of you get ready to go over."

They would wait until darkness, then cross the Rio Grande into Mexico. If that meant war and death, so be it.

CHAPTER 40

"KILL ALL YOU SEE"

As he waited to cross the river, Leander McNelly had to reconcile himself to the fact that he and his two dozen men would be completely on their own.[87] Clendenin had offered to at least protect the Rangers when they crossed the Rio Grande, but he would not touch Mexican soil.

At least some of the Bluebellies were not happy to be ordered to remain on the north side of the river. While in the past there had not been much fraternization between U.S. Army soldiers and Texans—with open hostility more the rule than the exception—this time there was more of a sense that they shared a common enemy. And there was

---

87 The captain's company had closer to fifty men on its roster, but as many as half had been out on "scouts," so in haste Lt. Robinson mustered what men he could and took off after McNelly.

grudging admiration among some of the soldiers for the frail but feisty Ranger captain who would not let red tape stop him from going after bandits who had no similar concerns about invading the United States and stealing American property for their own profit. McNelly could have done some recruiting among the troopers. But at least for now, they followed their orders.

Major Clendenin reminded the Ranger captain of the limit of the army's support: "If you are determined to cross, we will cover your return, but cannot cross at present to help you."

A constrained Capt. Randlett could offer only one thing—a delay in notifying his superiors of what was about to take place, because when he did, "they might order me to use the army to prevent you from crossing," he explained to McNelly. "You're making ready to violate two American laws—one is against mounting an armed invasion in Texas, the other is against committing suicide." Offering what little he could, Randlett added, "We'll bring the bodies back and bury you on this side."

The army soldiers watched the seemingly inadequate contingent of Texas Rangers go across the river. It was not necessarily a grand sight. Because of deep mud, only five horses could be brought across. The remaining Rangers had to float across two at a time in a dugout canoe. Among those in the invasion force following Capt. McNelly were his lieutenant (Robinson), George Durham, William Callicott, Jesus Sandoval, and Sergeants George Hall and John Armstrong.

"In single file and leading the horses, we gathered at the

beautiful river and in silence commenced the embarkation," Pidge later reported. "On each side of the crossing crouched the men, gun in hand, to protect the passage of the first boat; from below at another crossing echoed the sullen roar of the Springfields, where the regulars were making a feint, while we went over undiscovered; with very little assistance I could have made a feint myself about that time."

Finally, at four on the damp and chilly morning of November 19, the company gathered on the other side of the river. McNelly, Robinson, Sandoval, and the sergeants rode ahead of the rest of the Rangers, who trudged in their wake. From the north side of the river, the men of the Eighth Cavalry who had remained awake continued to watch them go until they were swallowed by the fog.

That fog was a portent of what was about to happen.

McNelly's target was Rancho Las Cuevas, which was owned by his adversary Juan Flores Salinas. He had to expect it was occupied by guards but had no idea how many. Entering an area of brush and scrub oak, the Rangers made their way on foot along a cattle trail. Even their man on point, Sandoval, had trouble seeing in the dense mist. After about three miles, the trail led them to a ranch. It was not the one they sought . . . but the Rangers did not realize this until it was too late.

According to George Durham, "The fog was still so heavy you couldn't tell the difference between a man and a tree, except when it moved, then you knew it was a man."

The Rangers were able to spot a lone sentry, who suddenly saw this apparition of men. He fired a shot, the bullet almost hitting Sgt. Armstrong. Immediately, McNelly fired back, killing the sentry.

Ahead, the captain could see vaqueros in the field and moving between the ranch buildings. Clearly, they were not expecting an attack. "I want you to kill all you see," McNelly told his men, "except old men, women, and children." The Rangers charged.

Estimates vary as to how many Mexicans were cut down in the surprise attack by the two dozen Rangers with guns blazing—as few as four, as McNelly later reported, or as many as a dozen, as local sources claimed.

"When we charged [there were] five on horseback and twenty-one on foot, with old 'Casuse' on his old Paint horse in the lead, yelling and shooting in every direction, and the other of us closed in behind," Callicott later recalled. "If the angels of heaven had flown down on them they could not have been any more surprised, as we were the first Rangers or soldiers that had been in Mexico since the old Mexican War."

Only when the firing stopped and the Rangers gathered together did McNelly learn that they had attacked the wrong ranch. This one was Rancho Cachattus, also known as Las Cucharas or "Ranch of the Spoons." Rancho Las Cuevas was another half mile away. In the fog, Sandoval had taken a wrong turn, and the Rangers had followed him.

They were not overly perturbed by the error. "The common perception among border Texans was that all Mexican males living close to the river were potential cattle rustlers," explains Darren Ivey, "so the Rangers did not pause to question whether they had killed innocent men. Instead, even though the gunfire had alerted everyone within hearing distance, they boldly moved on to Las Cuevas."

There was no getting around the fact that the company, and especially its captain, had blundered. But there was no sense waiting for Salinas's men to come to them. Arriving at Rancho Las Cuevas, McNelly saw Mexican militia there, as many as two hundred and fifty men, mounted and on foot. Robinson reported that "out from the houses poured the robbers by hundreds" and there was also "a column of cavalry, in sets of fours, which seemed to me to stretch to Matamoros." Whatever the true count of Mexicans led by Salinas, the Rangers were severely outnumbered.

So, of course, they attacked.

Shocked by the bold tactic and perhaps believing this was just the first wave of an army, the Mexicans retreated. Then they regrouped, but their ranks were being depleted by the accuracy of the Texans' Sharps rifles. Still, with such numbers in their favor, the Mexicans pressed forward.

Even with such firepower, McNelly knew his men risked being surrounded. Ten minutes was enough to send the message to Salinas that the Rangers meant business. He called for a retreat. With McNelly and the other mounted men covering them, the rest of the Rangers trotted back the way they came.

Robinson would report that both the Rangers and their opposites were uttering "fiendish yells" and "where the smoke came from the guns it hung like a pall, and I was not sorry to leave, for it had a very offensive odor to me. Back to the river we went."

On the way, they passed by the first ranch they had

attacked. The only people they saw were dead. "They lay like they fell, on the woodpiles and in the streets or roads," observed Callicott.

When the Rangers reached the Rio Grande, they did not cross it. Instead, they dropped down into the shallow water on the southern side. Leander McNelly was determined to make a stand—apparently, he was not done sending messages.

What would happen the rest of the day has been conveyed by several writers in several ways, thanks to an uncomfortable combination of shaky scholarship, less-than-reliable accounts, and supposition. Of some help, at least, is a lengthy account *The Daily State Gazette* published on January 19, 1876, that Lieutenant "Pidge" Robinson finally found time to write:

> I would have sent you an account of the invasion long, long ago, but was compelled by special orders to write out a *true* account of it, which has been awful straining to the mind; I am not accustomed to this, and have scarcely recovered from it yet; besides, I think I must have been sun struck in Mexico, or received some kind of shock; I have not felt well since; it may be the effect of the heavy dew on the river, but every time a shot is fired in my vicinity, a disagreeable chilly sensation starts with lightning speed from the back of my neck, and comes out at my boot heels.

That morning, Capt. McNelly had several men deployed as pickets while the rest of the Rangers dug in on the south bank of the river. "If they charge us," he advised his men, "they will have to come across that open field and we can stand here and mow them down with but little danger of even getting hit with a bullet unless it is in the head." He added, "And if you do, the pain won't last long."

The Rangers appreciated their captain's dry sense of humor, but they hoped that his view of death would not be put to the test. No matter what, they expected a long day.

CHAPTER 41

RIO GRANDE STANDOFF

On the Mexico side of the Rio Grande, Captain McNelly paced back and forth, occasionally pausing to peer south to spot the approach of riders. He did not have to wait long. About two dozen appeared, led by Juan Flores Salinas himself. Apparently, in a rush to overtake the Rangers or at least catch them in the vulnerable position of trying to cross the river, the rurales leader had set off, accompanied by only his fastest riders, leaving his main force behind.

Also spotting the approach of the Mexicans were U.S. Army officers and troopers. However, it was clear to McNelly that, at least for now, the Eighth Cavalry troopers on the north bank would be no more than spectators.

The Rangers lined the river's south bank, where they had carved out firing positions. Without hesitation, Salinas led his men toward the Rangers' position, yelling and shooting. "Not seeing any of us on top," Callicott reported, "they thought we had taken a scare and were swimming the river back to Texas. There was not a tree on the bank at that place on the river. It was an open field for one hundred fifty yards back to the thicket."

There may have been a fleeting moment when the rurales leader realized his terrible mistake . . . but by then it was too late.

"Come on, boys!" McNelly called out. "Open up on them as fast as you can." In the volley that followed, Salinas was shot off his horse and was dead when he hit the ground.[88]

The Rangers heard a few cheers from the cavalrymen across the river. When they quieted, McNelly prepared to remain on the Mexico side indefinitely. He posted two guards, one each fifty yards up and down the river.

The abrupt death of Gen. Salinas earned only a delay of hostilities. During it, the Ranger captain and the army officers conferred. McNelly wondered if there was a way that Clendenin and Randlett could justify to their superiors crossing into Mexico. Randlett had his answer ready: He would characterize it as a defensive maneuver. Once bullets from Mexican guns began hitting the ground and brush on the northern side of the Rio Grande, they feared an invasion would follow. A preemptive strike was the most sensible

---

88 Some consolation for members of Gen. Salinas's family was that he would be considered a national hero. A stone tablet would be installed at the site reading: "To citizen JUAN FLORES SALINAS who fighting Died for his country November 20, 1875." It was actually November 19, but it was the thought that counted.

and effective way to protect the United States. That all made sense to a nodding McNelly too.

For now, though, American soldiers would still not venture forth to Mexico. But Randlett offered to send a message. This one went to Major Andrew Alexander at Fort Ringgold. His presence at the Rio Grande was urgently requested.

The Rangers remained on guard as the sun rose higher. The warming light helped McNelly, who had returned to the south side of the river, to see that the main force of Mexicans was approaching. It appeared to consist of a motley mix of militia, vaqueros, and whoever else could be rounded up quickly from the men at Salinas's ranch. The captain estimated there may have been as many as three hundred armed men on their way toward the Rangers.

Warily, then with a little more confidence, the Mexicans moved closer. Then they began firing and coming on faster. No matter how well positioned the Rangers were, the odds against them were more than ten to one. The captain called across the river to the army commanders, "For God's sake, come over and help us."

The eyes of his men were fixed on the approaching enemy when they heard splashing behind them. This was the sound made by Capt. Randlett and some forty troopers as they hurried across the Rio Grande. A sergeant named Leahy and another soldier carried with them a Gatling gun. They set the weapon up atop the south bank with a clear line of fire. When Leahy opened up, swaths of Mexican men and horses fell.

Pidge Robinson was especially pleased with this turn of events: "Just here I would like to remark that if there is an inanimate object in this whole world for which I have a pure and unadulterated veneration, respect and love, that object is a Gatling gun; if Mr. Gatling has a daughter I would marry her tomorrow, if she would have me."

The charging Mexicans soon had enough of the sudden combined firepower of the Gatling gun and Sharps rifles and turned back, leaving behind dead and writhing bodies. For a time, there was an uneasy camaraderie between the Bluebellies and the Rangers . . . until Randlett ordered his men to return to U.S. soil.

Still, McNelly got to thinking: If Randlett could be further persuaded to bring the rest of his men back across, leaving Clendenin with a token force on the American side, the combined group of troopers and Rangers might then surprise the Mexicans and send them rushing back to Rancho Las Cuevas, which would in turn come under attack. It would be quite the battle indeed, and it would end only when the stolen cattle—or an equivalent number—were herded to and then across the Rio Grande by defeated Mexicans. The bureaucratic details could be worked out later.

But the army captain, despite his impetuous donation of some troops to the Ranger cause, continued to consider his career. Two dozen Texans venturing deeper into Mexico was one thing . . . a cavalry company with two Gatling guns doing so could not be seen as anything other than an invasion of a sovereign country. That decision was above his pay grade. He would wait to see if Major Alexander showed up.

Several times during the afternoon, the Mexicans, whoever was leading them, tried a few halfhearted attacks that were easily beaten back by the sharpshooting Texas Rangers. Alexander had still not arrived by five o'clock, when Capt. McNelly spotted a man riding toward the river holding aloft a white flag. Capt. Randlett, perhaps gritting his teeth, crossed over. He and McNelly rode out to meet the Mexican emissary. McNelly was especially eager to do so as he did not want it discovered how few men he had.

The group of five men bearing the white flag had as their spokesman a thirty-nine-year-old Englishman. Dr. Alexander Manford Headley had served in the British navy; emigrated to the United States, settling in Arkansas; and served as a Confederate surgeon during the war. By the time the conflict ended, the carnage he had witnessed had turned his hair and beard white. In Mexico, he would be known as *el doctor canoso,* the "gray-haired doctor." One of the Ranger reporters described him as a "tall, handsome man [and] his long hair was white as snow, giving him a most patriarchal appearance. A closer view showed he had a youthful, ruddy complexion and deep, soft blue eyes. He wore a fine, white linen suit and a broad, wide sombrero."

Headley was one of the many men who had tried Mexico after the South surrendered. In his case, he went with General Joseph O. Shelby, who had organized a group of "undefeated rebels" to go to Mexico. They crossed into Mexico at Eagle Pass and reached Mexico City in August 1865. Unlike many former rebels, Dr. Headley chose to stay in Mexico. In Camargo, he established a medical practice and a large mercantile business called Casa de Comercio.

He was later appointed military commandant of Camargo by President Lerdo de Tejada.

That was his role when McNelly's Rangers crossed into Mexico. To prevent further bloodshed, the doctor/commandant had grabbed a white flag and, with the modest entourage of Mexicans, ridden out to parley.

Dr. Headley offered a letter to McNelly, who refused it. As Pidge Robinson put it: "This Capt. M— refused to receive, as he only came over to receive property stolen from Texas, and if possible capture the robbers."

When the letter was offered to Randlett, he took it and opened it. He may have wished he hadn't when he saw that it was addressed to "Commander of the American forces on Mexican soil." It informed the Americans that efforts were underway to arrest and punish the rustlers who had stolen the cattle. The letter, signed by the mayor of Camargo, insisted that the Americans leave Mexico immediately. Randlett worried that if he remained after the receipt of this letter, their presence could be considered an act of war . . . or escalating the one that had already begun.

McNelly did not share those concerns. He told Dr. Headley that the Texas Rangers were not going anywhere until they had both the cattle and the rustlers. He did, however, agree to continue the truce until the next morning and allow the bodies of Salinas and others to be carted to Camargo. With that, the expatriate physician and his silent companions turned and rode away.

As the sun drifted lower, food was provided to the Rangers by supportive citizens in Rio Grande City, who floated a skiff of provisions down to them. Their bellies full, the night quiet, and sentries posted, most of the Rangers eased off to sleep on the south bank of the Rio Grande.

Much of the next day, November 20, was uneventful too. But this American invasion of Mexico was not yet ready to end. At 4 P.M., Dr. Headley and his party, again bearing a white flag, were back. He asked the Rangers to return to Texas. Otherwise, there would be more killing.

In fact, there was almost more killing right then and there. An alert Lt. Robinson had noticed that "the enemy is advancing on our right, in large numbers" and that he "expects firing to begin at any minute." This information was conveyed in a note to Sgt. Armstrong, who in turn read it out loud to the captain.

Fixing Dr. Headley and the others with a stare, McNelly said loudly, "Very well. Instruct your men to kill every one of this flag-of-truce party if there is a shot fired."

A frightened Dr. Headley said, "You don't intend to have us murdered, do you?"

"My men will do what they are ordered to do," McNelly replied.

Without hesitation, a message was written and sent to whoever was leading the advance, and it came to an abrupt halt.

While this meeting on the Mexican side of the river was taking place, on the American side, an irritable Major Alexander had finally shown up. He too carried a message, this one to Clendenin as well as Randlett. It was from Colonel Joseph Potter at Fort Brown, who in turn had been telegraphed by General Edward Ord in San Antonio: "Advise Captain McNelly to return at once to this side of the river. Inform him that you are directed not to support him in any way while he remains on Mexican territory. If McNelly is attacked by Mexican forces on Mexican soil, do not render him any assistance. Let me know if McNelly acts on this advice."

With Alexander now the senior army officer on the scene, it did not matter what Clendenin or Randlett thought. The major had the message brought across the river and handed to McNelly. The Ranger captain carefully read it and then issued four terse words. "The answer is no."

Major Alexander's next message reemphasized that American troops would not cross the Rio Grande under any circumstances. If the Rangers indeed wanted to commit suicide, they would not take U.S. Army soldiers with them. The troopers and their commanders were not happy about this—by now, there was much respect for the Texans' courage and stubbornness—but there was indeed nothing they could do.

Before long, the group of men headed by Dr. Headley was back. The physician told McNelly that every male over fourteen years old had been recruited and given a gun. He estimated that there could be as many as fifteen hundred armed and angry Mexican troops ready to march to the Rio Grande and rid their country of the Texan infestation. McNelly fixed a stare on him and said firmly that he and his men would not return to Texas without the stolen cattle.[89]

---

89 Dr. Headley had more adventures ahead. In 1880, he regained American citizenship and practiced medicine on both sides of the river. Four

At sundown, on the U.S. side of the river, another message arrived, addressed to Major Alexander: "Secretary of War [William W.] Belknap orders you to demand McNelly return at once to Texas. Do not support him in any manner. Inform the Secretary if McNelly acts on these orders and returns to Texas. Signed, Colonel Potter."

This was also transported across the river. In less than a minute, Capt. McNelly penned a reply that would become famous throughout Texas: "Near Las Cuevas, Mexico, Nov. 20 1875. I shall remain in Mexico with my rangers and cross back at my discretion. Give my compliments to the Secretary of War and tell him and his United States soldiers to go to hell. Signed, Lee H. McNelly, commanding."

It seemed as if, when the truce ended, hell was going to get more crowded.

---

years later, the forty-eight-year-old married Pilar Treviño, who was twenty-eight and his fourth wife, and they had a daughter. In Hidalgo County, Dr. Headley joined the Republican Party and was county commissioner of Precinct 3 in 1890. Contending the Republicans had won an election, Headley led an armed attack on the courthouse at Edinburg, evicted the Democrats, who fled to Mexico, and tried to establish his own government. When the wife of a political ally of Headley shot and killed a Hidalgo County judge and was arrested and sent to Matamoros, Dr. Headley rescued her from the police station and escaped back to Texas. But as he neared his ranch, one of his men served him black coffee laced with arsenic. The doctor knew enough to hurry to the ranch and swallowed a bottle of castor oil. Realizing he had too many enemies around, he sold his ranch, moved to Rio Grande City, and continued to practice medicine until his death in 1912, two months before his seventy-sixth birthday.

CHAPTER 42

"DEATH SQUAD"

Leander McNelly was not completely on his own while risking a new war between Mexico and the United States. Adjutant General William Steele was in the loop via telegrams . . . as was, possibly, President Ulysses S. Grant.

There was a telegraph line that ran from Fort Brown to Rio Grande City. One of the soldiers under Randlett's command had wriggled up the nearest pole and tapped into it. Thus, as Robert Utley puts it, "The drama being played out on both sides of the river involved tiers of officialdom all the way to Washington."

As impetuous as McNelly could be, he did not want to be viewed as a renegade Texas Ranger, acting completely on his own—even though for the most part that was true. He had sent a message to the adjutant general saying, "The Mexicans in my front are about four hundred. What should I do?"

Apparently, Steele chose not to tell him. He was certainly not about to sanction an invasion of another country that could provoke war, and anything other than that—with the possible exception of a suggestion to try not to get wiped out by the Mexican army—would probably be ignored by McNelly anyway.

The fact was—as the Ranger captain probably realized—no one in the governments of Texas and the United States was going to back his play. The consequences would be much greater than the fate of a few hundred cows. And a couple of dozen Rangers. According to Major Alexander, if the situation escalated there would be no help coming from the U.S. Army. Rather than start a new war with Mexico, McNelly's men were expendable.

The captain, though, was not inclined to wait for someone else to do something. A standoff was certainly not a victory to him. That afternoon, as the shadows on both sides of the Rio Grande grew longer, McNelly had a message delivered to whoever was now leading the Mexican forces. It declared that the Texans would attack in one hour unless there was a guarantee that at ten o'clock the next morning the missing cattle would be returned and the men who stole them surrendered to the Rangers in Rio Grande City.

Many a Mexican leader would have laughed at the bravado. And maybe such a message would have inspired an attack to get rid of these defiant Texan intruders once and for all. But this particular Ranger captain had proved to be unpredictable and quick to fight. There would be much loss of life on both sides—not only right away but in the ensuing second Mexican-American war.

McNelly did not have to wait long for a response to his threat. Word came from Camargo that his terms would be met. Still, the captain told his men that to continue to show the Mexicans they meant business the Rangers would remain at their positions.

Major Alexander was not about to have any of his soldiers cross the river, but he did not feel the same way about food. A boat laden with hot meals was steered across the Rio Grande. The victuals warmed the Rangers' stomachs as darkness descended and the mid-November temperature dropped. McNelly determined who would be on watch and when, then one by one the others, wrapped in blankets and rifles at the ready, drifted off to sleep. It had been another long day.

As soon as dawn of November 21 allowed McNelly's men to see well enough, and with no perceived activity among the Mexicans, they began crossing the Rio Grande, taking turns in the small boat. McNelly, astride his horse and perhaps daring anyone to take a shot at him, was the last to leave Mexican soil. In the Rangers' absence, the army troopers had fed and watered their horses, and more than a few Rangers were glad to be reunited with them. Once they were saddled up, they rode to Rio Grande City . . . where the planned return of the cattle went awry.

When the Rangers arrived at the riverbank just south of the city, they could see the cattle in question. The bad news was they were still in Mexico, milling about in pens guarded by armed Mexicans. McNelly gave a local man a message that was taken across the river to Diego Garcia, who reportedly was the chief magistrate of Camargo.

McNelly assumed there was a mix-up and requested that the cattle now be returned: "This agreement has not been complied with, and as the Commanding Officer of the United States forces is here awaiting your action in this matter I would be glad if you would inform me of the earliest hour at which you can deliver these cattle and any of the thieves you may have apprehended." It is amusing to note that McNelly implied he had army troopers at his disposal.

Garcia replied that he was too busy—so busy that he would not even take the time to write anything more than a message saying he was busy. However, the messenger told the Ranger captain that Garcia would put a little of his valuable time aside to see McNelly but not until the next day. While the captain pondered his next move, another man crossed the river, this one bearing a written message: Garcia would return the cattle, but he was still very busy, and that would not happen until the following morning.

McNelly, on his horse and gazing across the Rio Grande, thought upon this and then penned a note to Garcia: The agreement made the previous afternoon was for a delivery of the cattle by ten that morning. If that indeed was not going to happen, Garcia should have the courtesy to make it clear once more, since both the Ranger commander and the army officer in charge were waiting.

Probably, McNelly did not inform that army officer that he was being included in the flurry of cross-river correspondence, but the subtle ruse worked. The next note from Garcia reported that he was not quite as busy as he thought he was, and he would make sure the cattle were at the riverbank at three o'clock. Noting that the message contained nothing about turning over the rustlers or about which riverbank, the Ranger captain was not convinced. Thinking about it some more, McNelly concluded that Garcia was attempting a ruse of his own. This he could not abide.

But first, to feed his men. They followed McNelly into Rio Grande City, where he bought them a good Sunday breakfast at a café. After a leisurely interlude, the Rangers mounted up again, and this time McNelly led them back to the river. He got off his horse and signaled to the ferryman that he wanted to cross over to Camargo. He then instructed Sgt. Armstrong that he and Lt. Robinson and eight others were to accompany him. They labeled themselves the "Death Squad," because if just eleven men invading Mexico was not a suicide mission, nothing was.

After checking that their guns were loaded and they had plenty of ammunition, the abbreviated McNelly's Rangers boarded the ferry. It was low in the water as it traveled from the United States to Mexico. Disembarking, according to the account of Bill Callicott, who was a member of the Death Squad, they were greeted by two dozen uniformed and armed Mexican soldiers. McNelly shook the hand of the captain of the group and announced that it was closing in on three o'clock in the afternoon and the Texans were there to accept delivery of the stolen cattle. He asked that the officer order some men to bring the beeves down to the river.

And that was when a war almost began.

Right after the customs captain explained that it was Sunday and their religion prohibited that kind of work,

McNelly tugged his pistol out and cracked the captain's skull with it. Behind him, the Rangers drew their weapons. When one of the customs officials went for his weapon, he was shot.

For a few moments there was tense silence. Then the Mexicans, even though they were in Mexico, surrendered.

That was Durham's recollection. But the more reliable Callicott offered a less dramatic albeit risk-filled scene. Instead of employing the Sunday excuse, the captain said that the cattle could not be returned until they had been inspected. McNelly pointed out that they had been taken to Mexico without being inspected and could be taken back without that task being performed.

This reasoning did not persuade the Mexican captain. However, he was more impressed when the Rangers brandished their weapons. According to Pidge Robinson, McNelly had "exhausted all arguments with these gentlemen, except one, which he reserved for the very last, and which, as a dernier resorte in this country, is considered 'a clincher': 'prepare to load with ball cartridges—load!' The ominous 'kerchack' of the carbine levers as the long, murderous looking cartridges were chambered home, satisfied them as to the permit and the cattle allowed to cross over without one; such is the power of a fifty calibre argument, such the authority of Sharpe on International law."

The customs captain—whose skull, in this account, was still intact—was further impressed when he was told that if the cattle were not on their way to Texas immediately, he and his men would be dead. Specifically, in Callicott's colorful prose, McNelly said, "Tell the son of a bitch if he didn't cross them cattle in less than five minutes we would kill the last one of them."

Moments later, there was a burst of activity as Mexican soldiers and civilians opened the pens and began urging the cows toward the Rio Grande. Within minutes, they were back on U.S. soil again. As a tip for his trouble, the ferryman was awarded one of the animals. After the last cow crossed, McNelly and the rest of the Death Squad, very much alive, also crossed the river.

In reports written afterward about the incident, estimates varied widely, from seventy-five to four hundred, of how many cattle were recovered by the Rangers. However many beeves there were, they were not much return for all the riding and shooting and killing and risking a war. But many Texans did not see it that way. Word spread like a prairie fire from the Rio Grande to Austin that the Rangers had won what was already being called the "Las Cuevas War." And what mattered most was that McNelly's men had not hesitated to take the fight to Mexico itself and were willing to lose their lives rather than have thieves get away with raiding Texas and stealing cattle.

"Let the policy inaugurated at the Rancho *Cuevas* be followed on vigorously," Pidge Robinson advised, "and there will be some hope for Texas' citizens and some security for their property."

The Galveston Daily News lauded McNelly, "Instead of being surrounded by Mexicans and treating for surrender, he actually dictated the terms of his withdrawal from Mexico."

Even the faraway *New York Herald* weighed in: "What

Texas intends to do for her own protection may be gathered from the recent action of Captain McNally [*sic*]. She proposes to protect herself if the United States government will not protect her."

Back at the Rio Grande, of more practical and immediate concern after the crossing was returning the cattle to their rightful owners. McNelly was not terribly interested in this task, except for the beeves that displayed the brand of Richard King. About thirty of those animals were collected, and the captain assigned four men to escort them to the Santa Gertrudis Ranch. McNelly made sure one of them was George Durham, because he knew he was smitten with a young woman named Caroline, who was King's niece.[90]

For Leander McNelly, he had to wonder how much time on this earth he had left. His fragile health had certainly not improved during the Mexico adventure. He had to be contemplating that his days as a Ranger captain were dwindling and that, at least for the sake of his wife and children, he should ride back to Washington County and stay there.

Then those plans were interrupted. There was business to attend to up north.

---

90 In 1877 Durham left the Texas Rangers and went to work at Santa Gertrudis, eventually becoming a foreman. He and Caroline Chamberlain married, and they lived on the ranch with their ten children. Their six sons worked on the King ranch all of their lives. Durham was the last of McNelly's Rangers alive when he died in 1940 at age eighty-four.

CHAPTER 43

CAPTAIN McNELLY GOES TO WASHINGTON

Leander McNelly was expected in the nation's capital early in the new year. Before the captain left, he wanted to settle his Washington County company down for the winter. One of his more bothersome tasks was to make it plain that he and his men were still alive.

The captain learned that during the so-called Las Cuevas War, McNelly's Rangers had been reported killed in action—overwhelmed and murdered by the Mexican army. One of Eighth Cavalry's young officers had gotten agitated watching the Mexican force attack the small company of Rangers and, assuming the worst, had rushed to telegraph news of them being slain. As such news is wont to do, it spread fast. While the Rangers were in winter quarters in Retama, telegrams and letters arrived from relatives asking permission to come claim the bodies. The captain also learned that the cattleman Richard King was organizing a force of a hundred men to either rescue the remaining Rangers or avenge their deaths.

From not quite the afterlife, McNelly and Pidge Robinson wrote the relatives that their loved ones were alive and well. King received a similar message along with his returned cattle, and he disbanded his revenge riders.

The Rangers enjoyed the next round of rumors, which included taller and taller tales that the two dozen Texans had not only survived but also, after crossing the Rio Grande, had defeated the entire Mexican army and returned with hundreds—maybe thousands—of stolen cattle. Nearby farmers and ranchers were so honored to have such heroes that wagons bearing food arrived at the Rangers' camp. Better sustenance for the captain was that Carey McNelly was back near the border to help take care of her husband. When word circulated that goat milk would be good for him, gallons of it were donated.

The captain's health was once more of some concern. Most of the day-to-day responsibilities at the camp were overseen by Lt. Robinson and Sgts. Armstrong and Hall. The colder temperatures and more frequent rain upon the Nueces Strip were hazardous to a man with consumption. Somehow, though, while still in the middle of winter, McNelly gathered himself together and joined Colonel Rip Ford on a trip to Washington, D.C.

In the nation's capital, McNelly was viewed as a villain by some (especially Northerners) and a hero by others. Some lawmakers and military leaders were not pleased that this tubercular Texan had almost embroiled the United States in a war only ten years after the devastation of the

Civil War had finally ended. On the other side were those who saw the Ranger captain as something of a folk hero who, with a small but scrappy company of men, had taught those south-of-the-border thieves and ruffians a lesson.

It was a pleasant surprise that even newspapers in New York were praising his actions. *The New York Herald* informed readers that McNelly, "who is under thirty years of age, energetic, cool, brave and possessed of wonderful physical endurance"—the last part was a curious claim—"has already pursued into Mexico bands of thieves, recovering stolen property and showing no mercy to the robbers. His last exploit proves of what stuff he is made."

McNelly did not travel up from Texas for attention one way or the other but to give testimony. A committee in Congress was looking into the troubles along the border between the Lone Star State and Mexico. During the last week of January 1876, the captain testified before the committee, explaining tersely that, while his men had been effective, there were simply more rustlers than Rangers and that they kept popping up along the border like prairie dogs.[91]

He also pointed out the unique circumstances of the border—many of the Mexican residents on both sides of the Rio Grande were related to each other. The ones who owned ranches on the American side certainly opposed cattle rustling, but for them, McNelly said, "the risk is too

---

91 One member of the committee was Nathaniel Banks of Massachusetts, who had faced off against Confederates, including McNelly, during the war.

great" to go after the thieves themselves. "My position, in command of a company of troops, I do not consider half so hazardous as that of those men living on ranches."

He hoped the people in Washington who were far removed from the border trouble would at least understand the feelings of the people who lived there. "I speak as a soldier," the Washington County captain told the committee. "I served four years in the Confederate Army. I have met some of these Mexicans out there and they are men who stand killing splendidly."

Inevitably, McNelly was asked about his invasion of Mexico and how he justified it. He responded that if a nation of "turbulent people" committed crimes against a neighbor nation, the latter has the right to defend itself, even with an incursion.

Meanwhile, while the captain was away, his Rangers continued to patrol the border area. Still, ranchers were not completely safe from raids, and the activity threatened to rise to the level of depredations as before. Echoing the sentiments McNelly had expressed to Congress, *The San Antonio Express* advised that a force of fed-up Americans take bold action. "Push over the river soldiers, and citizens," the newspaper exhorted, "and destroy the whole nest of thieves, regardless of the consequences."

This was not a good time for an increase in banditry, but it is what the advent of spring brought.

There was yet another revolution underway in Mexico. This one was led by Porfirio Díaz. Born in Oaxaca in 1830, José de la Cruz Porfirio Díaz Mori pursued a military career and did quite well at it. By the time of the bloody

Battle of Puebla in May 1862, a big victory over an army of French invaders, Díaz was a general. He continued to fight against the forces of Emperor Maximilian, and by the time of the French ruler's eventual ouster, Díaz was considered a national hero.

That was enough fighting for Díaz . . . or so he thought. When Benito Juárez became the president of Mexico in 1868 and began to restore peace, Díaz was content to resign his military command and go home to Oaxaca. However, he could not shake that political itch and was soon openly opposed to the new administration. In 1870, when Díaz believed that Juárez was running for an illegal second term, he threw his own hat in the ring and ran against the president and his vice president, Sebastián Lerdo de Tejada. After Díaz lost, he made claims of fraud, and when they were not enough to topple Juárez, he launched a rebellion. In March 1872, however, Díaz's forces were defeated in the Battle of La Bufa.

But perhaps providence was on his side: Only four months later, Juárez died. His successor, Lerdo de Tejado, offered amnesty to the rebels. Díaz accepted and retired again, this time to Veracruz. In 1874, he was elected to Congress. Díaz did not like Lerdo de Tejado any more than he did Juárez and began to contemplate another rebellion. It was a tad dangerous to plan one in Mexico itself, so Díaz left for New Orleans, then relocated to Brownsville. Lerdo de Tejado was alarmed enough that he offered Díaz an ambassadorship in Europe as a way to remove him from the Mexican political scene, but Díaz refused. He put his energy instead to organizing a new revolution, which got off to a decent start when his forces captured Matamoros on April 2, 1875.[92]

This was not good news for McNelly's company. As Frederick Wilkins points out, "Many of the Mexican cattlemen and workers had no interest in reforming Mexico, or furthering Diaz's personal ambitions. They swarmed into Texas, bringing on an increase in stealing."

So the respite for the Rangers was short-lived. Stopping the rustlers from conducting raids was like trying to plug holes in a dam. None of the thefts were large-scale, but there were fifty beeves stolen here, seventy-five stolen there. Whatever had been discussed in Washington seemed to be of little use in the reality of the southern border.

On his way back to it, McNelly stopped off in Austin to brief Gov. Coke and Adjutant General Steele about the hearing of the congressional committee. Then he went to reunite with Carey, who was visiting a friend in DeWitt County. As the captain had predicted, the Sutton-Taylor feud had reemerged as a reason for violence, including killings. McNelly wrote to Austin that he felt compelled to stay on in the county "in case of any serious disturbance I might be of some service to the State if not the local officers."

He was instead ordered to rejoin his company. The escalating cattle raids was a more pressing matter. But the thievery did not end with McNelly's return.

---

92 Ultimately, Díaz would be successful at seizing and retaining power. Beginning later that year, he would serve three separate terms as president of Mexico. The final one lasted from 1884 to 1911. Díaz died in July 1915, two months before his eighty-fifth birthday.

In May 1876 his spies tipped him off to a raid, and his men took to their horses. By the time they found the rustlers at the Rio Grande, most of the cattle had crossed. Still, there was a fight, which resulted in the deaths of at least two bandits.[93]

That was not good enough for the captain. Accompanied by only three men, McNelly entered Mexico again. He followed a trail that took him to the outskirts of Reynosa, where, presumably, the stolen herd had been brought. But there was also a large military presence there, so McNelly chose not to take further action. He and his small squad rode back to Texas.

When asked later by a Mexican official how he could excuse sending armed men into Mexico, McNelly replied, "I didn't—I went and took men with me."

Not only was this particular mission frustrating but the prospect of spending the summer chasing thieves was not appealing. So it must have been with some relief that McNelly's Rangers—who had by the end of May relocated to Fort Ewell, south of the Nueces River—received a new assignment: They were to go after King Fisher.

The half rancher, half outlaw was about to meet his match in Leander McNelly . . . if the exhausted captain could survive one more campaign.

---

93 The already formidable firepower of the Rangers had been increased recently by the arrival of thirty Winchester repeating rifles, provided by Richard King.

CHAPTER 44

"THIS RASH YOUNG MAN"

"Gunfighter" was just one occupation listed on the résumé of John King Fisher.

He was the oldest of two sons born to Jobe Fisher, originally from Arkansas, and Lucinda Warren, in Collin County, Texas. He was nearing two years old in 1855 when his mother died giving birth to his brother. His father remarried and moved the family to Williamson County, where King's uncle lived. During the Civil War, Jobe served in the Confederate army until being mustered out in February 1864.

Jobe's second wife, Minerva, was a frail woman in poor health, so after a time, he decided to move the family again, this time to Goliad County, to be closer to the coast. Jobe was in the cattle business and frequently operated freight wagons along the Gulf of Mexico.

After the death of his second wife—clearly, the frontier

was especially hard on frail women—Jobe noticed that his older son was starting to surround himself with people whom he considered the wrong crowd—principally, the Bruton family. He decided to write a letter to relatives in Florence requesting that they allow John to stay with them and attend school. They accepted, and the boy made the 150-mile trip by himself, on a sorrel mule.

He was described as athletic, good looking, and popular with the ladies. He displayed talents for fistfighting, horseback riding, and breaking wild horses for extra money. Once, while riding horseback, he decided to stop to take a nap. While he was sleeping, his pony broke loose. To chase the pony down, Fisher borrowed a horse from a nearby pasture. The property owner pressed theft charges against him, making this his first brush with the law. Fisher managed to escape custody and sought refuge back in Goliad County.

Apparently not having learned his lesson, he continued a downward spiral into a life of crime, which included surrounding himself with the same crowd—members of the Bruton clan—that his father had initially tried to get him away from. He was eventually arrested for burglary, found guilty, and sentenced to serve two years in the state penitentiary at Huntsville.

Fisher was only sixteen years old at the time, so he was released from prison only a few months later, having been pardoned by the governor.[94] After his release, the teenager

---

94 Several accounts have John King Fisher killing his first man at age sixteen, but there does not appear to be factual corroboration for this.

aimed to become a cowboy and joined other Goliad residents who were migrating westward. They chose to establish a community on the Pendencia Creek, which flows through Dimmit County in the Nueces Strip, but it was hard going. As O. Clark Fisher writes, because of the lack of lawmen in the vicinity, "The frontiersmen became their own protectors, enforcing their own laws as best they could. The triple threat menace of Indians, cattle thieves, and Mexican bandits plagued the new settlement, and many of their cattle were stolen."[95]

Fisher adds, "The stage was set for the arrival of this rash young man"—whom many were referring to simply as King.

The job he was given by the settlers was to ride the ranges and keep an eye on their grazing livestock. Obviously, this was a lot of responsibility for a man barely shut of his teenage years. And often the bandits he had to chase off or hunt down were ones sent by Juan Cortina. But King took to it and was an effective stock guardian. "With him gunmanship seemed a natural gift," remarks O. C. Fisher. And the

---

95 The author Fisher's father was also named Jobe and was related to King Fisher, seemingly a great-nephew. In the late 1920s, O. C. Fisher practiced law in San Angelo in West Texas, and beginning in 1931 he served in several county and state positions. In 1942 Fisher was elected to the U.S. House of Representatives as a Democrat and served for thirty-two years. He was one of five U.S. representatives from Texas to sign the "Southern Manifesto" in protest of the U.S. Supreme Court's decision in *Brown v. Board of Education.* Because of a heart condition, Fisher did not run for reelection in 1974. However, he lived for another twenty years, dying at age ninety-one.

young cattleman enjoyed the freedom of the wide, open spaces.

The few times he was back at the settlement, he also enjoyed the company of Sarah Vivian. He courted the teenager and, perhaps thinking more seriously about his domestic future, determined that if he was to be spending most of his time protecting livestock, at least some of them should be his own. To that end, he established a ranch on Pendencia Creek, a region where cattle rustling had become routine. This was the kind of environment King could thrive in.

Soon, he "was becoming known in every saloon on the border, at cow camps, and on the range," according to O. C. Fisher. "His reputation as an expert horseman, gunslinger, and detective spread like wildfire up and down the border." Especially because of the "gunslinger" part, "No one wanted to tangle with him."

King acquired more cattle legitimately . . . but after a time, illegitimately as well given the tempting combination of hundreds if not thousands of unbranded beeves roaming around the Nueces Strip and a growing market to the north and east for beef. Also in the mix were men of questionable backgrounds and character arriving regularly in the area looking for work and not too particular about it. Needing more men to work his ranch and the ranges, King hired them.

Thus, his ranch became a sanctuary for criminals, rustlers, and drifters who came through the area. He was so feared that when travelers saw road signs near his ranch that read, "This is King Fisher's Road. Take the other," they did. The new empresario had created a sizable gang, having over a hundred men loyal to him.

"With this array of toughies," writes O. C. Fisher, "King had a formidable gang around him, all loyal, anxious, and willing to follow his commands. In an area infested with renegades and being invaded by Mexican *bandidos,* Fisher marshaled a superior force and laid the ground work for the building of an empire. Now respected and feared, the young man was prepared to consolidate his gains and capitalize upon the natural advantages afforded by an open, unprotected, and lawless area."

In the mid-1870s, most of the area near the border between Mexico and the U.S. remained unfenced. Using this to his advantage, King and his crew would frequently dash into Mexico, steal cattle and horses, then quickly return to his ranch. On one occasion, he found several Mexicans attempting to remove a horse from his ranch that they claimed had belonged to them. According to Major T. T. Teel, a criminal lawyer who frequently represented King in court, one of the Mexicans fired at King but missed. The rancher took the gun away from him, then killed all three of them with it.

There was no mistaking King Fisher when he was in town. He wore elaborate outfits that included tiger-skinned chaps and carried a pair of silver-plated, ivory-handled six-shooters. He was usually described as a tall and handsome man with black hair and with one black and one brown eye.

Despite their youth—or maybe because of it—the romance between Fisher, twenty-two, and Sarah, nineteen, moved quickly to marriage. The ceremony took place on April 6, 1876.[96]

As was true of Wild Bill Hickok to the north, King was deadly fast and accurate with either hand. This skill, combined with an intimidating personality, made King Fisher the most formidable figure in South Texas. His ranch became solidly established, and according to O. C. Fisher, "Between San Felipe and Brownsville, a distance of seven hundred miles, little evidence of law and order could be detected. On both sides of the Rio Grande conditions were intolerable. Cattle thieves, cutthroats, and other outlaws and gamblers and homesteaders wormed their way through the chaparral, all vying for supremacy and survival."

King Fisher, youthful, colorful, and resourceful, moved in to become the dominant figure. With a fast draw, steel courage, irrepressible ambition, and a truly magnetic personality and capacity for leadership, he carved out the empire that made of him a legend.

How was the increasingly fragile Leander McNelly going to be able to go up against such a young and powerful (and romanticized) specimen of precocious Texan manhood? It helped that the Ranger captain had amply demonstrated that he had no fear. But also helping was that in 1876, at the height of his infamy, King was becom-

---

96 The life of Sarah Fisher would span the presidential administrations from Franklin Pierce to Harry Truman. She died in August 1946, in her ninetieth year.

ing accustomed to being more of a family man, with Sarah. The couple would go on to produce four daughters.

But by then he had already attracted the attention of Governor Richard Coke and William Steele. Being a successful rancher was certainly no crime, but Fisher, according to Darren Ivey, had "provided his ranch as a sanctuary to fugitives and stock thieves operating on both sides of the Rio Grande. Leading his own gang of desperadoes, Fisher personally backed his control with his six-shooter." Or, in his case, two of them.

This was particularly galling to the administration in Austin. As McNelly had testified to Congress, it was believed that it was mostly Mexicans on both sides of the border who were responsible for the relentless rustling. However, here was a native Texan eclipsing other operations—and doing it with impunity, at the head of his own special force and sporting a pair of fancy firearms.

During the spring of 1876, local lawmen had given up trying to challenge King Fisher. That was where McNelly's Rangers came in.

CHAPTER 45

"TWO BEST PISTOL FIGHTERS IN TEXAS"

No doubt, the Ranger captain, despite the chronic misery of consumption, was itching for a new assignment. The intervals between missions meant catching up on reports and related paperwork, an exercise he loathed. "While Mc-Nelly's leadership qualities and bravery could not be questioned," writes Mike Cox, "and though popular with the Anglo ranchers in South Texas, he periodically received reprimands from headquarters for not keeping his financial records in order and for failure to keep Austin abreast of his location and activities."

Go up against the powerful King Fisher? McNelly and his men were more than ready.

As the captain and his men prepared to head to Dimmit County, he assured Adjutant General Steele, "You may depend on my not doing anything that will not be justifiable legally." Even better, he added in the May 31 message, "I shall have a duly authorized civil officer accompany each of my squads."

McNelly may have well been sincere about the latter, unaware that the local civil officers would much rather hide in the high chaparral than try to arrest Fisher or any of his many friends—especially on his own property.

Though his men would follow the captain anywhere, even to hell, there was some apprehension among the Rangers about the new mission. As one of his sergeants, John Armstrong, exclaimed, "Why, that is King Fisher country. When we go in there somebody might get hurt!"

By late spring 1876, Fisher's reputation was pretty widespread. A newspaper as far away as St. Louis expostulated, "Long the terror of the western border of Texas"—though not true geographically—"this king fishes for plunder and generally succeeds well in his catch."

Frederick Wilkins notes, "Like Hardin, [King Fisher] began his career during Reconstruction by killing Republican police. Just how many people he killed is unknown. Within his territory in the Eagle Pass country he became a leader; no one operated or moved anything without his approval. He was wanted by the state of Texas, and several of his workers were wanted on warrants from other states."

The Rangers knew that, once again, they would be outnumbered, but that did not stop them from heading toward the notorious ranch. After all, they had survived invading another country. "We made up in self-confidence and reckless disregard of danger what we lacked in numbers," wrote N. A. Jennings. "Our success on the lower Rio Grande gave us the feeling that we were invincible. We not only did not fear the result of a conflict with desperadoes, we were eager to try conclusions with them."

Still, for McNelly's men, this mission would be quite different from playing cat and mouse with Mexican border ruffians. This would be Texan versus Texan. And their twenty-two-year-old Texan target was at the height of his power.

Unfortunately, missing on this journey into harm's way was one of the Rangers' most loyal men, Lieutenant Pidge Robinson. He had undertaken a different mission—one that would turn out to be even more dangerous.

At the end of his last dispatch to *The Austin Gazette,* Robinson had written, "I am going home to spend my pay" and that he intended to leave on the next steamer. By "home," he meant returning to Virginia. His abrupt separation from McNelly's Rangers was not a sudden impulse but the result of a telegram he had just received: "I am in dire distress. Come home immediately," wired his sister, Lizzie May.

In mid-March, Pidge Robinson was in Brownsville, having visited with McNelly and the rest of his family. Next he was boarding a steamer, which took him to Galveston. Given the desperation expressed in the telegram, it could not have parted the water fast enough. From Galveston he went to New Orleans and then traveled to Virginia. When Robinson at last arrived at the family homestead on April 1, he was accompanied by a friend, Whitfield Clark, who may have joined him in Lynchburg. According to Chuck Parsons, in all likelihood that first night was spent with his father and sister.

It is not certain what Lizzie May was referring to in

her message of distress. However, it probably had something to do with Jesse Mitchell, because the next day Pidge Robinson went in search of him. It is possible that he was taking advantage of a lull in Rangers activity by resuming his romance with "Pidgie" Mitchell and that her brother's longstanding opposition had to be overcome, but that does not explain Lizzie May's urgency. Whatever the motivation, when Robinson set out, he did so with guns.

In Parsons's biography of Robinson, he includes a detailed account of the events that followed, taken from an article that appeared in *The Lynchburg Virginian*. It reported that "Truxton Robinson" searched that Sunday morning for Jesse Mitchell and found him "at a cabin on his father's land," about three hundred yards from the main house. Without hesitation, Pidge advanced and "within twenty paces of Mitchell he cocked a large Navy pistol. Mitchell, being strongly impressed at that moment with the first law of nature, drew his pistol."

Robinson kept coming, and the two men aimed their weapons and fired simultaneously. Though shot in the abdomen, Robinson continued advancing and pulled the trigger a second time. His first bullet had hit Mitchell's right hand, then ricocheted into his right cheek and continued to the back of his head. The second bullet hit him in the right breast and exited his back. Then, the report revealed, Mitchell "received a pistol shot in the bowels from a derringer in the hands of Robinson when it was so close to him it burned his clothing."

Both men collapsed to the ground. Two doctors were summoned to treat the young men "but the recovery of either of them is extremely doubtful." This turned out to be half true—despite his three serious wounds, Jesse Mitchell survived.

While such gunfights might have been routine fare for men like Wild Bill Hickok and John Wesley Hardin on the frontier, they were highly unusual in long-settled Virginia. It created headlines in major daily newspapers from *The Baltimore Sun* to *The St. Paul Pioneer Press* to *The New York Times,* which provided the simple headline, "A Fatal Duel in Virginia." Texas newspapers also carried the story, of course, which was probably how Leander McNelly learned of his lieutenant's sensational death.

Sadly, the shooting did not conclude the enmity between the Robinson and Mitchell families. Jesse recovered, and three years later, when Lizzie May, upon her father's death, inherited the 180-acre family farm, he began to prey upon her. Jesse's attempts to gain control of some or all of the Robinson land actually dated back to when the elder Robinson was alive, and may have been the reason for Lizzie May's desperate telegram to her brother.

Somehow, she had the fortitude to endure Jesse's ongoing efforts. And he overplayed his hand enough that Jesse and two other men were charged with extortion. Jesse was found guilty and was sentenced to five years in prison. Upon his release, he married a widow, and they lived in Lynchburg with their son. Jesse Mitchell died in May 1900 at age fifty-four.[97]

---

97 His sister, Pidgie, the object of Thomas Robinson Jr.'s affections, married in 1881 and lived to 1923, residing in the Blue Ridge Mountains.

As Leander McNelly had demonstrated before, once he decided upon a course of action, he did not hesitate. To prepare for whatever was to happen, he once more had some spying done. A. L. Parrott, one of the Rangers, had assumed the guise of a photographer roaming the borderlands and recording the places and people who occupied them. He just happened to find his way to the King Fisher ranch. Viewed as a harmless eccentric, Parrott was welcomed there. After taking several photographs, he wandered off . . . toward the Rangers' nearby camp. Thanks to Parrott's report, McNelly had a good idea of the layout of the ranch.

On June 4 the captain collected fifteen Rangers to ride to Fisher's ranch. Arriving around noon, they dismounted at the main house, nestled under cottonwood trees. They had their guns drawn as they surrounded the dwelling, but expecting that Sarah Fisher would be present, McNelly had instructed his men not to shoot unless fired upon.

Several of Fisher's men, who had been playing cards, emerged from a nearby shed. They were curious about the return of what one of them called "that damn picture man." A. J. Parrott informed them of his real occupation: "We're Texas Rangers."

The captain told a couple of his men to guard those who had been in the shed. One of them, Frank Porter, was indicative of the kind of man Fisher had attracted as friends and employees. Porter actually was Burd Obenchain, who had been a member of Quantrill's Raiders during the Civil War and was still wanted in Kansas for murder and rustling cattle.

Then, with McNelly leading, the Rangers rushed into the house. No shots were fired, and they emerged with King Fisher and several other men.

Outside, when Fisher and McNelly faced each other, the former smiled. With some hyperbole, George Durham recorded that "right there, facing each other at not more than five paces, were by long odds the two best pistol fighters in Texas." King Fisher was not intimidated, but he and his men were clearly outfoxed and outgunned.

The young rancher carefully removed his glinting guns from their holsters and presented them to McNelly. Then he locked his hands behind his head. Now it was the captain's turn to smile, which, according to Durham, was "something I never saw him do to a man he wanted."

McNelly said, "We had you."

Fisher acknowledged, "Yes, you had me. Pretty neat."

At that moment, Sarah Fisher emerged from the house. N. A. Jennings described her as "a pretty girl, with wonderfully fine, bold black eyes." She said to McNelly, "What are you doing to my husband?"

"Plenty," the captain replied.

She scoffed, "He's done nothing."

Fisher shooed his wife back inside, and giving McNelly another grin, he said, "I'm a law-abiding citizen."

There was not any part of the Ranger captain that believed this. However, he replied: "Make damn sure you stay law-abiding, King. You've got a nice wife. You could make a good citizen. You'd also make a nice corpse. All outlaws look good dead."

Once more, the Texas press lauded the Ranger captain, who was nearing legendary status. *The San Antonio Express* blared, "King Fisher and Seven of His Gang Captured." Right beneath the headline was, "Captain McNelly Did It." It also opined that Fisher was smart to surrender, because any resistance "would have been useless."

Arresting the criminal rancher was one thing . . . sending him to prison was another.

CHAPTER 46

THE NEW LIEUTENANT

There was no way that King Fisher would be convicted in his own Dimmit County backyard, even if witnesses were willing to testify. But before McNelly did anything else, there were some procedures to follow and paperwork to do. "Have arrested King Fisher and nine of his gang and turned them over to the sheriff," he telegraphed William Steele in Austin. "Will camp at Fort Ewell and scout country between here and Oakville until otherwise instructed. Country in most deplorable condition. All civil officers helpless."

Next, McNelly had to find those witnesses to Fisher's crimes and then ensure their safety—both tall tasks. The Rangers no longer had the element of surprise, as they had had at the Fisher ranch. By now, everyone in the Pendencia Creek area knew there were state lawmen present . . . and probably not enough of them to face Fisher's loyal followers.

But the captain had anticipated the possibility of interference. Before they had left the ranch, McNelly notified Fisher's angry wife that if there was any rescue attempt, "the prisoners will all be killed on the spot. That's our rule." Then the lawmen and their manacled prisoners left the ranch.

Fisher and the nine men arrested with him were turned over to the sheriff of Maverick County, C. J. Cook. Leander McNelly wanted to believe that the arrested men would stay in custody, but even though this was another county, he did not trust the local lawmen, including Sheriff Cook. Even if he and others were good, well-intentioned men, Fisher had amply demonstrated he could ride roughshod over them.

Hence, time was short. McNelly needed witnesses for what he hoped would be a quick trial. He put his Rangers to work with some local wranglers to round up several hundred head of cattle that he believed had been stolen. The beeves were unlikely to testify, but they were evidence. While this task was being pursued, the captain set off alone to round up witnesses. To boost his authority among local residents, McNelly had been appointed a special deputy sheriff by Cook.

After a circuit of some forty miles, McNelly was closing in on Eagle Pass, accompanied by several men who, albeit with some reluctance, had agreed to testify against King Fisher and his outlaw underlings. One can imagine the captain's surprise when he encountered a party of men on their way to the Fisher ranch. This group included King himself and the others who had been arrested.

Outraged, McNelly demanded to know why these men were not still in jail. Smiling amiably, the young rancher explained that the defense attorney had raised a number of technicalities about the arrest and the charges. While all this was being sorted out, and with Fisher not likely to leave the area, the judge saw fit to release all the defendants on a twenty-thousand-dollar bond.

McNelly suspected there was more to this, and he was right. During the couple of days that Fisher and his cohorts were behind bars, his supporters had fanned out to shopkeepers and other businesspeople in the area to suggest they put up bail money, lest their economic fortunes and health take turns for the worse.

In any event, whatever his status as a Ranger captain—and by that time, one of the most well-known ones—McNelly could not contradict a judge's decision. "Very well, if the people of this section want such men as you running over their country and stealing and murdering, they are welcome," McNelly growled. "There is no use working my men night and day for such a farce as this."

The captain moved his horse closer to Fisher. Fixing him with a stare, he said, "If we ever come up here again, we'll come to kill." Fisher's smile evened out as McNelly continued, "And if you keep up your system of robbery and murder, you'll be hearing from us."

According to Jennings, "Fisher said he would be

delighted to see the Rangers at any time and entertain them to the best of his ability."

Another frustration was being reminded of further friction in DeWitt County. McNelly traveled there to escort his wife, who had again been visiting a friend, home to Burton. He found that there had been more shootings, murders, and reported sightings of the man-killer John Wesley Hardin. McNelly wrote to William Steele that here was "an opportunity of ridding the State of these pests for good and all for I will deal with them without mercy."

No doubt he would have. However, the rumors about Hardin were untrue, and Steele was not about to authorize—and pay for—the Washington County company to return to DeWitt County. Instead, McNelly's Rangers were ordered back to Brownsville. There was still much to do along the border.

Cattle rustling continued at a steady pace. McNelly and his men were kept busy tracking down and apprehending— and in some cases, shooting—suspects and striving to return stolen beeves to their owners. It turned out, according to Parsons and Little, that "capturing outlaws did bring some satisfaction. Killing an occasional cattle thief crossing stolen cattle" made an impression too.

McNelly had every intention of taking another crack at King Fisher and affiliated lawbreakers who had eluded him that spring. He needed more power, though—not firepower, necessarily, but political and financial power. On June 21 the Ranger captain was in Austin, taking his case to the state legislature. His appearance had been arranged by a sympathetic Rip Ford, who was now a member of the legislature.

Though obviously not in good health, McNelly firmly testified about his experiences in DeWitt County and with King Fisher and his ilk. A big obstacle to strong law enforcement was weak local lawmen, he explained. How could Texas Rangers assist sheriffs and deputies who were not all that motivated to enforce the law?

The lawmakers not only listened to the esteemed lawman, they took action. In July, with Ford leading the way, they passed an act aimed at suppressing "lawlessness and crime in certain parts of the State." In a significant change to the way lawing had been done before, Captain McNelly and his Washington County volunteers were disbanded and then immediately restored as "Special State Troops." The new fifty-two-man company not only had more enforcement power but a bigger and stable budget of forty thousand dollars and, according to the act, the Rangers "shall have authority to make arrests"—wherever they were and without having to defer to local officers.

Something else of significance but less welcome came out of McNelly's appearance before the state legislature: It appointed Jesse Lee Hall to be the new company's lieutenant, replacing Pidge Robinson. It was troubling that the captain hadn't been left with the prerogative of selecting his own second-in-command. And worse, McNelly could see the writing on the wall.

It wasn't that Hall was not capable. He was both young and experienced. Hall had been born in October 1849 in Lexington, North Carolina, and twenty years later, like many young men drawn to the allure of Texas, he moved there.[98] His initial occupation was schoolteacher, but he soon turned to policing. He was hired as a marshal in Sherman, then served as a deputy sheriff in Denison, and then became known to members of the Texas legislature when appointed to be its sergeant at arms.

It was during his tenure in Denison that Lee Hall began to burnish his bona fides as a lawman. At that time, thanks to it being a terminus of the Missouri, Kansas & Texas Railroad, Denison was a boomtown, where riotous behavior was routine. The deputy sheriff, both holsters sporting revolvers and with a Winchester in his hands, was determined to establish at least a minimum of public safety. During the next eighteen months, Hall and several other peace officers who stood with him made over one thousand arrests. For several years, until moving on to Austin, Hall roamed the region, apprehending robbers, horse thieves, and other miscreants.

He was well qualified by the summer of 1876 to be a Texas Ranger. Still, taking the decision out of McNelly's hands was an extraordinary step. "The naming of an outsider was in part a response to his declining health," writes Robert Utley.[99] "But it also reflected an increasing irritation with McNelly's disdain of such paperwork as muster rolls

---

98 During the Civil War, Hall's father, a physician, was the regimental surgeon for the Twenty-second North Carolina Infantry. While he was away, the family home was burned by Northern sympathizers.

99 One can be certain that word had reached Steele and the governor, and at least some members of the state legislature, that in the aftermath of the King Fisher mission, McNelly's men had noticed their captain coughing up blood.

and vouchers and of his habit of reporting his operations only sporadically and in scant detail."

This had indeed been a burr under the adjutant general's saddle for quite some time. McNelly had apparently made the mistake of dismissing Steele and his bureaucracy for too long. George Durham had pointed out that his captain "was sent in by the governor not to write reports, but to bring law to a lawless country, to prove Texas was bigger than any gang or gangs of bandits. Other Texas Ranger outfits had failed to halt banditry. So had the military. Captain said reports weren't what bandits needed. He held that a well-placed bullet from a Sharps did more for law enforcement than a hundred reports."

But like it or not, policing on the frontier was changing. And whatever the real reason for Hall's appointment, he had not been a longtime member of McNelly's Rangers like Sgt. Armstrong, who should have been the one promoted. How would the newcomer and the revered captain negotiate the new arrangement the legislature had thrust upon them?

The men not only cared deeply for their captain, they knew it was a two-way street. They were well aware by now of an interview McNelly had given in June to a reporter for *The San Antonio Express*. In it, he praised the men under his command, declaring that he "would not hesitate to compare my company with a similar number of men anywhere, in any respect, regarding their qualifications as soldiers." He cited some examples of their abilities, then concluded, "I can rely on my men."

The *Express* had also noted that "several of Capt.

McNelly's boys were in the city yesterday. They are well mounted men, and armed to the teeth."

It turned out that there would not be a longstanding or divisive issue of competing command. As the Rangers prepared for their next mission, it became clear that their captain was not likely to accompany them. "You could see that," observed Durham about the consumption overtaking their commander. "His cheek bones was sunk in. His straight shoulders drooped. And he was breathing in them short gaps. Only his eyes had any life about them now."

That August of 1876, McNelly's Rangers—but without McNelly—were camped just below Oakville. One afternoon a redheaded stranger rode into camp. Jennings and a few of the others had heard that Hall "was a hard man to deal with." However, "we soon discovered that he was a splendid fellow, full of fun, of charming manners, and only 'nasty' when dealing with outlaws."

When the man they would come to call Red Hall asked for a chew of tobacco, "We invited him to get down and have something to eat."

After a couple of weeks during which the lieutenant and the men of the company got used to each other, the Rangers were given their next assignment. Hall was to lead some men to Goliad, take over for a sheriff who had been suspended for malfeasance, and go out and catch the outlaws the lawman was supposed to have caught.

The torch was being passed. "In the opinion of many," write Parsons and Little, "McNelly had accomplished great things in the two-and-one-half years of service under Governor Richard Coke. He had prevented additional battles between the Sutton and Taylor forces in DeWitt County; he had recovered stolen stock from the Las Cuevas stronghold; he had arrested the notorious John King Fisher and his gang as well as dozens of other but lesser known outlaws. These actions, which only the desperadoes could find fault, had resulted in both statewide and national attention."

When his men decamped on their next mission, they missed Capt. McNelly. They knew he was at the Menger Hotel in San Antonio being tended to by his wife. Carey had restored her husband before, and the Rangers believed she would do so again. With any luck, this new mission would be successful, and upon their return, a stronger, smartly-dressed-as-usual Leander McNelly would be waiting for them.

CHAPTER 47

"THE BRAVE WHO SINK TO REST"

Acting Captain Lee Hall decided to try his hand at putting King Fisher behind bars and keeping him there.

However, back in Dimmit County, he and the other Rangers had even less luck. At least Leander McNelly had been able to round up a few witnesses. This time, no one was willing to provide solid testimony of the rancher's alleged crimes. Seeing how Fisher had so brazenly avoided the justice system a few months earlier only made his neighbors even more timid and forgetful.

Still, Hall tried. He managed to get the local legal system to issue twenty-two indictments against Fisher, among them charges of murder and horse theft. This strategy, while not the equivalent of a prison cell, would at least annoy King Fisher for a while and inspire him to keep his head down.

Gradually, the men came to accept Red Hall, despite his understated leadership. "Although an imposing figure, he lacked McNelly's flamboyance and swashbuckling independence," writes Robert Utley. "The public applauded McNelly, even for indiscretions that displeased his superiors." Hall knew about the comparisons, but he persevered.

Next for McNelly's Rangers and their temporary commanding officer was a sweep through the Eagle Pass area to enforce the warrants for as many outlaws as they could train their guns on. They repeated these actions in Laredo and Corpus Christi. Within a few weeks, jailers had their hands and cells full.

There was also another dustup with Mexican authorities. Hall and his company were dispatched to Rio Grande City to track down Segundo Garza, a bandit charged with murder whose brother Rafael had sprung him from jail. This mushroomed into an international incident when the brother and some twenty others fled into Mexico. This time, though, the U.S. military made sure there was no new Texas Rangers invasion.

The company, with John Armstrong as Hall's lieutenant, fulfilled McNelly's wish of returning to DeWitt County and finally bringing peace to it. After a physician, Philip Brazell, and his twelve-year-old son had been executed by a masked group of vigilantes, the company was sent in. In November 1876, Hall and his Rangers arrested seven men, two of them deputy sheriffs, for the murders.

It was with great joy that McNelly's Rangers welcomed their real captain back. McNelly had rallied ... but he looked more sickly than ever. Only the fierce gaze of his eyes was undiminished. He had arrived in Clinton not to retake command of his company but to volunteer to do whatever he could. With some awkwardness, Hall asked his predecessor and five Rangers to escort the DeWitt County prisoners.

Because he was Leander McNelly, the captain did more than provide an escort. George Durham, who had been part of it, described how the prisoners joked with each other that the arraignment wouldn't take long and soon they would be drinking in the nearest saloon. A few considered not even waiting that long.

"Captain McNelly stepped from a door in the back and stopped at the end of the Judge's bench," reported Durham, further noting:

> He carried in his right hand his service pistol, with the hammer back. He stood there till the talk stopped and things got quiet. Then he spoke in a voice that carried fairly well. "This court is now opening for regular business. Any man who lifts a hand to hamper its functions will die."
>
> He waited what seemed an awful long time. He turned his head slow, trying to look every man in the eye. Finally he half-turned and nodded, and Judge Pleasants came in.

According to N. A. Jennings's recollection, "I had my carbine in my hand and, like the others, I threw a cartridge into the breech and cocked the gun in plain sight of all in the court-room. Then we stood at 'ready' while Judge Pleasants addressed the crowd of men in the room.

With supreme dignity he stood and looked at them for a full minute before he spoke."

Though only one of the suspects wound up being convicted, the bold actions of the company—which had included arresting one of the accused during his wedding—had made enough of an impression that the family feud finally petered out.

McNelly's taking control of the courtroom in Clinton was to be his last hurrah.

As his company continued to go on new missions ordered by Adjutant General Steele, McNelly was still officially in charge. But it became painfully obvious that he was too weak to resume his command, and he and Carey relocated to Austin.

There, despite visits from physicians, her ministrations, and the presence of his children, his health continued to decline. Every so often, a messenger arrived at their hotel to update him on the adventures of McNelly's Rangers. He would write notes of encouragement back, but as the weeks went by, it became clear that their captain would not rejoin them.

As the nation's centennial year drew to a close—a year that had seen a much-disputed presidential election and the battle that would come to be called "Custer's Last Stand"—McNelly rested, trying to regain his strength. Bizarrely, several newspaper editorials encouraged him to run for public office, even governor. Note Parsons and Little, "Popular and respected as he may have been, McNelly entertained no thoughts towards seeking a political office; it was more important for him to know that honest citizens of various communities in South Texas felt more secure due to his work."

And then, at the end of January, it became official. First, Governor Richard Hubbard had the Ranger company mustered out, with the reason being the term of service of the Special State Troops had ended.[100] On February 1, 1877, a new twenty-four-man company was formed. As part of this transition, McNelly was retired. There were newspaper editorials criticizing William Steele for cutting off the state medical coverage of the loyal captain, but he weathered the storm, maintaining that McNelly's medical bills were draining too much of the company's budget. Soon, even McNelly's most ardent supporters knew he would not be back in the saddle anytime soon, or perhaps ever again.

As the months passed, McNelly's consumption worsened. He was, even friends recognized, a dying man. As though confirming that there would not be one more rally, McNelly and Carey made the decision to go home to their farm in Burton.

That summer, Carey characterized her husband's condition as "gradually sinking." Eventually, the number of people allowed to see him dwindled down to Carey, Leander Jr., and Irene McNelly, and a small handful of others. He fretted about his family's financial future. They had the farm, but not much else. When he had resigned

---

100 The McNelly supporter Richard Coke had traded being governor for the U.S. Senate. This had allowed the four-hundred-pound lieutenant governor, "Jumbo" Hubbard, to take over in Austin.

as commander of the company at the end of January, between his debts to the state and what the state owed him, McNelly had netted only $390.

He was probably not informed that toward the end of August a couple of newspapers had already reported him dead. Soon, though, there was truth to the reports. Leander McNelly, with his wife and children and other family members present, passed away at home on September 4, 1877, just thirty-three years of age.[101]

His friend, the newspaperman Alfred Belo, editor of *The Galveston Daily News* (who later founded *The Dallas Morning News*), had been one of the few allowed to see McNelly in his last days. Belo later informed readers that the captain "prayed earnestly and fervently to God for many months for Christian fortitude to bear all He saw fit to send upon him, and was prepared for death." Belo also described the actual death, reporting that McNelly appeared to look at something on the wall opposite his bed "with the greatest astonishment," and "a beautiful expression beamed from his dying eyes just before the last fleeting breath."

During the funeral service, Colonel Rip Ford praised McNelly for his devotion to Texas and to being a lawman, including that he was an "energetic officer of great ability." A procession took the captain's body to the Mount Zion Cemetery outside Burton, where he was buried.

---

101 One of those on hand was John McNelly, a nephew who was at the time a Texas Ranger.

Richard King was among those present. Four months later, he had a fifteen-foot-tall granite monument mounted over McNelly's grave. After providing the basic biographical information, the inscription concluded: "How sleep the brave who sink to rest, by all their country's wishes blest."

EPILOGUE

*Courageous and gentlemanly, utterly devoted to his men and
his mission, a remorseless killer, and dead himself by the holy
age of thirty-three. From McNelly flows the rich blood of
Ranger lore.*

—*Texas Monthly*

For the next several years, John Barclay Armstrong had a
distinguished career as a lawman, including participating
in the arrest of John Wesley Hardin (see below for details)
and the killing of the bank robber Sam Bass. He left the
Texas Rangers in 1881 to become a U.S. marshal. He established and lived on a ranch in Willacy County, where he
died at age sixty-three in May 1913.

Jesse Lee "Red" Hall served as captain of the former
McNelly's Rangers until 1880, when he married and turned
over command to T. L. Oglesby. Hall managed several
failed businesses, and in the mid-1880s, while overseeing
the Dull ranch, he became involved in the fighting during
the Fence Cutting War. He later served as an agent for the

Kiowa-Comanche-Apache and Wichita Reservations; he was indicted for embezzlement, but the charges were dismissed in 1888 for lack of evidence.

For the ensuing decade, Hall was engaged in several more businesses. With the outbreak of the Spanish-American War, he then raised two companies for service. He left the military in October 1900 and was chief of security for the Giroux Consolidated Mining Company. Afterward, he and his wife settled in San Antonio, where he died in 1911 at age sixty-one.

The gunslinging career of John Wesley Hardin finally ended on August 23, 1877, on a train stopped at a station in Pensacola, Florida. After a tip from an informant, Armstrong spotted the outlaw in the smoking car of a train. The Ranger was being helped by local law enforcement and had deputies placed at both ends of the car. When Armstrong and another lawman burst in with guns drawn, Hardin was caught by surprise. But he was quick on the draw as usual . . . well, almost.

The gun caught in Hardin's fashionable suspenders that were holding up his pants. This gaffe allowed the lawmen the crucial few seconds they needed and probably saved Hardin's life—instead of shooting him, Armstrong clubbed Hardin to the floor, and he was soon in handcuffs.

Technically, the Texas Rangers had no authority in Florida. Nevertheless, with the help of the local lawmen, Armstrong took a chained-up Hardin back to Texas on the next train.

Four years after it had taken place, Hardin was tried for the murder of the deputy sheriff Charles Webb, and he was convicted. On June 5, 1878, he was sentenced to serve twenty-five years in the Huntsville prison. The following year, Hardin, not content to do his time, was caught along with some fifty other convicts as they were trying to tunnel out of the prison. Undaunted, he made several other attempts to escape. Meanwhile, the law was not quite finished with him. On February 14, 1892, Hardin was convicted of another manslaughter charge and given a two-year sentence to be served concurrently with his unexpired twenty-five-year sentence.

Finally accepting his home would be Huntsville for quite a while, Hardin began reading theological books. After becoming the superintendent of the prison Sunday school, he began a study of the law. Hardin ended up with more leisure time than anticipated to do this when, in 1883, the shotgun wound he had received in Trinity became reinfected, and he was bedridden for almost two years. He was still in prison in November 1892, when his wife, Jane, died. Perhaps this prompted periods of reflection because Hardin set out to write an autobiography. When it was published, it would be faulted for inventing or at least embellishing stories of his outlaw exploits.

After serving almost sixteen years of the original twenty-five-year sentence, Hardin was released from prison in February 1894. He was only forty years old when he set foot again in Gonzales. He must have presented a good argument that he had completely reformed because the governor of Texas, "Big Jim" Hogg, pardoned Hardin the following month. Next up was making a living. He had learned enough about the law while behind bars that in July of that year he passed the state's bar examination and obtained a license to practice law.

Also on the post-prison to-do list was remarrying. This did not go as well as the bar exam—his new wife, Callie Lewis, had just turned fifteen years old. The twenty-six-year age gap between her and Hardin quickly doomed the union, and the groom relocated to El Paso.[102]

The following year, Hardin found trouble with the law again. An El Paso lawman, John Selman Jr., arrested a female acquaintance of Hardin's for brandishing a gun in public. He confronted Selman, and the two men argued. Some accounts state that Hardin pistol-whipped the younger man. Selman's fifty-six-year-old father, Constable John Selman Sr. (himself a notorious gunman and former outlaw), approached Hardin on the afternoon of August 19, 1895, and the two men exchanged heated words.

That night, Hardin went to the Acme Saloon, where he began playing dice. Shortly before midnight, Selman Sr. entered the saloon, walked up to Hardin from behind, and shot him in the head, killing him instantly. Just to be sure, as Hardin lay on the floor, Selman fired three more shots into him. Hardin was buried the next day in the Concordia Cemetery.[103]

---

102 Callie would marry again in 1898, to Perry Allen Baze, and have a long life, passing away in 1963 at eighty-four in Mason County.
103 Hardin rested in peace for a century. Then, in August 1995, there was a confrontation between two groups at the site of his grave. One group, representing several of Hardin's great-grandchildren, sought to relocate his body to Nixon so it could be interred next to the grave of his first wife, Jane. The other group, consisting of El Paso citizens, sought to prevent the move. During the confrontation, Hardin's descendants presented a

Understandably, Selman Sr. was arrested for murder. At his trial, he claimed self-defense. He did not contend that the back of Hardin's head was about to attack his pistol; rather, Selman said, he saw Hardin attempting to draw his own gun. This was persuasive enough that there was a hung jury. A new jury was never convened, but their services would not be needed: Before Selman was returned for trial, he was killed in a shootout with U.S. Marshal George Scarborough during an argument following a card game.

The talking-to by Leander McNelly and the aggravation of the legal proceedings of Lee Hall appear to have had a profound impact on John King Fisher. He became a solid citizen and, more incredibly, a lawman.

In May 1881, the last of the charges against Fisher was dropped because of insufficient evidence. Two months later, he was acquitted of horse stealing in Laredo. He could now do as he pleased. But instead of returning to the life of a criminal empresario, King and Sarah and their family settled down.

His lawman career began in 1883, when he was the acting sheriff of Uvalde County. On his watch there was a stagecoach robbery. Fisher tracked down the two suspects, Tom and Jim Hannehan. When the brothers resisted arrest, Fisher shot and killed Tom, and Jim surrendered. The acting sheriff turned him in as well as the money stolen from the stagecoach.

---

disinterment permit for the body, while the locals presented a court order prohibiting its removal. Both sides accused the other parties of seeking tourist revenue. A subsequent lawsuit resulted in a ruling to keep what was left of John Wesley Hardin where he was.

In March of the following year, while in San Antonio, Fisher ran into Ben Thompson, a well-known gambler and gunfighter.[104] The two men had crossed paths before and decided to renew their friendship by attending a play at the Turner Hall Opera House and, afterward, a show at the Vaudeville Variety Theater. Fisher was unaware that the theater's owner, Joe Foster, had sworn vengeance against Thompson for the killing of his friend Jack Harris.

During the show, a local lawman named Jacob Coy sat with the two reunited friends. Thompson decided that he wanted to meet with Foster to clear the air, and Foster soon came down from his office. While some of the details have never been sorted out, the bottom line is that an ambush had been arranged. Suddenly, gunfire erupted from another theater box. Both Thompson and Fisher were hit. Thompson fell onto his side, and either Coy or Foster ran up to him and shot him in the head, killing him. Fisher was shot thirteen times, but managed to fire one round in retaliation, wounding Coy and crippling him for life. While drawing his pistol, Foster shot himself in the leg. It was soon amputated, but he died anyway.

Attempts to save King Fisher's life were unsuccessful. His body was taken to his ranch and buried there, in a tear-shaped casket. His distraught widow, Sarah, held on to the

---

104 For the full story of Ben Thompson's career and his friendship with Bat Masterson, grab a copy of *Dodge City: Wyatt Earp, Bat Masterson, and the Wickedest Town in the American West.*

ranch for as long as she could. She died in Carrizo Springs in August 1946, age eighty-nine.

As a young adult, Leander Rebel McNelly worked a variety of jobs . . . until he landed on the wrong side of the law. In 1891, he was charged with robbery, assault, and intent to murder a man in Brenham. He pled guilty to reduced charges and served less than the two years he was sentenced, thanks to a pardon from Gov. Hogg.[105] By then, Rebel was suffering from the symptoms of the same disease that had killed his father. He succumbed to tuberculosis on New Year's Day, 1907, in Tombstone, Arizona. He was buried in Austin's Oakwood Cemetery, where his mother would eventually join him.

Irene McNelly outlived her father by less than seven years. She was attending Baylor College in Washington County, when, in May 1884, at just sixteen years old, she was killed in a prank gone terribly wrong. Irene was standing on a chair, and another student yanked it out from under her. Her injuries proved to be fatal. Irene was buried next to her father.

Leander McNelly was right to be concerned about his wife's financial future. Carey struggled to hold on to the farm in Burton, but in 1895 she either lost or sold it. She relocated to Austin and obtained a position as a clerk in the State Land Office. In 1901, she became a member of the Albert Sidney Johnston chapter of the Texas

---

105 One of Rebel's acquaintances in the Huntsville prison was John Wesley Hardin.

Daughters of the Confederacy.[106] And eight years later, at age fifty-two, she married William Wroe, who had served in the Fifth Texas Cavalry during the war.

Carey became a widow again in 1933, when William Wroe died. Four years later, she entered the Women's Confederate Home in Austin. She died there in October 1938, age ninety, having outlived both her children and both her husbands.

During World War II, the liberty ship *L. H. McNelly* was named in the former captain's honor. And in 1976 Leander McNelly was a member of the first class inducted into the Texas Ranger Hall of Fame.

---

106 In 1945, the Carey McNelly Wroe chapter of the Children of the Confederacy would be established in San Antonio.

ACKNOWLEDGMENTS

I have long maintained that without librarians and curators at research centers I would not have a career. I mean this most sincerely. Once more, this time with *Follow Me to Hell,* my thanks go to those at libraries and historical societies in Texas and elsewhere who helped me along the arduous research road and whose unflagging courtesy made the trek less difficult. In particular, I want to express my gratitude to the Texas State Library and Archives Commission and the Tobin and Anne Armstrong Texas Ranger Research Center at the Texas Ranger Hall of Fame.

I am always both delighted and humbled by the expertise and enthusiasm of research professionals. Several I would like to cite are Raymond Bloxom, Shelly Crittendon, David Johnson, Tammy Murphy, Mark Phillips, Christina Stopka, Roy Young, and especially Ann Gaines Rodriguez. And I am grateful for the courtesy of Chuck

Parsons. Closer to home, I am also grateful for the efforts of staffers at the John Jermain Memorial Library for their longstanding assistance and kindness.

A special thanks also to Dr. Watson Arnold—and Heyward Taylor, for introducing us—who gave the manuscript a careful read and alerted me to errors. The ones that still managed to slip through are my responsibility.

This book would not have originated, let alone been completed, without the encouragement and steadfast support of my editor, Marc Resnick. Others at St. Martin's Press who have also made the journey a happy and productive one include Sally Richardson, Andy Martin, Rebecca Lang, Danielle Prielipp, Tracy Guest, Rob Grom, and Lily Cronig. Another "founder" of *Follow Me to Hell* is Nat Sobel, a friend as well as agent, and I appreciate everything done for me by his staff, especially Adia Wright.

My dear friends continue to wait for me to not work so much so we can get together more often. The support of Mike, Tony, John, Bob, Heather, Ed, Joe, another Bob, Ken, Lynne, Dave, Randye, Lisa, Maureen, and a bunch of others is a big reason why every day matters. And finally, my love to Leslie, Katy and James, Vivienne, and Edna, and another James for . . . well, keeping me in their lives.

SELECTED BIBLIOGRAPHY

BOOKS

Alexander, Bob. *Winchester Warriors: Texas Rangers of Company D, 1874–1901*. Denton: University of North Texas Press, 2009.

Alexander, Bob, and Donaly E. Brice. *Texas Rangers: Lives, Legend, and Legacy*. Denton: University of North Texas Press, 2017.

Alonzo, Armando C. *Tejano Legacy: Rancheros and Settlers in South Texas, 1734–1900*. Albuquerque: University of New Mexico Press, 1998.

Anderson, John Q., ed. *Tales of Frontier Texas, 1830–1860*. Dallas: Southern Methodist University Press, 1966.

Arnold, James R. *Jeff Davis's Own: Cavalry, Comanches, and the Battle for the Texas Frontier*. New York: John Wiley, 2000.

Barton, Henry W. *Texas Volunteers in the Mexican War*. Waco: Texian Press, 1970.

Bauer, K. Jack. *The Mexican War, 1846–1848*. New York: Macmillan, 1974.

Brice, Donaly E. *The Great Comanche Raid: Boldest Indian Attack of the Texas Republic*. Austin: Eakin Press, 1987.

Campbell, Randolph B. *Gone to Texas: A History of the Lone Star State*. New York: Oxford University Press, 2003.

Cantrell, Gregg. *Stephen F. Austin: Empresario of Texas*. New Haven: Yale University Press, 1999.

Collins, Michael L. *Texas Devils: Rangers and Regulars on the Lower Rio Grande, 1846–1861*. Norman: University of Oklahoma Press, 2008.

Cox, Mike. *The Texas Rangers*. Vol. I, *Wearing the Cinco Peso, 1821–1900*. New York: Forge Books, 2008.

Cummins, Merle. *A Gun in Every Hand: John Wesley Hardin and the Texas Rangers*. Xlibris, 2006.

Cutrer, Thomas W. *Ben McCulloch and the Frontier Military Tradition*. Chapel Hill: University of North Carolina Press, 1993.

Day, Jack Hays. *The Sutton-Taylor Feud*. San Antonio: Sid Murray and Son, 1937.

DeShields, James T. *Border Wars of Texas*. Austin: State House Press, 1993.

Dukes, Doug. *Firearms of the Texas Rangers: From the Frontier Era to the Modern Age*. Denton: University of North Texas Press, 2020.

Durham, George, as told to Clyde Wantland. *Taming the Nueces Strip: The Story of McNelly's Rangers*. Austin: University of Texas Press, 1962.

Duval, John C. *The Adventures of Big-Foot Wallace: The Texas Ranger and Hunter*. Lincoln: University of Nebraska Press, 1966.

Emmett, Chris. *Shanghai Pierce: A Fair Likeness*. Norman: University of Oklahoma Press, 1953.

Farrow, Marion Humphreys. *Troublesome Times in Texas*. San Antonio: Naylor Company, 1959.

Fehrenbach, T. R. *Comanches: The Destruction of a People*. New York: Da Capo, 1994.

Fisher, O. C., with J. C. Dykes. *King Fisher: His Life and Times*. Norman: University of Oklahoma Press, 1966.

Ford, John Salmon. *Rip Ford's Texas*. Edited by Stephen B. Oates. Austin: University of Texas Press, 1987.

Garst, Shannon. *Big Foot Wallace of the Texas Rangers*. New York: Julian Messner, 1952.

Gillett, James B. *Six Years with the Texas Rangers, 1875 to 1881*. New Haven: Yale University Press, 1925.

Glasrud, Bruce A., and Harold J. Weiss, Jr., eds. *Tracking the Texas Rangers: The Nineteenth Century*. Denton: University of North Texas Press, 2012.

Goebel, Patsy, and Rosemary Sheppard, eds. *The History of DeWitt County, Texas*. Dallas: Curtis Media Company, 1991.

González-Quiroga, Miguel Ángel. *War and Peace on the Rio Grande Frontier, 1830–1880*. Norman: University of Oklahoma Press, 2020.

Greer, James K. *Colonel Jack Hays: Texas Frontier Leader and California Builder*. College Station: Texas A&M University Press, 1987.

Guinn, Jeff. *War on the Border: Villa, Pershing, the Texas Rangers, and an American Invasion*. New York: Simon & Schuster, 2021.

Gwynne, S. C. *Empire of the Summer Moon: Quanah Parker and the Rise and Fall of the Comanches, the Most Powerful Indian Tribe in American History*. New York: Scribner, 2010.

Hardin, John Wesley. *The Life of John Wesley Hardin*. Norman: University of Oklahoma Press, 1961.

Hardin, Stephen L. *Texian Iliad: A Military History of the Texas Revolution, 1835–1836*. Austin: University of Texas Press, 1994.

Hatley, Allen G. *The Indian Wars in Stephen F. Austin's Colony, 1822–1835*. Austin: Eakin Press, 2001.

Haynes, Sam W. *Soldiers of Misfortune: The Somervell and Mier Expeditions*. Austin: University of Texas Press, 1990.

Ivey, Darren L. *The Ranger Ideal*. Vol. 1, *Texas Rangers in the Hall of Fame, 1823–1861*. Denton: University of North Texas Press, 2017.

———. *The Ranger Ideal*. Vol. 2, *Texas Rangers in the Hall of Fame, 1874–1930*. Denton: University of North Texas Press, 2018.

Jennings, N. A. *A Texas Ranger*. Norman: University of Oklahoma Press, 1977.

Knowles, Thomas W. *They Rode for the Lone Star: The Saga of the Texas Rangers*. Lanham, MD: Taylor Trade Publishing, 1999.

Lea, Tom. *The King Ranch*. Boston: Little, Brown, 1957.

McComb, David G. *Texas: A Modern History*. Austin: University of Texas Press, 1989.

McGiffin, Lee. *Ten Tall Texans: Tales of the Texas Rangers*. New York: Lee and Shepard, 1956.

Metz, Leon. *John Wesley Hardin: Dark Angel of Texas*. El Paso: Mangan Books, 1996.

Moneyhon, Carl H. *Texas after the Civil War: The Struggle of Reconstruction*. College Station: Texas A&M University Press, 2004.

Moore, Stephen L. *Savage Frontier: Rangers, Riflemen, and Indian Wars in Texas*. Vol. 1. Denton: University of North Texas Press, 2010.

Nelson, Megan Kate. *The Three-Cornered War: The Union, the Confederacy and Native Peoples in the Fight for the West*. New York: Scribner, 2020.

Nunn, William Curtis. *Texas Under the Carpetbaggers*. Austin: University of Texas Press, 1962.

Oates, Stephen B. *Visions of Glory: Texans on the Southwestern Frontier*. Norman: University of Oklahoma Press, 1970.

Parsons, Chuck, and Marianne E. Hall Little. *Captain L. H. McNelly, Texas Ranger: The Life and Times of a Fighting Man*. Austin: State House Press, 2001.

Parsons, Chuck. *"Pidge": A Texas Ranger from Virginia*. Wolfe City, TX: Henington Publishing Company, 1985.

Robinson, Charles M., III. *The Men Who Wear the Star: The Story of the Texas Rangers*. New York: Random House, 2000.

Smith, David Paul. *Frontier Defense in the Civil War: Texas Rangers and Rebels*. College Station: Texas A&M University Press, 1992.

Smith, F. Todd. *From Dominance to Disappearance: The Indians of Texas and the Near Southwest, 1786–1859*. Lincoln: University of Nebraska Press, 2005.

Smithwick, Noah. *The Evolution of a State, or, Recollections of Old Texas Days*. Independently published, 2016.

Sonnichsen, C. L. *I'll Die Before I'll Run: The Story of the Great Feuds of Texas*. Lincoln: University of Nebraska Press, 1961.

———. *Ten Texas Feuds*. Albuquerque: University of New Mexico Press, 1957.

Sowell, A. J. *Life of "Big Foot" Wallace: The Great Ranger Captain*. Austin: State House Press, 1989.

Swanson, Doug J. *Cult of Glory: The Bold and Brutal History of the Texas Rangers*. New York: Viking, 2020.

Thompson, Jerry. *Confederate General of the West: Henry Hopkins Sibley*. College Station: Texas A&M University Press, 1996.

———. *Juan Cortina and the Texas-Mexico Frontier, 1859–1877*. El Paso: Texas Western Press, 1994.

Tijerina, Andrés. *Tejano Empire: Life on the South Texas Ranches*. College Station: Texas A&M University Press, 1998.

Utley, Robert M. *Lone Star Justice: The First Century of the Texas Rangers*. New York: Oxford University Press, 2002.

Vestal, Stanley. *Big Foot Wallace: Texas Indian Fighter*. Cambridge, MA: Riverside Press, 1942.

Webb, Walter Prescott. *The Texas Rangers: A Century of Frontier Defense*. Austin: University of Texas Press, 1965.

Wilkins, Frederick. *Defending the Borders: The Texas Rangers, 1848–1861*. Austin: State House Press, 2001.

———. *The Law Comes to Texas: The Texas Rangers, 1870–1901*. Austin: State House Press, 1999.

———. *The Legend Begins: The Texas Rangers, 1823–1845*. Austin: State House Press, 1996.

Wooster, Ralph A. *Texas and Texans in the Civil War*. Austin: Eakin Press, 1995.

ARTICLES

Boggs, Johnny D. "On the Trail to Texas Statehood." *True West,* December 2020.

Dodson, Ruth. "The Noakes Raid." *Frontier Times,* July 1946.

Friberg, Ben. "Too Brave to Die." *True West,* May 2020.

Hagen, William. "The Nuecestown Raid of 1875: A Border Incident." *Arizona and the West,* Autumn 1959.

Lea, Tom. "Captain King of Texas: The Man Who Made the King Ranch." *The Atlantic,* April 1957.

Rosebrook, Stuart. "The Real Texas Rangers Armed and Dangerous." *True West,* May 2020.

Singletary, Otis A. "The Texas Militia during Reconstruction." *The Southwestern Historical Quarterly,* July 1956.

COLLECTIONS

Leander H. McNelly Papers: Albert and Ethel Herzstein Library, San Jacinto Museum of History, La Porte, TX.

Panhandle-Plains Historical Museum, Canyon, TX.

Texas Adjutant General's Department Ranger Records, Austin.

Texas Department of Public Safety, Austin.

Texas Historical Commission, Austin.

Texas Ranger Hall of Fame and Museum, Waco.

Texas State Historical Association, University of North Texas, Denton.

Texas State Library and Archives Commission, Austin.

NEWSPAPERS

The Advertiser (Bastrop)
Daily Commercial (Dallas)
The Daily Democratic Statesman (Austin)
The Daily Express (San Antonio)
The Daily Herald (San Antonio)
The Daily News (Galveston)
The Daily Republican (St. Louis)
The Daily State Journal (Austin)
The New York Herald
The Weekly Herald (Dallas)
The Weekly State Gazette (Austin)
The Weekly State Journal (Austin)

INDEX

Turn the page for a sneak peek at
Tom Clavin's new book

BANDIT HEAVEN

Available Fall 2024

The train station in Wilcox served the Union Pacific line. It was in the southern part of Wyoming and about ninety-five miles northwest of Cheyenne. Early in the morning of June 2, 1899, a gang known as the Wild Bunch planned to rob the No. 1 Overland Limited as it approached the station.

And that is what happened—but not exactly as planned.

It was 2:18 A.M. when W. R. Jones, the train's engineer, spotted a man standing beside the tracks waving a red lantern. For a moment, Jones, who had earned the nickname "Grindstone," hesitated. Bandits were known to do this as a trick to get a train to stop unnecessarily. But if there was a legitimate reason to stop, such as track damage ahead, and the engineer did not, the result could be catastrophic. He was not one to take chances.

He ordered the train to halt. For the right reason, he made the wrong choice. But it turned out not to matter. He would have stopped the train anyway when he caught sight of the man crawling over the coal tender and into the engine. The man held a pistol pointed at Grindstone. This was infinitely more persuasive than a lantern of any color.

To emphasize that, the man said, "Do what I say, you son of a bitch, or I will put light through you." Grindstone's guess at who the man was would be confirmed later that day: Butch Cassidy.

Immediately after the train stopped, four other men appeared trackside. One was George "Flat Nose" Curry. The other three were related: Bob Lee and his cousins, the brothers Lonie and Harvey Logan. The latter was more familiar to lawmen as Kid Curry. The man who had been swinging the lantern would be identified as Harry Longabaugh, who also had a juvenile nickname—the Sundance Kid. All six men, Grindstone noted, his dismay deepening, had long masks covering their faces, and each carried a Winchester rifle in addition to a Colt pistol.[1]

The plan, so far, was working perfectly. It would soon dawn on the passengers that the train stopping short of the Wilcox station might mean a robbery was in progress, and to be on the safe side, they would stay glued to their seats. The wild card in the Wild Bunch was always Kid Curry. He had a hair-trigger temper and could be unpredictable. Cassidy had to keep him on a short rein, and usually, he followed the plan.

As Cassidy had rehearsed with his crew, Grindstone Jones and his fireman were hauled down from the engine and escorted along the tracks to the mail car. Then the first deviation from the plan occurred: the men inside refused to open up. The mail car door remained fixed and locked even after Cassidy had shouted that they had two hostages and the gang had fired bullets into the car.

The second deviation caused even more consternation

---

1 At the time, there was a chain of restaurants founded twenty-three years earlier by Fred Harvey to cater to the growing number of train passengers. Members of the gang had most likely dined there before the robbery, because their masks were cloth napkins pilfered from a Harvey House.

to Cassidy: the lights of another Overland Limited train came into view, traveling toward them. Now what?

Cassidy wasn't keen on giving up just yet. He ordered his men to hop back on the train, and Grindstone Jones and the fireman were pushed back up into the engine compartment. Cassidy knew this section of track and that about a mile ahead was a gully where a bridge had recently been built spanning it. He had the train travel to the other side of it. Then, as it idled, billowing smoke disappearing into the dark sky, Cassidy ran back to the bridge. A minute later, an explosion of ten pounds of gunpowder turned it into a precarious structure that no train should risk crossing.

Thus far, Butch Cassidy had been such a cool customer that no one would guess this was his very first train robbery.

Cassidy told Jones to get the train rolling again. This he did, but the engine struggled a bit on an upgrade. As he nervously adjusted the controls, the engineer heard one of the men say, "I'll fix you!" With that, Kid Curry clunked Jones on the head with his Colt pistol. He went to strike again, but this time Jones deflected the blow with his hand. There would not be a third time—Cassidy told the Kid, "Calm down or you'll kill someone." So far in his criminal career, Cassidy had avoided doing that, and he was not about to start now.

Several miles later, the train stopped. Cassidy and his crew had to get back to work on that mail car. He could not know that the plan would go awry in another way, and that it would result in a death. The victim would be Josiah Hazen. The sheriff of Converse County would soon be pulling a posse together to chase the bandits down. The forty-four-year-old Illinois native had been the county sheriff for two years, and he and his wife had two young sons. Capturing any one member of the notorious Wild Bunch, possibly a few, would mean accolades showered on the determined lawman.

Instead, after Kid Curry killed him, Hazen received one of the largest funerals Converse County had ever seen, presided over by J. DeForest Richards, the governor of Wyoming. News of the sheriff's murder and the burial in the Pioneer Cemetery made headlines across America, which in turn inspired a push by lawmen to once and for all round up the gangs who called Bandit Heaven home.

The famous Pinkerton National Detective Agency was part of that effort. It assigned the best man they had, Charlie Siringo, to track down Butch Cassidy, Kid Curry, the Sundance Kid, and the others. Others, like Joe Lefors and Tom Horn, would be in on the pursuit too.

But Butch Cassidy was confident he could outwit and outrun any lawman. First, though, he and his gang had to finish this Wilcox train job. And that mail car door was still shut tight. He signaled to Sundance that it was time for more dynamite. . . .

Gordon M. Grant

TOM CLAVIN is a #1 *New York Times* bestselling author and has worked as a newspaper editor, magazine writer, TV and radio commentator, and reporter for *The New York Times*. He has received awards from the Society of Professional Journalists, the Marine Corps Heritage Foundation, and the National Newspaper Association. His books include the bestselling Frontier Lawmen trilogy—*Wild Bill, Dodge City*, and *Tombstone*—and, with coauthor Bob Drury, *Blood and Treasure* and *The Last Hill*. He lives in Sag Harbor, New York.

Investing in Cryptocurrency

by Kiana Danial

Investing in Cryptocurrency For Dummies®

Published by: **John Wiley & Sons, Inc.,** 111 River Street, Hoboken, NJ 07030-5774, www.wiley.com

Copyright © 2023 by John Wiley & Sons, Inc., Hoboken, New Jersey

Published simultaneously in Canada

For general information on our other products and services, please contact our Customer Care Department within the U.S. at 877-762-2974, outside the U.S. at 317-572-3993, or fax 317-572-4002. For technical support, please visit https://hub.wiley.com/community/support/dummies.

Wiley publishes in a variety of print and electronic formats and by print-on-demand. Some material included with standard print versions of this book may not be included in e-books or in print-on-demand. If this book refers to media such as a CD or DVD that is not included in the version you purchased, you may download this material at http://booksupport.wiley.com. For more information about Wiley products, visit www.wiley.com.

Library of Congress Control Number: 2023941888

ISBN 978-1-394-20083-2 (pbk); ISBN 978-1-394-20085-6 (ebk); ISBN 978-1-394-20084-9 (ebk)

SKY10051365_071823

Contents at a Glance

Table of Contents

Introduction

More than 20,000 cryptocurrencies currently exist at the time of writing, ten times more than the number of cryptocurrencies that existed in 2018. It's likely that the number will continue growing in the coming years.

Cryptos gained their first round of mainstream hype in 2017, when Bitcoin's value increased by 1,318 percent. This surge was nothing compared to the gains of some other digital assets, such as Ripple, which went up (hold your breath) a whopping 36,018 percent! These returns are more than what a stock investor could normally make in a lifetime, and they generated enough interest to create a true frenzy.

However, the bubble burst at the beginning of 2018, leaving many late investors, who bought cryptocurrencies at a very high price, at a loss. That was enough for some newbie investors to label the whole industry a scam and either give up on investing altogether or go back to traditional financial assets like stocks.

Regardless, the cryptocurrency market continued evolving, became more stable, and caught the attention and support of many major financial institutions in the United States and globally. As more people get their hands on cryptocurrencies, more sellers feel comfortable accepting them as a payment method, and that's how the whole industry can flourish.

For instance, after the 2018 crash, Bitcoin, along with other cryptocurrencies, continued their roller-coaster ride: Bitcoin gained another 1,903 percent from 2019 to 2021 and then crashed again to just above its highest price from back in 2017.

Investors who continued holding Bitcoin throughout the years, and continued dollar cost averaging without panic selling, are likely still in a profitable position. But many more sold at a loss, turning against this new category of financial assets altogether, and reverted back to their old methods of investing or not investing at all.

The foundation of cryptocurrencies such as Bitcoin lies in a relatively new technology called *blockchain* (the infrastructure that cryptocurrencies are built on). Blockchain is a disruptive technology that many argue is bigger than the advent of the internet. The applications of blockchain don't end with cryptocurrencies, though, just like the applications of the internet don't end with email.

The unique thing about cryptocurrency investing and trading is that a crypto is a cross between an asset (like stocks) and a currency (like the U.S. dollar). Analyzing the fundamentals behind a cryptocurrency is typically very different from analyzing any other financial asset. The traditional ways of measuring value don't work in the crypto industry, mainly because, in many cases, the crypto data isn't stored in a central hub somewhere. In fact, most cryptocurrencies and their underlying blockchains are *decentralized*, which means no central authority is in charge. Instead, the power is distributed among the members of any given blockchain or crypto community.

About This Book

You may have heard of some of the famous cryptocurrencies, like Bitcoin, but the industry doesn't end there — far from it. And although the crypto market has a ton of volatility, it also has the potential for you to make real money by investing wisely and developing strategies that suit your personal risk tolerance. In this book, I tap into the risks involved in cryptocurrency investing and show you the different methods you can use to get involved.

The topic of cryptocurrencies and their underlying blockchain technologies can be a bit confusing. That's why I try my best to keep this book easily accessible and relatable, and free of intimidating terminology. But it does contain some serious information about strategy development, risk management, and the whole industry in general.

As you dip into and out of this book, feel free to skip the sidebars (shaded boxes) and the paragraphs marked with the Technical Stuff icon. They contain interesting information but aren't essential to becoming a crypto investor.

This book contains a lot of web addresses to steer you toward additional information about certain topics. Some of the web addresses are affiliate links, meaning that if you click them and start using a company's services through that specific web address, I may earn an affiliate payment for making the introduction.

You also may note that some web addresses break across two lines of text. If you're reading this book in print and you want to visit one of these web pages, simply key in the web address exactly as it's noted in the text, pretending as though the line break doesn't exist. If you're reading this work as an e-book, you've got it easy: Click the web address to be taken directly to the web page — just like magic!

Foolish Assumptions

I've made some assumptions about you and your basic knowledge of investing and the cryptocurrency market:

» You may have heard of or even own some cryptocurrencies, but you don't really know how they work.

» Though you may have invested in other markets like the stock market before, you aren't necessarily familiar with the terminology and the technical aspects of trading and investing in cryptocurrencies.

» You know how to operate a computer and use the internet. If you don't have high-speed access to the internet now, be sure you have it before trying to get involved in the cryptocurrency market. You need high-speed access to be able to work with many of the valuable online tools I recommend in this book.

Icons Used in This Book

For Dummies books use little pictures, called *icons*, to mark certain chunks of text. Here's what they mean:

If something is particularly important for you to take away from this book, I mark it with this icon.

REMEMBER

TIP

Watch for these little flags to get ideas on how to improve your crypto-investing skills or where to find other useful resources.

WARNING

The cryptocurrency market and investing in general have many risks. Some mistakes can cost you a ton of money, so I use this icon to point out particularly dangerous areas.

TECHNICAL STUFF

This icon designates some interesting facts and sometimes funny anecdotes that I feel you may enjoy reading but that aren't essential to your crypto-investing journey.

Where to Go from Here

What you're holding in your hands isn't your typical book, where you start from the beginning and read through to the end. Depending on your interest, knowledge on the matter, and investment goals, you can start anywhere you want. For example,

>> If you're already familiar with cryptocurrency basics and know how they work, where to buy them, and where to securely store them, you may want to start with Part 3 to explore different investment and trading tactics.

>> Chapter 15 gives you an overview of things to consider before you start your cryptocurrency journey and cross-references to other chapters if you need further information.

>> Chapter 3 is a great (and essential) place to explore methods of risk management before pulling the trigger and jumping on the crypto wagon.

1

Getting Started with Cryptocurrencies

Know what you're getting into before buying, investing, or trading cryptocurrencies.

Check out the perks of cryptocurrency investing, and understand the risks involved in the cryptocurrency market and how to manage them.

Discover how *blockchain* (the underlying technology behind cryptocurrencies) makes them unique and revolutionary.

Familiarize yourself with how different types of cryptocurrencies operate.

Chapter **1**

Introducing the World of Cryptocurrencies

So, you've picked up this book, and your first question is probably this: "What the heck is a cryptocurrency, anyway?" Simply stated, a *cryptocurrency* is a new form of digital money. You can transfer your traditional, non-cryptocurrency money like the U.S. dollar digitally, but that's not quite the same as how cryptocurrencies work. When some cryptocurrencies become mainstream, you may be able to use them to pay for stuff electronically, just as you do with traditional currencies.

However, what sets cryptocurrencies apart is the technology behind them. You may say, "Who cares about the technology behind my money? I only care about how much of it there is in my wallet!" The issue is that the world's current money systems have a bunch of problems. Here are some examples:

» Payment systems such as credit cards and wire transfers are outdated.

» In most cases, a bunch of intermediaries, such as banks and brokers, take a cut in the process, making transactions expensive and slow.

>> Financial inequality is growing around the globe.

>> Your assets could be confiscated.

>> Around 3 billion unbanked or underbanked people can't access financial services. That's a big chunk of the planet's population!

Cryptocurrencies aim to solve some of these problems, if not more. This chapter introduces you to crypto fundamentals.

Beginning with the Basics of Cryptocurrencies

You know how your everyday, government-based currency is reserved in banks? And that you need an ATM or a connection to a bank to get more of it or transfer it to other people? Well, with cryptocurrencies, you may be able to get rid of banks and other centralized intermediaries altogether. That's because cryptocurrencies rely on a technology called *blockchain*, which is *decentralized* (meaning no single entity is in charge of it). Instead, every computer in the network confirms the transactions. Turn to Chapter 4 to find out more about the blockchain technology that enables cool things like cryptocurrencies.

In the following sections, I go over the basics of cryptocurrencies: their background, benefits, and more.

The definition of money

REMEMBER

Before getting into the nitty-gritty of cryptocurrencies, you need to understand the definition of money itself. The philosophy behind money is a bit like the whole "Which came first: the chicken or the egg?" thing. In order for money to be valuable, it must have a number of characteristics, such as the following:

>> Enough people must have it.

>> Merchants must accept it as a form of payment.

>> Society must trust that it's valuable and that it will remain valuable in the future.

Of course, in the old days, when you traded your chicken for shoes, the values of the exchanged materials were inherent to their nature. But when coins, cash, and credit cards came into play, the definition of money and, more important, the trust model of money changed.

Another key change in money has been its ease of transaction. The hassle of carrying a ton of gold bars from one country to another was one of the main reasons cash was invented. Then, when people got even lazier, credit cards were invented. But credit cards carry the money that your government controls. As the world becomes more interconnected and more concerned about authorities who may or may not have people's best interests in mind, cryptocurrencies may offer a valuable alternative.

TECHNICAL STUFF

Here's a fun fact: Your normal, government-backed currency, such as the U.S. dollar, must go by its fancy name, *fiat currency*, now that cryptocurrencies are around. Fiat is described as a legal tender like coins and banknotes that have value only because the government says so.

Some cryptocurrency history

The first-ever cryptocurrency was (drumroll, please) Bitcoin! You've probably heard of Bitcoin more than any other thing in the crypto industry. Bitcoin was the first product of the first blockchain developed by some anonymous entity who went by the name Satoshi Nakamoto. Satoshi released the idea of Bitcoin in 2008 and described it as a "purely peer-to-peer version" of electronic money.

TECHNICAL STUFF

Bitcoin was the first established cryptocurrency, but many attempts at creating digital currencies occurred years before Bitcoin was formally introduced.

Cryptocurrencies like Bitcoin are created through a process called *mining*. Very different from mining gold, mining cryptocurrencies involves powerful computers solving complicated problems.

Bitcoin remained the only cryptocurrency until 2011. Then Bitcoin enthusiasts started noticing flaws in it, so they decided to create alternative coins, also known as *altcoins,* to improve Bitcoin's design for things like speed, security, anonymity, and more. Among the first altcoins was Litecoin, which aimed to become the silver to Bitcoin's gold. But as of the time of writing, more than 20,000 cryptocurrencies are available, and the number is expected to increase in the future. That includes active, valuable, and nonactive cryptocurrencies. Nonactive cryptocurrencies are also referred to as *dead cryptocurrencies*, which means they don't have any investors or people using them anymore. Check out Chapter 8 for just a sampling of cryptocurrencies available now.

Key crypto benefits

Still not convinced that cryptocurrencies (or any other sort of decentralized money) are a better solution than traditional government-based money? Here are a number of solutions that cryptocurrencies may be able to provide through their decentralized nature.

Reducing corruption

With great power comes great responsibility. But when you give a ton of power to only one person or entity, the chances of their abusing that power increase. The 19th-century British politician Lord Acton said it best: "Power tends to corrupt, and absolute power corrupts absolutely."

Cryptocurrencies aim to resolve the issue of absolute power by distributing power among many people or, better yet, among all the members of the network. During the crypto boom, some people have been able to manipulate the market, but when things are truly decentralized, corruption could go lower. That's the key idea behind blockchain technology anyway (see Chapter 4).

Eliminating extreme money printing

Governments have central banks, and central banks have the ability to simply print money when they're faced with a serious economic problem. This process is also called *quantitative easing*. By printing more money, a government may be able to bail out debt or devalue its currency. However, this approach is like putting a bandage on a broken leg. Not only does it rarely solve the problem, but the negative side effects also can sometimes surpass the original issue.

For example, when a country like Iran or Venezuela printed too much money, the value of its currency dropped so much that inflation skyrocketed and people couldn't even afford to buy everyday goods and services. Their cash became barely as valuable as rolls of toilet paper. Most cryptocurrencies have a limited, set amount of coins available. When all those coins are in circulation, a central entity or the company behind the blockchain has no easy way to simply create more coins or add on to its supply.

Giving people charge of their own money

With traditional cash, you're basically giving away all your control to central banks and the government. If you trust your government, that's great, but keep in mind that at any point, your government can simply freeze your bank account and deny you access to your funds.

For example, in the United States, if you don't have a legal will and own a business, the government has the right to all your assets if you pass away. Some governments can even simply abolish banknotes the way India did in 2016. With cryptocurrencies, you and only you can access your funds. (Unless someone steals them from you, that is. To find out how to secure your crypto assets, turn to Chapter 7.)

Cutting out intermediaries

With traditional money, every time you make a transfer, an intermediary such as your bank or a digital payment service takes a cut. With cryptocurrencies, all the network members in the blockchain are that intermediary; their compensation is formulated differently from that of fiat money intermediaries and, therefore, is minimal in comparison. Turn to Chapter 5 for more on how cryptocurrencies work.

Serving the unbanked

A vast portion of the world's citizens has no access or limited access to payment systems like banks. Cryptocurrencies aim to resolve this issue by spreading digital commerce around the globe so that anyone with a mobile phone can start making payments. And yes, more people have access to mobile phones than to banks. In fact, more people have mobile phones than have toilets, but at this point the blockchain technology may not be able to resolve the latter issue! (Turn to Chapter 2 for more on the social good that can come from cryptocurrencies and blockchain technology.)

Common crypto and blockchain myths

During the 2017 Bitcoin hype, a lot of misconceptions about the whole industry started to circulate. These myths may have played a role in the cryptocurrency crash that followed the surge. The important thing to remember is that both the blockchain technology and its by-product, the cryptocurrency market, are still in their infancy, and things are rapidly changing. Let me get some of the most common misunderstandings out of the way:

» **Cryptocurrencies are good only for criminals.** Some cryptocurrencies boast anonymity as one of their key features. That means your identity isn't revealed when you're making transactions. Other cryptocurrencies are based on a decentralized blockchain, meaning a central government isn't the sole power behind them. These features do make such cryptocurrencies attractive for criminals; however, law-abiding citizens in corrupt countries can also benefit from them. For example, if you don't trust your local bank or country because of corruption and political instability, the best way to store your money may be through the blockchain and cryptocurrency assets.

» **You can make anonymous transactions using all cryptocurrencies.** For some reason, many people equate Bitcoin with anonymity. But Bitcoin, along with many other cryptocurrencies, doesn't incorporate anonymity at all. All transactions made using such cryptocurrencies are made on public blockchain. Some cryptocurrencies, such as Monero, do prioritize privacy, meaning no outsider can find the source, amount, or destination of transactions. However, most other cryptocurrencies, including Bitcoin, don't operate that way.

» **The only application of blockchain is Bitcoin.** This idea couldn't be farther from the truth. Bitcoin and other cryptocurrencies are a tiny by-product of the blockchain revolution. Many people believe Satoshi created Bitcoin simply to provide an example of how blockchain technology can work. As I explore in Chapter 4, almost every industry and business in the world can use blockchain technology in its specific field.

>> **All blockchain activity is private.** Many people falsely believe that blockchain technology isn't open to the public and is accessible only to its network of common users. Although some companies create their own private blockchains to be used only among employees and business partners, the majority of the blockchains behind famous cryptocurrencies such as Bitcoin are accessible by the public. Literally anyone with a computer can access the transactions in real time. For example, you can view the real-time Bitcoin transactions at www.blockchain.com.

Risks to know about

WARNING

Just like anything else in life, cryptocurrencies come with their own baggage of risk. Whether you trade cryptos, invest in them, or simply hold on to them for the future, you must assess and understand the risks beforehand. Some of the most talked-about cryptocurrency risks include their volatility and lack of regulation. Volatility got especially out of hand in 2017, when the price of most major cryptocurrencies, including Bitcoin, skyrocketed above 1,000 percent and then came crashing down. This pattern repeated itself in the 2022 market crash. Although these crashes provide investing opportunities for those who missed the boat in previous years, they can be painful for those who invested at the peak and have to remain patient for the markets to move back up.

Regulations are another major topic in the industry. The funny thing is that both lack of regulation and exposure to regulation can turn into risk events for cryptocurrency investors. I explore these and other types of risks, as well as methods of managing them, in Chapter 3.

Gearing Up to Make Transactions

Cryptocurrencies are here to make transactions easier and faster. But before you take advantage of these benefits, you must gear up with crypto gadgets, discover where you can get your hands on different cryptocurrencies, and get to know the cryptocurrency community. Some of the essentials include cryptocurrency wallets and exchanges.

Wallets

Some *cryptocurrency wallets*, which hold your purchased cryptos, are similar to digital payment services like Apple Pay and PayPal. But generally, they're different from traditional wallets and come in different formats and levels of security.

REMEMBER

You can't get involved in the cryptocurrency market without a crypto wallet. I recommend that you get the most secure type of wallet, such as a hardware or paper wallet, instead of using the convenient online ones. Turn to Chapter 7 to explore how these wallets work and how you can get them.

Exchanges

After you get yourself a crypto wallet (see the preceding section), you're ready to go crypto shopping, and one of the best destinations is a cryptocurrency exchange. These online web services are where you can transfer your traditional money to buy cryptocurrencies, exchange different types of cryptocurrencies, or even store your cryptocurrencies.

WARNING

Storing your cryptocurrencies on an exchange is considered high risk because many such exchanges have been exposed to hacking attacks and scams in the past. When you're done with your transactions, it's recommended to move your new digital assets to your personal, secure wallet. On the flip side, when storing all your crypto in a wallet, you become the only person responsible for them. Meaning you could lose your assets if there's a theft in your house or if your housekeeper mistakenly throws your wallet into the trash along with a pile of papers. This is why some investors spread their cryptocurrency assets among a combination of hard wallets and online wallets provided by exchanges.

Exchanges come in different shapes and forms:

>> Some are like traditional stock exchanges and act as intermediaries — something crypto enthusiasts believe is a slap in the face of the cryptocurrency market, which is trying to remove centralized intermediaries.

>> Others are decentralized and provide a service where buyers and sellers come together and transact in a peer-to-peer manner, but they come with their own sets of problems, like the risk of locking yourself out.

>> A third type of crypto exchange is called *hybrid,* and it merges the benefits of the other two types to create a better, more secure experience for users.

Turn to Chapter 6 to review the pros and cons of all these types of exchanges and get to know other places where you can go cryptocurrency shopping.

Communities

TIP

Getting to know the crypto community can be the next step as you're finding your way in the market. The web has plenty of chat rooms and support groups to give you a sense of the market and what people are talking about. Here are some ways to get involved:

>> **Crypto-specific Telegram groups:** Many cryptocurrencies have their very own channels on the Telegram app. To join them, you first need to download the Telegram messenger app on your smartphone or computer; it's available for iOS and Android.

>> **Crypto chat rooms on BitcoinTalk, Discord, or Reddit:** BitcoinTalk (https://bitcointalk.org), Discord (https://discord.com), and Reddit (www.reddit.com) have some of the oldest and hottest crypto chat rooms around. You can view some topics without signing up, but if you want to get involved, you need to log in. (Of course, Discord and Reddit aren't exclusive to cryptos, but you can search for a variety of cryptocurrency topics.)

>> **TradingView chat room:** One of the best trading platforms out there, TradingView (www.tradingview.com) also has a social service where traders and investors of all sorts come together and share their thoughts, questions, and ideas.

WARNING

Be aware that many scammers target these kinds of platforms to advertise and lure members into trouble. Keep your wits about you!

TIP

If you're looking for a fun, done-with-you community to help you with your investments (without having to pay a financial advisor), check out my most popular free Masterclass at https://investdiva.com/masterclass.

Making a Plan Before You Jump In

You may just want to buy some cryptocurrencies and save them for their potential growth in the future. Or you may want to become more of an active investor and buy or sell cryptocurrencies more regularly to maximize profit and revenue. Regardless, you must have a plan and a strategy. Even if your transaction is a one-time thing and you don't want to hear anything about your crypto assets for the next ten years, you still must gain the knowledge necessary to determine things like the following:

>> What to buy

>> When to buy

>> How much to buy

>> When to sell

The following sections give you a quick overview of the steps you must take before buying your first cryptocurrency.

Select your cryptos

More than 20,600 active and nonactive cryptocurrencies are out there at the time of writing, and the number is growing. Some of these cryptos may vanish in five years. Others may explode over 1,000 percent and may even replace traditional cash. In Chapter 8, I go through all different types of cryptocurrencies, including the most famous ones right now, such as Cardano, Chainlink, Ethereum, Monero, and Ripple.

As I discuss in Chapter 9, you can select cryptocurrencies based on things like category, popularity, ideology, the management behind the blockchain, and its economic model.

TIP

Because the crypto industry is pretty new, it's still very hard to identify the best-performing cryptos for long-term investments. That's why you may benefit from diversifying among various types and categories of cryptocurrencies in order to manage your risk. By diversifying across 15 or more cryptos, you can stack up the odds of having winners in your portfolio. On the flip side, overdiversification can become problematic as well, so you need to take calculated measures. Turn to Chapter 10 for more on diversification.

Analyze, invest, and profit

When you've narrowed down the cryptocurrencies you like, you must then identify the best time to buy them. For example, in 2017, many people started to believe in the idea of Bitcoin and wanted to get involved. Unfortunately, many of those people mismanaged the timing and bought when the price had peaked. Therefore, they not only were able to buy fewer bits of Bitcoin (pun intended), but also had to sit on their losses and wait for the next price surge.

Now, I'm not saying that by reading Part 3 of this book, you're going to become some sort of new age Cryptodamus. However, by analyzing the price action and conducting proper risk management, you may be able to stack the odds in your favor and make a ton of profit in the future. In addition to reading this book, you can grab my free risk-management toolkit (https://investdiva.com/masterclass) and dive into the world of cryptocurrencies in style and with confidence.

Chapter **2**

Checking Out the Benefits of Cryptocurrency Investing

Whether you're a seasoned investor who has been exposed only to investment assets other than cryptos or you're just starting to invest (in anything!) for the first time, you're probably wondering why you should consider including cryptocurrencies in your portfolio. You've probably heard about Bitcoin. Heck, you may have even heard of other cryptocurrencies such as Ethereum and Litecoin, or meme coins like Dogecoin. But what's the big deal about all these funny-sounding coins anyway? Is Litecoin just a very light coin that won't take much space in your physical wallet? Is Dogecoin the type of money your pet can pay its bills with? Is a Bitcoin made of bits and pieces of other valuable coins? Why on earth should you invest in bits of coins?

You can read all about the different types of cryptocurrencies, what they're made of, and what their purpose is in Chapter 8. Here, I give you a general overview of the market as a whole. That way, you can decide whether the cryptocurrency industry is the right route for you to grow your wealth.

Cryptocurrency investing may make sense for many investors, for a growing number of reasons — from things as simple as diversification to more exciting stuff like taking control of your own money without relying on central banks, or joining the revolutionary movement toward the future of technology and infrastructure. In this chapter, I show you some exciting features of this (fairly) new investment kid on the block.

TIP

Although you can read this book in any order, I encourage you to read Chapter 3 right after this one. That's where I explain the other side of the coin, which involves the risks surrounding cryptocurrencies.

Diversifying from Traditional Investments

Diversification is the good ol' "don't put all your eggs in one basket" thing. You can apply this advice to literally anything in life. If you're traveling, don't put all your underwear in your checked luggage. Put an emergency pair in your carry-on in case your luggage gets lost. If you're grocery shopping, don't buy only apples. Even though they say, "An apple a day keeps the doctor away," you still need the nutrition in other kinds of vegetables and fruits.

REMEMBER

You can go about investment diversification in so many ways. You can diversify with different financial assets, like stocks, bonds, commodities, real estate, and so on. You can diversify based on industry, like technology, health care, and entertainment. You can allocate your investment by having multiple investment time frames, both short term and long term (see Chapters 11 and 12 for details). Adding cryptocurrencies to your investment portfolio is essentially one way of balancing that portfolio. Especially because the cryptocurrency industry is vastly different from traditional ones, this diversification may increase the potential of maximizing your portfolio's growth. One of the main reasons for this higher potential is that the cryptocurrency market may react differently to various geopolitical and financial events.

In the following sections, I explain more by briefly looking into some of the traditional markets and exploring their differences from the cryptocurrency market. (Find out more about diversification in Chapter 10.)

Stocks

The stock market gives you the opportunity to take a bite of the profits a company makes. By buying stocks of that company, you become a part owner of that firm. The more stocks you buy, the bigger your slice of the cake. And of course, the higher the risk you face if the whole cake is thrown out in the garbage.

The stock market is perhaps one of the most appealing investment assets. Novice investors may pick up a stock or two just because they like the company. For most investors, the charm of stock investing is the possibility that the prices will increase over time and generate significant capital gains. Some stocks even provide you with a periodic income stream through something called *dividends.* (I explain more about capital gains and dividend income in Chapter 3.) Regardless, for most stocks, the dividends paid within a year are nothing compared to the increase of the stock's value, especially when the economic environment is upbeat.

REMEMBER

This is precisely what stocks and cryptocurrencies have in common: When their respective markets are strong, you can generally expect to benefit from price appreciation.

Make no mistake, though: Both markets have their bad days and sometimes even bad years. The stock market has a longer history that can guide investors through navigating the future. For example, even though it may not always seem like it, bad days happen less often than good ones. For the 100 years between 1922 and 2022, the Dow, one of the main stock market indexes, ended the year at a lower price only 32 percent of the time (32 years). The other 68 years, it went up.

WARNING

However, stock investing naturally has some disadvantages. For example:

>> **Stocks face different types of risks.** Even the most awesome stocks have risks that you can't easily eliminate, such as the following (see Chapter 3 for details):

- Business and financial risk
- Purchasing power risk

- Market risk
- Global pandemic risk
- Government control and regulations
- Foreign competition
- The general state of the economy

>> **The stock selection process can be a pain in the neck.** You have literally thousands of stocks to choose from. Predicting how the company will perform tomorrow can also be very difficult. After all, the price today only reflects how the market participants feel about the current or future state of the company or that industry.

By investing in the cryptocurrency market, you may be able to balance out some of the preceding risks. The cryptocurrency selection process is also different from that of stocks, as I explain in Chapter 9.

The final disadvantage of stock investing, however, is similar to that of crypto investing. They both generally produce less current income than some other investments. Several types of investments, such as bonds, or investing in yourself and starting a side hustle, pay more current income and do so with much greater certainty.

TECHNICAL STUFF

Rightly timed, crypto investing can produce an enormous return on investment (ROI). For example, if you bought 1 Bitcoin in 2019 (when Bitcoin's price was at $3,409) and sold your Bitcoin in November 2021 when Bitcoin reached $68,009 in price, you would've made $64,600. That's a 1,895 percent ROI in just two years! However, there is a very small likelihood that anyone could time the market like that. By contrast, the best-performing stock in the same time period, Tesla, had a 2,950 percent ROI. Both assets have since fallen from their highs at the time of writing this book.

Bonds

Bonds are also known as *fixed-income securities*. They're different from cryptocurrencies and stocks in that you loan money to an entity for a period of time, and you receive a fixed amount of interest on a periodic basis — hence, its categorization as "fixed income."

Just like with cryptocurrencies and stocks (see the preceding section), you can also expect capital gains from bonds. But these capital gains work a bit differently. Because the companies issuing bonds promise to repay a fixed amount when the bonds mature, bond prices don't typically rise in correlation with the firm's profits. The bond prices rise and fall as market interest rates change.

Another similarity among bonds, cryptocurrencies, and stocks is that they're all issued by a wide range of companies. Additionally, many governmental bodies issue bonds. So, if you're looking to diversify only within the bonds market, you still can choose from a range of relatively safe ones to highly speculative ones.

Compared to cryptocurrencies and stocks, bonds are generally less risky and provide higher current income. But they still are subject to a variety of risks. Some of the risks involved with bond investing are similar to those of cryptocurrencies and stocks — namely, purchasing power risk, business and financial risk, and liquidity risk. Bonds have an additional type of risk known as the *call risk* or *prepayment risk*. Call risk is the risk that a bond will be *called* (retired) long before its maturity date. If the bond issuer calls its bonds, you'll have to find another place for your funds.

REMEMBER

The potential for very high returns on bonds is much lower compared to cryptocurrencies and stocks, respectively. But the risk involved with bonds is also comparatively lower. You can find more about cryptocurrency risks in Chapter 3.

Foreign exchange

Have you ever traveled to another country? Have you noticed the exchange booth in the airport allowing you to exchange your country's currency to your destination country's currency? Did you notice that depending on the rate, you could either lose or gain money when you do the transactions between the two currencies? Congratulations! You now understand the foreign exchange (or forex) market!

In the early 2000s, many retail investors got introduced to online forex trading. By participating in the forex market, you buy and sell currencies in hopes of a profit — not cryptocurrencies, but fiat currencies such as the U.S. dollar, the euro, the British pound, the Australian dollar, or any other currency any government issues. A *fiat currency* is a country's legal tender that's issued by the government.

Participating in the forex market as an investor mainly consists of short- to medium-term trading activity between different currency pairs. You can buy the euro versus the U.S. dollar (the EUR/USD pair), for example. If the euro's value appreciates relative to the U.S. dollar's, you make money. However, if the U.S. dollar's value goes higher than the euro's, you lose money.

Analyzing the forex market needs a very different approach when compared to stock and cryptocurrency analysis. When looking at the forex markets, you need to focus on the issuing country's economic state, its upcoming economic figures such as its *gross domestic product* (GDP, or the value of the goods produced inside the country), unemployment rate, inflation, interest rate, and so on, as well as its political environment.

However, just like the cryptocurrency market, you need to trade forex in pairs. In my online education course, the Invest Diva's Make Your Money Work For You PowerCourse (learn more at https://investdiva.com/masterclass), I compare these pairs to dancing couples — international couples who push each other back and forth. Traders can make money by speculating which direction the couple will move next.

You can apply a similar concept to the cryptocurrency market. For example, you can pair up Bitcoin (BTC) and Ethereum (ETH) against each other.

Technically, when you buy Bitcoin (or anything else for that matter, like a house, clothes, or food) using your fiat currency like the U.S. dollar, you're *pairing them up* in your act of exchange. That's why you need to measure their relative value against each other and see if the potential return is worth your investment.

TIP

You can also consider cryptocurrencies as a cross between stocks and forex. Though many investors invest in cryptocurrencies for capital gains purposes, you can also trade different cryptocurrencies against each other, the way you can in the forex market. I explore cross-cryptocurrency trading in Chapter 10.

Precious metals

Time to compare one of the most recent man-made means to buy stuff (cryptocurrencies) to one of the most ancient ones! No, I'm not going back all the way to *bartering*, where people exchanged their goods and services to fulfill their needs. In the following sections, I talk about the stuff with a bling. Before the advent of paper money, precious metals such as gold and silver were long used to make coins and to buy stuff.

The precious metals comparison is actually the best argument when someone tells you cryptocurrencies are worthless because they don't have any intrinsic value. In fact, this is why most Bitcoin enthusiasts believe Bitcoin is way more valuable than gold.

Getting a little background

Back in the days of bartering, people would exchange stuff that provided real value to their human needs: chickens, clothes, or farming services. Supposedly, people in the ancient civilization of Lydia were among the first to use coins made of gold and silver in exchange for goods and services. Imagine the first shopper who tried to convince the seller to accept a gold coin instead of three chickens that could feed a family for a week. This change was followed by leather money, paper money, credit cards, and now cryptocurrencies.

Some may argue that precious metals like gold also have intrinsic value. They're durable. They conduct both heat and electricity and, therefore, have some industrial application. I know I used some gold and silver in experiments back in the day when I was studying electrical engineering in Japan. But in reality, most people don't invest in precious metals because they're trying to conduct electricity. They primarily buy them to use as jewelry or as a store of value.

Today, market sentiment mainly determines the value of gold and silver. In other words, gold (which is a type of shiny dirt!) only has value because we as a society collectively decided that gold is valuable. If an alien from a planet that's made of gold instead of dirt visits the earth, it's going to be very surprised that we treat gold as a store of value. This is true about any form of transaction. However, the anti-Bitcoiners use the exact same logic to defend their position.

To me, Bitcoin, and many other cryptocurrencies are far more than a transactional currency. I explain more in the following sections.

Silver has more use as an industrial metal than gold does. Silver is used in batteries, electrical appliances, medical products, and other industrial items. However, despite the additional demand, silver is valued lower than gold. For example, at the time of writing, silver is priced at $19 per ounce, while gold is traded above $1,751 per ounce.

Keep in mind that England didn't establish gold as its standard of value until 1816. (*Standard of value* means tying the value of the currency to its value in gold.) In 1913, the United States finally jumped on board through its Federal Reserve system. It backed its notes by gold and aimed to ensure that notes and checks would be honored and could be redeemed for gold.

Even though precious metals don't have an arguable intrinsic value, they have long been a favorite investment tool among market participants. One of the main reasons is their historical association with wealth. Often, when investments such as bonds, real estate, and the stock market go down or the political environment is uncertain, people flock to precious metals. People prefer to own precious metals at these times because they can actually physically touch metals and keep them in their homes right next to their beds. However, this is nothing more than a *feeling* of security rather than real intrinsic value.

Comparing precious metals to cryptocurrencies

Besides the fact that you need to mine in order to get your hands on precious metals and some cryptocurrencies, one key similarity between precious metals and cryptocurrencies is that both categories have unregulated characteristics. Gold has been an unregulated currency at various times and in various places. Unregulated currencies become more valuable when investors don't trust the official currency, and cryptocurrencies just seem to be another example of this trend.

Investing in precious metals comes with a number of risk factors you need to keep in mind. For example, if you're buying physical precious metals as an investment, you must consider their portability risk. Transferring precious metals can be expensive, given their weight, high import taxes, and the need for a high level of security. In contrast, you don't need to make a physical transfer with cryptocurrencies besides the hardware crypto wallets I discuss in Chapter 7. But moving cryptocurrencies is much faster and less expensive, even with a hardware wallet, than transferring precious metals.

On the other hand, cryptocurrency prices have been more volatile in the short time they've been available on the markets than have all precious metals combined.

One factor that gives Bitcoin enthusiasts hope for future gains is supply and demand. There are only ever going to be 21 million Bitcoins available to be mined. This number was decided by the anonymous creator(s) of Bitcoin who go by the name of Satoshi Nakamoto, and means the maximum number of Bitcoins that can be issued (or *mined*) is capped at 21 million. At the time of writing, 19 million of those Bitcoins had already been mined. This means that although the demand for Bitcoin could remain the same or even go higher, the supply of Bitcoin is always going to be a fixed number. Compare that to the U.S. dollar or gold. The Fed can print new $100 bills out of thin air. We have no idea how much gold there really is. In fact, we could get hit by an asteroid made of gold, giving us enough gold to give all the people on the planet five bags full of gold; if that were ever to happen, thanks to supply and demand, the value of gold would go lower. This is also the reason why many investors consider Bitcoin to be a hedge against inflation.

Gaining Capital Appreciation

Capital appreciation refers to the increase in the price or value of cryptocurrencies. And it's one of the reasons many investors (and noninvestors, for that matter) look to jump on the cryptocurrency train.

Initial Bitcoin owners waited years before they saw any sort of capital appreciation. Personally, I was one of the skeptics of the whole thing. Back in 2012, one of my investor friends in Switzerland told me to buy some Bitcoin. I decided not to invest in Bitcoin because I didn't feel confident in its value — a decision that makes sense from a risk-management point of view but cost me a ton of profit.

I started investing in cryptocurrencies when the price of Bitcoin had surged significantly. However, using my Invest Diva Diamond Analysis (IDDA) research, and thanks to the ups and downs in the cryptocurrency markets, I was able to find more affordable cryptocurrencies that were expected to have similar capital appreciation and to identify bargain prices to Bitcoin and other digital assets that suit my risk tolerance. I explain how the IDDA works in Chapter 9 and in my free 90-minute Masterclass at https://investdiva.com/masterclass.

In the following sections, I look at the history of capital appreciation for cryptocurrencies and discuss their growth potential — a big reason to consider investing in them.

REMEMBER

With great expectations of capital appreciation and huge growth potential come great expectations of capital losses. That's why I strongly recommend reading Chapter 3 before starting your investing activity in the cryptocurrency market.

Knowing it's a wild ride

The gains and losses in the cryptocurrency market have been a wild ride. Even as the industry becomes more established, we still witness multiple bubbles and crashes in most cryptocurrencies. Most of the bubbles are created by hype and FOMO (fear of missing out), and most of the crashes have been created out of FUD (fear, uncertainty, and doubt).

This simply indicates that the cryptocurrency market is still largely driven by emotions. The same can be said about any market, but the cryptocurrency market, still in its infancy and largely a mystery to the general public, is more sensitive to investors' feelings. I know this because I only ever get asked to go on national TV and talk about crypto when the markets are crashing or when the markets are seeing unrealistic gains. Never do they ever ask me to go on when everything is steady! In that way, the media has been playing a big role in adding fuel to the market fire, which impacts the uneducated investors who are simply investing based on what they hear in the news. So, congratulations on picking up this book, allowing you to create a strategy that is suitable for you, your risk tolerance, and your level of confidence if you choose to invest in cryptocurrencies.

Playing "coulda woulda shoulda"

Let's play a game of "coulda woulda shoulda": How much would you have had if you invested in crypto early?

In 2013, many people bought Bitcoin as its price approached $1,000 for the first time. Shortly after, its price crashed to around $300, where it stayed for the following two years. The next big wave of growth came in January 2017, when Bitcoin's price broke above the $1,000 level.

If you had bought one Bitcoin at $300 at the end of 2015, by January 2017 (when the price hit $1,000) you would've had $700 worth of capital appreciation. But, of course, the gains didn't stop there. After the break above $1,000, Bitcoin's price managed to go all the way up to close to $20,000 by the end of 2017, when it came crashing down to a range around $6,000.

For people who had bought (or mined) Bitcoin when it was valued at around $300 and held on to it throughout the volatility, the crash to $6,000 wasn't that big of a deal. For every Bitcoin they'd bought at $300, they had around $5,700 worth of capital appreciation even if they didn't cash their Bitcoins in when the value reached above $19,000.

People who bought Bitcoin at around $1,000 and cashed it out at $19,000 at its 2017 peak would've made $18,000 for every Bitcoin they owned. Of course, many people who bought Bitcoin at $19,000 felt angry and thought they were scammed by investing in Bitcoin.

But those who had entered the cryptocurrency market from an IDDA approach knew that patience is a profitable virtue. They held on to their cryptocurrency assets through the 2018 to 2020 crypto winter (outlined in Chapter 3). They then enjoyed the next wave of capital gains that pushed the price of Bitcoin to almost $65,000. But once again, Bitcoin crashed, this time just touching the 2017 "hype" price of around $20,000.

REMEMBER

Do you see the pattern? The Bitcoin price shoots up to a new high after a period of winter or little activity. Then it comes crashing down to the same level as the previous period's high. A variation of this pattern has been playing out over and over again through Bitcoin's short life. This could give investors some insights on when to buy and when to sell to make a profit. The geek name for this is *technical analysis*.

This means, if you bought Bitcoin at the highest price of the 2017 bubble ($20,000) and didn't do anything for five years (neither buying more at lower prices nor selling at the higher prices), you would be at a "break-even" point. Considering the increased inflation during this time period (which tends to devalue your fiat currency), this could still be considered a win.

REMEMBER

Inflation is the reason you pay a higher price for things like gas and milk than your parents did. During times of high inflation, keeping your fiat currency in the bank means that your one dollar is worth less and less every year. It's essentially like setting your money on fire. We were always told by our parents that it's a good idea to "save." But no one ever became a millionaire by investing in a savings account. That's why I'm so passionate about helping people make their money work for them through investing. Cryptocurrency is one vehicle that can take you to your financial destination and is certainly worth paying attention to.

Knowing that history doesn't always repeat itself

Many market participants compare Bitcoin and other cryptocurrencies' appreciation to the dot-com bubble from the mid-1990s and early 2000s. According to *Fortune* magazine, since its creation in 2009 until March 2018, Bitcoin saw four bear (falling) waves, where prices dropped 45 percent to 50 percent, typically rebounding an average of 47 percent afterward. During the dot-com bubble, the Nasdaq Composite Index had five of those waves, averaging 44 percent declines followed by 40 percent rebounds. Trading volume patterns are also eerily similar.

Nasdaq has clearly rallied nicely from its low in 2002. Though history and past performance aren't indicative of future behavior, crypto enthusiasts have reasons to believe that growth potential for cryptocurrencies may be similar to the Nasdaq rebound, if not better.

WARNING

Most people have no clue what's really going on in the cryptocurrency market, or any market for that matter. Ever since online retail trading became popular among the "non-Wall Street" crowd, most people seek their investing advice from news sources, Twitter, or TikTok gurus. Unfortunately, "They said so" is not a real investing strategy! The majority of those interested in the market are taking their cues from market noise, making it way easier for the prices to fall when the big movers downplay for their own benefit.

"Going against the crowd" is one of the key pillars in my IDDA, which I cover in Chapter 9, as well as my free Make Your Money Work For You Masterclass (found at `https://investdiva.com/masterclass`). When the majority of the market panics about the drops in the value of an asset, it's often the best time to stack up on it. You can say the same about the cryptocurrency market. For the cryptocurrencies with strong blockchain technology, ideology, and future growth potential behind them, when the price bottoms out, there could be a high potential for their value to go up.

Increasing Income Potential

Although gaining capital appreciation is one of the most attractive features of cryptocurrency investing (as I explain earlier in this chapter), you can also take advantage of some cryptocurrencies that pay something similar to dividends in the stock market.

A bit about traditional dividends

By definition, a *dividend* is a sum of money public companies pay their shareholders on a regular basis. U.S. corporations pay billions of dollars' worth of dividends every year. Yet in spite of these numbers, many investors (especially young ones) don't pay much attention to dividends. They prefer capital gains because the rewards can be quicker and can way exceed any amount of dividend payment.

In the traditional stock market, companies typically pay dividends on a quarterly basis. A firm's board of directors decides how much to pay shareholders in dividends or whether to pay dividends at all. Sometimes, the directors decide to pay dividends because the stock value isn't doing so well. So, they select a higher dividend rate to keep investors interested in buying the stocks.

Investors with lower risk tolerance, and those approaching retirement, may prefer dividend payments to capital gains because dividend payments don't fluctuate as much as the value of stocks do. Furthermore, if the markets crash as they did in 2020, dividends can provide nice protection. The best way to accumulate dividends is to hold onto your assets long-term.

The basics on crypto dividends

During the crypto mania of 2017, many cryptocurrency platforms were quick to realize the importance of regular payments to keep investors happy. But these payments can be a bit different from traditional stock dividends. You can generate regular, passive income in the crypto market in several ways. Here are the two most popular ones:

>> **HODLing:** No, this term is not a typo for *holding*, although it has a similar meaning. It was a typo on the word *hold* back in 2013 that turned into one of the most popular words in the crypto world. One of the reasons it became so popular could also be that it can be used as an acronym for "hold on for dear life." HODLing is buying and holding the tokens of a crypto exchange (explained in Chapter 6) that pays dividends in crypto. It's the closest payment to traditional dividends. Some cryptocurrencies pay out the HODLers, who simply purchase and carry the digital coins in their wallets.

>> **Proof of stake (PoS):** Staking and getting passive income from crypto is a lighter version of proof of work in cryptocurrency mining, which I explain in Chapter 7. When you *stake* a crypto, it means you put it aside so it can't be used in the blockchain network. If you have a ton of stakes, you have a higher chance of getting paid at a random selection by the network. Annual returns for staking vary between 1 percent and 5 percent, depending on the coin.

REMEMBER

Receiving cash (or digital coins) just for holding onto your assets is pretty cool, but sometimes it makes more sense to cash out and reinvest your holdings to get a better return.

WARNING

If the dividend payments sound too good to be true, beware. At the time of writing, this remains a highly irregulated industry. That means often times you don't have any protection if the exchange behind the dividend payments goes bankrupt — and you may lose all your money. This is exactly what happened with the massive collapse of the popular crypto exchange FTX in 2022. FTX became popular via aggressive marketing strategies and high-yield payments for parking your money with them, much higher than you would earn from parking your money in a traditional bank. Needless to say, this too-good-to-be-true frenzy came crashing down when customers rushed to withdraw their funds just to find out the exchange didn't have sufficient assets in reserve to pay back its customers.

Fueling Ideological Empowerment

Just as oil is the lubricant that allows a machine to operate, blockchain technology is the lubricant that enables the cryptocurrency market. *Blockchain* is the underlying technology for cryptocurrencies, not to mention one of those breakthrough developments that has the potential to revolutionize nearly every industry in the world completely. (I cover blockchain further in Chapter 4.)

Blockchain can offer so much more because it's aiming to resolve many economic and financial problems in the world today, from dealing with the flaws of the sharing economy to banking the unbanked and underbanked. Here are some of the kinds of social good that come through cryptocurrencies and the blockchain technology.

The economy of the future

We live in an era where the *sharing economy* is exploding. The sharing economy allows people to rent out their own property for use by others. Internet giants such as Google, TikTok, and Twitter rely on the contributions of users as a means to generate value within their own platforms. If you've ever taken an Uber or Lyft rather than a taxi or rented a room on Airbnb instead of a hotel, you're part of the sharing economy crowd.

However, the traditional sharing economy has its issues, such as the following:

>> Requiring high fees for using the platforms.

>> Hurting individual users but benefitting the underlying corporation. In most cases, the value produced by the crowd isn't equally redistributed among all who have contributed to the value production. All the profits are captured by the large intermediaries who operate the platforms.

>> **Playing fast and loose with consumer info.** Some companies have abused their power by getting access to private data without customers knowing.

As the sharing economy expands in the future, its problems will likely become more complicated.

In order to combat these issues, several companies are developing blockchain-based sharing economy platforms. These platforms are much more affordable to use and provide much-needed transparency. They limit, and sometimes completely cut out, the need for a centralized intermediary. This shift allows true peer-to-peer interactions, eliminating the 20 percent to 30 percent transaction fees that come with centralized platforms. Because all transactions are logged on blockchains, all users can audit the network's operations.

This approach is possible because of the decentralized nature of blockchain technology, which is ultimately a means for individuals to coordinate common activities, interact directly with one another, and govern themselves in a more trustworthy and decentralized manner.

WARNING

Some cryptocurrency transactions aren't entirely free. In many cases, every time there is a transaction on a blockchain, you have to pay the "network fees," which are funds payable to the blockchain network members who are mining your coins/transactions. If you take into consideration the time "wasted" waiting for a transaction to clear (for example, it takes anywhere from one minute to several hours for a Bitcoin transaction to reach consensus), then in reality, you may not save anything in fees by going to some blockchain applications.

Blockchain remains the fuel behind the economy of the future, and cryptocurrencies are a by-product to pave the way by distributing the global economy.

This is the exact reason why I finally came about to participate in the cryptocurrency market. I first learned about Bitcoin in 2012 (when it was only $11), but its value didn't fully resonate with me. It wasn't until 2016, when I got hired to do market research for a UK-based crypto news company, that I learned this about Bitcoin: No matter what happens to your government and as long as you own your own Bitcoin keys, the government can't touch your Bitcoin.

Potential hedge against inflation

The rise of Bitcoin and other cryptocurrencies as a trillion-dollar asset class in 2017 was spurred without the oversight of a central bank or monetary authority guaranteeing trust or market conduct. Unlike fiat currencies such as the U.S. dollar and the euro, most cryptocurrencies will never be subject to money printing (officially called *quantitative easing*) by central banks. Most cryptocurrencies operate under controlled supply, which means no printing of money. In fact, networks limit the supply of tokens even in cases where the demand is high. For example, Bitcoin's supply will decrease in time and will reach its final number somewhere around the year 2140. All cryptocurrencies control the supply of the tokens by a schedule written in the code. Translation: The money supply of a cryptocurrency in every given moment in the future can roughly be calculated today.

The lack of government control over cryptocurrencies can also help with lower inflation risk. History has shown over and over again that when a particular government applies bad policies, becomes corrupt, or is faced with crisis, the country's individual currency suffers. This fluctuation in the currency value can lead to the printing of more money. Inflation is the reason why your parents paid less than $1 for a gallon of milk while you have to pay at least $3. How awesome would it be if cryptocurrencies could get rid of government-controlled inflation so your grandchildren don't have to pay more for stuff than you do?

Help for the unbanked and underbanked

One of the most noble problems cryptocurrencies can solve is banking the *unbanked*. According to Cointelegraph, "2 billion people in the world still don't have a bank account. Most of them live in low- and middle-income emerging markets, but even in high-income countries, large numbers of people are unable to use banks to meet their day-to-day financial needs. This means they don't have access to the convenience, security, and interest that banks provide."

Moreover, many people are *underbanked*; they have access to a bank account but don't have adequate access to the financial services that banks can provide. Even in the United States, for example, an estimated 4.5 percent of U.S. households (approximately 5.9 million households) were unbanked in 2021. Without access to savings and credit, these people can't participate in the cycle of economic growth.

REMEMBER

Cryptocurrencies, with the help of blockchain technology, have the potential to help the unbanked and underbanked by letting them create their own financial alternatives efficiently and transparently. All someone needs to start using cryptocurrencies such as Bitcoin and send and receive money is a smartphone or laptop and an internet connection. (Turn to Chapter 6 for an introduction on how to buy cryptocurrencies.)

IN THIS CHAPTER

» **Understanding the concept of return in crypto investing**

» **Getting to know cryptos' risks**

» **Considering cryptocurrency return versus risk**

» **Exploring different types of cryptocurrency risks**

» **Applying your risk tolerance to your investment strategy**

Chapter **3**

Knowing the Risks of Cryptocurrencies

S o, you're excited to jump on the crypto wagon, perhaps because you expect a gigantic *return* (profit) on your investment! That's basically the reward for investing. However, you can't consider return without also looking at risk. *Risk* is the uncertainty surrounding the actual return you generate.

In my investment education course, I spend a lot of time speaking about risk and how everyone should approach it individually. What may represent high risk for me may not be as risky for you due to our unique lifestyles and financial circumstances.

Cryptocurrencies have shown their fair share of volatility, which has made some investors millions of dollars while wiping out some others' initial investment. In this chapter, I look at cryptocurrencies' price volatility from 2017 to 2022. I also define cryptocurrency rewards and risk, describe different types of risk, and give you pointers on managing risk.

Reviewing Cryptocurrency Returns

Different assets generate different types of returns. For example, one source of return is the change in the investment's value. When you invest in the stock market or the real estate market, you may generate an income in the form of dividends, interest, or rent. Investors call these two sources of return *capital gains* (or *capital losses*) and *current income*, respectively.

REMEMBER

Although most people invest in the cryptocurrency market for capital gains, some cryptocurrencies actually offer current income opportunities. You get an introduction to cryptocurrency returns in Chapter 2.

Capital gains (or losses)

The most popular reason for crypto investing is to see gains in the coins' value. Some people associate the coins with precious metals such as gold. Doing so makes sense because, just like gold, a limited amount is available for some cryptocurrencies, and one way to extract many of them is to mine. (Of course, you don't need to gear up with a pickax and headlamp when mining cryptocurrencies.)

With that, many investors consider cryptocurrencies to be assets even though they're technically currency tokens that can be used in transactions. Most people buy these tokens in the hopes of selling them when the prices rise more. If the value of your cryptocurrency token goes higher from the time you purchase, you get capital gains when you sell the token. Congrats! If the prices go lower, and you decide to sell at those lower prices, you end up with capital losses.

Income

Income is a lesser-known and higher-risk type of return in the cryptocurrency market. Income is generated from something called *crypto yields*, which are marketed to work like traditional dividends.

Traditionally, dividends occur when public companies distribute a portion of their earnings to their shareholders. Traditional types of dividends include cash payments, shares of stock, or other property.

Earning dividends in the crypto market can get a bit more complicated and way riskier. Different currencies have different operating systems and their own rules and regulations. However, the concept still remains the same. Crypto dividend payments are becoming increasingly popular among altcoins, which are the alternative cryptocurrencies besides Bitcoin. When choosing a cryptocurrency for your portfolio, you can consider looking into crypto dividends, as well as the potential of capital gains (discussed in the preceding section).

Two of the most popular ways to earn crypto dividends are

>> **Staking:** Holding a proof-of-stake coin in a special wallet

>> **Holding:** Buying and holding a crypto in any wallet

I talk more about staking and holding in Chapter 7.

At the time of writing, the majority of crypto lending platforms have gone bankrupt. That includes the popular FTX and Celsius exchanges. Their collapse and bankruptcy left many investors shirtless, and the stories created a huge wave of uncertainty in the cryptocurrency market. It also gave investors another reason to look deeper into the fundamentals of their investments and avoid investing based on hype and FOMO (fear of missing out).

Compounding

The ultimate reason to invest in online financial assets is to take advantage of compounding. *Compounding* is the process of reinvesting capital gains, interest, or dividends to generate additional earnings. It's basically the act of making your money have babies!

There are three ways you can multiply your money by compounding:

>> **Buy low, sell high.** Buy an asset at a low, sell it at a higher price, and then go back in with more money to buy at the low prices. As you do this over and over again, your investment portfolio compounds and grows larger. However, the risk associated with this type of compounding is very high, especially if you're buying low and selling high in short periods of time.

TIP

>> **Reinvest dividends or interest.** You can manually or automatically reinvest the dividend payments you receive from your cryptocurrency or stocks. This will expose you to more potential future capital gains and dividend payments.

>> **Make regular contributions.** My favorite method of compounding is by increasing my income through side hustles and then investing the increased income in online financial assets such as cryptocurrencies and stocks regularly. It's the lowest-risk method of compounding because it eliminates the need for timing the market price.

Risk: Flipping the Other Side of the Coin

Investment returns are exciting, but you can't consider return without also looking at risk. The sad truth about any type of investment is that the greater the expected return, the greater the risk. Because cryptocurrencies are considered riskier than some other assets, they may also provide higher returns. The relationship between risk and return is called the *risk–return trade-off*.

REMEMBER

Cryptocurrency investing isn't a get-rich-quick scheme. You shouldn't invest in cryptocurrencies by using your life savings or taking out a loan. You must consider your risk tolerance, understand the different sources of cryptocurrency risks, and then develop an investment strategy that's suitable for you — just you, not anyone else — because you're unique, and so is your financial situation.

Also, keep in mind that early Bitcoin investors waited years to see any returns. If you don't have the patience required to see meaningful returns on your investment, you may need to forget about investing altogether.

That being said, a healthy amount of risk appetite is essential not only when investing but also in life. Don't get so paranoid about risk that you never leave the house for fear of getting into an accident!

The lowest-risk, highest-return investment is always an investment in yourself to learn a high-income-creating skill. Because no matter where you go, no matter the economic conditions, there you are! You can always use your own skills to increase your income. So, congratulations on picking up this book and investing in yourself by increasing your knowledge!

Glimpsing Cryptocurrencies' Reward versus Risk

One of the main reasons cryptocurrency investing has become such a hot topic since 2017 is the crazy surge in the value of major cryptocurrencies such as Bitcoin.

Although you may have heard of Bitcoin the most, it wasn't even among the ten best-performing crypto assets back in 2017. Bitcoin's value grew by more than 1,000 percent, but other, lesser-known cryptocurrencies such as Ripple and NEM were among the biggest winners, with a whopping 36,018 percent and 29,842 percent growth, respectively.

Where did Bitcoin stand on the performance list? Fourteenth!

These returns made investors and noninvestors alike super excited about the cryptocurrency market. By the beginning of 2018, almost everyone you knew — your doctor, your rideshare driver, perhaps even your grandmother — was probably talking about Bitcoin, whether or not the person had any experience in any sort of investing. Even my 8-year-old nephew was asking me about it.

However, as is true of any type of investment, what goes up must come down, including the cryptocurrency market. Because the cryptocurrency prices had gone up so much, so quickly, the crash was as hard and as speedy. For example, by January 2019, Bitcoin dropped back to the lows of $3,000 from highs of nearly $20,000.

This became known as *crypto winter*. All the buzz about cryptocurrency and Bitcoin shut down and many people started calling it a scam. It wasn't until July 2020 that cryptocurrency became a hot topic again as its price started to surge. By the end of 2021, Bitcoin's price had risen to over $68,000. Everyone was talking about it again, and people were catching FOMO again. Until (surprise, surprise!) the new bubble also burst, and Bitcoin's price dropped back to $20,000. The media went quiet on Bitcoin again. But ironically, this new low was the same value as the high of 2018!

In the geeky investing world, we call this a *support level.* A support level is the price that the asset's price has had difficulty going lower than in the past. In this case, in the crypto winter of 2018 to 2020, the price had difficulty breaking below $3,000.

At the time of writing, Bitcoin's price had difficulty going lower than $20,000 and the next support level for it is identified at around $13,000 and $7,000, respectively. Conducting technical analysis identifies the key support levels an asset's price could drop to, so you can mitigate your risk of buying at higher prices.

REMEMBER

Many analysts considered the great appreciation of major cryptocurrencies' value to be a bubble. This fluctuation is a heck of a roller-coaster ride in such a short period of time! The returns were great for those who invested early and took profit at the highs. But just imagine investing in the market when the prices were up and watching the value of your investment going lower and lower. That's one of the major risk factors in any type of investing and the reason the majority of crypto investors prefer to hold their crypto assets long term instead of trying to time the market and compound by buying low and selling high.

Digging into Different Kinds of Risk

Getting educated about risk puts you right on top of your game. Knowing your risk tolerance, you can create a strategy that protects you and your wealth. The risks associated with cryptocurrencies come from many different sources. Here are the various types of crypto risks.

Crypto hype risk

Seizing opportunities is a big characteristic of wealthy people, but investing based solely on hype and Twitter trending topics may not be a good thing!

The main reason cryptos have a lot of hype is that most people get lazy in educating themselves about the underlying value of a cryptocurrency, so they blindly follow the advice of their favorite celebrity. Crypto bubbles between 2017 and 2022 were mainly caused by market hype. After the initial hype came an adjustment in the market price (which is normal) and people panicked and started selling at a loss, resulting in a crash and a crypto winter (covered earlier in this chapter).

Unfortunately, this is the exact opposite of how investors should be investing. The first method of compounding (explained earlier in this chapter) is "Buy low and sell high," not the other way around!

TIP

This type of behavior became so popular that crypto geeks created their very own lingo around it. Here are a few terms:

>> **FOMO:** Short for "fear of missing out." It happens when you see a massive surge in a crypto you don't own, and you hurry in to get your hands on it as the price goes up. *Hint:* Don't do it! What goes up must come down, so you may be better off waiting for the hype to calm down and buy at lower prices.

>> **FUD:** Short for "fear, uncertainty, and doubt." You can use this in a Reddit post when you hear one of those Doctor Doomsdays talking down the market. JPMorgan Chase's CEO, Jamie Dimon, spread one of the biggest FUDs in September 2017 by calling Bitcoin a fraud. In May 2022, he said Bitcoin's slide has created a "significant upside" for crypto investors.

>> **ATH:** Short for "all-time high." Whenever the price of an asset reaches the highest point in its history, you can say, "It's reached an ATH." This is also known as a *bubble*.

>> **Bag holder:** You don't want this to be your nickname! Bag holders are those investors who bought out of FOMO at an ATH and missed the chance of selling. Therefore, they're left holding a bag (wallet) filled with worthless coins.

>> **Diamond hands:** The positive version of a bag holder! This is an investor who has high confidence in their investment and, therefore, refrains from selling during the downturns and stays the long course.

>> **BTFD:** This one stands for "Buy the f@#&ing dip!" When you're confident in an asset's long-term potential growth, you've got to BTFD when its price drops lower.

Before falling for the market noise, arm yourself with knowledge on the specific cryptos you're considering. You have plenty of opportunities to make lots of money in the crypto market. Be patient and acquire the right knowledge instead of betting on the current hype. An investor who trades on the hype probably doesn't even have an investment strategy — unless you call gambling a strategy! You can find different methods of strategy development in Parts 2 and 3.

Security risk

Scams! Hacking! Theft!

These issues have been a common theme in the cryptocurrency market since Bitcoin's inception in 2009. And with each scandal, the cryptocurrencies' values are compromised as well, although temporarily. Your cryptocurrency can be compromised in several main ways, which I outline in the following sections. You should definitely follow safety precautions in every step of your cryptocurrency investing strategy.

Safety check #1: Bitcoin investing schemes

If you're on any social media, you may have seen a version of this. Scammers pretend to be an influencer and offer to pay Bitcoin. This, unfortunately, has even happened to many of my followers. Every time I post content on Instagram, Facebook, YouTube, TikTok, or even Twitter, my comment section gets flooded by impersonators pretending to be me by using my photo and a version of my name or my company's name, direct messaging (DMing) my followers, and offering Bitcoin in exchange for their investment.

To avoid such scams, before ever handing your money to anyone, do a quick Google search and go to the source. You can often find influencers' social media handles on their website. In my case, my social media handles have a verified check mark. When in doubt, always contact the customer service of the business to ensure you're not falling for a scammer. These scammers are often very skilled in making you believe they're actually who you think you're talking with.

WARNING

Crypto-investing scams don't end with public social media impersonators. You can even find scammers on dating apps and other social networks where people can contact you directly via DM. These scammers typically start building trust through long-distance conversations, and then over time, they convince their victims to buy or give money in some form of cryptocurrency. After getting the money, the dating scammer disappears. These scams are also known as *pig-butchering scams,* because the scam system works kind of like fattening a hog before slaughter. The scammers may open up the conversation with a simple "Hello" as the first step in a process of taking the friendly chat to an online investment that will result in your money disappearing.

Safety check #2: The cryptocurrency itself

WARNING

Hundreds of cryptocurrencies are already available for investments, with thousands of new initial coin offerings (ICOs) on the way. When choosing a cryptocurrency to invest in, educate yourself on the blockchain's protocol and make sure it isn't a rug-pull scam or a pump-and-dump scam:

>> A *rug-pull scam* is when scammers "pump up" a new cryptocurrency project to get funding. But after they get the money, they disappear with them, pulling the rug out from under investors.

>> A *pump-and-dump scam* is similar to a rug-pull scam, but the difference is the scammers create hype around their cryptocurrency and get people to buy, which drives its price higher. When the price reaches a considerably high price, the scammers start selling, reaping profits and leaving the investors with losses in a coin that has otherwise no intrinsic value.

TIP

One way to avoid falling for these scams is to read the cryptocurrency's protocol on its white paper on its website. The white paper is an official document that the crypto founders put together before their ICO, laying out everything there is to know about the cryptocurrency. Make sure you actually understand the cryptocurrency before investing in it. If the protocol or your promised return on investment (ROI) is too good to be true, or you don't fully understand how it works, then stay far away from it. There's no substitute for confidence when it comes to managing your investment risks.

In Chapter 9, I explain the best ways to analyze crypto assets from a fundamental point of view, so you can progress with confidence.

Safety check #3: The exchange

Exchanges are where you can buy cryptocurrency tokens (see Chapter 6 for an introduction). You need to make sure that your crypto exchange is trustworthy and credible. Countless numbers of security incidents and data breaches have occurred in the crypto community because of the exchanges.

One of the famous initial hacks was that of Japan-based Mt. Gox, the largest Bitcoin exchange, in 2013. At the time, Mt. Gox was handling 70 percent of the world's Bitcoin exchanges. However, it had many issues, such as lack of a testing policy, lack of a version control software, and lack of a proper management. As all these problems piled up, in February 2014 the exchange became the victim of a massive hack, where about 850,000 Bitcoins were lost. Although 200,000 Bitcoins were eventually recovered, the remaining 650,000 have never been recovered.

Many exchanges have learned a lesson from this incident and are keeping up with the latest safety measures. However, exchange hacks still happen almost on a monthly basis.

WARNING

Centralized exchanges are the most vulnerable to attacks. Turn to Chapter 6 for methods to spot red flags in cryptocurrency exchanges.

TIP

I'm not trying to scare you with these stories. As time goes by, the market learns from previous mistakes and works on a better and safer future. However, you still need to take matters into your own hands as much as possible. Follow these tips:

» **Before choosing an exchange, take a look at its security section on its website.** Check whether it participates in any bug bounty programs to encourage safety. These programs are deals offered by many websites, organizations, and software developers. People who find bugs can get recognition and compensation.

» **Check if the exchange has insurance and uses Security Operations Center (SOC)-compliant cold storage.** *SOC compliance* means that a company has completed a third-party audit to show that it has certain controls in place.

>> **Check whether the exchange uses a multisig wallet.**
A *multisig wallet* is a digital wallet that needs more than
one private key to sign a crypto transaction. This means
that more than one person is needed to sign the transaction
for it to happen, which adds to its security.

>> **Ask the right people about the exchange.** In Invest
Diva's Make Your Money Work For You PowerCourse, we
keep an eye on the latest developments in the market and
keep our members informed about any shady activities
(https://investdiva.com/masterclass).

Safety check #4: Your wallet

TIP

The final round of security checks is all in your own hands because
the kind of crypto wallet you use is entirely up to you. Though you
don't physically carry your crypto coins, you can store them in a
secure physical wallet. You actually store the public and private
keys, which you can use for making transactions with your altcoins, in these wallets as well. You can take your wallet's security
to a higher level by using a backup. I explore wallet safety methods
more in Chapter 7.

Volatility risk

Volatility risk is essentially the risk of unexpected market movements. Though volatility can be a good thing, it can also catch you
off guard sometimes. Just like any other market, the cryptocurrency market can suddenly move in the opposite direction from
what you expected. If you aren't prepared for the market volatility, you can lose the money you invested in the market.

The volatility in the cryptocurrency market has resulted from
many factors. For one, it's a brand-new technology. The inception of revolutionary technologies — such as the internet — can
create initial periods of volatility. The blockchain technology (see
Chapter 4) and its underpinning cryptocurrencies take a lot of
getting used to before they become mainstream.

REMEMBER

The best way to combat the cryptocurrency volatility risk is looking at the big picture. Volatility matters a lot if you have a short-
term investing horizon (see Chapter 11) because it's an indicator
of how much money you may make or lose over a short period. But
if you have a long-term horizon (see Chapter 12), volatility can
turn into an opportunity.

Liquidity risk

By definition, *liquidity risk* is the risk of not being able to sell (or *liquidate*) an investment quickly at a reasonable price. Liquidity is important for any tradable asset. If you trade currencies with very low volume, you may not even be able to close your trade because the prices just won't move!

Cryptocurrencies can also see episodes of illiquidity. Heck, the liquidity problem was one of the factors that led to the high volatility in Bitcoin and other altcoins described earlier in this chapter. When the liquidity is low, the risk of price manipulation also comes into play. One big player can easily move the market to their favor by placing a massive order.

TIP

The crypto community refers to these types of big players as *whales*. In the cryptocurrency market, whales often move small altcoins by using their huge capital.

On the bright side, as cryptocurrency investing becomes more available and acceptable, the market may become more liquid. The increase in the number of trusted crypto exchanges will provide opportunity for more people to trade. Crypto ATMs and payment cards are popping up, helping raise the awareness and acceptance of cryptocurrencies in everyday transactions.

Another key factor in cryptocurrency liquidity is the stance of countries on cryptocurrency regulations. If the authorities are able to define issues such as consumer protection and crypto taxes, more people will be comfortable using and trading cryptocurrencies, which will affect their liquidity.

REMEMBER

When choosing a cryptocurrency to invest in, you must consider its liquidity by analyzing its acceptance, popularity, and the number of exchanges it has been traded on. Lesser-known cryptocurrencies may have a lot of upside potential, but they may put you in trouble because of lack of liquidity. I explore different types of cryptocurrencies and their characteristics in Part 2.

Vanishing risk

No, I'm not talking about disappearing into the ever-magical blockchain industry! Quite the contrary. Thousands of different cryptocurrencies are currently out there. More and more cryptocurrencies are being introduced every day. In ten years' time, many of these altcoins may vanish while others flourish.

A familiar example of vanishing risk is the dot-com bubble. In the late 1990s, many people around the world dreamed up businesses that capitalized on the popularity of the internet. Some, such as Amazon and eBay, succeeded in conquering the world. Many more crashed and burned. Following the path of history, many of the booming cryptocurrencies popping up left and right are destined to bust.

REMEMBER

To minimize the vanishing risk, you need to analyze the fundamentals of the cryptocurrencies you choose to invest in. Do their goals make sense to you? Are they solving a problem that will continue in the years to come? Who are their partners? You can't vanish the vanishing risk entirely (pun intended), but you can eliminate your exposure to a sudden bust. Check out Part 2 for more on fundamental analysis.

Regulation risk

One of the initial attractions of cryptocurrencies was their lack of regulation. In the good old days in cryptoland, crypto enthusiasts didn't have to worry about governments chasing them down. All they had was a white paper and a promise. However, as the demand for cryptocurrencies grows, global regulators are scratching their heads on how to keep up — and not lose their shirts to the new economic reality.

REMEMBER

To date, most digital currencies aren't backed by any central government, meaning each country has different standards.

You can divide the cryptocurrency regulation risk into two components: the regulation event risk and regulation's nature itself.

>> The *regulation event risk* doesn't necessarily mean that the cryptocurrency market is doing poorly. It just means the market participants reacted to an unexpected announcement. Between 2018 and 2022, every seemingly small regulation announcement drove the price of many major cryptocurrencies and created a ton of volatility.

>> At the time of writing, the U.S. Securities and Exchange Commission (SEC) and the Commodity Futures Trading Commission (CFTC) have enforced dozens of regulatory actions. Some crypto investors are happy about the regulations, while others (who are mainly interested in cryptocurrencies for their decentralized nature) aren't. But at large, substantial government regulations have yet to be put in place.

REMEMBER

The future of cryptocurrency regulations seems to be bright at this writing, but it may impact the markets in the future. As the market grows stronger, though, these impacts may turn into isolated events.

Tax risk

When cryptocurrency investing first got popular, hardly anyone was paying taxes on the gains. A lot of underreporting was going on. However, as the market gets more regulated, the authorities may become stricter on taxation.

REMEMBER

As of 2022, the U.S. Internal Revenue Service (IRS) treats gains on cryptocurrencies the same way it treats any kind of capital gains. That means, just like capital gains from investing in stocks, you'll have to pay ordinary tax rates on any gains realized within a year. But for assets held longer than a year, you'll pay long-term capital gains, which is typically lower. In other countries, tax risk can get more complicated. Always be sure to consult with your tax accountant as you build your investment portfolio.

Turn to Chapter 14 for more details on taxes in relation to cryptocurrencies.

Exploring Risk Management Methods

The only way you can achieve your investment goals is to invest at a risk level consistent with your risk tolerance assessment. That's why I talk a lot about methods to calculate your unique risk tolerance in my Invest Diva education courses. You can measure your risk tolerance by considering objective measures like your investment goals, your time horizon for each goal, your need for liquidity, and so on. You can increase your risk tolerance by setting longer-term goals, increasing your income using methods other than online investing, lowering your need for current liquidity, and most important, increasing your confidence in the asset you're planning to invest in by educating yourself about it.

These things are certainly easier said than done, especially considering you never know when you're going to get hit financially. The following sections provide guidance on how to manage risk by building an emergency fund, being patient with your investments, and diversifying.

MEASURING YOUR OWN RISK TOLERANCE

If you ask a traditional financial advisor, they'd tell you your risk tolerance has two main components:

- Your willingness to risk
- Your ability to risk

But throughout my years of investing and helping my students build their investment portfolios, I've come to realize there's a missing component in calculating your risk tolerance the traditional way. And that is: your confidence in the asset you're planning to invest in.

In other words, you can, indeed, increase your willingness to take a risk by increasing your confidence in the asset you're investing in.

A financial planner is likely to have you fill out a risk tolerance questionnaire that measures your willingness to risk. This questionnaire evaluates your willingness to take on risk by asking about risk issues. It can help you determine whether you're risk averse or risk tolerant. A *risk-averse* investor requires significantly more return in order to consider investing in a higher-risk investment. A *risk-tolerant* investor is more willing to accept risk for a small increase in return.

However, to really get an understanding about the amount you can invest in the markets, you must also find out your ability to risk based on your unique financial situation and living circumstances. To calculate your risk tolerance, you must prepare your financial statements and analyze some ratios such as

- **Your emergency fund ratio:** You can calculate this by dividing your accessible cash by your monthly necessary spending. The result must be greater than 6.

- **Your housing ratio:** Divide your housing costs by your gross pay. If you live in the United States, the result must be below 28 percent.

- **Your debt ratio:** This one calculates your total debt divided by your total assets. The benchmark varies depending on your age and financial goals.

(continued)

(continued)

- **Your net worth ratio:** You can calculate this by dividing your net worth (which is all your assets minus your debt) by your total assets.

Using these ratios and comparing them to benchmark numbers, you can then fill out a simple questionnaire to figure out your risk tolerance.

TIP

Download my free risk-management toolkit to calculate your exact risk tolerance: https://investdiva.com/masterclass. See the nearby sidebar for more information, too.

Build your emergency fund first

A few years ago, my family was exposed to an unpredicted financial burden. After a year of financial success for both of us, we went ahead and upgraded our budget, bought a new house in an awesome neighborhood, and added some luxury expenses we normally wouldn't go after. It was good times!

Then an unexpected tax law change in the United States put us in a higher tax bracket than usual and took away some of our previously sought tax exemptions and deductions. Right after that, our daughter was born, and our plans to have our parents take care of her for the first six months fell through because of sudden health issues on both sides of the family. As the saying goes, when it rains, it pours — figuratively and literally. Our area got hit by a few storms, which flooded our basement, damaged our trees, and dropped a few branches on our house. We now needed an additional budget for the damages.

I tell this story simply to point out the importance of having an emergency fund, no matter what you're investing in or what your strategy is. Thanks to our emergency fund, we were able to overcome this financially challenging time and turn our focus back on raising our little bundle of joy. Of course, now we had to rebuild the fund from scratch.

TIP

You can calculate your emergency fund by dividing the value of your total immediately accessible cash by your necessary monthly expenses. That will give you the number of months you can survive with no additional cash flow. The result *must* be greater than six months. But the more the merrier. For more on risk tolerance calculation, visit https://investdiva.com/masterclass.

You must have an emergency fund before creating an investment portfolio, let alone adding cryptocurrencies to it.

Be patient

The risks involved with cryptocurrencies are slightly different from those of other, more established markets such as equities and precious metals. However, you can use similar methods for managing your portfolio risk regardless of your investments.

The most common reason many investors lose money online is the fantasy of getting rich quick. I can say with confidence (verifiably) that the vast majority of my long-term students made money, and in many cases a lot of money. In fact, many of our students have received our $100K Diva, $500K Diva, and even Millionaire Diva awards! These are awarded to my students who have built such a portfolio using my strategies.

But if you need a shortcut, here it is: The key has been patience.

"Patience is a profitable virtue" is the mantra of the Invest Diva movement. The majority of my students' portfolio holdings have been equities and cryptocurrencies. This works because, over time, markets usually go up, even if they're more volatile in the short term. If you're super busy, you can set your portfolio to take advantage of the long-term gains instead of getting stressed over short-term ups and downs.

That being said, the patience mantra doesn't help only long-term investors. It also goes for short-term traders and speculators. Although short-term trading is not something I recommend, very often, that investment or speculative position you took may go down or sideways for what seems like forever. Sooner or later, the market will take note of the sentiment and either erase losses or create new buy opportunities.

In Figure 3-1, you can see the role patience can play in an investor's returns. Of course, you'd love for the markets to just march up to your profit target (that is, exit) price level straightaway. But more often than not, it just doesn't work that way:

» The chart on the left shows a fantasy most traders have when they buy an asset. They hope the price will march up toward their profit target within their trading time frame, whether short term or long term, and make them money.

>> The chart on the right shows the reality. Traders and investors alike often see a lot of dips in the price before the market reaches their profit target. Some investors panic on the dips and call it quits. But in the end, those who were patient and held their position through the rough times win. This can be true to both short-term and long-term investors, so the chart's time frame doesn't really matter.

© *InvestDiva.com*

FIGURE 3-1: Demonstrating why patience is a profitable virtue.

REMEMBER

Success follows a bumpy road. Your portfolio may even turn into negative territory at times. However, if you've done your due diligence of analyzing your investment, you must make time your friend in order to see long-term profit. See Chapter 12 for full details on long-term investing strategies.

A great example of this Idea is the crash of 2008 and 2020. Almost all markets around the world, including the U.S. stock market, dropped like a hot rock because of economic issues such as the mortgage crisis in 2008 and the COVID-19 pandemic in 2020. Most people panicked and started to get out of their investments with massive losses. Had they given it some (well, a lot of) patience, they would've seen their portfolios in positive territory in around five years. By 2022, they would've more than doubled the returns on the very same investments.

Diversify outside and inside your cryptocurrency portfolio

As I note in Chapter 2, diversification is the "don't put all your eggs in one basket" rule, and this age-old investing advice remains true to the revolutionary cryptocurrency market. Besides diversifying your portfolio by adding different assets such as stocks, bonds, or exchange-traded funds (ETFs), diversification within your cryptocurrency portfolio is also important. (See Chapter 10 for some diversification ideas.)

For example, Bitcoin is perhaps the celebrity of all cryptocurrencies, so everyone wants to get hold of it. But Bitcoin is also the oldest cryptocurrency, so it has some unresolvable problems. Every day, younger and better-performing cryptocurrencies make their way into the market and offer exciting opportunities. (I'm not trying to say younger is better in all facets of life. I'm talking about cryptocurrencies here, not people!)

Besides age, you can group cryptocurrencies in several different ways for diversification purposes. Here are some examples (see Chapter 8 for full details):

>> **Major cryptocurrencies by market cap:** This category includes the ones in the top ten. At the time of writing, these options include Bitcoin, Ethereum, Ripple, and Litecoin.

>> **Transactional cryptocurrencies:** This group is the original category for cryptocurrencies. Transactional cryptocurrencies are designed to be used as money and exchanged for goods and services. Bitcoin and Litecoin are examples of well-known cryptos on this list.

>> **Platform cryptocurrencies:** These cryptocurrencies are designed to get rid of intermediaries, create markets, and even launch other cryptocurrencies. Ethereum is one of the biggest cryptos in this category. It provides a backbone for future applications. Such cryptocurrencies are generally considered good long-term investments because they rise in value as more applications are created on their blockchains.

>> **Privacy cryptocurrencies:** These options are similar to transactional cryptocurrencies, but they're heavily focused toward transaction security and anonymity. Examples include Monero, Zcash, and Dash.

>> **Application-specific cryptocurrencies:** One of the trendiest types of cryptos, application-specific cryptocurrencies, serve specific functions and solve some of the world's biggest problems. Some examples of such cryptos are Vechain (used for supply chain applications), IOTA (Internet of Things Application), and Cardano (cryptocurrency scalability, privacy optimizations, and so on). Some get super-specific, such as Mobius, also known as Stripe for the blockchain industry, which was seeking to resolve the payment issues in the agriculture industry in 2018. Depending on the specifics of each project, a number of these cryptos may prove highly successful. You can pick the ones that are solving issues closer to your heart; just be sure to analyze their usability, application performance, and project team properly.

One key problem the cryptocurrency market faces when it comes to diversification is that the whole market appears to be extremely correlated. The majority of cryptocurrencies go up when the market sentiment turns bullish (upward), and vice versa. Despite this tendency, you can diversify away risk in a crypto-only portfolio by adding more crypto assets to your portfolio. By investing in multiple crypto assets, or the top cryptocurrencies in each crypto category, you can spread out the amount of risk you're exposed to instead of having all the volatility of the portfolio come from one or a few assets. Turn to Chapter 10 for the full scoop on diversification in cryptocurrencies.

Chapter **4**

Looking at Blockchain Technology

Most people have probably heard about Bitcoin more than they have blockchain. Many people who *have* heard of blockchain think it's just the technology that powers Bitcoin. Although Bitcoin became one of the most famous outcomes of blockchain technology, blockchain is capable of so much more. It is perhaps one of the most interruptive technologies in decades and may change our lives forever.

Simply put, the relationship between Bitcoin and blockchain is similar to the relationship between email and the internet. To be able to send and receive emails, you need the internet. Similarly, to be able to use any crypto, you need blockchain technology.

In this chapter, I take a look at how blockchain technology works, why it matters, and how it can impact your life in the future. Having a better understanding of blockchain technology may help reshape your view on the cryptocurrency market. That way, you can make better investment decisions in the industry.

Breaking Down Blockchain Technology Basics

Modern technologies allow people to communicate directly. You can use them to directly send emails, text messages, pictures, and videos to others without the use of an intermediary. This way, you can maintain trust with others no matter where they are in the world. Long-distance relationships aren't as hard and heart-wrenching anymore. For example, my family has maintained years and years of long-distance relationships only possible due to the advent of the internet. I attended my sister's wedding in Los Angeles via Skype when I was in Tokyo. My Australia-based in-laws, who weren't able to travel due to a terminal illness, were able to attend our wedding in Hawaii via FaceTime.

Despite this advancement, people still have to trust a third party to complete a financial transaction. But blockchain technology is challenging this setup in a radical way. I explain the basics of blockchain technology in the following sections.

What is a blockchain, and how does it work?

Simply put, a *blockchain* is a special kind of database. According to the Center for International Governance Innovation (www. cigionline.org), the term *blockchain* refers to the whole network of distributed ledger technologies. According to Oxford Dictionaries, a *ledger* is "a book or other collection of financial accounts of a particular type." It can be a computer file that records transactions. A ledger is actually the foundation of accounting and is as old as writing and money.

Now imagine a whole suite of incorruptible digital ledgers of economic transactions that can be programmed to record and track not only financial transactions but also virtually everything of value. The blockchain can track things like medical records, land titles, and even voting (as you find out later in this chapter). It's a shared, distributed, and immutable ledger that records the history of transactions starting with transaction number one. It establishes trust, accountability, and transparency.

Blockchain stores information in batches called *blocks*. These blocks are linked together in a sequential way to form a continuous line. A chain of blocks. A blockchain. Each block is like a page of a ledger or a record book. As you can see in Figure 4-1, each block mainly has three elements:

>> **Data:** The type of data depends on what the blockchain is being used for. In Bitcoin, for example, a block's data contains the details about the transaction, including sender, receiver, number of coins, and so on.

>> **Hash:** No, I'm not talking about *that* kind of hash. A *hash* in blockchain is something like a fingerprint or signature. It identifies a block and all its content, and it's always unique.

>> **Hash of previous block:** This piece is precisely what makes a blockchain! Because each block carries the information of the previous block, the chain becomes very secure.

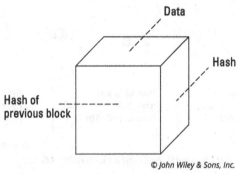

© *John Wiley & Sons, Inc.*

FIGURE 4-1: Three main elements of a block.

Here's an example of how a bunch of blocks come together in a blockchain. Say you have three blocks.

Block 1 contains this stuff:

>> **Data:** 10 Bitcoins from Fred to Jack

>> **Hash (simplified):** 12A

>> **Previous hash (simplified):** 000

Block 2 contains this stuff:

>> **Data:** 5 Bitcoins from Jack to Mary

>> **Hash (simplified):** 3B4

>> **Previous hash:** 12A

Block 3 contains this stuff:

>> **Data:** 4 Bitcoins from Mary to Sally

>> **Hash (simplified):** C74

>> **Previous hash:** 3B4

As you can see in Figure 4-2, each block has its own hash and a hash of the previous block. So, block 3 points to block 2, and block 2 points to block 1. (*Note:* The first block is a bit special because it can't point to a previous block. This block is the *genesis block.*)

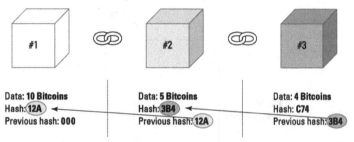

Data: **10 Bitcoins**
Hash: 12A
Previous hash: **000**

Data: **5 Bitcoins**
Hash: 3B4
Previous hash: 12A

Data: **4 Bitcoins**
Hash: **C74**
Previous hash: 3B4

© John Wiley & Sons, Inc.

FIGURE 4-2: Simplified version of how a blockchain works.

The hashes and the data are unique to each block, but they can still be tampered with. The following section lays out some ways blockchains secure themselves.

How does a blockchain secure itself?

Interfering with a block on the blockchain is almost impossible to do. The first way a blockchain secures itself is by hashing. Tampering with a block within a blockchain causes the hash of the block to change. That change makes the following block, which originally pointed to the first block's hash, invalid. In fact, changing a single block makes all the following blocks invalid. This setup gives the blockchain a level of security.

However, using hashing isn't enough to prevent tampering. That's because computers are superfast, and they can calculate more than 100 trillion hashes per second. Technically, a hacker can change the hash of a specific block and then calculate and change all the hashes of the following blocks in order to hide the tampering.

That's why on top of the hashes, blockchains have additional security steps, including things like proof of work and peer-to-peer distribution. A *proof of work* (PoW) is a mechanism that slows down the creation of the blocks. In Bitcoin's case, for example, it takes about ten minutes to calculate the required PoW and add a new block to the chain. This timeline makes tampering with a block super difficult because if you interfere with one block, you need to interfere with all the following blocks. A blockchain like Bitcoin contains hundreds of thousands of blocks, so successfully manipulating it can take more than ten years! I explore more about PoW in Chapter 5.

Another way blockchains secure themselves is by being distributed. Blockchains don't use a central entity to manage the chain. Instead, they use a *peer-to-peer* (P2P) network. In public blockchains like Bitcoin, everyone is allowed to join. Each member of the network is called a *validator* or a *node*. When someone joins the network, they get the full copy of the blockchain. This way, the node can verify that everything is still in order.

Here's what happens when someone creates a new block in the network:

1. The new block is sent to everyone in the network.

2. Each node verifies the block and makes sure it hasn't been tampered with.

3. If everything checks out, each node adds this new block to their own blockchain.

All the nodes in this process create a consensus. They agree about which blocks are valid and which ones aren't. The other nodes in the network reject blocks that are tampered with. So, to successfully mess with a block on a blockchain, you'd need to tamper with all the blocks on the chain, redo the PoW for each block, and take control of the P2P network!

REMEMBER

Blockchains are also constantly evolving. One of the most recent developments in the cryptocurrency ecosystem is the addition of something called a smart contract. A *smart contract* is a digital computer program stored inside a blockchain. It can directly control the transfer of cryptocurrencies or other digital assets based on certain conditions. Find out more on smart contracts in Chapter 5.

Why is blockchain revolutionary?

Here are three main reasons blockchain is different from other kinds of database and tracking systems already in use.

Blockchain may eliminate data tampering because of the way it tracks and stores data

REMEMBER

If you make a change to the information recorded in one particular block of a blockchain, you don't rewrite it. Instead, the change is stored in a new block. Therefore, you can't rewrite history — no one can — because that new block shows the change, as well as the date and time of the change. This approach is actually based on a century-old method of the general financial ledger.

I can explain the difference through an example. Suppose Joe and his cousin Matt have a dispute over who owns the furniture shop they've been comanaging for years. Because the blockchain technology uses the ledger method, the ledger should have an entry showing that George first owned the shop in 1947. When George sold the shop to Mary in 1976, he made a new entry in the ledger, and so on. Every change of ownership of this shop is represented by a new entry in the ledger, right up until Matt bought it from his uncle in 2009. By going through the history in the ledger, Matt can show that he is, in fact, the current owner.

Now, here's how blockchain would approach this dispute differently from the age-old ledger method. The traditional ledger method uses a book or a database file stored in a single (centralized) system. However, blockchain was designed to be *decentralized* and distributed across a large network of computers. This decentralizing of information reduces the ability for data tampering.

WARNING

Blockchain attacks in the past show that data tampering can't be completely eliminated on the blockchain database as is. If 51 percent of miners decide to rewrite the ledger, it would be possible, and as a result, they can do whatever they want with the transaction: They can delay it, double-spend the coins, postpone it, or simply remove it from the block. Several blockchain networks are currently working on a custom solution for this. Even some of the traditional tech giants such as IBM have now dedicated a whole arm to blockchain services and consulting to help blockchain networks address their security and governance issues. (For more information, see www.ibm.com/topics/blockchain-security.)

Blockchain creates trust in the data

The unique way blockchain works creates trust in the data. I get more into the specifics earlier in this chapter, but here's a simplified version to show you why. Before a block can be added to the chain, a few things have to happen:

1. A cryptographic puzzle must be solved to create the new block.

2. The computer that solves the puzzle shares the solution with all the other computers in the network. This solution is the PoW I discuss briefly in the earlier section "How does a blockchain secure itself?" and in more detail in Chapter 5.

3. All the computers involved in the network verify the PoW. If 51 percent of the network testifies that the PoW was correct, the new block is added to the chain.

The combination of these complex math puzzles and verification by many computers ensures that users can trust each and every block on the chain. Heck, one of the main reasons I'm a big supporter of cryptocurrencies is that I trust in the blockchain technology so much. Because the network does the trust-building for you, you now have the opportunity to interact with your data in real time.

Centralized third parties aren't necessary

In my previous example of the dispute between Joe and Matt, each of the cousins may have hired a lawyer or a trusted *centralized* third party to go through the ledger and the documentation of the shop ownership. They trust the lawyers to keep the financial information and the documentation confidential. The third-party lawyers try to build trust between their clients and verify that Matt is, indeed, the rightful owner of the shop. (For the details of the example, check out "Blockchain may eliminate data tampering because of the way it tracks and stores data.")

The problem with centralized third parties and intermediaries such as lawyers and banks is that they add an extra step to resolving the dispute, resulting in spending more time and money.

If Matt's ownership information had been stored in a blockchain, he would've been able to cut out the centralized intermediary, his lawyer. That's because all blocks added to the chain would've been verified to be true and couldn't be tampered with. In other words, the blockchain network and the miners are now the third party, which makes the process faster and more affordable. So, Matt could simply show Joe his ownership information secured on the blockchain. He would save a ton of money and time by cutting out the centralized intermediary.

This type of trusted, P2P interaction with data can revolutionize the way people access, verify, and transact with one another. And because blockchain is a type of technology and not a single network, it can be implemented in many different ways, as I explain later in this chapter.

Perusing Problems with Blockchain

The blockchain technology I describe earlier in this chapter is all sexy and revolutionary, but it sure has a bunch of problems it has to deal with before it becomes truly adapted to daily life. Here are some of the issues and barriers that blockchain has to overcome before you get too excited or too involved.

Scalability problems

Scalability is perhaps one of the most immediate problems that blockchain technology faces. Earlier in this chapter, I talk about how the blockchain secures itself, and how hackers would need a long time to be able to tamper with the system successfully. Well, this security comes at a cost for the users, too. Blockchain transactions are slow and expensive. For example, the Bitcoin network is capable of processing a maximum of seven transactions per second — for the millions of users worldwide. Additionally, to increase payment security, Bitcoin-blockchain transactions are recorded only once every ten minutes. Now imagine everyone on the planet using Bitcoins for transactions and having to wait this long for each throughput. Scary, isn't it?

However, at the time of writing, data shows that Bitcoin Lightning Network has finally solved the scalability problem. The Lightning Network is a way to make Bitcoin better. It makes it faster and easier to use. This is done by adding a second layer to the Bitcoin network and is the scaling solution that everyone in the crypto world is focused on.

Other solutions include using things like a hard fork (explained in Chapter 5), the Lightning Network, and sharding:

>> According to CoinDesk, "the Lightning Network effectively creates a layer on top of Bitcoin, enabling fast and cheap transactions, which can net settle to the Bitcoin blockchain." The concept "is based on a network that sits on top of the Bitcoin blockchain and eventually settles on it. The network is comprised of user-generated channels that send payments back and forth in a secure and trust-less fashion (*trust-less* means that you don't need to trust or even know your counterparty)." Essentially, the Lightning Network takes the transactions away from the main blockchain and, therefore, reduces transaction fees and time.

>> *Sharding* is another proposed solution for the blockchain's scalability problem and is a concept that's widely used in databases to make them more efficient. Simply put, for cryptocurrencies sharding assigns random nodes rather than the entire network to validate a transaction on the blockchain network. The idea is that smaller sets of nodes can crunch the data faster and that the random distribution means nobody is stuck doing all the work. Sharding as a technology raises some concerns, the most basic being whether an unethical actor can manipulate a shard and whether members of a shard should be compensated.

With all the possible solutions being proposed left and right, investors can be hopeful that the blockchain's scalability problem can be solved sooner rather than later.

Environmental problems

One of the biggest problems environmentalists have with blockchains such as Bitcoin that use the PoW mining system is the amount of energy they waste at the environment's cost. Many investors refuse to add cryptocurrencies to their portfolio purely for this reason.

According to the *New York Times*, the Bitcoin network uses around 91 terawatt-hours (91 TWh) of electricity annually, which is more energy used than countries like Finland. Other sources put this number at 150 TWh per year, which is more energy than Argentina, a nation of 45 million people.

That being said, in reality, calculating the carbon footprint of cryptocurrency is more complicated. As cryptocurrency and blockchain technology evolve, more efficient hardware will be introduced that requires less energy. For example, blockchains that use the proof-of-stake (PoS) method of mining new coins don't use expensive computer powers and are, therefore, more environmentally friendly.

TECHNICAL STUFF

New methods of mining cryptocurrency are being introduced, such as *proof of burn*, which is a mix of PoW and PoS. At the time of writing, these new methods haven't yet caught on in any significant way, but such new ideas and research shows that we may at least be headed in the right direction when solving the environmental issues caused by blockchain. In fact, the Crypto Climate Accord has gathered 250 signatures from individuals and companies who have committed themselves to reducing their carbon emissions to net zero by 2030 and eventually decarbonizing the entire cryptocurrency industry by 2040.

TIP

If you want be a part of the solution to blockchain environmental issues, check out https://cryptoclimate.org/solutions.

Fraud problems

The blockchain industry has had a ton of hype around it, particularly regarding the cryptocurrency market (as I talk about in Chapter 3). Some companies in the financial world are trying to take advantage of the excitement surrounding blockchain. In 2018, Nasdaq delisted one company due to concerns that the company made "public statements designed to mislead investors and to take advantage of general investor interest in Bitcoin and blockchain technology." And the Securities and Exchange Commission (SEC) has taken action against companies that have made false and misleading statements about blockchain technology in an effort to pump up the price of the stock. This isn't a new kind of fraud; it's the same old story where a company changes its game, takes advantage of a hot trend, and makes baseless claims to attract new investors to pump, and then dump, the stock.

Additionally, some fraudsters have attempted to capitalize on the mystery and excitement around the term *blockchain* to target investors. Scammers have posed as legitimate websites that provide services to cryptocurrency users to target unknowing users.

The list goes on. These stories only prove the importance of being educated on the subject matter before getting too hyped up and overly involved. You have the right book in your hands to get you started with that!

Political problems

Earlier in this chapter, I talk about how blockchain technology cuts out the intermediary. Now consider how big this intermediary industry is. All the banks, brokers, lawyers, you name it — all of them make huge profits from playing the intermediary role. As of now, because the cost is distributed among millions of customers, end users usually pay very little individually. But if blockchain continues to replace these roles, it may pose a serious danger to their business — unless they join the movement, that is.

In most countries, including the United States, banks carry huge lobbying power with governments and legislators. The established financial services industry could dramatically reduce blockchain's usefulness and restrict its availability (if not kill it altogether) should it decide doing so is to the industry's benefit. But then again, the people have power, too. And the more people know about the advantages of using blockchain technology, the harder time politicians and the financial establishment will have standing in the way of its growth.

Discovering What Blockchain Can Be Used For

The creation of the blockchain technology has piqued a lot of people's interest. Supposedly, someone called Satoshi Nakamoto invented blockchain in 2008. Blockchain's original intent was Bitcoin. Or perhaps Satoshi used Bitcoin as a tool to introduce blockchain to the masses. Regardless, soon people realized blockchain technology can be used for different purposes, such as identity verification and storing medical records. The following sections explain how a few different categories can use blockchain and, more important, how the cryptocurrency market uses it.

TECHNICAL STUFF

No one knows who Satoshi Nakamoto is. It may be a man, a woman, or a team of anonymous geeks. In fact, a women-on-the-block movement is out to prove that Satoshi is female!

Payments

As I cover throughout this book, money transferring was the first and most popular usage of the blockchain technology. For more than 40 years, economists have been seeking the holy grail of a digital currency that can eliminate the problem of double-spending and circumvent the issue of needing to trust an unknown third party. And then — bam! — Satoshi's white paper was published in October 2008 and removed banks from the equation, just like that. Disregarding the scalability problem that I describe earlier in this chapter, with banks removed from transactions, most payments processed over a blockchain can be settled within a matter of seconds.

Voting

Voting fraud has been an ongoing theme in democratic, and not-so-democratic, countries. Blockchain technology can put you (and all your political debaters on social media) at ease. Digital voting through the blockchain can offer enough transparency that anyone would be able to see whether something was changed on the network. It combines the ease of digital voting with the security of blockchain to make your vote truly count.

Supply chain monitoring

Are you one of those people who must know where their food comes from? Is it organic, kosher, halal? Is there a foodborne illness you need to be aware of immediately? With the help of the blockchain, you can trace your food from its origin to your plate. It can help you make ethical, healthy choices about the things you buy.

Blockchain can also help consumers view how products performed from a quality-control perspective as they traveled from their place of origin to the retailer. Furthermore, it can help businesses pinpoint their inefficiencies within their supply chains quickly. The blockchain removes the paper-based trails and locates items in real time.

Identity verification

This is an era where people are stuck between their digital identity and their actual physical presence. Credit agencies and social networks such as Facebook and Instagram act as the main gatekeepers for online identity. Meanwhile, consumers are longing for a reliable digital identity system to maintain credit records and prove who they are to employers, banks, or car rental companies without letting private corporations make money from selling their data.

To overcome this challenge, many companies are already using blockchain technology and creating a secure digital identification system that would give users a way to control their digital identities. Some examples include Microsoft's Authenticator app and Deloitte's Smart Identity platform.

Legal ownership of stuff

You can get into legal trouble in so many ways. Family disputes. Lost legal paperwork. Lost assets that aren't easily traceable. Most of people's assets are currently documented on paper. And as I talk about earlier in this chapter, blockchain is hard at work to keep paper, and all the intermediaries attached to it, out of the way. So, if you're buying or selling land, a house, or a car, the blockchain can store titles on its network, allowing for a transparent view of this transfer and legal ownership.

Additionally, if your high-value, portable assets such as bikes, jet skis, luxury handbags, and so on are stolen, you may be able to trace them back using companies who are working on providing such blockchain-based services.

Health care

One major problem with medical records has been paper record-keeping, which the medical sector (at least in the United States) has been trying to move away from for years. Another issue has been medical identity theft. In the United States alone, the National Health Care Anti-Fraud Association estimates the loss owing to health-care fraud to be about $300 billion annually.

Blockchain to the rescue! All medical information related to a patient — such as past and present ailments, treatments, and family history of medical problems — will be stored on the block-chain. This approach will make every record permanent, transferable, and accessible, which will prevent the medical records from being lost or modified. Additionally, the patient, who possesses the key to access these digital records, will be in control of who gains access to that data.

Entertainment

It's not all dull around the block. The many branches of the entertainment industry can benefit from blockchain technology, if they haven't already started. The music and e-sports industries are a couple of examples.

The internet democratized content creation in the early 2000s, but a new type of intermediary has emerged in digital content. Platforms like YouTube (2.4 billion users), SoundCloud (176 million), Spotify (433 million), and Netflix (around 223 million) are now the intermediaries controlling users and artists.

This amount of control has caused a ton of disputes around artists' compensation. Even someone as famous as Taylor Swift had to go at it with Apple Music and Spotify. As artists grow increasingly disillusioned with such platforms, blockchain technology can be an exciting new option.

The blockchain can give label companies the ability to have completely encrypted records of ownership. When applied to media consumption, the technology can solve the problems surrounding content access, distribution, compensation, managing assets, and digital rights, among others.

Another example of blockchain in the entertainment industry is e-sports betting. Though I don't encourage this type of gambling entertainment, e-sports betting was pretty popular in the United States in 2018 and is now gaining popularity in Europe and Asia, too.

Energy

Using blockchain, people can trade energy among themselves, cutting out the energy companies (yep, the intermediary or middleman). According to Renewable Energy World (www. renewableenergyworld.com), "this shift [to P2P distribution of energy] will stimulate more renewable energy projects as a whole, ultimately forwarding our transition from carbon-emitting electricity generation. Tokenizing renewable energy allows wind, solar, and hydro producers to seamlessly connect with investors, who are willing to pay up front for the right to consume renewable energy. As a distributed system, the middleman is removed."

Internet of Things

The *Internet of Things* (IoT) is basically the fact that most of your stuff is connected to the internet. For example, we control almost everything in our house, from bedside lamps to air-conditioning to the microwave oven and even the baby's crib, through the internet! While my parents were staying with us to help with our newborn, my husband would sometimes mess with them, turning off the light or TV remotely, using his phone, without their knowing. Of course, I don't think we'll get them to come back for help if we have another baby.

Besides acting as a control freak, the IoT helps you send and receive data within the network of your physical devices. If you can directly integrate your physical world into computer-based systems, you may be able to reduce human exertions and improve your efficiency. According to an article in the IEEE *Internet Initiative* newsletter, "IoT capabilities are considered as 'game-changing' when combined with the concepts of big data analytics and cloud computing" (other hot topics of the tech world). Put it next to blockchain, and you may be taking the true next step into the future.

Chapter **5**

Understanding How Cryptocurrencies Work

I n Chapter 4, I explain how blockchain technology works. Cryptocurrencies, and more specifically Bitcoin, have been one of the first use cases for blockchain technology. That's why most people may have heard about Bitcoin more than they have about the underlying blockchain technology.

In this chapter, I go into more detail about how cryptocurrencies use blockchain technology, how they operate, and how they're generated, as well as some crypto-geek terms you can impress your date or teenage kids with.

Explaining Basic Terms in the Cryptocurrency Process

Cryptocurrencies are also known as digital coins, but they're quite different from the coins in your piggy bank. For one thing, they traditionally aren't attached to a central bank, a country, or a regulatory body.

Here's an example: Say you want to buy the latest version of *Investing in Cryptocurrency For Dummies* from your local bookstore. Using your normal debit card, this is what happens:

1. You give your card details to the cashier or the store's point-of-sale system.

2. The store runs the info through, essentially asking your bank whether you have enough money in your bank account to buy the book.

3. The bank checks its records to confirm whether you do.

4. If you have enough, the bank gives a thumbs-up to the bookstore.

5. The bank updates its records to show the movement of the money from your account to the bookstore's account.

6. The bank gets a little cut for the trouble of being the intermediary.

Now if you wanted to remove the bank from this entire process, who else would you trust to keep all these records without altering them or cheating in any way? Your best friend? Your dog walker? (I hope you didn't say the crown prince of Nigeria.) In fact, you may not trust any single person. But how about trusting *everyone* in the network?

REMEMBER

As I explain in Chapter 4, blockchain technology works to remove the intermediary. When applied to cryptocurrencies, blockchain eliminates a central record of transactions. Instead, you distribute many copies of your transaction ledger around the world. Each owner of each copy records your transaction of buying the book.

Here's what happens if you want to buy this book using a cryptocurrency:

1. You give your crypto details to the cashier.

2. The shop asks everyone in the network to see whether you have enough coins to buy the book.

3. All the record holders in the network check their records to see whether you do. (These record holders are called *nodes*; I explain their function in more detail later in this chapter.)

4. If you have enough, each node gives the thumbs-up to the cashier.

5. The nodes all update their records to show the transfer.

6. At random, a node gets a reward for the work.

That means no organization is keeping track of where your coins are or investigating fraud. In fact, cryptocurrencies such as Bitcoin wouldn't exist without a whole network of bookkeepers (nodes) and a little thing known as cryptography. In the following sections, I explain that and some other important terms related to the workings of cryptocurrencies.

Cryptography

Shhh. Don't tell anyone. That's the *crypto* in *cryptography* and *cryptocurrency*. It means "secret." In the cryptocurrency world, it mainly refers to being "anonymous."

Historically, cryptography is an ancient art for sending hidden messages. (The term comes from the Greek word *krypto logos*, which means *secret writing*.) The sender *encrypts* the message by using some sort of key. The receiver then has to *decrypt* it. For example, 19th-century scholars decrypted ancient Egyptian hieroglyphics when Napoleon's soldiers found the Rosetta Stone in 1799 near Rosetta, Egypt. In the 21st-century era of information networks, the sender can digitally encrypt messages, and the receiver can use cryptographic services and algorithms to decrypt them.

REMEMBER

What does Napoleon have to do with cryptocurrencies? Cryptocurrencies use cryptography to maintain security and anonymity. That's how digital coins, even though they're not issued by any central authority or regulatory body, can help with security and protection from double-spending, which is the risk of your digital cash being used more than once.

Cryptography uses three main encryption methods:

>> **Hashing:** I talk about hashing briefly in Chapter 4, explaining how it's something like a fingerprint or signature. A *hash function* takes your input data (which can be of any size), performs an operation on the original data, and returns an output that represents the original data but has a fixed (and generally smaller) size. In cryptocurrencies such as Bitcoin, it's used to guess the combination of the lock of a block. Hashing maintains the structure of blockchain data,

encodes people's account addresses, and makes block mining possible. You can find more on mining later in this chapter.

>> **Symmetric encryption cryptography:** *Symmetric encryption* is the simplest method used in cryptography. It involves only one secret key for both the sender and the receiver. The main disadvantage of symmetric encryption is that all parties involved have to exchange the key used to encrypt the data before they can decrypt it.

>> **Asymmetric encryption cryptography:** *Asymmetric encryption* uses two keys: a public key and a private key. You can encrypt a message by using the receiver's public key, but the receiver can decrypt it only with their private key.

Nodes

I mention nodes in the examples in this chapter and in Chapter 4. A *node* is an electronic device doing the bookkeeping job in the blockchain network, making the whole decentralized thing possible. The device can be a computer, a cellphone, or even a printer, as long as it is connected to the internet and has access to the blockchain network.

Mining

As the owners of nodes (see the preceding section) willingly contribute their computing resources to store and validate transactions, they have the chance to collect the transaction fees and earn a reward in the underlying cryptocurrency for doing so. This process is known as *mining,* and the owners who do it are *miners.*

REMEMBER

Let me make something clear: Not all cryptocurrencies can be mined. Bitcoin and some other famous ones can. Some others, such as Ripple (XRP), avoid mining altogether because they want a platform that doesn't consume a huge amount of energy in the process of mining; power usage is one of the issues with blockchain that I bring up in Chapter 4, actually. Regardless, for the most part, mining remains a huge part of many cryptocurrencies to date.

Here's how mining works: Cryptocurrency miners solve cryptographic puzzles (via software) to add transactions to the ledger (the blockchain) in the hopes of getting coins as a reward. It's called *mining* because of the fact that this process helps extract new cryptocurrencies from the system. Anyone, including you, can join this group. Your computer needs to "guess" a random number that solves an equation that the blockchain system generates. In fact, your computer has to calculate many 64-character strings or 256-bit hashes and check with the challenge equation to see whether the answer is right. That's why it's so important that you have a powerful computer. The more powerful your computer is, the more guesses it can make in a second, increasing your chances of winning this game. If you manage to guess right, you earn Bitcoins and get to write the "next page" of Bitcoin transactions on the blockchain.

Because mining is based on a form of guessing, for each block a different miner guesses the number and is granted the right to update the blockchain. Whoever has the biggest computing power combined, controlling 51 percent of the votes, controls the chain and can arguably win. Thanks to the law of statistical probability, the same miner is unlikely to succeed every time. On the other hand, this game can sometimes be unfair because the biggest computer power will be the first to solve the challenge equation and "win" more often. That being said, it would be very, very difficult to control 51 percent of the Bitcoin network, and even then, you wouldn't win every time, so this may not even be an issue.

Proof of work

If you're a miner and you want to actually enter your block and transactions into the blockchain, you have to provide an answer (proof) to a specific challenge. This proof is difficult to produce (hence, all the gigantic computers, time, and money needed for it), but others can very easily verify it. This process is known as *proof of work* (PoW).

For example, guessing a combination to a lock is a proof to a challenge. Going through all the different possible combinations to come up with the right answer may be pretty hard, but after you get it, it's easy to validate — just enter the combination and see whether the lock opens! The first miner who solves the problem for each block on the blockchain gets a reward. The reward is basically the incentive to keep mining and gets the miners competing to be the first one to find a solution for mathematical problems. Bitcoin and some other minable cryptocurrencies mainly use the PoW concept to make sure that the network isn't easily manipulated.

As I talk about in Chapter 4, this whole PoW thing has some downsides for blockchain technology. One of the main challenges is that it consumes a lot of computing power and electricity just for the sake of producing random guesses. That's why new cryptocurrencies have jumped on an alternative wagon called proof of stake, covered in the next section.

Proof of stake

As PoW consensus started to get more heat from environmentalists, a new protocol, proof of stake (PoS), was created. Unlike PoW, a PoS system requires you to show ownership of a certain amount of money (or *stake*). That means the more crypto you own, the more mining power you have. This approach eliminates the need for an expensive mining extravaganza. And because the calculations are pretty simple to prove, you own a certain percentage of the total amount of the cryptos available.

Another difference is that the PoS system offers no block rewards, so the miners get transaction fees. That's how PoS cryptos can be several thousand times more cost-effective than PoW ones. (Don't let the PoS abbreviation give you the wrong idea.)

Some famous PoS blockchains at the time of writing include Polkadot (DOT), Avalanche (AVAX), and Cardano (ADA).

But of course, PoS also can have its own problems. For starters, you can argue that PoS rewards coin hoarders. Under the PoS model, nodes can mine only a percentage of transactions that corresponds to their stake in a cryptocurrency. For example, a PoS miner who owns 10 percent of a cryptocurrency would be able to mine 10 percent of blocks on the network. The limitation with this consensus model is that it gives nodes on the network a reason to save their coins instead of spending them. It also produces a scenario in which the rich get richer because large coin holders are able to mine a larger percentage of blocks on the network and may have an excessive influence on transaction validation.

Delegated proof of stake

The crypto world is constantly evolving, and a popular evolution of the PoS concept is the *delegated proof of stake* (DPoS). In this mechanism, users of the network vote and elect delegates to validate the next block. For each new block, the network chooses a limited number of delegates. For most protocols, this number is anywhere between 20 and 100. It's a bit more democratic than PoS, if you will.

WARNING

Although DPoS is praised for being more democratic, there's still a chance that a network could become more centralized than traditional blockchain mechanisms. This also means voters with a larger number of staked tokens have more power, and if the power falls into the hands of bad actors, they could abuse their power. Another issue with DPoS is related to network security. Because fewer people are responsible for maintaining the network, it's easier for hackers to organize a 51 percent attack and screw the network over.

DPoS was first coined by EOS's former chief technology officer, Dan Larimer, in 2014. Some other blockchains that use DPoS include TRON (TRX) and Lisk (LSK).

Proof of authority

A *proof-of-authority* (PoA) consensus is all about the value of identity and reputation. The validators on a PoA blockchain don't stake coins; instead, they stake their reputation. That means PoAs are secured by elected nodes who were voted as trustworthy entities.

This consensus mechanism is typically used by private networks and companies who want to maintain their privacy while reaping the benefits of blockchain without the need for a native currency or the need for mining. This means PoAs waste a whole lot less energy to operate.

Supply chain networks and Microsoft Azure are examples of where PoA is being implemented. Microsoft Azure is using PoA in its Ethereum-powered cloud-computing system, offering solutions for GE Aviation. In supply chain, Walmart collaborates with the VeChain blockchain to help address food safety issues and optimize product recalls.

TECHNICAL STUFF

The other consensus mechanisms mentioned here gear towards decentralization, but PoA is centralized (find out more about decentralization later in this chapter). It's primarily an attempt to improve the efficiency of traditional centralized systems. It sacrifices decentralization to achieve high output and scalability. But that doesn't mean it's immune to censorship and blacklisting.

Proof of history

Also known as a *clock for blockchain*, the *proof-of-history* (PoH) mechanism aims to address the time-stamp problem.

What's the time-stamp problem, you ask? Let me ask you a question before answering your question:

> Which came first, the chicken or the egg?

PoH may not be able to answer that question, but in our normal time-bounded world, it can prove that a transaction occurred sometime before or after an event (instead of trusting the time stamp on the transaction).

I know, the world of blockchain has lots of trust issues! That's mainly due to the fast speed at which the networks can operate and the complexity of the distributed systems.

Think of it as an international airport. For all the airplanes to operate in a timely manner and for the destination airport to know the exact time of arrival, there must be a centralized clock. With the advent of the internet and as our communications got even faster than airplanes, there was even more need for a standardized time. For example, when you land in your new destination that has a different time zone than your departing location, your phone checks back with a centralized clock to make sure it's accurate at your new location. (Yes, your phone is pretty clever!)

TECHNICAL STUFF

PoH is like a clock that stamps transactions with a hash. The hash shows when the transaction happened and makes it valid. This means the network doesn't need to worry about verifying the time claims of nodes. It can rely on the system to do this instead. This makes it easier for nodes to process blocks and put them in the ledger. PoH, and its first web-scale blockchain, Solana, rose to fame to eliminate the "talking between validators" to agree that time has passed. Instead, each validator in PoH blockchains such as Solana has its own clock and encodes the passage of time in a sequential-hashing verifiable delay function (VDF).

How is this different from traditional blockchains such as PoW? The traditional blockchain infrastructure relies on sequential block production, but the structure could get delayed as the network waits for confirmation across the board before it can move on to the next block. According to Anatoly Yakovenko, cofounder of Solana Labs, in a PoH system, "every block producer has to crank through the VDF to get to their assigned slot and produce the block." This helps the blockchain to validate information a lot quicker and with a higher level of confidence.

PoH still has its own drawbacks compared to traditional consensus systems. For one, to become a validator in a PoH system, your hardware needs to meet strict specifications described in the Solana documents (see `https://docs.solana.com/running-validator/validator-reqs`).

At the time of writing, Solana is the most famous PoH-based blockchain, and there are concerns about the extent of its decentralization competitiveness. Although Solana does have features of decentralization, it appears to be more centralized than Ethereum, its biggest competitor (find out more about decentralization later in this chapter).

Proof of importance

Proof of importance (PoI) was first introduced by a blockchain platform called NEM to support its XEM cryptocurrency. In some ways PoI is similar to PoS because participants (nodes) are marked as "eligible" if they have a certain amount of crypto "vested." Then the network gives a "score" to the eligible nodes, and they can create a block that is roughly the same proportion to that "score." But the difference is that the nodes won't get a higher score only by holding onto more cryptocurrencies. Other variables are considered in the score, too, in order to resolve the primary problem with PoS, which is hoarding. The NEM community in particular uses a method called *harvesting* to solve the PoS "hoarding" problem.

Here's how Investopedia defines harvesting: "Instead of each miner contributing its mining power in a cumulative manner to a computing node, a harvesting participant simply links his account to an existing supernode and uses that account's computing power to complete blocks on his behalf." (I talk about harvesting later in this chapter.)

Transactions: Putting it all together

Here's a summary of how cryptocurrencies work (check out the preceding sections for details on some of the terminology):

1. When you want to use cryptos to purchase something, first your crypto network and your crypto wallet automatically check your previous transactions to make sure you have enough cryptocurrencies to make that transaction. For this, you need your private and public keys (explained in Chapter 7).

2. The transaction is encrypted, broadcast to the cryptocurrency's network, and queued up to be added to the public ledger.

3. Transactions are recorded on the public ledger through mining. The sending and receiving addresses are wallet IDs or hash values that aren't tied to the user identification, so they're anonymous.

4. For PoW cryptos, the miners have to solve a math puzzle to verify the transaction. PoS cryptos attribute the mining power to the proportion of the coins held by the miners, instead of utilizing energy to solve math problems, in order to resolve the "wasted energy" problem of PoW. The PoI cryptos add a number of variables when attributing the mining power to nodes in order to resolve the "hoarding" problem that's associated with PoS.

Cruising through Other Important Crypto Concepts

Earlier in this chapter and in Chapter 4, I talk about the basics of cryptocurrencies and how they're related to blockchain technology. I dig into more details about brokers, exchanges, wallets, and different types of cryptocurrencies in Part 2, but here I want to get a few more concepts out of the way, just in case someone starts talking to you about them. Other factors make cryptocurrencies special and different from your government-backed legal tender, also known as *fiat currency*, such as the U.S. dollar.

Adaptive scaling

Adaptive scaling is one of the advantages of investing in cryptocurrencies. It means that it gets harder to mine a specific cryptocurrency over time. It allows cryptocurrencies to work well on both small and large scales. That's why cryptocurrencies take measures such as limiting the supply over time (to create scarcity) and reducing the reward for mining as more total coins are mined. Thanks to adaptive scaling, mining difficulty goes up and down depending on the popularity of the coin and the blockchain. This can give cryptocurrencies a real longevity within the market.

Decentralization

As I explain in Chapter 4, the whole idea behind blockchain technology is that it's *decentralized*. This concept means no single entity can affect the cryptocurrencies.

TECHNICAL STUFF

Some people claim cryptocurrencies such as Ripple aren't truly decentralized because they don't follow Bitcoin's mining protocol exactly. Ripple has no miners. Instead, transactions are powered through a "centralized" blockchain to make it more reliable and faster. Ripple, in particular, has gone this route because it wants to work with big banks and, therefore, wants to combine the best elements of fiat money and blockchain cryptocurrency. Whether nonminable currencies such as Ripple can be considered true cryptocurrencies is up for discussion, but that fact doesn't mean you can't invest in them, which is the whole purpose of this book anyway!

Harvesting

Harvesting is an alternative to the traditional mining used to maintain the integrity of a blockchain network. It was designed by a blockchain platform called NEM to generate its own currency called XEM.

According to Finder (www.finder.com), this is how harvesting works: "Every time someone carries out a transaction, the first computer to see and verify the transaction will notify nearby users of that transaction, creating a cascade of information. This process is called 'generating a block.' Whenever someone with more than 10,000 vested XEM generates a block in NEM, they receive the transaction fees on that block as payment." Also, as I explain earlier in this chapter, harvesting uses a PoI system rather than PoS or PoW.

Open source

Cryptocurrencies are typically *open source*. That means that miners, nodes, and harvesters alike can join and use the network without paying a fee.

Public ledger

As I explain in Chapter 4, a ledger is the age-old recordkeeping system for recording information and data. Cryptocurrencies use a *public ledger* to record all transactional data. Everyone in the world can access public blockchains and see entire transactions happening with cryptocurrencies.

Note that not all blockchains use a public ledger. Some businesses and financial institutions use private ledgers so that the transactions aren't visible to the world. However, by doing so, they may contradict the original idea behind blockchain technology.

Smart contracts

Smart contracts are also called *self-executing contracts, blockchain contracts,* or *digital contracts.* They're just like traditional contracts except that they're completely digital. Smart contracts remove the intermediary between the buyer and the seller (as I talk about in Chapter 4), so you can implement things like automatic payments and investment products without the need for a central authority like a bank.

A smart contract is actually a tiny computer program that's stored and runs on a blockchain platform. Because of that, all the transactions are completely distributed, and no centralized authority is in control of the money. Also, because it's stored on a blockchain, a smart contract is *immutable.* Being immutable means that after a smart contract is created, it can never be changed again; it can't be tampered with, which is an inherited feature from blockchain technology.

However, being immutable comes with its own disadvantages. Because you can't change anything in the smart contract, that means that if the code has any bugs, you can't fix them either. This makes smart contract security more difficult. Some companies aim to combat this problem by auditing their smart contracts, which can be very costly.

As time goes by, we can expect better coding practices and development life cycles to combat smart contract security problems. After all, smart contracts are still a pretty young practice with their whole life of trial and error ahead of them.

Stick a Fork in It: Digging into Cryptocurrency Forks

What you get from a cryptocurrency fork won't fill your tummy, but it may fill your crypto wallet with some money! Many popular cryptocurrencies were born as a result of a *fork* (split) in another cryptocurrency like Bitcoin. The following sections explain the basics of these cryptocurrency forks and how you may be able to profit from them.

What is a fork and why do they happen?

Sometimes when a group of developers disagrees with the direction a specific cryptocurrency is going, the members decide to go their own way and initiate a *fork.* Imagine an actual physical fork. It has one long handle, and then it divides into a bunch of branches. That's exactly what happens in a cryptocurrency fork.

Some cryptocurrencies are implemented within open-source software. Each of these cryptocurrencies has its own protocol that everyone in the network should follow. Examples of such rule topics include the following:

>> Block size

>> Rewards that miners, harvesters, or other network participants get

>> How fees are calculated

REMEMBER

But because cryptocurrencies are essentially software projects, their development will never be fully finished. There's always room for improvement. Crypto developers regularly push out updates to fix issues or improve performance. Some of these improvements are small, but others fundamentally change the way the original cryptocurrency (which the developers fell in love with) works. Just as in any type of relationship, you either grow together or grow apart. When the disagreements among a group of developers or network participants intensify, they can choose to break up, create their own version of the protocol, and cause a potential heartbreak that requires years of therapy to get over. Okay, the last part doesn't really happen.

Hard forks and soft forks

Two types of forks can happen in a cryptocurrency: a hard fork and a soft fork.

Most cryptocurrencies consist of two big pieces: the protocol (set of rules) and the blockchain (which stores all the transactions that have ever happened; see Chapter 4). If a segment of the crypto community decides to create its own new rules, it starts by copying the original protocol code and then goes about making changes to it (assuming the cryptocurrency is completely open source). After the developers have implemented their desired changes, they define a point at which their fork will become active. More specifically, they choose a block number to start the forking. For example, as you can see in Figure 5-1, the community can say that the new protocol will go live when block 999 is published to the cryptocurrency blockchain.

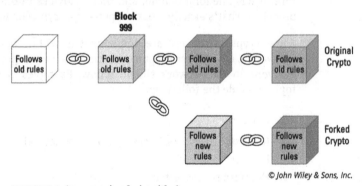

FIGURE 5-1: An example of a hard fork.

When the currency reaches that block number, the community splits in two. Some people decide to support the original set of rules, while others support the new fork. Each group then starts adding new blocks to the fork it supports. At this point, both blockchains are incompatible with each other, and a *hard fork* has occurred. In a hard fork, the nodes essentially go through a contentious divorce and don't ever interact with each other again. They don't even acknowledge the nodes or transactions on the old blockchain.

On the other hand, a soft fork is the type of breakup where you remain friends with your ex. If the developers decide to fork the cryptocurrency and make the changes compatible with the old one, then the situation is called a *soft fork.* You can see the subtle difference in the example shown in Figure 5-2.

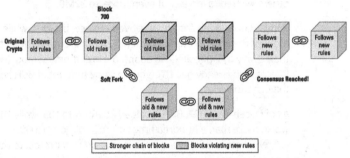

© John Wiley & Sons, Inc.

FIGURE 5-2: An example of a soft fork.

Say the soft fork is set to happen at block 700. The majority of the community may support the stronger chain of blocks following both the new and old rules. If the two sides reach a consensus after a while, the new rules are upgraded across the network. Any non-upgraded nodes (that is, stubborn geeks) who are still mining are essentially wasting their time. The community comes back together softly, and everyone lives happily ever after — until the next major argument, of course.

Free money on forks

Because a new fork is based on the original blockchain, all transactions that previously happened on the blockchain also happen on the fork. The developers of the new chain take a "snapshot" of the ledger at the specific block number where the fork happened (like 999 in Figure 5-1) and, therefore, create a duplicate copy of the chain. That means if you had a certain amount of cryptocurrencies before the fork, you also get the same amount of the new coin.

A FORKING EXAMPLE: BITCOIN VERSUS BITCOIN CASH

Even the celebrity of cryptocurrencies, Bitcoin (BTC), has seen forks. One of the well-known Bitcoin forks happened on August 1, 2017. That's the birthday of Bitcoin Cash.

In this case, the developers couldn't agree on what the size for a block should be. Some wanted the block size to go from 1MB to 2MB, but others wanted to increase it even more, to 32MB.

Some people in the community loved the new big idea, while others thought the other group was crazy. So, both groups decided to go their own ways. Bitcoin Cash adapted a brand-new symbol (BCH), too. People who already had BTC got the same amount of BCH added to their crypto wallets.

As of December 2022, BCH is valued at around $109, while BTC is worth more than a hundred times more, around $16,000. Only time will tell whether BCH ever surpasses the original protocol's value. But, hey, at least the forkers got some value out of it!

REMEMBER

To get free coins from a fork, you need to have the cryptocurrency on a platform that supports the fork before the block number at which the fork occurs. You can call this free money. But how valuable the coins are depends on how well the new fork performs and how popular it gets within the community.

2

Crypto-Investing Fundamentals

Pick an appropriate investing partner by finding an exchange or broker who's suitable for your level of involvement in the market.

Select a secure cryptocurrency wallet for your digital assets based on your needs.

Find background information on a number of current cryptocurrencies.

Identify the best cryptocurrencies to invest in at any given time.

Explore diversification methods across crypto and non-crypto assets to minimize risk in your investment portfolio.

Chapter **6**
Buying Cryptocurrencies

I f you've familiarized yourself with cryptocurrencies' risks and rewards (check out Chapters 2 and 3) and decided that cryptocurrency investing is right for you, you're ready to go crypto shopping!

As you may guess, most of crypto shopping, investing, and trading occurs online; after all, we're talking about digital assets. There are ways to pay cash to purchase digital currencies, but such transactions are uncommon. I mean, sure, if you have a friend who became a crypto millionaire and is looking to sell some crypto assets, you can simply give that person your cash in exchange for the cryptocurrencies.

The most popular way to buy cryptocurrencies, though, is to go directly through an online cryptocurrency exchange. By doing so on decentralized exchanges, you'll eliminate third-party interference in your transaction. However, depending on your cryptocurrency investing goals, you may need to consider alternative methods. For example, if you're an active crypto trader, you may find a traditional cryptocurrency broker easier to use. But if you want just to buy some cryptos and park them in your wallet, a trusted online/local exchange can do the job.

In this chapter, I tell you all about different types of exchanges, brokers, and other cryptocurrency providers and show you how to choose the right one(s) for your cryptocurrency goals.

Choosing a method to get your hands on these hot digital assets can be a lengthy process. However, with the changing regulatory stance, increasing adoption and acceptance, and overall market confidence in cryptocurrencies, the hard work may very well pay off. Regardless of the method you use to purchase cryptocurrencies, you must have a cryptocurrency wallet ready to store your digital assets. You find out all you need to know about cryptocurrency wallets in Chapter 7.

Overviewing the Steps in Buying Cryptocurrencies

Unlike the stock market, the crypto market is open 24 hours a day, seven days a week. This means you can participate in the cryptocurrency market at a Saturday night party after consuming ten tequila shots on an empty stomach. But I'd highly recommend that you not do that.

If you decide that buying a certain cryptocurrency is a smart investment, take the following steps to secure your position:

1. **Choose the place to buy.**

   You can select from cryptocurrency exchanges operating in your country, crypto brokers, or ATMs.

2. **Choose a payment method.**

   Most exchanges allow you to purchase crypto using the fiat currency of your country (like the U.S. dollar). One of the easiest methods for buying is connecting your bank account or other payment option to the exchange. But before being able to pay, most exchanges require personal identification methods, including pictures of your driver's license or Social Security card. You sometimes need to pay a fee for the transaction. The fees vary depending on your payment method and the exchange's policy.

3. **Search for the cryptocurrency you've decided to invest in.**

   Turn to Chapter 8 to discover different types of cryptocurrencies and how to select the ones that are most suitable to your risk tolerance.

4. **Select the price and the amount of cryptocurrency you'd like to invest in.**

   Most crypto exchanges and brokers allow you to set something called a *buy-limit order* to purchase your crypto assets at your optimal price. By conducting technical analysis and combining that with your risk tolerance (outlined in Chapter 3) you may decide to purchase your favorite crypto asset at the current market price or set a buy-limit order to purchase at a future, potentially lower price.

COMPARING BROKERS, EXCHANGES, AND WALLETS

When you invest in stocks, your choice of where to buy them is typically very clear. Ever since online brokers became a thing, almost anyone can access the stocks listed on big stock exchanges such as the New York Stock Exchange (NYSE) and the National Association of Securities Dealers Automated Quotations (Nasdaq). A broker serves as an intermediary that gives you access to financial assets so you can buy and sell.

When it comes to cryptocurrencies, however, you have more choices. Instead of using a broker as an intermediary, you can go directly to the source — the cryptocurrency exchange — to buy and sell.

The main difference between crypto brokers and a crypto exchange is that exchanges provide a wider selection of crypto and other digital assets. However, as a result, they sometimes charge higher transaction fees, and they may also be susceptible to cyberattacks (because it's still a new industry). At the time of writing, most cryptocurrency exchanges are expanding their services and level of security. However, the best way to protect your cryptocurrency assets is by using a crypto wallet.

In short, a *crypto wallet* is a program that allows you to store your cryptocurrency. Turn to Chapter 7 for different types of cryptocurrency wallets and how you can use them.

A buy-limit order is kind of like preordering food from your favorite restaurant. You basically tell your online broker or exchange that you want to buy an asset such as Bitcoin at a specific future price (that is lower than the current price). The broker will then automatically execute your order when the price reaches your ideal level.

Voilà! You've now successfully participated in the most disruptive market since the internet — the crypto market!

Distinguishing Crypto Exchanges

A *cryptocurrency exchange* is also called a *digital currency exchange* (DCE). It's a web service that can help people exchange their cash into cryptocurrencies and vice versa. Most exchanges are more focused on providing services to help you exchange a cryptocurrency such as Bitcoin into other digital currencies like Ethereum, Dogecoin, and so on.

Most exchanges operate online. However, a number of brick-and-mortar businesses do exist; they provide customers services to exchange traditional payment methods and cryptocurrencies. Those options are similar to the currency exchange booths at international airports where you exchange your country's money into the currency of the country you're visiting.

The most distinguished forms of cryptocurrency exchanges are the following:

>> **Centralized cryptocurrency exchange (CEX):** CEXs are similar to traditional stock exchanges.

>> **Decentralized cryptocurrency exchange (DEX):** DEXs aim to stay true to the pure philosophy behind the cryptocurrency industry.

>> **Hybrid cryptocurrency exchange:** Hybrid exchanges are known to be the next-generation crypto-trading marketplace. They combine the best of CEXs and DEXs.

In the following sections, I give you the lowdown on CEXs, DEXs, and hybrid exchanges. Finally, I give you guidance on choosing an exchange.

Centralized exchanges

CEXs are like traditional stock exchanges. The buyers and sellers come together, and the exchange plays the role of an intermediary. These exchanges typically charge a commission to facilitate the transactions made between the buyers and the sellers. In the crypto world, *centralize* means "to trust somebody else to handle your money."

Here's how a CEX typically works:

1. You give your money to the exchange.

2. The exchange holds it for you (like a bank or a trusted intermediary).

3. You watch the prices of the available cryptocurrencies on the exchange.

4. Depending on the exchange, you can trade your *fiat currency* (a traditional currency, such as the U.S. dollar) for a cryptocurrency (such as Bitcoin). With most exchanges, however, you find better luck exchanging two cryptocurrencies for one another. I talk more about cryptocurrency pairings in Chapter 10.

5. You place your order.

6. The exchange finds a seller to match your buy order. If you're selling, the exchange finds you a buyer.

7. Ta-da! You just crypto-shopped on an exchange.

Most CEXs have crypto/crypto pairings. But not all of them provide fiat/crypto pairings:

>> A *crypto/crypto pairing* involves exchanging one cryptocurrency (such as Bitcoin) for another cryptocurrency (such as Ethereum).

>> A *fiat/crypto* pairing involves exchanging a traditional currency (such as the U.S. dollar) for a cryptocurrency (such as Bitcoin).

One of the main issues with CEXs is their vulnerability to hacks. In some past hacking scandals, however, the exchange has paid the customers back out of pocket. That's why choosing a CEX wisely, knowing it has the financial ability to combat hackers and pay you in case it gets hacked, is important. Of course, with the popularity of cryptocurrencies, more CEXs are bound to pop up in the market. Some will succeed, and some may fail. Therefore, you need to pick your crypto shop wisely. I talk about methods for picking the best exchange later in this chapter.

TIP

CEXs are typically user-friendly and offer a support system to beginner investors. If you're new to crypto investing, starting at an exchange that offers fiat/crypto pairings may make the most sense.

That's precisely the reason why exchanges that provide this service have become some of the most popular ones. At the time of writing, some of the most popular CEXs that offer fiat/crypto pairings include the following:

>> **Binance:** This exchange has grown to become the largest crypto exchange since it was founded in 2017 (although more limited in the United States). However, its exponential growth also brought about tons of regulatory issues, making it a risky place to use for your crypto investments. Binance offers an online crypto wallet for traders to store their assets. It also supports interest-earning services.

At the time of writing, Binance supports more than 600 cryptocurrencies globally, but only 100 cryptocurrencies in the United States. Binance offers almost all types of transactions.

On top of having regulatory issues, in my experience, Binance has not been the most user-friendly for beginner investors. On the bright side, it's one of the cheapest platforms to use because transaction fees are pretty low. If you use my referral link when signing up, we'll both earn $10 each after you complete $100 worth of trading in 30 days: www.investdivabinance.com.

>> **Coinbase:** This exchange is one of the most beginner-friendly cryptocurrency platforms and offers basic transactions, a digital wallet, and easy withdrawals. For more complicated investment methods, they also have a pro platform.

At the time of writing, Coinbase supports 179 cryptocurrencies and is insured up to $250,000. This means, in the unlikely event of hacks or scams, Coinbase exchange will pay for damages up to this amount as long as it's their fault. You can use the U.S. dollar (USD), the euro (EUR), the Australian dollar (AUD), or the British pound (GBP) to fund your account and to buy and sell cryptocurrencies.

Coinbase also offers a Visa debit card that is accepted at more than 40 million merchants worldwide.

>> **Gemini:** Gemini was launched in 2014 by the Winklevoss brothers with high regulation standards. The exchange is focused on security and ease of use and supports more than 120 cryptocurrencies.

Gemini offers a credit card that could give you up to 3 percent cash back in Bitcoin or other cryptocurrencies.

Other top cryptocurrency exchanges at the time of writing include OKX, KuCoin, Kraken, and Bitfinex. For an up-to-date list of cryptocurrency exchanges, visit https://investdiva.com/crypto-exchanges.

Decentralized exchanges

A DEX is an exchange that doesn't rely on an intermediary to hold your funds. It's a marketplace where buyers and sellers come together and process the transactions directly between one another. In other words, DEXs facilitate peer-to-peer trades.

On a DEX, you can buy and sell your crypto assets directly from other market participants. You're able to make the deals through things like smart contracts and atomic swaps. *Smart contracts*, as explained on Investopedia, are "self-executing contracts where the terms of the agreement between buyer and seller are directly written into lines of code." They're the underlying technology for *atomic swaps*, which enable the exchange of one cryptocurrency for another without using CEXs. With the DEX, smart contracts, and atomic swaps, instead of giving your cryptocurrencies to the CEX, you'll give them to an escrow that's centralized by the network running the exchange. Escrow still exists because transactions take as long as five days to clear. As a buyer, you'll have your cash taken out from your account immediately, although the funds aren't moved to the seller's account until the crypto transaction clears.

You may think that a DEX makes more sense to buy and sell cryptocurrencies on because the whole market is often billed as decentralized. Heck, cryptocurrencies became popular because they allow you to become your own bank and be in charge of your own assets. That's why many DEX fans argue that if you utilize CEXs, you're essentially jeopardizing the whole point of using cryptocurrencies.

The following sections give you more information on some of the issues facing DEXs, plus a rundown of some noteworthy DEX options.

Potential problems

Though DEXs may replace CEXs completely in the future, at this point DEXs have their own problems.

WARNING

DEXs are harder to hack than CEXs are. On the flip side, you're more vulnerable to locking yourself out of your money. That means if you forget your login info, you may get your account locked because the system thinks you're a hacker! Other problems with DEXs include low volumes and low liquidity. *Liquidity* is how fast you can buy or sell cryptocurrencies on the marketplace. Because DEXs are less popular than CEXs (at least for now), you may face more difficulty finding someone to match your buy/sell orders on a DEX. This issue is a vicious cycle because as long as DEXs are less popular, their liquidity remains low. As long as the liquidity is low, DEXs may remain less popular. That's why, at least for now, CEXs are more popular than DEXs.

WARNING

Additionally, most DEXs don't offer services to deposit or withdraw fiat currencies such as the U.S. dollar. They can also be expensive and slow. Everything from canceling orders to transferring crypto requires paying a fee and waiting for block confirmations; these take at least a few minutes (sometimes hours).

Popular decentralized exchanges

Regardless of possible DEX issues, the highest-ranked DEXs according to traffic, liquidity, and trading volume include the following:

>> **Curve (Ethereum):** Curve is a popular automated market-maker (AMM) platform. This platform offers a very efficient way to exchange tokens. It has low fees and low slippage. This is because it works only with liquidity pools made up of assets that have similar behavior patterns.

- **DODO:** DODO is a decentralized exchange that uses Ethereum and Binance Smart Chain. It aims to make decentralized finance (DeFi) liquidity more accessible. Unlike many other DEXs, which use an automated market-maker algorithm, DODO uses its own proactive market-maker algorithm.

- **PancakeSwap:** PancakeSwap is a place where people can trade NB Chain ecosystem and one of the top DEXs by market share. The exchange employs an AMM model, allowing users to trade against a liquidity pool. You can become a liquidity provider (LP) and receive LP tokens, which entitle users to a share of the exchange's trading fees.

- **Uniswap:** With Uniswap, you can easily trade cryptocurrency tokens without having to create an account. Additionally, you can earn interest on your crypto through Uniswap's liquidity pools. Like the other DEXs, Uniswap also uses an AMM. However, Uniswap doesn't permit buying or selling of cryptocurrency. You also can't buy crypto using regular money on this exchange — you can only use crypto that you already have in a digital wallet.

WARNING

Liquidity mining is a way to earn more money with your cryptocurrency. Some liquidity pools offer annual percentage yields (APYs) of 100 percent or more, which means you can grow your holdings by a lot. But there is also a risk that you may lose money if the value of the cryptocurrency changes while it's in the pool; this is called *impermanent loss*. Impermanent loss is more likely to happen with more volatile cryptocurrencies, but those are often the ones where you can earn the most money. So, when you're choosing a liquidity pool, make sure you pick cryptocurrencies that are aligned with your risk tolerance and have strong fundamentals first, and then see if you can use them for liquidity mining. Turn to Chapter 3 for more on risk tolerance and attend my free Masterclass to learn how to pick the right assets for your portfolio: https://investdiva.com/masterclass.

The DEXs I mention in this section are the purest form of DEXs. They're entirely *on-chain*, which means all orders interact with each other directly through the blockchain (see Chapter 4 for more about this technology). However, these kinds of exchanges have their own sets of problems. Many of those problems don't exist in the CEXs that I describe earlier; therefore, DEXs are less suitable for beginner investors.

Hybrid exchanges

The hybrid approach to cryptocurrency exchanges aims to merge benefits from both CEXs and DEXs to give consumers the best of both worlds. More specifically, hybrids seek to provide the functionality and liquidity of a CEX with the privacy and security of a DEX. Many people believe such exchanges are the real future of the cryptocurrency trading experience. A hybrid crypto platform gives you access to *private keys* (a secret number that is used in cryptography, similar to a password; turn to Chapter 7 for more information) and allows you to trade for a lower fee.

Hybrid exchanges look to provide cryptocurrency trading services with the speed, ease, and liquidity institutional users are used to in traditional exchanges. A hybrid exchange connects its centralized elements to a network of decentralized elements. This approach allows users to access the trading platform the way they do in a CEX and then engage in peer-to-peer trading activity as they do in a DEX. The hybrid then provides confirmation and record transactions on the blockchain.

TECHNICAL STUFF

Hybrids are also called *semi-decentralized exchanges* because they incorporate both on-chain and off-chain components. An *off-chain* transaction moves your cryptocurrency value outside the blockchain.

The first-ever hybrid exchange was Qurrex (www.qurrex.com), which launched in 2018. The Qurrex team got together in 2016, consisting of experts who had years of experience working in the foreign exchange (forex) markets, developers of trade terminals, and founders of successfully operating stock and futures exchanges. They all saw the significant potential in applying the best practices of the traditional exchanges to create a new generation of cryptocurrency exchange, providing a harmonious merge of centralized and decentralized elements.

Another hybrid cryptocurrency exchange that's gaining attention is NEXT.exchange (https://next.exchange). If you own its native token, NEXT, you can trade between fiat and crypto pairs such as Bitcoin (BTC) versus the euro (EUR), or Ethereum (ETH) versus the U.S. dollar (USD).

How to choose an exchange

First-time investors are better off doing their research on the cryptocurrencies first and then choosing an exchange. But when you become more experienced, you can simply choose cryptos to trade based on the current market conditions.

TIP

Personally, I'm a big fan of diversification in anything. Because many of these exchanges offer different sets of pros and cons, you may be wise to diversify your cryptocurrency activities across a number of exchanges, just as many people do when they go grocery shopping. You may go to one store for its better-quality meat but get all your produce from another.

Security

REMEMBER

Security is one of the biggest issues in the cryptocurrency industry. Exchanges are at constant risk of hacks, frauds, and pump-and-dump schemes. A *pump-and-dump scheme* is when someone encourages investors to buy a crypto asset in order to artificially inflate its value (the "pumping" part) and then sells their own assets at a high price (or "dumps"). That's why one of the most important things to do before choosing your crypto shop(s) is to do your research. Word of mouth and online reviews on sites like Reddit or news organizations like Forbes are some of the ways to help you choose a legitimate and secure platform. Some other safety features you must check on the exchange include the following:

>> **Two-factor authentication (2FA):** *Two-factor authentication* is a method of confirming your claimed identity by using a combination of two different factors: something the exchange knows (like your password) and something it has (like a six-digit number it sends to your mobile phone or your email address for the second step of the verification).

>> **Multifactor authentication (MFA):** *Multifactor authentication* is an authentication method that requires the user to provide two or more verification factors to gain access to a resource such as an application, an online account, or a virtual private network (VPN). It's a more secure way to make sure that someone is who they say they are. They need to give two things that show it is them — for example, their name and a password.

- **Cold storage for the majority of funds:** This term means the exchange stores your funds offline, so risk of online hacking is lower. I explain more about this feature in Chapter 7.

- **Proof of reserve:** This element requires the exchange to be audited to verify that the total amount of funds held by the exchange matches the amount required to cover an anonymized set of customer balances.

Supported currencies (crypto and otherwise)

When you decide which of the thousands of available cryptocurrencies are right for you, you must make sure your exchange carries them. You can read more about various crypto options in Chapter 8.

Additionally, if you're looking to purchase cryptocurrencies for the very first time, you probably need an exchange that allows you to deposit your country's fiat currency.

Some exchanges use solely cryptocurrency for purchases, and some allow you to use fiat currencies such as the U.S. dollar, the euro, or your country's currency.

Liquidity

Without sufficient liquidity, the prices and the speeds of your transactions may be compromised. After you decide which cryptocurrencies you want to purchase, make sure your exchange offers sufficient liquidity and trading volume for fast and easy transactions. Liquidity also ensures you're able to buy and sell without the cryptocurrency's price being significantly affected by big market movers. The more buyers and sellers there are, the more liquidity that exists.

TIP

The best way to measure an exchange's liquidity is to look up its most recent trading volume. CoinMarketCap (https://coinmarketcap.com) and CoinGecko (www.coingecko.com) are two of the many cryptocurrency information websites that rank exchanges based on their volume and liquidity.

Fees

Exchanges charge their customers in a number of different ways. It would be great if they didn't, but exchanges aren't charities. Charging customers fees is precisely how they make money to stay in business. The most common method is taking a small percentage of the amount you trade. Most exchanges charge a low percentage to stay competitive; some exchanges go as low as around 0.2 percent. Often, a sliding scale decreases the fee percentage as the user's monthly trading volume rises. At the time of writing, Coinbase and Gemini charge a 1.49 percent fee for trades above $200.

REMEMBER

Paying less is always attractive, but prioritize security and liquidity over fees. Your investment will defeat its purpose if you pay next to nothing on transaction fees and then lose all your funds in a hacker's attack. Some exchanges also have wider bid–ask spreads than others, so even though the fees could be lower, you're still paying more depending on the trading pair and order type.

Ease of use

This one is especially important for newbies. You want your exchange to provide you with an easy-to-use, intuitive, and fast user interface. This factor also depends on what kind of device you want to use for your cryptocurrency investing activities. If you're always on the go, you may want to choose an exchange with great mobile app services.

A good user experience helps you take more informed and more efficient actions on the exchange. Another benefit of exchanges with great interface and mobile support is that they're more likely to grow more quickly and, therefore, provide more trading volume and liquidity in their markets.

Location

Depending on where you live, you may find a specific exchange that works better for you in your country than another, more popular one on an international level does. Some of the things to keep in mind are issues like which fiat currency exchanges accept and what fees they charge locals compared to international customers.

Additionally, the location of the exchange dictates the laws it has to comply with. At the time of writing, many countries don't have any specific regulations on cryptocurrencies. However, if and when they start to regulate, any restrictions may significantly affect your ability to participate in the market through the exchanges in those countries.

Method of payment

Look into the methods of payment the exchange accepts. Some exchanges require deposits by bank transfer, some use PayPal, and some accept credit and debit cards.

REMEMBER

Typically, the easier it is for you to pay, the more fees you're going to have to pay. For example, few services allow you to pay with a credit or debit card, and the ones that do will make you pay for the convenience. (Head to the earlier section "Fees" for more on fee issues; the later section "PayPal" has info on that option.)

Customer support

Poor customer support was precisely the reason I decided not to go with one of the major exchanges when I first started crypto investing. I always feel more comfortable knowing that the place I'm trusting with my funds has a responsive customer support service.

You can check this factor either by directly contacting the customer support department and asking any questions that you haven't been able to find on the exchange's FAQ page or by perusing online cryptocurrency forums like BitcoinTalk (https://bitcointalk.org). You may find complaints about the exchanges in these forums. However, keep in mind that fast-growing exchanges often combat these complaints by improving their customer service, which is always a good thing.

TIP

Another point you may be able to find on forums is whether an exchange has spurred complaints about locking people out of their accounts. If it has, you may want to consider other options.

Trading options

WARNING

Trading options are especially important for active and advanced traders. For example, depending on your risk tolerance and financial goals, you may want to have access to certain order types or margin trading. On these occasions, make sure you understand the risks involved with such trading activities (check out Part 3) before getting yourself in trouble.

Transaction limits

Most exchanges have a daily withdrawal/deposit limit. Unless you're an institutional trader who wants to make millions of transactions per day, these restrictions may not be an issue. But these limits are still something you may need to keep in mind, depending on your investing style and goals. You can typically find out about the exchanges' transaction limits on their websites without having to create an account.

Understanding Crypto Brokers

If you're looking to purchase cryptocurrencies online and invest in them as an asset, then cryptocurrency exchanges (covered earlier in this chapter) are the way to go. However, if you're thinking of simply speculating the price action of cryptocurrencies, then you may want to consider brokers.

As cryptocurrencies became more popular, some traditional forex currency brokers started extending their services to cryptos. But keep in mind that the concept of a "broker" doesn't really exist in pure cryptocurrency investing. You can't purchase cryptocurrencies such as Bitcoin through traditional forex brokers. Even though the brokers may carry them, all they're really doing is streaming a tradable price on their platform. That way, you may be able to take advantage of the market volatility and make (or lose) money based on your speculated trading orders.

In the following sections, I explain how traditional brokers work. Then I get into the pros and cons of utilizing them in your crypto-trading activities.

REMEMBER

When you search the internet for cryptocurrency brokers or exchanges, you often get a list that has all types mixed together. You need to take a second look to identify which is an exchange and which is a brokerage. Do this by going to each website's "About" page or simply adding the keywords "broker or exchange" next to their name in your search box.

How brokers work

Traditional brokers are market intermediaries who help traders execute trades on their platforms. They're the intermediaries between an individual retail trader and networks of big banks. Stockbrokers take orders from customers and try to fill them at the best price possible. In the case of forex brokers, they typically get a price from one or multiple banks for a specific currency. They then offer you the best price they've received from their banks. You can then trade your favorite currencies based on the prices that are streaming on your broker's platform.

Such brokers operate on something called the *over-the-counter* (OTC) *markets*. This means that the currencies are traded via a dealer network as opposed to on a centralized exchange. The brokers unload their trading risk to third-party or internal back-end warehouses called *liquidity providers*. When it comes to cryptocurrency services on their platforms, these liquidity providers are often cryptocurrency exchanges (which I talk about earlier in this chapter).

Forex brokers mainly make money through transparent — and sometimes hidden — commission fees. Some brokers even make money when their customers lose money. That's one reason the forex industry as a whole started getting a bad reputation; some such brokers started getting caught by government regulators. I explain more about forex brokers and the scams involved with the industry in my book *Invest Diva's Guide to Making Money in Forex* (McGraw Hill). But my short, takeaway message right here, right now is if you have a low risk tolerance (based on what you calculate in Chapter 3), then you may want to stay away from trading forex!

The pros and cons of using a broker

Forex brokers who provide cryptocurrency services have started hard-core marketing to advertise speculative crypto trading. Here are some of the advantages of trading through a broker as opposed to using a cryptocurrency exchange:

>> **You get improved liquidity.** Because the brokers get their quotes from multiple exchanges, they're able to provide increased liquidity to customers. That means you have a

higher chance of getting your buy/sell orders fulfilled in a timely manner. You also may be able to get a price closer to your initial buy/sell order because the broker has multiple channels to find a buyer and a seller to fulfill your order.

>> **You can start trading immediately.** If you go through an exchange, you sometimes need to wait for days before your account is confirmed. With most brokers, the account confirmation can be quicker.

And here are some of the disadvantages of trading through a broker:

>> **You can't invest in cryptos as an asset.** By trading through a broker, you're simply speculating on the price volatility of the market. You aren't actually purchasing or investing in the cryptocurrency market. This distinction means you don't own your cryptos even if you buy them on the brokerage account.

>> **You don't have access to wallets.** For the same reason as in the preceding point, no real portfolio or wallet is available for you. This fact also means you can't realize your transfers or cryptocurrency acquisitions.

REMEMBER

In addition to these pros and cons, some conditions can be both advantages and disadvantages of trading cryptocurrencies through a broker. Of course, if you go to the brokers' websites, they've featured these characteristics as advantages. However, you must understand the risks beneath the surface, outlined in the next sections.

Pro or con: You can take advantage of a down market

This tricky advantage is one that many brokers advertise. Because you aren't actually purchasing the currencies (fiat or crypto), you can bet on the markets going down. If the prices do go down as you predicted, you can make money.

WARNING

This process is called *short-selling.* Short-selling is actually also available on exchanges and traditional stock markets as well. However, it involves a lot of risk because you need to borrow money from your broker, exchange, or whoever is providing your trading services.

Pro or con: You can trade on leverage

Trading on leverage means borrowing money from your broker to trade. With some brokers, you can open an account with $100 and then use 50-times leverage (or even more), which means you control a $5,000 account with your mere $100! But unless you're Nostradamus or you have a crystal ball, using leverage can be problematic because leverage enlarges the risks of gains and losses by the same magnitude.

WARNING

Here's how leverage can make or break your account: Say you have a $1,000 account. You place a trade order without using any leverage, and you end up making $50. If you'd used a 10-times leverage, you would've made $500 instead. That's awesome! But (and that's a very big but) on the flip side, if the markets go *against* your speculation when you're trading on that leverage, you lose $500 rather than $50, wiping half of your account. Newbie traders often wipe out their accounts completely within the first few days. Sometimes, depending on the broker's policy, investors' losses can even exceed their initial deposits, which means they actually *owe* the broker money!

REMEMBER

Using leverage can be an advantage if you know what you're doing and you have high enough risk tolerance to be prepared for a worst-case scenario, which means losing parts or all of your initial investment through the broker.

Here are the two traditional brokers that offer cryptocurrency trading services; I personally use them for a portion of my investment portfolio.

>> **Robinhood:** This is my favorite beginner's app thanks to its ease of use. Despite going through a rough patch of scandals in 2020, Robinhood is, like most other brokers, regulated by the Securities and Exchange Commission (SEC) and insures your assets by up to $250,000.

Robinhood's trading app originally offered stocks and exchange-traded fund (ETF) services but now provides fiat pairings to Bitcoin (BTC) and Ethereum (ETH) alongside other cryptocurrencies.

An important note about Robinhood is that it only allows you to take a position on the cryptocurrency's price and enter either a buy or sell position with the hopes of making a profit. However, by trading on Robinhood you won't actually own the cryptocurrency asset. That means you aren't able to transfer them to your own cryptocurrency wallet. If you're only interested in position trading, then Robinhood is a commission-free choice, and their app is very easy to use. If you use my referral link, we'll both get some free stocks in our portfolio: https://earn.investdiva.com/robinhood.

>> **Interactive Brokers:** This platform is available in more than 200 countries and offers one of the largest selections of financial assets, including stocks, cryptocurrencies, options, and bonds.

I personally started my stock-investing journey with Interactive Brokers and continue to hold some of my assets with them. At the time of writing, Interactive only lets you trade four cryptocurrencies. You can get up to $1,000 of free IBKR stock when opening an account at Interactive Brokers if you use my link. Check it out here: https://earn.investdiva.com/ib.

How to choose a broker

You may notice the internet has no lack of cryptocurrency exchanges and brokers! And more variations of exchanges are bound to make their way into the market. Which type of platform is best for you to buy and sell cryptocurrencies: brokers, CEX, DEX, or hybrid? Even then, which one of the many platforms in each category should you choose?

I can't answer these questions for you, but I can offer ways to cycle through some of the most important characteristics in exchanges and brokers to help you make the best decision.

Here are a few things to consider when choosing a cryptocurrency exchange or a broker:

>> **Make sure it's regulated.** Each country has strict international regulatory authorities that audit brokers on a regular basis to ensure their security. Your best bet is often to make sure the broker is regulated by two or more regulatory bodies in your country. You can find regulation information on brokers' websites.

>> **Consider ease of deposits and withdrawals.** Good brokers will allow you to deposit funds and withdraw your earnings without a hassle. Brokers really have no reason to make it hard for you to withdraw your profits, because the only reason they hold your funds is to facilitate trading.

>> **Make sure they have insurance.** Banks, brokers, and exchanges alike have a limited amount they guarantee to insure in the event of a theft, hack, or system breakdown. This amount is typically $250,000, but some brokers offer more insurance. Before choosing a place to store your financial assets, confirm their insurance amount by visiting their policy page or contacting their customer service.

   If your financial assets exceed the amount they insure, consider spreading your assets among various platforms. For example, I spread my over-$5 million portfolio across more than seven platforms.

>> **Beware of promotions.** Some brokers have discovered that people love discount sales, so they use such promotions to attract customers. Nothing is wrong with promotions, but be careful — sometimes brokers use these promotions to push new traders into making risky investments or using unreliable products and signals. That's why you need to do your due diligence and know your broker before you take advantage of a promotion.

Looking at Other Methods for Buying Cryptos

I cover some of the most popular methods for purchasing or investing in cryptocurrencies earlier in this chapter. However, these options aren't the only ones. Check out the following sections for a few other handy ways to buy cryptos. (I explain where to store your cryptocurrencies after you purchase them in Chapter 7.)

Funds

Many people seek exposure to the cryptocurrency market but don't want to invest in a specific cryptocurrency such as Bitcoin or Ethereum. They may be looking for an equivalent of a mutual fund or an ETF, which tracks a basket of different assets such as stocks and indexes.

Several ETFs now offer direct or indirect exposure to cryptocurrency prices, stocks of digital payment companies, crypto brokers and exchanges, or blockchain technology. These funds can hold cryptocurrency future contracts or stocks of companies that are involved with crypto. Some non-U.S. ETFs even offer spot cryptocurrency in offline storage. *Spot cryptocurrency* is when you buy and sell assets right away; it's like day-trading in the stock market, where people buy and sell assets within one day.

The upside of a fund is that it's somewhat diversified. That's because you get to invest in a number of popular cryptos in one fund, without the hassle of selecting just a few. The downside of most funds is their costs and restrictions.

Here are some cryptocurrency ETFs available at the time of writing:

» **Amplify Transformational Data Sharing ETF (BLOK):** This ETF is focused on companies that are involved with cryptocurrencies or that offer indirect exposure to crypto prices. It has $555 million under its asset management at the time of writing.

» **Fidelity Crypto Industry and Digital Payments ETF (FDIG):** This index tracks the performance of global cryptocurrency, blockchain, and digital payment companies. At the time of writing, FDIG owns 35 stocks and has around $16 million under its management. Three of its major holdings include Block, Inc. (SQ); Coinbase Global, Inc. (COIN); and Marathon Digital Holdings (MARA). This fund has a passive investing strategy for its fund. Its expense ratio is 0.39 percent.

TECHNICAL STUFF

An *expense ratio* is a number that shows how much it costs to manage, advertise, and distribute a mutual fund or an ETF. The expense ratio is usually a percentage of the fund's average net assets.

» **Global X Blockchain ETF (BKCH):** This is another passively managed fund that can give you exposure to companies that may benefit from the adoption of blockchain technology. This includes Bitcoin mining companies such as Marathon Digital (MARA) and leading crypto exchange Coinbase (COIN). At the time of writing, BKCH has around $80 million under management.

A quick Google search will give you a list of the newest crypto-related ETFs. Always make sure you then separately check the ETF and all its holdings.

I personally don't like investing in ETFs because you never know what assets may be hidden in their basket. I'm a huge fan of moral investing, and I avoid investing in assets or companies that don't comply with my moral beliefs. Investing in ETFs is mainly a lazy approach to participating in the online financial markets. With just a little bit of research, you can instead create an investment portfolio that's suitable to you, your risk tolerance, and your moral beliefs, and that allows you to avoid paying that unnecessary management fee.

Credit card

Financial services such as Coinmama allow you to buy cryptocurrencies like Bitcoin (BTC) and Ethereum (ETH) using a credit card. But they aren't available in all countries yet at the time of writing.

PayPal

Earlier in this chapter, I touch on various methods of payment that cryptocurrency exchanges may offer, including transferring money from your bank account and using your credit card or debit card. PayPal is another online payment system that supports money transfers and serves as an electronic alternative to traditional money.

PayPal started out working on Bitcoin integration earlier than many other financial services, back in 2014. At the time of writing, Coinbase is the only exchange that accepts PayPal money transfers, and it's only available to customers in the United States. This means you can use PayPal to indirectly buy cryptocurrencies.

This type of information is constantly subject to change due to cryptocurrencies' volatile current state. The best way to stay on top of cryptocurrency news is on websites such as CoinDesk (www.coindesk.com) or simply by typing the most relevant keywords into your chosen search engine. Some keywords include "how to buy cryptocurrency," "best methods to buy crypto," and "best crypto funds today."

Cash

The process for paying cash to buy cryptocurrencies such as Bitcoin is to find someone who owns cryptocurrencies and is willing to sell them in exchange for cash. Some sites connect buyers and sellers in a way where the seller provides bank details that let the buyer make a cash deposit at the bank. You must keep the receipt to provide proof, and the seller can send you the Bitcoins. Some options in this vein include www.bitquick.co (part of Athena Bitcoin based in Chicago) and https://paxful.com (based in Delaware).

TIP

If you do an internet search on how to buy cryptocurrencies with cash, you may get directed to a mobile app called Cash App, which is indeed an app that helps you buy and sell Bitcoin from friends! However, this isn't the type of cash payment I'm talking about in this section.

Cryptocurrency ATMs

Cryptocurrency ATMs are becoming more popular. Many individuals are even trying to start their own such machines to make passive income. Bitcoin (and other cryptocurrency) ATMs work like any other ATM. The first step in the process is to find one near you, something you can do via a quick online search or at https://coinatmradar.com.

There are several different brands of ATMs with differing methods of verifying your ID and *cryptocurrency address* (a code in your cryptocurrency wallet). Naturally, you need to do some research to find a secure and trustworthy ATM with a good online reputation. One simple research method is entering the ATM name on Google or Bing, and checking whether it has any negative press.

The process of buying cryptocurrencies at an ATM may vary from machine to machine. However, here are the general steps most ATMs require:

1. Verify your identity (using an ID card, for example).
2. Select the cryptocurrency you want to purchase.
3. Provide a cryptocurrency address for deposit (Chapter 7 has more on this).

4. Select the amount of cryptocurrency you want to purchase.
5. Insert cash into the cryptocurrency ATM.
6. Confirm the operation.

REMEMBER

Some cryptocurrency ATMs even provide services to sell and buy digital coins. Keep in mind that these types of cryptocurrency machines aren't ATMs in the traditional sense, where they help you connect with your bank account. Instead, they're machines that are connected to the internet and direct you to a cryptocurrency exchange in order to provide you with your cryptocurrency.

Chapter **7**

Putting Cryptocurrency Wallets to Use

A traditional wallet is where you keep your valuable personal items such as cash, credit cards, and identification cards. But now that you're using the most advanced, futuristic form of money (cryptos, baby!), you're going to need a brand-new type of wallet to go with it: a cryptocurrency wallet.

With a cryptocurrency wallet, you can not only store the value of your digital money but also send and receive currencies. Additionally, you can monitor your balance the way you'd do with your bank account. In this chapter, I walk you step-by-step through understanding and choosing your very first cryptocurrency wallet.

Defining Cryptocurrency Wallets

A *cryptocurrency wallet* is a software program that helps you manage your digital money. Though you may be the type of person who doesn't like to carry around traditional wallets and would rather put your cash and credit cards right in your back pocket, you must have a digital cryptocurrency wallet if you want to use any type of cryptocurrency. There's no way around it. Cryptocurrencies aren't stored in a bank reserve like other types of traditional assets such as gold and cash. Without crypto wallets, the whole idea of cryptocurrencies dies! Cryptocurrency wallets are the air that keeps the system alive.

In theory, Bitcoin is decentralized and nobody controls anything, but it's in fact run by a network that's controlled and maintained by someone (whoever is hiding behind the name Satoshi Nakamoto). In other words, Bitcoin is distributed and miners are somewhat anonymous, but the actual blockchain is stored in its entirety by the network. It's so large in size that miners have maybe 30 days' worth of transactions and blocks stored on their devices; the full blockchain is actually stored somewhat centralized by the network.

A few important terms

Before you get started, take a look at some geek terms that you may encounter as you explore the world of crypto wallets:

>> **Hot wallet:** A wallet connected to the internet.

>> **Cold wallet:** A wallet not connected to the internet.

>> **Wallet address:** A number that functions something like a traditional bank account number.

>> **Public key:** A code that allows you to receive cryptocurrencies into your account or wallet. It's mathematically linked to your wallet address, but it isn't identical.

>> **Private key:** A code that's coupled with the public key to ensure your security. It's something like your own private password you use to enter your bank account in the real world.

The following section explains how some of these items work together so you can complete crypto transactions.

How a wallet works

Crypto wallets don't actually store the cryptocurrency itself; instead, they store the cryptocurrency's private and public keys. These keys are something like the personal identification number (PIN) you use to access your bank account.

No two wallet addresses are ever the same. They're something like fingerprints. This distinction means that there is a very low chance that somebody else can get your funds by mistake. Also, you have no limit to the number of wallet addresses you can create.

There have been cases where a wallet ID was intercepted and changed and funds went to the wrong wallet. For example, some malware recently replaced wallet IDs in the clipboard of a computer, so when the user cut and pasted the IDs of the intended recipient, the wrong ones were actually pasted — that of the perpetrator.

To give you an example of what a cryptocurrency address looks like, here's the wallet address believed to belong to the creator of Bitcoin, Satoshi Nakamoto!

1A1zP1eP5QGefi2DMPTfTL5SLmv7DivfNa

As you can see, it uses a combination of numbers and letters, both uppercase and lowercase. Don't worry — as long as you have a safe and secure wallet, you don't have to memorize your crypto wallet address. I keep my wallet address and other keys in a locked document on a secure computer. You can also consider printing your keys and storing them somewhere safe that you won't forget about.

A private key does the job of a unique individual password to your individual crypto wallet address. A public key then adds an extra layer of security and ensures that your wallet can't be hacked. Here's a quick example of what the keys look like:

Private key: 03bf350d2821375158a608b51e3e898e507f
e47f2d2e8c774de4a9a7edecf74eda

Public key: 99b1ebcfc11a13df5161aba8160460fe1601d541

These addresses look completely different to the eye, but the software technology knows that the two keys are specifically linked to each other. That proves that you're the owner of the coins and allows you to transfer funds whenever you want.

When someone sends you any type of cryptocurrency, they're essentially signing off ownership of those cryptos to your wallet's address. To be able to spend those cryptos and unlock the funds, the private key stored in your wallet must match the public address the currency is assigned to. If the public and private keys match, the balance in your wallet increases, and the sender's balance decreases accordingly. No exchange of real coins actually occurs. The transaction is signified merely by a transaction record on the blockchain (see Chapter 4) and a change in balance in your cryptocurrency wallet.

Looking at Different Types of Wallets

First, let me clear up the difference between a traditional digital wallet and a cryptocurrency wallet. You may already be using digital wallets, also known as e-wallets, through your mobile phone. I use wallet apps for my train tickets, parking tickets, Apple Pay (a mobile payment and digital wallet service run by Apple that allows users to make payments in person, in iOS apps), and Venmo (a mobile payment service you can pay your babysitter, friends, and family with).

Cryptocurrency wallets are a whole different animal; furthermore, they come in several different species catering to different needs. The following sections cover the five most popular types of cryptocurrency wallets, in order of their security level (from least secure to most).

In Figure 7-1, you can see a summary of the most common crypto wallets and their examples that I share with Invest Diva students.

SUMMARY OF CRYPTOCURRENCY WALLETS

	SOFTWARE	ONLINE	HARDWARE	PAPER
PROS	User-controlled Security For POS coins, allows minting	High convenience Accessible from any browser without needing to download the Blockchain	Protects user's private keys, which are stored on the device Can be recovered with PIN and seed	Extremely secure Can't be hacked using digital means Great for long term storage
CONS	Must download entire Blockchain for each type of coin/token	Susceptible to key logging hacks Can't stake POS coins Unknown level of security	Doesn't support all coins/tokens Can't stake POS coins	Inconvenient to use for transactions
EXAMPLES	Electrum Armory	Blockchain MyEtherWallet	Ledger Trezor	

© John Wiley & Sons, Inc.

FIGURE 7-1: Popular cryptocurrency wallet types.

TIP

According to Bitcoin Wiki, a "seed phrase, seed recovery phrase, or backup seed phrase is a list of words which store all the information needed to recover a Bitcoin wallet. Wallet software will typically generate a seed phrase and instruct the user to write it down on paper. If the user's computer breaks or their hard drive becomes corrupted, they can download the same wallet software again and use the paper backup to get their bitcoins back." *PoS* stands for proof of stake, a mining concept I explain in Chapter 5.

REMEMBER

Specific wallet brands I mention here aren't the only options available, and you shouldn't take their inclusion as a recommendation. Do your own research to find the best options available in your area and for your needs and chosen cryptocurrencies. I discuss choosing a crypto wallet in more detail later in this chapter.

Online wallet

Online wallets may be less secure, but they do have a bunch of advantages for small amounts of cryptocurrencies. An *online* (or *web*) *wallet* allows you access to your cryptos via the internet. Therefore, as long as you're connected to the internet (the cloud), you can reach and store your coins and make crypto payments. The online wallet provider stores your wallet's private key on its server. The provider may send you the crypto code but store your keys and give you the ability to access your keys. Different services offer various features, with some of them linking to multiple devices, such as your mobile phone, tablet, and computer.

Advantages of online wallets include the following:

>> They enable fast transactions.

>> They may be able to manage multiple cryptocurrencies.

>> They're convenient for use on the go and for active trading.

WARNING

Disadvantages include the following:

>> They risk your online security because of potential vulnerability to hacks and scams.

>> They risk your personal security because of potential exposure to computer viruses.

>> You aren't storing your cryptos; a third party is.

Mobile wallet

Mobile wallets are available on your cellphone through an app. You can use mobile wallets when shopping in physical stores as cryptocurrencies become more acceptable.

Note: Other types of wallets, such as online wallets (see the preceding section), offer mobile versions as well. But some wallets are specifically and only used for mobile phones.

Mobile wallets (which fall into the category of software wallets) have their advantages:

>> They can be safer than online wallets.

>> They're convenient for use on the go.

>> They offer additional features such as QR code scanning.

Some disadvantages of mobile wallets include the following:

>> You risk losing your crypto assets if your phone is lost or damaged, unless you at least have your seed phrase secured someplace other than your phone (so you can create a new digital wallet).

>> They run the risk of getting mobile viruses and malware.

Desktop wallet

You can download a *desktop wallet* and install it on your computer. Some people argue that desktop wallets are safer if your computer isn't, or even better, has never been connected to the internet. If a desktop computer has never been connected to the internet, it essentially becomes a cold wallet. On the other hand, a computer that has never been connected to the internet may expose you to malware that may automatically move from the wallet drive that you connect to the computer and infect the desktop because it has never been patched with software updates that require an internet connection. Talk about a catch-22!

To set up your wallet on a computer that has never been connected to the internet, you must first download the latest version of the wallet on a computer that *is* connected to the internet. You then move the file to a USB drive or something similar in order to move it to your offline computer.

Some advantages of desktop wallets (which fall into the category of software wallets) include the following:

>> They're a convenient choice if you trade cryptos from your computer.

>> You aren't storing your private keys on a third-party server.

>> If your computer has never been connected to the internet, a desktop wallet can be safer than an online wallet.

WARNING

But desktop wallets do come with some disadvantages:

>> Using your crypto assets on the go is more difficult.

>> If you connected the wallet to the internet, it turns into a less secure hot wallet.

>> If you don't back up your computer and it dies, you lose your cryptos.

POPULAR ONLINE, MOBILE, AND DESKTOP WALLETS

Some of the cryptocurrency exchanges I mention in Chapter 6 offer online, mobile, or desktop crypto wallets where you can store the cryptocurrencies you purchase through them. Here are some of most popular ones at the time of writing:

- **Binance.us:** This wallet may be a better fit for more experienced crypto investors. Binance.us incorporates high security and is regulated by the Financial Conduct Authority (FCA) in the United Kingdom and the Securities and Exchange Commission (SEC) in the United States. In April 2019, when hackers stole more than $40 million in funds from the platform, Binance covered the entire amount for its customers. The U.S. branch of Binance regulations are fierce, but this is not yet true for Binance global at the time of writing. If you use my referral link when signing up, we'll both earn $10 each after you complete $100 worth of trading in 30 days: https://investdivabinance.com.

(continued)

(continued)

- **Coinbase:** Just like Coinbase exchange (see Chapter 6), Coinbase online wallet is user-friendly and easy to use. It supports more than 170 digital assets and offers multi-signature and two-factor authentication support. You can use the Coinbase Wallet on mobiles and tablets, as well as the Chrome extension on your computer.

- **MetaMask:** This decentralized online wallet was launched in 2016. With the advent of nonfungible tokens (NFTs), the MetaMask wallet became even more popular. This wallet is mainly used for storing Ethereum (ETH) and can be linked to most NFT marketplaces. The wallet supports thousands of decentralized applications and is compatible with other blockchain solutions and Web3 networks, including Polygon, Binance Smart Chain, and Avalanche. On a desktop, you can use the MetaMask wallet on Google Chrome, Microsoft Edge, Mozilla Firefox, and Brave browsers. On mobiles you can use MetaMask on Android or Apple devices. You can download the MetaMask wallet here: https://metamask.io.

- **Trust Wallet:** This wallet is owned by Binance, and it has one of the most user-friendly mobile apps for storing your crypto. According to its website, Trust Wallet supports more than 160,000 coins and tokens. Just for holding your cryptocurrency, you can earn up to an 11 percent annual percentage rate (APR) in 12 different cryptos. Like MetaMask, Trust Wallet is also popular with NFT and decentralized app enthusiasts. You can check out Trust Wallet here: https://trustwallet.com.

Always beware of the amount of risk you're willing to take to gain high-APR earnings. Risk and reward are directly correlated, and when companies promise such high earnings, there's always a risk involved. Turn to Chapter 3 to calculate your risk tolerance.

Hardware wallet

A *hardware wallet* can arguably be one of the safest types of crypto wallets out there. These wallets store your private keys on a device like a USB drive. You're still able to make online transactions, but the wallets are offline most of the time, so you can consider them cold wallets.

For security purposes, a hardware wallet is an absolute must (and a bare minimum) for large crypto amounts. Keeping a ton of your assets on other, less secure types of wallets increases your risk of unrecoverable hacking attacks. Even safer than hardware wallets are paper wallets, which I talk about in the next section.

Here are some advantages of hardware wallets:

>> They're one of the safest crypto wallet options.

>> They're great for storing large amounts of cryptocurrencies that you don't want to use on a day-to-day basis.

Some disadvantages of hardware wallets include the following:

>> They're the most expensive type of wallet.

>> They aren't as user-friendly as other wallets, especially for beginners.

Paper wallet

A *paper wallet* is a super-cold crypto wallet. To use it, you print out your private and public keys. You can send funds by transferring the money to the wallet's public address, and you can withdraw or send your currencies by entering your private keys or by scanning the QR code on the paper wallet.

Some of the advantages of paper wallets include the following:

>> They're ultra hacker-proof.

>> You don't store them on a computer, mobile phone, or third-party server.

Paper wallets do have some disadvantages, though:

>> They aren't user-friendly for nongeeks.

>> They're harder to use for day-to-day transactions than other wallet types are.

>> They can catch fire.

POPULAR HARDWARE AND PAPER WALLETS

Some of the most popular hardware wallets to store your cryptocurrency include, at the time of writing:

- **Ledger:** Ledger Nano S hardware wallet (priced at $99) is one of the most popular and highly rated secure wallets out there. I use Ledger hardware wallets to store my cryptocurrency assets. It isn't the most user-friendly wallet out there, but it has kept my crypto secure. You can also connect your wallet to Ledger's mobile app, Ledger Live, to track your crypto assets and their value as the market goes up and down. If you use my personalized link you can get the best deal: https://earn.investdiva.com/ledger.

- **Trezor:** This is another popular hardware wallet, storing your cryptocurrency with a high level of security. The maker of this wallet is a part of SatoshiLabs and is headquartered in Prague, Czech Republic. This wallet is on the pricier side and pairs with your mobile app through Trezor Suite. You can check it out here: https://trezor.io.

Paper wallet generators include www.bitaddress.org and https://paperwalletbitcoin.com (one of the oldest BTC paper wallet generators that still remains active at the time of writing). Another popular choice offering a variety of crypto-related services is Bitcoin.com (www.bitcoin.com), which has gained recognition recently and provides different services, including wallets, an exchange, and crypto news. You can create a paper wallet using its wallet generator: https://paperwallet.bitcoin.com.

Choosing a Crypto Wallet

Depending on your cryptocurrency needs and goals, you may need more than one type of cryptocurrency wallet. I use cold wallets to store my larger crypto reserves and hot wallets for active trading. Regardless, you can choose your cryptocurrency wallet(s) based on different characteristics, some of which I discuss in the following sections.

Make sure you've gathered everything you need to know about a given wallet before committing to getting one.

Based on security

Even if you're an active crypto trader, I recommend that you have a super-secure cold wallet where you store your larger amounts of crypto assets. As I note earlier in this chapter, online wallets aren't the most secure option, however convenient they may be. You can always transfer your assets to an online wallet if you need immediate access to your cryptocurrencies for an investment/shopping opportunity.

Another point to keep in mind is that the most secure hardware wallets are normally the most expensive ones. So, you should calculate whether spending that much money for a particular wallet makes sense for the amount of crypto you're going to store in it.

Some questions you must ask before choosing the most secure wallet include the following:

>> What sort of authentication does the wallet use?

>> Is the website secure?

>> What do online reviews say?

CoinCentral (https://coincentral.com), 99Bitcoins (https://99bitcoins.com), and CryptoCompare.com (www.cryptocompare.com) are among the websites that provide an annual crypto wallet review. I normally check with two or more websites before making a decision.

Based on your crypto ownership

Not all crypto wallets can handle your different types of cryptocurrency assets. In fact, some wallets are purpose-built for just one cryptocurrency; many cryptocurrencies have their own official wallets, which can handle only that one crypto. For example, Bitcoin-specific hot wallets include Bitcoin Core Wallet (https://bitcoin.org/en/choose-your-wallet), Mycelium (https://wallet.mycelium.com), and Electrum (www.electrum.org). For Ethereum, you have options such as Ethereum Wallet (https://ethereum.org), MetaMask (https://metamask.io), and MyEtherWallet (which is a paper wallet; see www.myetherwallet.com).

If you're not planning to diversify among other types of cryptocurrencies, a singular official cryptocurrency wallet may be right for you. Most of the time, you can find the official wallet of a cryptocurrency on the company's website.

Multicurrency wallets are an option for people who want to hold more than one cryptocurrency. The majority of online wallets provided on the exchanges (introduced in Chapter 6) give you the opportunity to store and transact among multiple cryptos. However, if you're using these wallets to store your crypto assets, know that your wallet security may be compromised.

I do *not* recommend leaving a large amount of coins in an online exchange wallet.

Coinomi (www.coinomi.com) is a popular multicoin mobile wallet. It supports more than 200 different digital tokens and a number of blockchains. It's a great multiasset cryptocurrency wallet, but at this writing, it's available for mobile devices only. Exodus (www.exodus.com) is another multicoin wallet, available only on desktop. Your private keys remain secure on your device and never leave it. Exodus can even encrypt the private keys for you.

Based on transaction fees

If you're planning to do a lot of crypto shopping and use digital coins on the go, you may need to be mindful of the transaction fees you're paying along the way. This point is especially true for active traders. If you're a day-trader and you're paying more on transaction fees than what you're making in the market, doesn't that defeat the purpose of trading?

Based on anonymity

Anonymity is an extra layer of security you can take into consideration when choosing a crypto wallet. If you use an anonymous wallet, you can separate your personal information from your funds, making it harder for anyone to track down your cryptos and potentially steal them. This factor is something that can be very personal. Some wallets offer full anonymity, while others don't. If anonymity is something that's really important to you, choose among more-private wallets. Note that prioritizing anonymity may affect transaction fees and the price of the wallet.

To find the latest, most popular anonymous wallets, you can simply search the web for the term "anonymous cryptocurrency wallets." Anonymous wallets come in the forms of mobile, hardware, software, and so on. With that, you can have one or more anonymous wallets based on your needs. Some of the popular anonymous wallets at the time of writing include these:

>> **BitLox:** This hardware Bitcoin wallet ensures both security and anonymity. It's capable of holding more than 100 wallets with the ability to create millions of addresses for each wallet. Check it out here: www.bitlox.com.

>> **Electrum:** This desktop Bitcoin wallet appears to be one of the most trusted software wallets by the cryptocurrency community. Check it out here: www.electrum.org.

>> **Samourai:** This wallet is a mobile Bitcoin wallet. According to the Samourai website, the aim is to "to keep your transactions private, your identity masked, and your funds secure." You can check out the company here: www.samouraiwallet.com.

Keeping Your Wallet Secure

After you've selected the cryptocurrency wallet(s) aligned with your goals, you want to actively keep your investment safe. No matter how secure a wallet is, you still need to take personal steps to enhance that security, just as you'd do with your traditional personal wallet. Because you may be storing a higher value in your cryptocurrency wallets, keeping them safe becomes that much more important. This effort is basically the price you pay for wanting to manage your own money without having to rely on third parties, governments, and big banks. Here are some tips on keeping your wallet safe.

Back up your wallet

A famous *Sex and the City* episode has main character Carrie Bradshaw losing her journalism portfolio because she didn't back up her computer. Don't let that happen to your crypto portfolio. Back up your cryptocurrency wallets just as you back up your photos, work files, and computer data.

A backup of your wallet can protect you against computer failures and many human mistakes. It can also allow you to recover your wallet if your mobile phone or computer is stolen. Of course, you need to keep your backup wallet in a safe place, away from your original wallet. And make sure you back up regularly to ensure that all recent crypto addresses are included in your original wallet.

Additionally, you should also consider keeping a backup of PINs, usernames, and passwords if your wallet provides these features. This measure is just in case it has been long enough for you to forget these things. I keep a hidden file with these items on a secure local cloud for my personal use that is almost impossible to hack.

Have multiple wallets

It's diversification time, baby! If you're having a hard time choosing among the many secure wallets, don't worry. Keeping your assets across multiple wallets is actually a great practice anyway. That way, if any of your wallets are somehow compromised, you don't go bankrupt of cryptocurrencies.

A good combination is using two or more hardware wallets for larger crypto amounts, with the rest of your smaller amounts spread across mobile, desktop, or online wallets, depending on your everyday use of cryptocurrencies. Of course, all these need to have their own specific backups (as I explain in the preceding section).

Add more security levels

You can add to the security level of your wallets in a number of ways. Here are some suggestions:

>> **Use two-factor authentication (2FA).** If your wallet allows it, 2FA is a great way to take the security of your wallet to the next level. It's simply a double authentication of who you are, though it can be done in different ways. I use the Google Authenticator app, which provides a six-digit code that changes every minute and is unique to you.

>> **Encrypt your wallet.** Encrypting your wallet or your smartphone allows you to set a password for anyone trying to withdraw funds. This act helps protect against thieves, though it can't protect against keylogging hardware or software (which tracks your keystrokes). You should also consider encrypting your backups. *Note:* Some methods to encrypt may need a bit more technical familiarity. The best way to encrypt your wallet is to contact your wallet provider for more information.

>> **Use a strong password.** A strong password must contain letters, numbers, and symbols and must be at least 16 characters long. Avoid passwords that contain only letters, only numbers, or only symbols. Recognizable English words are also a no-go because they're easy to break.

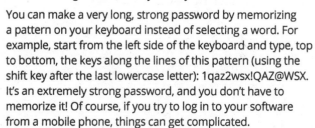

You can make a very long, strong password by memorizing a pattern on your keyboard instead of selecting a word. For example, start from the left side of the keyboard and type, top to bottom, the keys along the lines of this pattern (using the shift key after the last lowercase letter): 1qaz2wsx!QAZ@WSX. It's an extremely strong password, and you don't have to memorize it! Of course, if you try to log in to your software from a mobile phone, things can get complicated.

Update your software

If you're using mobile or desktop wallets, make sure you're using the latest version of the wallet's software. Reputable companies constantly send stability and security fixes. By updating your software regularly, you can make sure that you're using the newest safety features that can prevent problems from minor to severe. (Updating your wallet's software isn't the same as backing it up, which I discuss in the earlier section "Back up your wallet.")

Remember where you hide it!

This suggestion may sound a bit silly, but you have no idea how many times I've tried to hide something valuable, just to lose it forever! If you're one of those people who hides things so well that even *you* can't remember where they are, make sure you choose a location you won't forget. If you lose your cryptocurrency wallets, you may very well lose your shirt as well in the long run.

Chapter **8**

Surveying Different Types of Cryptocurrencies

By now, you've probably heard of the cryptocurrency that started it all: Bitcoin. But Bitcoin is hardly the only famous or even investment-worthy cryptocurrency out there anymore. Heck, some people even think that Bitcoin may be the worst cryptocurrency to own or invest in. So many other digital coins are available that have made massive improvements to the Bitcoin model to avoid its disadvantages.

TIP

Personally, I still see value in Bitcoin for various reasons: It's the only truly decentralized cryptocurrency, which can give you the ultimate control over your wealth and free you from governments globally. It is a *category king* (it created an entirely new industry and is the most well known in its category) and has value simply for its brand recognition. There will only ever be 21 million Bitcoins out there, so if it remains a category king, its value has nowhere to go but up due to the law of supply and demand. However, there are investors who'd rather avoid investing in Bitcoin due to its high energy consumption, slow and costly transactions, and lack of real utility.

In this chapter, I go over some of the most famous cryptos as of 2022. But because the cryptocurrency market is ever-changing, I explain how you can navigate your way through all the up-and-coming cryptos for years to come.

Distinguishing Coins, Altcoins, and Tokens

If you've scrolled through any crypto-related article, you may have caught them referring to cryptocurrencies using different terms such as *coins, altcoins,* and *tokens.* Some people use these terms interchangeably, but there's an actual difference between them.

The following sections present a quick overview of what each term really means.

Coins

Coins are the native cryptocurrencies of the specific blockchain they run on (for more on blockchains, check out Chapter 4). For example, Bitcoin is a coin because it runs on the Bitcoin blockchain. Because Bitcoin was the first ever cryptocurrency, all other coins that are native to a blockchain are considered alternative coins. Therefore, in the world of cryptocurrency, *coin* only refers to Bitcoin.

REMEMBER

Some people also consider Ethereum to be a coin because it was the second cryptocurrency out there and it runs on its own blockchain. As cryptocurrencies gained popularity in the 2010s, most other cryptocurrencies were formed as a result of Bitcoin or Ethereum forks — a splitting from the original blockchain (explained in Chapter 5). As blockchain is becoming more mainstream, there are many more novel blockchains popping up.

Altcoins

All cryptocurrency coins other than Bitcoin (and for some people, Ethereum) that run on a native or their own independent blockchain are called *altcoins.* Examples include Litecoin, Dogecoin, and Binance Coin.

TECHNICAL
STUFF

The first ever altcoin was Namecoin, which was created in April 2011. Namecoin is a decentralized open-source information registration and transfer system.

Tokens

A *token* is a digital representation of an asset or utility in a blockchain. Tokens usually reside on top of another blockchain (rather than their own independent blockchain). Tokens are meant to serve a different purpose to money, which is what coins and altcoins are all about. They can represent any asset that's fungible. Being *fungible* means that you can replace it with an identical item. For example, you can interchange your $100 bill for any other $100 bill. This makes it fungible.

Tokens can represent all fungible and tradable assets, from commodities to loyalty points and cryptocurrencies. You can even *tokenize* real estate.

REMEMBER

To figure out whether you're dealing with a crypto coin or token, you need to find out whether the cryptocurrency has its own blockchain. If it does, then it's a *coin*. If it doesn't, but it operates on an existing blockchain, then it's a *token*.

Celebrating Celebrity Cryptocurrencies by Market Cap

One of the fastest ways to navigate through popular cryptocurrencies is to check out their ranking based on their *market capitalization* (or *market cap* for short). Traditionally, market cap is the value of a company that's traded on the stock market. You can calculate it by multiplying the total number of shares by the present share price.

REMEMBER

In the cryptoworld, market capitalization shows the value of all units of a specific cryptocurrency that are for sale right now. To calculate a cryptocurrency's market cap, simply multiply the cryptocurrency's current price by its *circulating supply*. Circulating supply is the best approximate number of coins that are circulating in the market and in the general public's hands. Here's the formula:

Market cap = Price × Circulating supply

Knowing about a crypto's market cap and its ranking versus other coins is important because that info can quickly show you how popular the coin is and how much money you may be able to make from it. You can find out about all cryptocurrencies' market caps by visiting websites such as CoinMarketCap (https://coinmarketcap.com), CryptoCompare (www.cryptocompare.com), CoinCodex (https://coincodex.com), and CoinGecko (www.coingecko.com).

Market cap can't tell you everything about a cryptocurrency's investment potential, however. Lots of other factors (such as forks, regulations, rumors, blockchain, community, utility, mission, and so on) can affect a cryptocurrency's value. I talk more about analyzing a cryptocurrency's performance in Chapter 9.

A higher market cap isn't necessarily a good thing. Investors who can take higher risks may prefer cryptocurrencies with a lower market cap because they may offer more room for the market cap to increase. However, if you want to play it safe and avoid volatility or vanishing risk (as I explain in Chapter 3), you may prefer going with cryptocurrencies with a higher market cap.

With a knowledge of what role a coin's market cap plays in the industry, you can start to evaluate cryptocurrencies based on that metric. I discuss Bitcoin and other major cryptocurrencies in the following sections.

Bitcoin

Ranking number one on the list, Bitcoin was developed in 2008. As of September 2022, Bitcoin's market cap is around $385 billion. For comparison, in October 2018, Bitcoin's market cap was $115 billion. So, even though at the time of writing, Bitcoin has technically crashed from its 2021 all-time highs, its value has tripled within these four years!

A bit of Bitcoin background

An entity called Satoshi Nakamoto invented Bitcoin. Satoshi claimed to be a man living in Japan, born on April 5, 1975. I was actually living in Japan, completing my studies in electrical engineering in Tokyo, when Bitcoin hit the scene. I can tell you that Bitcoin wasn't really a big thing in Japan at that time. That's why most speculation about the true identity of Satoshi points to a number of cryptography and computer science experts of non-Japanese descent living in the United States and various European countries.

But Satoshi's anonymity isn't really a big deal, because Bitcoin (and most other cryptocurrencies, for that matter) are supposed to be open source and decentralized, as I explain in Chapter 5. In fact, according to Bitcoin.org, no single person or entity "owns the Bitcoin network much like no one owns the technology behind email." Bitcoin users around the world control Bitcoin, with the developer improving the software and the forkers making some radical changes. However, the main idea behind Bitcoin and Bitcoin's protocol can't be changed.

Almost ten years after Satoshi published Bitcoin's white paper, Bitcoin's market cap went up to as much as $320 billion by the end of 2017. If you had invested $100 to buy one Bitcoin in 2011 (something my investor friends told me to do that I ignored), you would've had $20,000 worth of Bitcoin by the end of 2017. Of course, many initial investors bought more than one Bitcoin at the time, which is exactly how all those Bitcoin millionaires were made. If you had bought 100 Bitcoins in 2011, by the end of 2017 they would've been worth $2 million.

But by the time everyone started talking about Bitcoin, it went crashing down to around $120 billion and stayed there until 2020. Then came another Bitcoin boom, which brought its market cap to over $1 trillion! Then it fell back down, but this time to the highs of 2017. Throughout the roller-coaster ride over the years, however, Bitcoin has maintained its number-one ranking among all other cryptocurrencies. The main reason behind this position may be that most people have heard a lot (relatively speaking) about Bitcoin but not so much about other cryptocurrencies. So, even though they have several hundred other altcoins to choose from, even some that may be better long-term alternatives to Bitcoin, most newbies who want to get involved in the market start out with Bitcoin.

Another reason for Bitcoin's huge market cap is its accessibility. I can pretty safely say that all cryptocurrency exchanges (see Chapter 6) carry Bitcoin. But not all exchanges list all altcoins, at least for now.

Bitcoin characteristics

Here are some main features of Bitcoin:

» Bitcoin's trading symbol is BTC.

» Bitcoin is minable.

» Coin creation occurs through proof of work (PoW; see Chapter 5).

» Transaction time is between 30 minutes and 24 hours.

» Transactions aren't fully anonymous.

» Bitcoin is decentralized.

» Mining Bitcoin requires a lot of (wasted) energy.

TIP

Because Bitcoin has been the superstar of all cryptocurrencies, it tends to pull the entire market along. Generally speaking, the whole market sentiment follows the volatility of Bitcoin in longer-term time frames (with many past exceptions). You can use this piece of information in technical analysis for investing. You can find out more about Bitcoin on its website, https://bitcoin.org.

Ethereum

Move over Bitcoin, here enters Ethereum! Celebrity cryptocurrencies such as Bitcoin and Ethereum were often criticized for their mining process and the amount of wasted energy they required to exist. That was until September 15, 2022, when Ethereum successfully made an upgrade to its entire network, cutting down its energy consumption by more than 99 percent. Ethereum has maintained its number-two rank behind Bitcoin based on coin market cap over the years and at the time of writing. With that, it's safe to say that Ethereum is a major cryptocurrency. As of September 2022, its market cap is around $177 billion — a significant jump from its $23 billion market cap in 2018.

WARNING

Note that past performance is not indicative of future results!

In mid-September 2022, Ethereum went under a major shift to improve the security and scalability of its blockchain network. These improvements were referred to as Ethereum 2.0 or ETH2.0 before September 2022. This new version uses a different method to verify transactions, called proof of stake (PoS) instead of

PoW. Then, something called The Merge happened in September 2022, when the old Ethereum (ETH1.0, the one that's been around since the beginning) joined the new Ethereum (ETH2.0). Now that they've merged, there is only one version of Ethereum.

A brief background of Ethereum

Compared to Bitcoin, Ethereum is a younger currency; Russian American Vitalik Buterin proposed it in 2013. It's almost five years younger than Bitcoin, which in the cryptoworld is still a big deal.

Ethereum uses the old Bitcoin's wisdom and philosophy, but it has a different purpose and capability. According to its website, https://ethereum.org, "Ethereum is a decentralized platform that runs smart contracts." As I explain in Chapter 5, *smart contracts* allow people to create agreements without an intermediary. Ethereum creates these smart contracts by employing the same blockchain technology as Bitcoin. Just as Bitcoin's blockchain and network validate Bitcoin ownership, Ethereum's blockchain validates smart contracts, which the encoded rules execute.

Ethereum versus Bitcoin

Once people learned about the underlying technology that supports Bitcoin, they were eager to utilize it for purposes other than a decentralized payment network. Ethereum was proposed as a network for creating tamper-proof contracts and applications. This means Ethereum is technically not a competitor of Bitcoin, but a complement to it.

The main difference between Ethereum and Bitcoin is that Ethereum wants to be the place users go to execute their decentralized applications. In fact, its goal is to be a sort of massive, decentralized computer that executes smart contracts. That's why many other cryptocurrencies can run on the Ethereum platform. The Ethereum blockchain forms a decentralized network where these programs can be executed.

Bitcoin is different in this sense. It was the granddaddy of all crypto, and its goal is to radically change the definition of money as we know it and introduce us to a new type of money that operates outside the control of any government or centralized institution. Its platform gets the miners to compete and solve the complicated blockchain math problems I talk about in Chapter 4. The first one who solves the problem is the winner and gets rewarded. But miners can use Ethereum's platform as a coworking space to create their own products. They get compensated for providing the infrastructure so inventors can cook their own new types of products.

TIP

In fact, even major technology players like Intel and Microsoft and financial behemoths like JPMorgan and Credit Suisse are using the Ethereum platform to create new stuff of their own. Along with other giant founding members, various blockchain start-ups, research groups, and Fortune 500 companies have created a group called the Enterprise Ethereum Alliance (EEA). By September 2022, the alliance had more than 500 members, including Accenture, AMD, Credit Suisse, Dash, FedEx, Pfizer, Samsung, and Toyota, to name a few. You can find out more about the EEA at https://entethalliance.org.

Ethereum characteristics

Here are some main attributes of Ethereum:

>> Ethereum's token symbol for investors is ETH.

>> Ethereum is minable.

>> Coin creation used to be through PoW, but after its September 2022 update, Ethereum got rid of the PoW mechanism and is now using a new mechanism called PoS that gets rid of puzzles and mining and, thus, reduces the network's energy consumption by 99.9 percent.

>> Transaction time can be as little as 14 seconds, although it can go higher based on confirmation requirements.

>> Transactions aren't fully anonymous.

>> Ethereum is arguably less decentralized than Bitcoin, although different crypto enthusiasts may have different takes on this.

Ripple

During the first crypto bubble/crash era between 2017 and 2020, Ripple was the third-largest cryptocurrency by market cap. It even surpassed Ethereum at the beginning of 2018, temporarily ranking number two. However, after getting into trouble with the U.S. Securities and Exchange Commission (SEC) in 2020, its ranking has dropped to number seven at the time of writing. Regardless, it remains a project with many enthusiasts in its community, a unique mechanism, and governmental issues, making it worthy of being mentioned in this book.

Some Ripple background

The idea of Ripple actually goes all the way back to 2004. That's way before Satoshi and Bitcoin. In 2004, Ryan Fugger founded a company called RipplePay. According to `https://blog.bitmex.com/the-ripple-story`, the idea behind the protocol was a "peer-to-peer trust network of financial relations that would replace banks." (If that sounds familiar, that's probably because it's also how blockchain works, as I discuss in Chapter 4.)

By 2011, Ripple's target demographic started paying attention to Bitcoin, which was just becoming popular and was doing a better job as a peer-to-peer payment network than Ripple. Ripple's architecture started to shift when an early Bitcoin pioneer, Jed McCaleb, joined the Ripple network in May 2011. Others hopped on the Ripple bandwagon as time went by.

Finally, Ripple's XRP, a cryptocurrency that also acts as a digital payment network for financial institutions, was released in 2012, according to its website, `https://ripple.com/xrp`. Like many other cryptocurrencies, XRP is based on a public chain of cryptographic signatures. That being said, Ripple is very different from traditional cryptos like Bitcoin and even Ethereum.

REMEMBER

Some people don't consider Ripple a true cryptocurrency. Also, Ripple as a company and Ripple the cryptocurrency are two different things, although they're connected:

>> Ripple the company does business as Ripple Labs, Inc.; is a money transfer network designed to serve the needs of the financial services industry; and provides global payment solutions for big financial institutions using blockchain technology.

>> Ripple the cryptocurrency, which trades as XRP, is the native cryptocurrency on the Ripple network that is used with some of the company's payment systems to facilitate transactions on the network.

Ripple versus Bitcoin

Here are some of the key differences between these two cryptocurrencies:

>> **Purpose and usage:** Bitcoin is a cryptocurrency based on a decentralized blockchain intended as a means of payment for goods and services. Ripple (XRP) runs on the XRP ledger, a blockchain that uses a distributed consensus mechanism via a group of bank-owned servers. XRP's main utility is to allow fast transactions between big financial institutions.

>> **Ownership and decentralization:** As I talk about earlier in this chapter, Bitcoin is owned by no particular person or entity, and Bitcoin the cryptocurrency is pretty much the same as Bitcoin the open-source platform. That's why Bitcoin is highly decentralized and open source, owned by a community that agrees on changes. This setup can make upgrades tough, and it's why Bitcoin has had a ton of forks (hard and soft; see Chapter 5) in its history.

By contrast, Ripple is a private company called Ripple Labs, with offices all over the world. Ripple's digital asset (cryptocurrency) is called XRP and is also owned by Ripple Labs. The company constantly looks to please everyone (especially its partners) and come up with consensus, which can allow for faster upgrades. It has an amendment system with which the developers seek consensus before making changes to the network. In most cases, if an amendment receives 80 percent support for two weeks, it comes into effect, and all future ledgers must support it. Basically, Ripple is a democracy that tries to avoid hard forks and nasty splits!

TIP

You can find out more about Ripple and its most recent updates at https://ripple.com.

>> **Transaction speed and fees:** This area is where Ripple really starts to shine. Bitcoin's transaction speed can sometimes go up to an hour, depending on fees. And the fees can reach $40 depending on demand.

Ripple's transactions, on the other hand, can settle in as little as four seconds. Fee-wise, even when the demand was super high at the end of 2017, Ripple's transaction fees averaged $0.007 — a fraction of that of Bitcoin. XRP transactions are faster than Ethereum but not faster than Solana, a cryptocurrency that became an investor favorite in 2021.

You can compare different cryptocurrencies' historical transaction fees at https://bitinfocharts.com/comparison/transactionfees-btc-xrp.html.

>> **Number of transactions per second:** At any given second, you can make around ten Bitcoin transactions. Enter Ripple, and raise the number to 1,500. Although some Bitcoin forks aim to resolve this issue, at the time of writing, Ripple appears to be ahead of the game.

>> **Coin amount limits:** Bitcoin and other minable cryptocurrencies have finite numbers of coins, which come into the market only through mining. But XRP is limited to the 100 billion coins in circulation now, largely to appeal to Ripple's (the company's) biggest clients, which are large financial institutions.

Ripple characteristics

The following list gives you a summary of Ripple's main features:

>> Ripple's token symbol for investors is XRP.

>> Ripple's XRP isn't minable. No miners whatsoever.

>> Coin creation and algorithm processing happens through consensus, *not* PoW.

>> Transaction time can be as little as 4 seconds.

>> Transactions can be made anonymously.

>> Ripple isn't fully decentralized.

>> Energy cost per transaction is minor.

Because these unique features are so different from Bitcoin's, some people believe Ripple's XRP isn't truly a cryptocurrency. Ripple is actually a strange hybrid of a *fiat currency* (the traditional form of currency backed by a local government, such as the U.S. dollar) and a traditional cryptocurrency. This deviation is because Ripple primarily has been seeking to serve financial institutions like American Express instead of focusing on the spread of Ripple's XRP among everyday users. This may very well change in the future.

Cardano

Cardano entered the cryptocurrency game as an alternative to Ethereum by (surprise, surprise) the cofounder of Ethereum, Charles Hoskinson, in 2015. Both Ethereum and Cardano have the same goal of providing a platform for other applications and building a connected and decentralized system.

Cardano considers itself an updated version of Ethereum; however, at the time of writing, Cardano still remains under construction. Regardless of that, Cardano and Charles Hoskinson have been able to gain momentum, which has brought the market cap of Cardano's cryptocurrency, ADA, into the top ten largest cryptocurrencies.

TIP

Check out my interview with Cardano founder Charles Hoskinson to learn more about the network: https://investdiva.com/charles-hoskinson-interview-from-ethereum-to-cardano-and-iohk.

Cardano versus Ethereum 2.0

Cardano is a direct competitor to Ethereum and especially the new version of Ethereum. Ethereum 2.0 moved the platform from a PoW system (which is what Bitcoin uses) to a PoS system (which is what Cardano uses). You can use both Cardano and Ethereum for peer-to-peer transactions and run custom programming logic (also known as *smart contracts*). Here are some of the differences between the two:

>> **Coin limitation:** Ethereum has no coin limitation. Kind of like oxygen that can be produced by trees, Ethereum can produce an unlimited number of ETH coins only capped on an annual basis. That means Ethereum can grow by 4.5 percent per year. However, Cardano has a total limited supply of 45 billion tokens. Some may argue that having a supply limit may increase the coin's value.

>> **Scalability:** Cardano and Ethereum are both dedicated to managing smart contracts and decentralized apps. However, Cardano focuses on functionality by using a dual-layer design. Ethereum focuses on mass adoption by using a single-layer solution.

Cardano characteristics

Cardano's main traits include the following:

>> Cardano's token symbol for investors is ADA.

>> Cardano works on a PoS system.

>> Transaction time is around 5 minutes.

>> Transactions are comparatively anonymous, but if you purchase from an exchange or a trading platform, they will know your details.

>> Cardano is decentralized.

>> Cardano is one of the most eco-friendly coins and uses only an estimated 0.00277429 terawatt-hours per year. Compare that to Bitcoin, which uses an estimated 127 terawatt-hours. This makes Cardano 47,200 times more energy-efficient than Bitcoin!

TIP

Most crypto enthusiasts typically argue that their platform is the best. The best way to go about your investment strategy may be to diversify your assets not only between these options but also among the other categories of cryptocurrencies I cover in this chapter. Find out more about diversification in Chapter 10.

Other top ten major cryptos

In the previous sections, I introduce some of the most well-known cryptocurrencies that also have some of the largest market caps on average. But being famous doesn't mean they're necessarily better. In fact, many analysts and investors believe some of these celebrity cryptocurrencies may vanish within ten years (as I explain in Chapter 3). For example, Litecoin was listed in the top ten in 2018, but at the time of writing, Litecoin has dropped to number 23 based on market cap, and there's not much clout going on about it. Also, having a bigger market cap doesn't necessarily mean having a brighter future. Their current popularity may just be the proverbial 15 minutes of fame, and they may, therefore, have lower growth opportunities compared to those that are less known.

REMEMBER

Chances are, if anything should happen to a core cryptocurrency, a hard fork may come along that saves it. As I explain in Chapter 5, if you've already invested in a cryptocurrency when it forks, you get the same amount of new coins anyway. That's why

I recommended to my Premium Investing Group (Invest Diva PIG) members in 2017–2018 to start their cryptocurrency portfolio by first diversifying among the top ten largest ones by market cap and then getting into other, different categories.

One of the biggest cryptocurrencies in 2021–2022 was Dogecoin, for example, which got a lot of hype from Elon Musk and his followers. Personally, I believe Dogecoin only has value because Elon Musk said so! At the time of writing, Dogecoin doesn't solve any core problems, besides making crypto fun. When it comes to long-term investing, I prefer to invest in projects that solve a tangible problem. Regardless, Dogecoin has remained in the top ten list by market cap.

Table 8-1 shows some cryptocurrencies (listed alphabetically) that were on the top 20 list more consistently during 2022. Please note that I have not personally invested in some of these cryptocurrencies.

TABLE 8-1 **Some Top Twenty Cryptos as of 2022**

Crypto	Symbol	Description
Avalanche (www.avax.network)	AVAX	Another of Ethereum's competitors that aims to have a higher transaction output while not compromising scalability.
Binance Coin (www.binance.com)	BNB	The cryptocurrency of the largest global crypto exchange in the world, Binance.
Chainlink (https://chain.link)	LINK	One of the first networks to allow the integration of off-chain data into smart contracts, and one of the major players in the data procession field.
Dogecoin (https://dogecoin.com)	DOGE	A popular internet meme coin that features a Shiba Inu on its logo. It started as a joke and was promoted by Tesla CEO Elon Musk during 2021–2022.
Polkadot (https://polkadot.network)	DOT	The leading protocol for Web3, a decentralized internet of blockchains that can be interoperable with each other.
Solana (https://solana.com)	SOL	Launched in March 2020 in Switzerland, Solana is one of the fastest-growing blockchains focused on decentralized finance (DeFi).

Top 100 major cryptos

You can dive into the top 100 major cryptocurrencies and still not find *the one* you want to have a long-term relationship with. At this point, selecting cryptocurrencies that match your portfolio really becomes like online dating. You've got to make some decisions based on first impressions and then go on dates (start making small investments and do more research) to discover whether a currency is worthy of a bigger chunk of your crypto portfolio.

TIP

You can find the list of all cryptocurrencies ranked based on their market cap at any given time here: https://coinmarketcap.com.

Cryptocurrencies by Category

As an alternative to selecting cryptocurrencies by market cap, the best way to truly diversify your portfolio, for both value and growth purposes, may be to go about selecting cryptocurrencies by category. After you've flipped through the categories and selected the finalists that best fit your risk tolerance (see Chapter 3), you can then move on to the advanced techniques I discuss in Chapters 9 and 10 and in Part 3.

Here are some of the most popular cryptocurrency categories and the leading cryptos in each space. I list these based on their popularity and total market cap as of 2022. Some popular cryptocurrency categories include the following:

- >> Decentralized finance (DeFi)
- >> Utility
- >> Exchange
- >> Payment
- >> Privacy
- >> Stablecoins
- >> Platform
- >> Financial technology (fintech)/finance
- >> Legal/property
- >> Nonfungible tokens (NFTs)/collectibles
- >> Metaverse

>> Gaming/gambling

>> Supply chain

>> Transportation

>> Medical/health care

The following sections describe just a few examples of these categories in the exciting cryptocurrency world; you may recognize some of the currencies from their coverage earlier in this chapter. Other people may categorize these cryptos differently.

REMEMBER

Keep in mind that some categories are hotter as of this writing, but others may have become more popular by the time you're reading this book. Also know that some cryptos are hybrids of multiple categories and are hard to fit in only one box. You can find the latest different crypto categories by searching "cryptocurrency categories" on your favorite search engine.

Decentralized finance cryptos

DeFi aims to allow anyone with access to the internet to lend, borrow, and bank without going through traditional intermediaries. DeFi is an unregulated financial system that many people believe will potentially revolutionize the way we conduct financial transactions.

WARNING

However, because DeFi is still primarily unregulated, investors don't enjoy the same protection that they do in traditional financial markets. That being said, despite some risks, the benefits of DeFi could be considered numerous because of the sheer level of transparency involved in transactions and because no banks or other financial institutions are needed to oversee your money.

Ultimately, DeFi works to replace the traditional role of financial systems through its smart contracts. In summary, any cryptocurrency that has its main focus on finance or decentralization can be considered a DeFi.

Here are some examples of DeFi cryptos:

>> **Avalanche (AVAX):** Avalanche is a smart contract–capable blockchain platform that focuses on lightning-fast transaction speed, low costs, and overall eco-friendliness. Avalanche is aiming to deliver an easily scalable blockchain that doesn't

sacrifice security or decentralization. See www.avax. network.

>> **Uniswap (UNI):** Uniswap is the largest decentralized exchange (DEX) operating on the Ethereum blockchain. It allows worldwide users to trade crypto without involving an intermediary. See https://uniswap.org.

>> **Chainlink (LINK):** Chainlink is a decentralized oracle network that provides real-world data to smart contracts on the blockchain. Smart contracts are predetermined agreements on the blockchain that evaluate information and then automatically execute when certain specific conditions are met. LINK tokens are, therefore, the digital asset token used to actually pay for services on the network. Chainlink's sophisticated technology has so far proven to be one of the most important pillars of the DeFi and wider crypto ecosystem. See https://chain.link.

Utility cryptos

Utility tokens are a type of cryptocurrency designed to be used for a specific purpose in a certain ecosystem. Utility tokens allow users to do certain things on a specific blockchain network or decentralized application.

Utility tokens are different from other kinds of tokens, because they can only be used in certain ecosystems. For example, the Basic Attention Token (BAT) is useful only on the Brave browser. BAT can be used to tip content creators on the Brave browser or in other applications that have a BAT wallet. You also need to understand that BAT doesn't have any other use than being traded for its value. It's just like other utility tokens. Utility tokens are also premined and created in a certain quantity, which is determined by the team behind the project.

Exchange-specific cryptos

Exchange-specific cryptos are the cryptos that (mainly) the cryptocurrency exchanges introduce and use. You can think of these cryptos as incentives that bring people to the exchanges' platforms.

TIP

To select the best exchange-specific cryptocurrency, you can consider taking the steps I introduce in Chapter 6 for choosing the best cryptocurrency exchange.

Here are a few examples of these currencies:

>> **Binance Coin (BNB):** Issued by the Binance exchange, Binance Coin runs on the Ethereum platform and has a strict maximum limit of 200 million BNB tokens. See www.binance.com.

>> **KuCoin Shares (KCS):** KuCoin Shares is just like Binance Coin but for the KuCoin exchange. See www.kucoin.com.

>> **Cronos Token (CRO):** Cronos is a utility token designed by Crypto.com and issued on the Crypto.com exchange to facilitate transactions within its blockchain. It's a full-service DeFi provider and exchange. See https://crypto.com.

Payment cryptos

Payment cryptos are by far the biggest category in terms of total market cap. In this group, you find cryptocurrencies that mainly aim to be used as a store of value, transactions, and payments, just like fiat currencies like the U.S. dollar. Examples of cryptocurrencies that fall into this category include the following:

>> Algorand (ALGO)

>> Bitcoin (BTC)

>> Bitcoin Cash (BCH)

>> Dash (DASH)

>> Litecoin (LTC)

>> OMG Network (OMG)

>> Ripple (XRP)

>> Stellar (XLM)

>> Tether (USDT)

TIP

With Bitcoin as the pioneer, no wonder this category started out so popular. But as I say multiple times throughout this book, blockchain technology can be applied to so much more than just payment systems, so be on the lookout for the next big thing within other hot categories!

Privacy cryptos

Privacy cryptos are heavily focused toward transaction security and anonymity, a lot more than those in the payment category are. In fact, the idea that Bitcoin and other cryptocurrencies in the payment category are fully anonymous and untraceable is a common misconception. Many blockchains only disguise users' identities while leaving behind a public record of all transactions that have occurred on the blockchain. The data in the ledger often includes how many tokens a user has received or sent in historical transactions, as well as the balance of any cryptocurrency in the user's wallet.

WARNING

Privacy cryptos can be a bit controversial because authorities see them as an illicit tool that criminals could use to engage in illegal activities, such as money laundering. Nonetheless, some of them have gained popularity. Here are some examples:

>> **Monero (XMR):** Monero is the most famous privacy crypto as of 2022. See www.getmonero.org.

>> **Zcash (ZEC):** Zcash is similar to Monero but has a different protocol (set of rules). See https://z.cash.

>> **Decred (DCR):** Decred is a cryptocurrency primarily designed for community input, open governance, privacy, and sustainable funding for development. It also operates a hybrid consensus mechanism. See https://decred.org.

Stablecoin cryptos

Stablecoins are a type of cryptocurrency, a digital asset whose value is *pegged* (directly linked) to an external and generally stable asset class such as a specific fiat currency like the U.S. dollar or gold. The cryptocurrency market is fairly volatile, so stablecoins can offer a less risky way of storing money on the blockchain because they maintain a predictable price range.

REMEMBER

Stablecoins are used completely differently from other cryptocurrencies that people tend to buy as an investment. They're often used to send money digitally to another party in the world. They're also used as a way of transferring your own funds between cryptocurrency exchanges, as well as storing funds on an exchange so you can quickly use them to purchase other cryptocurrencies. Some online platforms even allow you to lend out your stablecoins in order to earn high rates of interest.

Here are some popular examples of stablecoins:

>> **Binance USD (BUSD):** BUSD is a stablecoin founded by Paxos and Binance. It's a regulated, fiat-backed stablecoin pegged to the U.S. dollar. For every unit of BUSD, there is one U.S. dollar held in reserve. The supply of BUSD is pegged to the U.S. dollar at a ratio of 1:1. As an example, when the price of the U.S. dollar rises or falls, the price of BUSD also does in equal amounts. This is the most traditional model of stablecoin. See www.binance.com/en/busd.

>> **Tether (USDT):** Tether is designed to provide a stable price point at all times. The Tether stablecoin was created to function as the internet's "digital dollar," with each token being worth $1 USD and backed by $1 USD in physical reserves. See http://www.tether.to.

>> **USD Coin (USDC):** USD Coin is another popular stablecoin like Tether and has similar characteristics. USDC is often described as a potentially safer stablecoin because it places huge emphasis on transparency of its fully backed reserves and goes to great effort to comply with government regulation and audits. See www.circle.com/en/usdc.

Platform cryptos

Platform cryptos are also referred to as *decentralized application protocol cryptos, smart contract cryptos,* or a hybrid of all three. In this category, you can find cryptocurrencies that are built on a centralized blockchain platform; developers use them to build decentralized applications. In other words, such cryptocurrencies act as platforms where people build upon blockchain applications (and, thus, other cryptocurrencies).

TIP

In fact, some analysts suggest you may want to forget about payment cryptocurrencies and invest in crypto platforms instead. They're generally considered good long-term investments because they rise in value as more applications are created on their blockchain. As blockchain technology becomes more mainstream, the number of applications and their usage will increase, along with the price of such coins.

The most famous example in this category is Ethereum (ETH). Others include the following:

>> **Ark (ARK):** Ark wants to provide an all-in-one blockchain solution for developers and start-ups. See https://ark.io.

>> **EOS (EOS):** Another smart contracts platform similar to Ethereum, EOS has performance and scalability benefits.

>> **Icon (ICX):** Icon wants to "hyperconnect the world" by building one of the largest decentralized global networks. See https://icon.community.

>> **Lisk (LSK):** Lisk is a smart contracts platform similar to Ethereum but based on JavaScript. See https://lisk.com.

>> **NEO (NEO):** A smart contracts ecosystem similar to Ethereum, NEO wants to be a platform for a new smart economy. NEO is China's largest cryptocurrency. See https://neo.org.

>> **Qtum (QTUM):** Qtum is a Singapore-based Ethereum and Bitcoin hybrid. See https://qtum.org.

>> **Substratum (SUB):** Substratum wants to create a new generation of internet. See https://substratum.net.

>> **VeChain (VEN):** VeChain is a blockchain-based platform that gives retailers and consumers the ability to determine the quality and authenticity of products they buy. See www.vechain.org.

These are just a few of the hundreds of cryptocurrencies that are emerging in this category.

Finance and fintech cryptos

In this section, I group pure financial cryptos with fintech cryptocurrencies. These cryptos facilitate the creation of a financial system for the blockchain and for people around the world:

>> **Bancor (BNT):** Bancor lets you convert between two cryptocurrencies of your choice without another party. See https://bancor.network.

>> **Crypto.com (CRO) (formerly Monaco, MCO):** This cryptocurrency-funded Visa debit card allows you to spend your coins on everyday purchases. See https://crypto.com.

- ❯❯ **OMG Network (OMG):** OMG Network is designed to enable financial services for people without bank accounts. It works worldwide and with both traditional money (fiat currency) and cryptocurrencies. See `https://omg.network`.

- ❯❯ **Quoine (QASH):** Quoine wants to solve the liquidity problem in the cryptocurrency market through its LIQUID platform. See `www.liquid.com`.

- ❯❯ **Ripple (XRP):** Ripple is a blockchain payment system for banks, payment providers, digital asset exchanges, and other companies. It's designed to move large amounts of money quickly and reliably. See `https://ripple.com`.

- ❯❯ **Stellar (XLM):** Stellar aims to develop the world's new financial system. It's building an open system where people of all income levels can access financial services. See `www.stellar.org`.

Legal and property cryptos

More cryptocurrencies are emerging in the two categories of legal and property cryptos. But because they're related, I've grouped them together here for now. Here are a couple of examples:

- ❯❯ **Polymath (POLY):** Polymath helps provide legal advice for token investors and smart contract developers. See `https://polymath.network`.

- ❯❯ **Propy (PRO):** Propy solves problems of purchasing properties across borders when using fiat currencies or cryptocurrencies. It's the first company ever to sell a property on the blockchain and using Bitcoin. See `https://propy.com`.

TECHNICAL STUFF

Other up-and-coming property cryptocurrencies include REAL and REX, but at the time of writing they're way down on the cryptocurrency market cap ranking list.

NFTs and collectibles cryptos

NFTs are cryptographic assets on a specific blockchain with unique identification codes and metadata that distinguish them from each other. NFTs are, therefore, not able to be replicated, but they can represent collectible real-world items, the most popular and well-known being artwork.

Here are a few of examples of NFT-related crypto coins/tokens:

>> **ApeCoin (APE):** ApeCoin is a token that serves many functions within the APE ecosystem, which is made up of individual token holders and the products and services utilizing the token. It's closely affiliated with an NFT project known as the Bored Ape Yacht Club (BAYC), a hugely successful and highly valuable collection of 10,000 uniquely different cartoon-styled ape drawings each with a distinctive look! See https://apecoin.com.

>> **Chiliz (CHZ):** Chiliz is an Ethereum token that powers Socios.com, a platform that lets users trade tokens to show their support and appreciation for professional sports teams. It runs on an Ethereum-based Chiliz blockchain, and the token effectively serves as currency, which allows users to purchase NFTs at Chiliz's Socios fan token marketplace. See www.chiliz.com.

>> **Flow (FLOW):** Flow is a blockchain platform that allows for fast, low-cost transactions and supports smart contracts. It powers blockchain applications including NBA Top Shot, an NFT offering. See https://flow.com.

Metaverse cryptos

The integration of metaverse cryptos with blockchain infrastructure enables them to make virtual items exchangeable for real economic value beyond the confines of the metaverse. These cryptocurrencies are especially popular in the gaming world.

The metaverse is the perfect collision between the physical world and digital worlds when virtual reality and augmented reality bridge the gap and allow the physical and virtual worlds to interact closely.

Here are some examples:

>> **Decentraland (MANA):** Decentraland is a virtual-reality blockchain-based platform. It allows for a virtual world where users can buy, develop, and sell virtual land and estates (LAND), as well as gain access to Avatar wearables and names in the Decentraland Marketplace. See https://decentraland.org.

>> **The Sandbox (SAND):** The Sandbox is an Ethereum-based metaverse and gaming ecosystem where users can create, share, and monetize in-world assets and many other different types of gaming experiences. Users have the option of buying and selling virtual land and creating virtual communities, as well as purchasing NFT collections and digital avatar accessories. See www.sandbox.game.

Gaming cryptos

Gaming cryptos are cryptocurrencies that are used on gaming platforms. These platforms reward gamers with cryptos for playing games or being active on the platform.

Crypto gaming tokens are special items that represent gaming assets, such weapons, skins, skills, and customizations. Some of the famous gaming coins at the time of writing include Decentraland (MANA), Sandbox (SAND), and Axie Infinity (AXS).

Other crypto categories

Blockchain technology can be used in almost any project, including supply chain, transportation, and the medical industries. For example, for the supply chain industry, blockchain technology is a way to make sure that companies can track all types of transactions more securely and transparently. This is important because it can help companies figure out where products came from and where they are now. Every time a product changes hands, the transaction is documented on the blockchain, creating a permanent history. This can be helpful for companies that work together on one platform because it reduces the time delays, costs, and human error associated with transactions.

Blockchain technology is also used for many purposes in the health-care industry, including securing patient data and managing the pharmaceutical supply chain.

TIP

You can always learn about the most recent developments in each crypto category by searching the web for the name of the category and adding "crypto" in your favorite search engine. My team and I also regularly update our most recent strategies here: https://investdivapig.com.

Chapter **9**

Identifying Top Cryptocurrencies

I n Chapter 8, I open a huge window to all the different categories of cryptocurrencies because this whole industry isn't just about Bitcoin or a few other famous cryptos you may have already heard of. Having so many options to choose from is exciting! But just like dating in the digital age, having too many options can be tricky. You're always keeping an eye open for the next best thing.

The good news is that you can have multiple "right" cryptocurrencies for you. But swiping through so many cryptocurrencies can become challenging, especially if you don't know exactly what you're looking for.

In this chapter, I guide you through finding your best crypto match(es) by introducing you to my golden strategy development method, the Invest Diva Diamond Analysis (IDDA), and a few other techniques.

Introducing the Invest Diva Diamond Analysis

Most individual investors learn one or two methods for analyzing the markets before pulling the trigger and actually executing an investment strategy. For example, most newbie investors rely on things like technical analysis and their favorite economic news anchors on TV. Unfortunately, depending on only one type of analysis can be incredibly dangerous.

Enter the IDDA! The IDDA suggests analyzing the markets from five different points, as you can see in Figure 9-1:

>> Intentional analysis

>> Capital analysis (personal risk management)

>> Fundamental analysis

>> Technical analysis

>> Sentimental (market sentiment) analysis

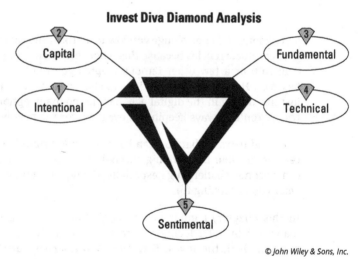

Invest Diva Diamond Analysis

© John Wiley & Sons, Inc.

FIGURE 9-1: Five points of the Invest Diva Diamond Analysis.

Turn to Chapter 3 to read about risk management (part of the capital analysis point); for a comprehensive Masterclass on the IDDA, visit https://investdiva.com/masterclass. In the rest of this chapter, I discuss fundamentals and market sentiment analysis and introduce technical analysis to help you pick the right cryptocurrencies at the right prices for your portfolio. Here's a brief overview of these concepts:

>> **Fundamental analysis:** As a fundamental analyst, you look at the fundamental value a blockchain or cryptocurrency project produces, and evaluate data from facts to rumors to decide whether that asset is worth buying.

>> **Technical analysis:** As a technical analyst, you look at how an asset's price has been performing, identify the past key psychological prices the market as a whole has been eyeing, and then you make an investment decision that's right for you.

More specifically, you analyze the price action of your favorite cryptocurrency to see the best time to jump into a relationship and a good time to call it quits. You can see the history of the crypto price actions on something called *charts* that are available on your cryptocurrency exchange.

>> **Sentimental analysis:** *Market sentiment* gauges the emotions and attitudes of traders in the market about a specific asset. Using sentimental analysis, even non-animal-lovers in the investing world compare market expectations to bulls and bears.

REMEMBER

If traders expect upward price movement of a specific security, the sentiment is said to be *bullish.* On the contrary, if the market sentiment is *bearish,* most traders expect downward price movement.

Using Fundamental Analysis to Pick Cryptocurrencies

Fundamental analysis is the art of making sense of all the gossip, stories, and facts about an asset; the problems it's solving; its long-term value; whether it's going to be relevant in the time frame you'd want to be invested in it; its financial situation; and upcoming risk events that may move the market. You can apply the same fundamental analysis approach to cryptocurrencies that you'd use for stocks.

Going back to the dating metaphor at the start of this chapter, finding the right crypto category is like picking your type in a significant other. Except in this case, you should most certainly think with your brain and maybe a little bit with your gut, but nothing more than that (if you catch my drift). Here are some methods you can use to cherry-pick the best crypto assets for you.

Go with what you know

Going with what you know is a golden yet simple method also used in the stock market. If you've already been exposed to certain types of cryptocurrencies or, better yet, used them in real life and liked their performance, consider adding them to your portfolio. In the stock market, for example, many newbie investors make several profitable investments by simply observing their own buying habits. If they prefer to buy from healthier fast-food services like Chipotle (CMG on the New York Stock Exchange [NYSE]) rather than McDonald's (NYSE: MCD), they may consider adding CMG to their portfolio.

Similarly, say you notice that your favorite online store has already added a cryptocurrency payment option to its checkout page and you place an order with it smoothly. That success may be an indication that the trading volume for that cryptocurrency will increase in the future, and the crypto may become a valuable asset for your portfolio.

TIP

Investing in what (or who) you know is by far my favorite investing strategy development method. This goes far beyond investing in online financial markets. Think about who you know the most about — who would that be? It's likely that the one person you know the most about in the world is yourself. That's why on the top level of the Invest Diva Movement, we prioritize investing in yourself. Investing in yourself can mean investing in your health, investing in your relationships, or learning high-income generation skills that can increase your wealth. For example, right now you're investing in yourself by reading this book to learn about the next generation of investing (congratulations!). As you accumulate high-income-producing skills, no matter what direction the world or the economy goes, you're always going to be there for yourself. For more about investing in yourself to acquire high-income-producing skills and building generational wealth, visit https://wealthdiva.com.

Choose the right categories

In Chapter 8, I talk a huge deal about crypto categories and where you can find them. Certain categories perform better at certain times in the overall market, not just the crypto market. So, for example, if you notice that the decentralized finance (DeFi) sector is heading higher in equities and that everyone is talking about artificial intelligence (AI), you may want to consider browsing through the AI category and finding cryptocurrencies that are involved with it.

Another way to pick the best categories for medium-term investments is to choose from categories that are already outperforming the overall market. I'm not talking about a category that did well just today but rather something that either has been doing well for a few months or even years or is showing signs of picking up. You can pick the hottest category as your top pick and then add on the second and third ones for diversification purposes. I talk more about diversification in Chapter 10.

REMEMBER

The cryptocurrency categories may not always follow the rest of the market. Because cryptocurrency is a very new industry to begin with, you may find opportunities in it that you may not necessarily find in the more traditional equities market. Heck, the crypto industry may turn into a safety net if the stock market crashes.

Exchange-traded funds (ETFs) normally consist of a basket of a number of assets in the same category. They're super popular in the equities market because they make the choosing process much easier. They're also cheaper to purchase than their big, fancy hedge-fund equivalents, mutual funds.

WARNING

Personally, I'm not the biggest fan of ETFs or index funds because it doesn't give me enough control over my portfolio. Investing in index funds is kind of like taking the bus: If you don't have a driver's license, you'd better take the bus because if you try to drive a car, you're likely gonna crash. But if you've educated yourself on investing principles (like you're doing now), you may consider building your own portfolio. Investing in individual assets is like driving your own car. You don't have to stop at every bus stop, you have more control over the route you take to reach your destination, and you can even have multiple destinations as you please!

Check out cryptos' websites

Whether you have a number of cryptocurrencies in mind based on your own experience or you've picked a category and you now want to choose the best crypto within that sector, you must now start a more detailed analysis on your finalists.

If you've ever watched *The Bachelor* or *The Bachelorette* on TV (guilty as charged — I'm addicted), you're probably already familiar with the process. You start out with around 30 potential matches for your portfolio. By the time you're down to the three or four finalists, you're ready to see what their worlds are all about. In the cryptocurrency world, the company's website is the equivalent of the TV hometown dates. Here are a few ideas to consider when you're picking your crypto sweethearts that don't involve visiting their high schools and getting a grilling from their families.

Flip through their white papers

TIP

A *white paper* is something like a business proposal for new cryptocurrencies. It includes everything potential investors need to know about the crypto, such as technology, purpose, financial details, and so on. More-established cryptocurrencies may already have a page that breaks down all this critical information into easy-to-understand video clips and cool infographics on tabs titled "About" or "How It Works." For others, you may just need to find the white paper on the website and try to digest the information by reading. The good news is that white papers are often written in a language that people who aren't experts in the field can understand.

Identify their teams

No one really knows who created Bitcoin, but the rest of the cryptocurrencies out there normally have a team behind them that guides the company and its blockchain technology (see Chapter 4). The team behind the crypto is important even if its platform is completely open source, which means anyone can access and modify it.

When you invest in anything, whether it's stocks, a new start-up, or a hot date, understanding the background and how it came to life can play a major role. Here are some things to look for in the management:

>> Bios

>> Résumés

>> Experience in the field

In addition to the core management, I also like to check the backgrounds of the members of the board of advisors if the company has it. You normally can find such information on the company's website, under tabs labeled things like "About Us" or "Our Team."

When you invest in a cryptocurrency, you're essentially investing in a start-up company, an entrepreneur, and its community of people. Sometimes these entrepreneurs are young with no qualifying résumé, just like Facebook founder Mark Zuckerberg or Ethereum founder Vitalik Buterin. That's when the creator's personality can become a factor in your decision-making. As Mark Cuban (*Shark Tank* investor and Dallas Mavericks owner) told CNBC, "When you invest in an entrepreneur, you get the personality. And if that's not appropriate or you don't think it's right, buy another stock" (or in this case, crypto).

Playing the devil's advocate here, I think it's also important to note that the leader of any movement (whether it's a company, a blockchain, or a government) is essentially the "attractive character" that has the power to either attract or repel the kind of people they want in the community as defined by their culture. Sometimes, the more polarizing an attractive character, the stronger the community and, therefore, the greater the chance of success.

Browse their partnerships

If you're not willing to take a lot of risk, seeing who in the industry has put their trust in the hands of the cryptocurrency you're considering buying is very important. More established blockchains have been able to team up with traditional giants like IBM and Microsoft and banks like Goldman Sachs. These companies have expert analytic teams perform due diligence before jumping on board with new investments and partnerships. Having reputable partners can be a sign that the company is solid and on the right track to get ahead of the competition.

Another good thing about having partners in the traditional world is that the cryptocurrency may have a higher chance of getting accepted by the masses. If a cryptocurrency has established partnerships with other companies, they're normally listed under a tab called "Our Partners" or "About Us."

Familiarize yourself with their technology

Many cryptocurrencies are tokens from blockchain companies with multiple products. Well-developed websites walk you through their technology and their products in a not-so-intimidating way. The more you get to know the products and the technology behind the cryptocurrency, the easier you can make your decision about the finalists on your cryptocurrency list. Chapter 5 can be your go-to "cryptionary" along the way.

Check out their contribution to society

What problems are your short-list cryptocurrencies trying to solve? Does it matter to you? Are they just here to get rich quick, or do they have a long-term plan for the betterment of society? Finding an answer to these questions can also help you narrow down your list of finalists. Companies like Ripple describe their social contributions under a subtab called "Ripple for Good." Other companies often use a similar format or simply put their core social contributions first thing on their home page.

Analyze their road maps

Many companies behind cryptocurrencies have sections on their websites dedicated to their road maps: where they come from, what they've achieved, and what they're planning to accomplish in the future. If available, road maps are a great way to discover a ton of fundamental information about the crypto in a few minutes.

Get to know their community

A big part of peer-to-peer blockchains and their tokens are the people. People are the heart and soul of crypto projects, and oftentimes they're also the cause of creating hype and FOMO ("fear of missing out") around a specific crypto project. Often these communities of people become so passionate about their own projects that they start bashing the other projects.

I recommend keeping emotions away from investment decisions and looking into the communities from above, taking notes on what they stand for, and deciding if they're aligned with your own values and moral beliefs.

Get involved

You can take the previous step to the next level and start participating in the communities. Just like dating, the more you get involved, the more you get to know about the dirty secrets. The majority of cryptocurrency platforms love to increase their followings and encourage people to get involved right there on their websites. Depending on the cryptocurrency, getting involved can mean anything from mining to joining its social forums or even starting a new cryptocurrency project on its blockchain platform (like Ethereum)! Of course, getting involved also means investing more of your time, so you need to find a balance there.

Trying Technical Analysis to Select Cryptos

When you've got your heart set on a few cryptocurrencies to add to your portfolio, you're ready to decide the best time to buy them. The golden rule to any type of investment comes down to four important words:

"Buy low, sell high."

But how can you decide when the price is at its lowest point to buy? That's where technical analysis, the third point of IDDA, comes in. *Technical analysis* is the art of using history to predict the future. Here's a brief introduction to price action and the best price analysis methods:

>> **Technical analysis basics:** So many fabulous tools and gadgets can help you understand the historical movements and patterns of a cryptocurrency's price. By discovering how each pattern and indicator works, you can have a higher degree of accuracy in predicting future price actions.

>> **Recent price action:** Although the current price of one coin isn't a very good indicator of a cryptocurrency's overall value, analyzing the price action becomes *very* important when you're trying to figure out when to buy and sell. You can check the most recent price action of your selected cryptocurrency on websites such as CoinMarketCap (https://coinmarketcap.com) to see how much the price has dropped or surged in the past day, week, or even months.

Analyzing recent price action is more important for short-term traders who are looking to get in and out of the market more rapidly (say, within a day or a week). Chapter 11 has more on short-term trading strategies.

>> **Big picture:** If you're a long-term investor like I am, you may find looking at the big picture more useful in your technical analysis. Many cryptocurrencies are too young to have a well-developed price history, but you still can use similar techniques by comparing older cryptocurrencies in the same category and applying big-picture analysis to the new ones. In Chapter 12, I discuss technical analysis methods for long-term investors.

Choosing Cryptos with Sentimental Analysis

After you've done the essential background check on your prospective cryptocurrencies, you can move on to the fifth point of IDDA, sentimental analysis. *Sentimental analysis* is the study of the love–hate relationship with cryptocurrencies and traders.

Key sentimental elements

Without getting too sentimental, here are some essential elements to check before setting your heart on your favorite cryptocurrencies.

The crypto community

The company behind the cryptocurrency can play a role in the direction the crypto goes, but the network that participates in the currency's blockchain technology (see Chapter 4) is an important key to its success. Many cryptocurrencies directly depend on the participation of their communities, like miners and developers. Most of the crypto communities have their own forums on places such as the following:

>> Reddit (www.reddit.com)

>> BitcoinTalk (https://bitcointalk.org)

>> Steemit (https://steemit.com)

These forums are great not only because they give you a sense of what type of people are involved in the cryptocurrency but also because you can find out more about the cryptocurrency itself.

TIP

More and more cryptocurrencies use their Telegram or Discord channels as a way to communicate with their user base. To join, you must download the Telegram app (https://telegram.org) or the Discord app (https://discord.com).

Exchanges that carry the crypto

REMEMBER

As I discuss in Chapter 6, cryptocurrency exchanges are a big part of the whole ecosystem. You want to make sure your cryptocurrency exchange carries your cryptos of choice, but choosing cryptos that are listed on many different exchanges is also a good idea. Most exchanges choose the cryptocurrencies they carry carefully. Finding your finalists on many different exchanges may be a sign that many exchanges have found that crypto to be valuable enough to carry. Therefore, the demand for it may be higher, and you may be able to do more with your investment. You can discover which exchanges carry your crypto of choice on websites such as https://coinmarketcap.com.

For example, say you want to know which exchanges carry Ripple's XRP. After selecting Ripple's XRP on https://coinmarketcap.com, go the tab labeled "Markets"; you may need to scroll down the web page a bit to find it. There you can view the full list of exchanges that carry XRP.

Volume

TIP

Volume means how much cryptocurrency got traded in a specific time frame. It's important because it tells you how easily you can buy or sell that cryptocurrency. The higher the volume, the more easily you can trade it off. You can check and compare cryptocurrency volume on websites such as www.cryptocompare. com and https://coinmarketcap.com, where they show the number of coins that have been traded in the last 24 hours. You can also examine which exchanges had what volume. Generally, the biggest and most popular coins are traded the most. But if you're trying to choose a cryptocurrency within a specific category (and not simply going for the celebrity cryptos), trading volume can be a very important indicator in making your decision.

Coin market capitalization

One of the fastest ways to navigate through cryptocurrencies is to check out their ranking based on their *market capitalization* (*market cap* for short). A bigger market cap shows a higher value of all units of a specific cryptocurrency that are for sale right now. This metric can again come in handy when you're trying to select "the one" within a specific category of cryptos. For more on market cap analysis, turn to Chapter 8.

Circulating supply

Circulating supply (CS) is the number of coins or tokens that people have mined or that companies have generated. The key is that the CS number shows you how many of these coins are currently in the market and that the general public has access to.

You can look at the importance of the CS in a couple of different ways:

>> **Some crypto investors believe less is more in terms of the CS.** That's if you look at it as an oversupply issue. Any market generally moves based on a principle called *supply and demand*. For example, when stores have a lot of apples and not enough people to buy them, they drop their apple prices because they want to get rid of their stock before it goes bad. The same theory can apply to cryptocurrencies. Although most coins don't have an expiration date (unless the company goes bankrupt, that is), a smaller CS may be more attractive if you're looking to invest short term to medium term. Fewer coins available and a higher demand may signal that the prices may go higher in the future.

>> **On the other hand, a lower CS number may indicate a lack of popularity.** Fewer people have put in the effort to mine the coin, which may impact the long-term forecast of the cryptocurrency.

>> **In some cases, the CS may not even matter.** For example, Ripple's XRP has a CS of almost 40 billion, while Dash has a CS of only 8 million. Meanwhile, they both gained around 3,000 percent in 2017!

You can find out about cryptocurrencies' circulating supply on websites such as `https://coinmarketcap.com`.

Total supply

When you add the newly mined cryptocurrencies to the circulating supply (see the preceding section), you get the *total supply* number. In other words, total supply is the total number of coins currently in existence, not just those circulating. For several reasons, some coins are reserved or locked and aren't sold in the public market. Total supply doesn't really impact a coin's price and isn't more important than the CS. I just threw it out here in case you come across it on a website and wonder what it is.

Stuff to check in the news

The news has the power to make someone or something so incredibly popular. Just take a look at reality stars or the latest Instagram sensation.

The same thing goes for cryptocurrencies. The media was behind the whole cryptocurrency hype and bullish market sentiment of 2017 and then again in 2021. Just as you may do a quick cyber check on your potential date before agreeing to meet, you may want to consider looking into the following about your finalist coins.

Recent coverage

TIP

Has your finalist been in the news a lot lately? Is it a hot topic? If the answer is yes, find out whether the news coverage is organic or paid. Of course, crypto companies are aware of the impact of the media, so they pay a ton of money to popular search engines to bring them right up on top of the search results ranking system. Some crypto news providers include CoinDesk (`www.coindesk.com`), Nasdaq (`www.nasdaq.com/news-and-insights/cryptocurrency`), and of course, `https://investdiva.com/investing-guide/category/cryptocurrencies`.

Another way you can approach this task is to simply go to the "News" tab in your search engine. When you search a topic on Google, for example, you're automatically directed to the "All" tab, which includes everything, from advertisements to news and general information. Find the "News" tab, and you'll get the relevant news coverage that's less likely to be paid ads.

Just because a crypto asset is getting a ton of hype that doesn't mean it's worthy of your investment. Sometimes, hyped-up cryptocurrencies simply become a pyramid where the price goes higher and higher for no reason other than FOMO, and the last person who buys at the highest price becomes the victim. This happened during the nonfungible token (NFT) craze of 2021 with all the Bored Ape NFTs being sold to celebrities for millions of dollars, just for the whole thing to crash down and the status of owning an NFT to be immediately wiped out.

Upcoming events

You can look for upcoming events in the early stages of finding your crypto soul mate or right at the very end:

>> For the first method, you can check out websites such as https://coinmarketcal.com and www.newsbtc.com/crypto-calendar and see which cryptos have a busy lineup of announcements and events that may impact the crypto in a positive way. Then take the other approaches I talk about earlier in this chapter to see whether that crypto is right for your portfolio.

>> For the second method, compile the list of your finalists, and then you can either check the cryptocurrency's website to see whether it has a blog where it shares its upcoming events or check out the third-party crypto calendars for additional information.

Of course, you can also combine both approaches.

Negative press

Public Relations 101 says any press is good press. The reason for that is that people tend to enjoy reading about negative stuff more. Then they get passionate about it and are more likely to remember the entity associated with the bad press in the future — but not necessarily in a bad way anymore. That certainly is the mentality of some celebrities, who believe any coverage of them, good or bad, will bring them positive outcomes in the long run.

And it certainly can be true in cryptocurrency investing as well. During the period when the negative press is a hot topic, the prices are likely to plummet. However, contrary to what you may think, that exact period may be a good time to purchase because everyone is likely dumping the asset. Catch them when they're down, and go to the top with them. A perfect romantic fairy tale, eh?

WARNING

Buying during negative press works only if all the other IDDA analysis points indicate the cryptocurrency is worthwhile long term. If the negative press consists of something ultra-damaging that the crypto is unlikely to recover from, go ahead and pass.

Chapter **10**

Using Diversification in Cryptocurrencies

I talk a lot about diversification throughout this book, specifically in Chapters 3, 8, and 9, and in my education products and seminars. In this chapter, I get to the bottom of what diversification means for your crypto portfolio, why it's important, and how you can manage your portfolio's risk by properly diversifying your assets.

Breaking Down Some Basics on Diversification

Small investors regularly hear about the topic of diversification for their personal stock portfolios. One of the first things a financial expert tells you when you want to get started with investing is "Don't forget to diversify!" You don't want to put all your eggs in one basket, regardless of whether that basket is stocks or cryptos. The following sections dig into what that really means, especially for cryptocurrency investing.

What is traditional diversification?

When you're building your personal stock portfolio, *diversification* often means having more than one or two stocks. The most conventional diversification method in a personal stock portfolio is to have around 15 to 20 stocks that are spread across different industries.

REMEMBER

When you diversify among industries, assets, or investment instruments that aren't correlated, you're less likely to see major drops in your portfolio when one of the categories is doing poorly. Diversification doesn't *eliminate* the risk of losses; it just reduces that risk if done correctly.

TIP

Although diversification appears to be a logical general rule to follow, throughout my years of investing I've come to realize that nothing beats having confidence in your investment. Investing in what you know and what you're confident in not only increases your risk tolerance, but also prevents you from having unnecessary stress when the markets move against you. In other words, diversifying by investing in assets you don't really know much about, just for the sake of diversifying, is not recommended.

How does diversification reduce risk?

You encounter two types of risk in a stock portfolio: unsystematic and systematic.

REMEMBER

Unsystematic risk is the type of risk that you can mitigate by combining multiple industries into one portfolio. Unsystematic risk includes the following:

>> **Business risk:** This risk is associated with a company's earnings and its ability to meet its financial obligations. This risk is also tied to the company's industry, because sometimes all the businesses within a category are exposed to a similar degree of uncertainty.

>> **Country risk:** This is the risk of political and economic instability in the country where the company does business.

>> **Default risk:** This is the risk that a company isn't able to repay its debt and, therefore, is subject to default.

- **Executive risk:** This risk is associated with the moral character of the executives who run the company. If they get into legal or ethical trouble, the company's stock may suffer both short term and long term.

- **Financial risk:** This risk is associated with the amount of *leverage* (a measure of the amount of debt) a company uses in its financial structure. The more debt the company has, the more leverage it's using and, therefore, the higher the risk.

- **Government/regulation risk:** This is the risk that a country may pass a new law or regulation that negatively impacts the industry that a company is in.

Systematic risk you can't get rid of simply by diversifying across various industries. That risk category includes

- **Market risk:** The risk that the market moves against your position due to various reasons, such as political reasons, social reasons, or general change in market sentiment

- **Exchange rate risk:** The risk that the exchange rate goes higher or its movements negatively impact your investments

- **Interest rate risk:** The chance that changes in interest rates adversely affect the asset's value

- **Political instability risk:** The risk that political uncertainties or changes negatively impact the market

- **Reinvestment risk:** The chance that you won't be able to reinvest your funds at a favorable rate of return

- **Event risk:** The chance of something unpredictable (like bankruptcy and hacker attacks) happening to the company, exchange, broker, or wallet that holds your asset, therefore contributing to negative market fluctuation

Traditional diversification in a stock portfolio helps reduce unsystematic risk. This is when things get interesting. You can't diversify away systematic risk within your stock portfolio, but how about diversifying across other markets? This approach is actually how I got into investing in the first place during the crash of 2008. (You can read about the details in the nearby sidebar "My foray into forex.")

MY FORAY INTO FOREX

In 2008, I was a mere college student studying electrical engineering at a university in Tokyo. I had no idea how the financial markets operated. But all I could hear was that the stock market was crashing and that the U.S. dollar's value was dropping versus the Japanese yen. That refers to the *exchange rate risk* portion of systematic risk (see the earlier section "How does diversification reduce risk?"). No amount of diversification could prevent the exchange rate risk in a U.S. stock portfolio, but investors did have one avenue to take advantage of the falling U.S. dollar: selling it against the appreciating Japanese yen. It was a brand-new investing opportunity called *forex* (short for *foreign exchange*).

That's exactly what I did (with the help of a friend), which led me to doubling my initial investment within a month while the rest of the market was crashing down. As a college student, making $10,000 within a month in a crashing market was enough for me to want to ditch my electrical engineering degrees (and six years of education!) and get on with finance and investing.

The rest is history. I came to New York to pursue my new dream and ended up empowering more women to join the movement in this male-dominated industry. Since then, I've stopped trading forex and have instead expanded my personal portfolio to stocks, exchange-traded funds (ETFs), and cryptocurrencies.

REMEMBER

As we get closer to the next inevitable stock market crash, I think adding unconventional investment instruments such as cryptocurrencies to your portfolio is more important than ever. Here's why: At the time of writing, the cryptocurrency market couldn't be more different from the traditional markets. It's new. It's unregulated and, therefore, traditional systematic risks such as political instability or interest rate risks don't really apply to it. In fact, investors may well see cryptocurrencies as a safety net for when things go south in other markets during a major economic crisis.

Using Cryptocurrencies in Long-Term Diversification

When it comes to adding cryptocurrencies to your portfolio, keep the following two types of long-term diversification in mind:

» Diversifying with non-cryptocurrencies

» Diversifying among cryptocurrencies

Here's a bit more about these two types of crypto diversification. (I talk more about diversification from traditional markets such as stocks, bonds, and forex in Chapter 2.)

Diversifying with non-cryptocurrencies

You have so many financial instruments to choose from when you consider diversifying your portfolio across the board. Stocks, commodities, precious metals, and bonds are just a few examples. As I explain in Chapter 2, each of these assets has its unique traits. Some assets' inherited risks can offset the risks of the other ones through long-term market ups and downs. The following sections provide guidance on how to use cryptos and non-cryptos together in the long term.

REMEMBER

No single golden diversification rule works for all investors. Diversification percentages and the overall mix greatly depend on the individual investor and their unique risk tolerance, as I talk about in the sidebar in Chapter 3 and in my free Masterclass (https://investdiva.com/masterclass).

TIP

The more risk you're willing to take, the higher the chances of a bigger return on investment, and vice versa. If you're just starting out and you have a lower risk tolerance, you may consider allocating a bigger portion of your portfolio to bonds and then systematically adding stocks, precious metals, and cryptocurrencies. For tips on calculating your unique risk tolerance, check out the sidebar in Chapter 3.

Some background on trading fiat currencies

Fiat currencies are the traditional money that different countries' authorities declare legal. For example, the U.S. dollar is the official currency of the United States. The euro is the official currency of the European Union and its territories. The Japanese yen is backed by Japan. You get the idea.

The *forex market* is a huge market where traders trade these fiat currencies against one another. Even though I no longer trade forex due to its high risk, time consumption, and low return on investment (ROI) compared to other types of income-creating activities, having a bit of a background in forex can help you better understand the cryptocurrency market and how you can trade the different types of currencies against one another, especially in shorter time frames.

I compare this market to a big international party where all the couples are made up of partners from different regions. So, if one is the Japanese yen (JPY), her partner may be the euro (EUR). I call them Ms. Japan and Mr. Euro. If one is the U.S. dollar (Ms. USA), her partner can be British, Portuguese, or Japanese.

In the forex market, these international pairs get together and start "dancing." But oftentimes, the paired-up partners aren't compatible, and their moves aren't correlated. For example, every time Ms. USA makes a good move, her partner screws up. Every time her partner picks up the rhythm, she's stuck in her previous move. These incompatibilities gain some attention, and a bunch of people who are watching the dancers start betting on which of the partners is going to screw up next. Those folks are the forex traders. You can watch this forex metaphor in action in my video here: https://investdiva.com/forex-coffee-break-with-invest-diva-education-course-info.

REMEMBER

The point is that when trading currencies — fiat or crypto — you can only trade them in pairs. For example, you can trade the U.S. dollar (USD) versus the Japanese yen (JPY); this is the USD/JPY pair. You can trade the Australian dollar (AUD) versus the Canadian dollar (CAD); that's the AUD/CAD pair.

Quote currency versus base currency

When trading currency pairs, the *base currency* is listed first, and the *quote currency* is listed second. Which currency in a given pair is the base currency and which is the quote currency is normally fixed across the trading markets. For example, when talking about trading the U.S. dollar versus the Japanese yen, the currency of the United States always comes first, followed by the currency of Japan (USD/JPY). In the EUR/USD pair, the euro always comes first, followed by the U.S. dollar.

REMEMBER

These set patterns have nothing to do with whether a certain currency's country is more important or whether one currency in a pair is more popular than the other. It's just how the trading crowd sets things up. The system doesn't change, which means everyone is on the same page and navigating through the pairs is easier.

As the base and quote come together, the currency pair shows how much of the quote currency is needed to purchase one unit of the base currency. For example, when USD/JPY is trading at 100, that means 1 U.S. dollar is valued at 100 Japanese yen. In other words, you need 100 Japanese yen (the quote currency) to buy 1 U.S. dollar (the base currency).

The same concept applies to cryptocurrency pairs. Many cryptocurrency exchanges offer a select number of quote currencies, mainly popular ones such as a fiat like the USD and cryptos such as Bitcoin, Ethereum, and their own exchange cryptos. Then they offer trading opportunities versus all the hundreds of other cryptocurrencies they may carry versus these quote currencies. I talk more about this topic later in this chapter.

Trading cryptos versus fiat currencies

Similar to the forex market, you can trade cryptocurrencies versus other currencies. The most common approach at the time of writing is trading them versus a fiat currency, typically the one backed by the country you live in.

For example, in the United States, most people trade Bitcoin versus the USD. They don't really think of it as trading these currencies in pairs because it feels a lot like buying a stock. But the fact is that when you buy Bitcoin using the U.S. dollar in hopes of capital gain, you're essentially betting that the value of Bitcoin will move higher against the U.S. dollar in the future. That's why if the U.S. dollar decreases in value (not only against Bitcoin but also against other currencies) at the same time that Bitcoin increases in value, you're likely to make more return on your investment.

This is where diversification can help you reduce your trading risk. As I explain in the next section "Diversifying among cryptocurrencies," most cryptos are correlated to Bitcoin in shorter time frames. That's why you can diversify your portfolio with the fiat currencies you trade them against. For example, if you think that at the time you're trading, the U.S. dollar and the Japanese yen aren't correlated, you can open up two Bitcoin trades: one versus the U.S. dollar and one versus the Japanese yen. Of course, in order to do so, you should make sure your exchange or broker carries these different fiat currencies and offers such trading opportunities.

WARNING

Speculating the markets and short-term trading carry a lot of risk. They may not be suitable for all investors, and you may end up losing all your investment. Before deciding to trade such assets, you should carefully consider your investment objectives, level of experience, risk tolerance, and risk appetite. Also, you should *not* invest money that you can't afford to lose. (If you're still curious, I delve more into short-term trades later in this chapter and in Chapter 11.)

Diversifying among cryptocurrencies

The majority of cryptocurrency exchanges offer a wider selection of cross-crypto pairs than they do fiat/crypto pairs. In fact, some exchanges don't even accept any type of fiat currencies altogether. That's why many traders have no choice but to trade one cryptocurrency against another. This is also called *cross-crypro trading*. Bitcoin (BTC) versus Ethereum (ETH) gives you the BTC/ETH pair, for example.

As you can imagine, the thousands of different cryptocurrencies available to trade mean the mixes and matches can be endless. Many cryptocurrency exchanges have categorized these mixes by creating different "rooms" where you can trade the majority of the cryptos they carry versus a number of more popular cryptos. For example, the Binance exchange has created four rooms or categories for the main cross-cryptos: Bitcoin (BTC), Ethereum

(ETH), Binance Coin (BNB), and Tether (USDT). By clicking each of these categories, you can trade other cryptos versus the selected quote currency that I talk about earlier in this chapter.

TIP

When trading currency pairs, fiat or crypto, the best bet is always to pair a strong base currency versus a weak quote currency and vice versa. This way, you maximize the chances of that pair moving strongly in the direction you're aiming for.

As I talk about earlier in this chapter, the reason you diversify your portfolio is to reduce its exposure to risk by including assets that aren't fully correlated. The big problem with diversifying within your cryptocurrency portfolio is that, at least at the time of writing, most cryptocurrencies are heavily correlated to Bitcoin. On most of the days where Bitcoin is having a bad day, the majority of other cryptocurrencies (that are not stablecoins or exposed to extreme media hype) are, too. In the crypto market, this type of short-term market correlation has become the norm.

During the second week of December 2022, for example, the majority of the top 15 cryptocurrencies (including Bitcoin) surged. The only exceptions were Tether (a stablecoin that isn't supposed to move that much), Binance Coin (an exchange coin that was having a lousy PR month due to scandals), and Dogecoin (a meme coin).

EXCHANGE-TRADED FUNDS OR INDIVIDUAL ASSETS?

ETFs are the lazy approach to investing. Although investing in ETFs may save you from having to do the proper research on individual assets, it also takes away your control over what you're investing in and how much you're allocating to each individual asset.

Personally, it's very important for me to only invest in assets that are aligned to my moral beliefs. When you invest in an index fund or an ETF, you'll never fully know what asset the fund managers may sneak into the basket. If you have to stay on top of everything that's happening in the fund, you may as well invest in each asset individually and become your own money manager!

REMEMBER

Such correlations are typically more substantial long term compared to the short term. This is also one key reason short-term trading cryptocurrencies is riskier than many other financial instruments. Considering long-term investments when adding cryptocurrencies to your portfolio may be best. That way, you can reduce your investment risk by diversifying within different crypto categories.

On the bright side, as the cryptocurrency market continues to develop, the diversification methods can also improve, and the whole market may become less correlated to Bitcoin.

Tackling Diversification in Short-Term Trades

If you've calculated your risk tolerance based on the information in Chapter 3 and the results are pretty aggressive, you may want to consider trading cryptocurrencies in shorter time frames. Here are some suggestions to keep in mind. To read more about developing short-term strategies, turn to Chapter 11.

WARNING

>> **Beware of commissions.** Cryptocurrency trading exchanges generally require lower commissions and transaction fees than brokers who offer forex or stocks. But you shouldn't completely ignore the commission cost to your wallet. When you're day-trading, you may end up paying more in commissions than what you're actually making by trading if you trade way too often, getting in and out of trades way too fast without calculating your returns! Also, as I talk about in Chapter 6, cheaper isn't always the best option when choosing an exchange. You always get what you pay for.

TIP

>> **Keep expanding your portfolio.** Some people invest a lump sum in their investment portfolios and then either wipe it out in dangerous day-trading actions or get stuck in a strategy that's working but isn't maximizing their returns. A healthy portfolio requires nourishment. Consider leaving a monthly investment fund aside out of your paycheck in order to expand your portfolio and make your money work for you.

» **Observe the rule of three.** You have a ton of options when trading currencies. You can mix and match crypto/crypto and fiat/crypto pairs like there's no tomorrow if your account size lets you.

However, the key in having a healthy diversified portfolio is to avoid double-dipping the same quote currency in your trades. Try to limit your open short-term positions against each quote currency to three. For example, trade one crypto versus Bitcoin, another crypto versus Ethereum, and a third crypto versus your exchange's cryptocurrency. This approach also helps you keep your portfolio at a reasonable size so it's not too big to monitor.

3
Essential Cryptocurrency Strategies and Tactics

Explore the differences between short-term trading and long-term investing, and decide which is the right route for you.

Dig into different investment strategy development methods, and incorporate your risk tolerance into your plan for minimizing losses and maximizing gains.

Make sure you're not getting burned by taxes.

Chapter **11**

Short-Term Crypto-Trading Strategies

et me set this straight: I'm not a big fan of short-term trading. It's a personality thing. Some traders thrive on the thrill of short-term trading adventures, or *speculative trading*. I sweat on speculations. I prefer to invest long term, sit back, relax, have nights of peaceful sleep, and let the markets do their thing. (You can discover some long-term investing strategies in Chapter 12.)

That being said, I have many students who ask me for short-term strategies. And being the awesome coach that I am, I deliver. In this chapter, I go through some methods I use to develop short-term strategies that have worked for my students in the past. Although the basics of short-term trading are similar across different assets, crypto trading requires you to consider some additional steps to stack the odds in your favor.

Distinguishing Three Short-Term Time Frames

Short-term trading can also be called *aggressive trading*. Why? Because you're taking more risk in the hopes of making more profit. As I discuss in Chapter 3, investment of any kind requires a constant balancing and trade-off between risk and return. To earn more return, you must take more risk. When aiming to make money in the short term, you must be prepared to lose your investment (and maybe even more!) in that time frame as well, especially in a volatile market like cryptocurrencies.

Short-term trading can be divided into different categories within itself based on how quickly you realize the profits — hours, days, or weeks. Generally speaking, the shorter the trading time frame, the higher the risk involved with that trade. The following sections spell out the three most common short-term trading time frames for cryptocurrencies.

Profiting within hours

If you've ever wondered what a day-trader does, this is it! *Day-trading* is one form of aggressive short-term trading. You aim to buy and sell cryptos within a day and take profit before you go to bed. In traditional markets like the stock market, a trading day often ends at 4:30 p.m. local time. But the cryptocurrency market runs 24/7, so you can define your day-trading hours to fit your schedule. Pretty neat, right? With this great power comes great responsibility, though. You don't want to lose your shirt and make your spouse angry at you.

REMEMBER

Here are a few questions to ask yourself to determine whether day-trading is, indeed, the right crypto route for you:

>> **Do you have the time to dedicate to day-trading?** If you have a full-time job and can't stick to your screen all day, day-trading probably isn't right for you. Make sure you don't use your company time for trading! Not only can you get fired, but you also won't be able to dedicate the required time and energy to trading either. Double the trouble.

>> **Do you have sufficient risk tolerance for day-trading?** Check out Chapter 3 for more on risk management, and attend this free Masterclass to get my risk-management toolkit: https://investdiva.com/masterclass.

>> **Even if you can financially afford to potentially lose money day-trading, are you willing to do so?** Do you have the stomach to see your portfolio go up and down on a daily basis? If not, perhaps day-trading isn't right for you.

If you've made up your mind that day-trading is the right crypto route for you, the following sections share some tips to keep in mind before getting started.

Define crypto-trading sessions

Because cryptocurrencies are traded internationally without borders, one way you can define a trading day is to go by the trading sessions in financial capitals of the world like New York, Tokyo, the *eurozone* (made up of the European countries whose official currency is the euro), and Australia. Figure 11-1 shows these sessions. This method follows similar trading sessions as in the foreign exchange (forex) market.

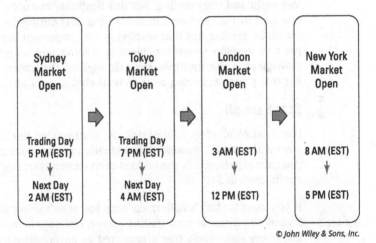

© John Wiley & Sons, Inc.

FIGURE 11-1: Cryptocurrency trading sessions based on international time zones.

Some sessions may provide better trading opportunities if the cryptocurrency you're planning to trade has higher volume or volatility in that time frame. For example, a cryptocurrency based in China, such as NEO, may see more trading volume during the Asian session.

Know that day-trading cryptos is different from day-trading other assets

When you're day-trading traditional financial assets such as stocks or forex, you can follow already-established fundamental market-movers such as a company's upcoming earnings report or a country's interest rate decision. The cryptocurrency market, for the most part, doesn't have a developed risk-event calendar. That's why conducting fundamental analysis (see Chapter 9) to develop a day-trading strategy is way harder for cryptos.

Set a time aside

Depending on your personal schedule, you may want to consider scheduling a specific time of the day to focus on your trades. The idea of being able to trade around the clock is pretty cool in theory. You can just get on your trading app during a sleepless night and start trading. But this flexibility can backfire when you start losing sleep over it. Remaining alert during day-trading (or night-trading, for that matter) is very important because you need to develop strategies, identify trading opportunities, and manage your risk multiple times throughout the trading session. For many people, having a concrete discipline pays off.

Start small

Day-trading involves a lot of risk. So, until you get the hang of it, start with a small amount and gradually increase your capital as you gain experience. Some brokers even let you start trading with a minimum of $50.

If you start trading small, make sure you aren't using margin or leverage to increase your trading power. Leverage is one of those incredibly risky tools that's projected as an opportunity. It lets you manage a bigger account with a small initial investment by borrowing the rest from your broker. If you're trying to test the waters by starting small, using leverage will defeat that purpose.

Don't take too much risk

According to Investopedia, most successful day-traders don't stake much of their account — 2 percent of it, max — with each trade. If you have a $10,000 trading account and you're willing to risk 1 percent of your capital on each trade, your maximum loss per trade is $100. So, you must make sure you have that money set aside for potential losses and that you aren't taking more risk than you can afford.

Secure your crypto wallet

One major problem with day-trading cryptocurrencies is securing your crypto wallet. As I explain in Chapter 7, the least-secure cryptocurrency wallets are online wallets. Because you're going to need your capital handy throughout the trading day, you may have no choice but to leave your assets on your exchange's online wallet, which can expose you to risk of hacking.

TIP

One way to enhance your security here is to not actually buy and sell cryptocurrencies but rather to speculate the price action and crypto market movements by using brokers who facilitate such services, as I discuss in Chapter 6.

Stay away from scalping

WARNING

Scalping is the shortest-term trading strategy some individual traders choose. It basically means jumping in and out of trades frequently, sometimes in a matter of seconds. If you're paying commission fees for every trade, not only are you exposing yourself to a ton of market risk when scalping, but you can also get burned out by the fees before you make any profit. Individual traders rarely make any profit scalping. Now, if you're part of an enterprise that has access to discount commission fees and huge trading accounts, the story may be different.

Profiting within days

If you want to trade short term but you don't want to stick to your computer all the time, this time frame may be the right one for you. In traditional trading, traders who hold their positions overnight are categorized as *swing-traders*. The most common trading strategy for swing-traders is *range trading*, where instead of riding up a trend, you look for a crypto whose price has been bouncing up and down within two prices. The idea is to buy at the bottom of the range and sell at the top, as you can see in Figure 11-2. If you're using a broker who facilitates short-selling services, you can also go the other direction.

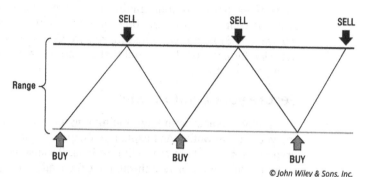

FIGURE 11-2: A simplified range-trading strategy.

Of course, in real life, the ranges aren't as neat and pretty as what you see in the example I put together for Figure 11-2. To identify a range, you must be proficient in technical analysis. A number of technical chart patterns and indicators can help you identify a range. For more on technical analysis, check out my Masterclass at https://investdiva.com/masterclass.

REMEMBER

If you choose swing-trading rather than day-trading, one downside is that you may not be able to get an optimized tax rate that's created for day-traders in some countries. In fact, swing-trading is in the gray area for taxation because if you hold your positions for more than a year (long-term investing; see Chapter 12), you also get an optimized tax rate. For more on tax optimizations, turn to Chapter 14.

TIP

If you're trading the cryptocurrency market movements without actually buying them, make sure you aren't paying a ton of commission fees for holding your positions overnight. Consult with your broker before developing your swing-trading strategy.

Profiting within weeks

This time frame falls into the category of *position trading* in traditional markets. Still shorter than a long-term investing strategy but longer than day-trading, this type of short-term trading can be considered the least risky form of short-term trading. But it's still risky. (Turn to Chapter 3 to read more about risks involved in trading cryptocurrencies.)

For this type of trade, you can identify a market trend and ride it up or down until the price hits a resistance or support. A *resistance level* is a psychological market barrier that prevents the price from going higher. A *support level* is the opposite: a price at which the market has difficulty "breaking below."

WARNING

To hold your positions for weeks, you need to keep your crypto assets in your exchange's online wallet, which may expose you to additional security risk (as I explain in Chapter 7). You may be better off utilizing a broker that provides price-speculation services for this type of trading strategy so you don't have to own the cryptocurrencies.

One popular position-trading strategy involves the following steps, as you can also see in Figure 11-3:

1. Identify a trend (using technical analysis).

2. Wait for a pullback.

3. Buy at the pullback within the uptrend.

4. Take profit (sell) at a resistance.

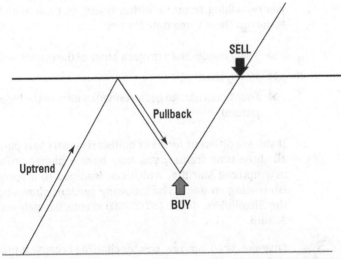

© *John Wiley & Sons, Inc.*

FIGURE 11-3: Buying at the pullback in an uptrend market and taking profit at resistance.

Trying Short-Term Analysis Methods

You can't become a successful short-term trader just by reading the news. Short-term trading is an art that combines active risk management with a great understanding of crowd psychology and price actions that goes beyond the scope of this book. Also, the cryptocurrency market isn't as established as other markets, so trading the lesser-known cryptos on a short-term basis can be even riskier. You can compare that to trading penny stocks or gambling, which are almost sure ways to lose money.

Regardless, the following sections present some analysis methods that professional traders with large accounts and a high risk tolerance can use.

WARNING

According to Medium.com, day-trading the cryptocurrency market has brought some investors profits between 1 percent and 2 percent, while on other values they *lose* money. For most, day-trading the crypto market has been a zero-sum game.

Deciphering chart patterns

I normally check with three different time frames when developing a trading strategy. If I'm analyzing the markets for more rapid profit-taking, I look at three short time frames. For example, if you're looking to profit within hours, you can analyze the price action on these three time frames:

>> Thirty-minute chart (to get a sense of the market sentiment)

>> Hourly chart

>> Four-hour chart (to get an understanding of the bigger picture)

If you see different forms of bullish reversal chart patterns across all three time frames, you may have a higher probability of a new uptrend starting, which can lead you to a successful bullish trading strategy. The following sections show an example of the Bitcoin/U.S. dollar (BTC/USD) crypto/fiat pair on September 5, 2018.

TIP

I use www.tradingview.com for charting because it provides many technical analysis tools and customizable charts.

A 30-minute chart

You're looking at the 30-minute chart, and at 9:30 a.m., you suddenly see a massive drop that brings Bitcoin's price down from approximately $7,380 to $7,111, as you can see in Figure 11-4. This formation is called a *bearish engulfing candlestick pattern* among technical analysts. Is this the beginning of a new downtrend?

© *TradingView, Inc.*

FIGURE 11-4: BTC/USD 30-minute chart on September 5, 2018.

An hourly chart

By switching from the 30-minute chart (see the preceding section) to the hourly chart, you notice the same drop (shown in Figure 11-5). But because now you can see the bigger picture, you discover that this drop was after a period of uptrend in the market, which may be a signal of a pullback during an uptrend. But how low can the pair go?

A four-hour chart

By switching from the hourly chart (see the preceding section) to the four-hour chart, you notice that the bearish engulfing pattern is formed in a much longer uptrend that has been moving up since the middle of August. By observing the four-hour chart, you can pinpoint the key support levels, shown at $6,890 and $6,720, that the price can pull back toward within this newly established bearish market sentiment. In Figure 11-6, I've used the Fibonacci retracement levels to identify the key price levels with higher accuracy.

© TradingView, Inc.

FIGURE 11-5: BTC/USD hourly chart on September 5, 2018.

© TradingView, Inc.

FIGURE 11-6: BTC/USD four-hour chart on September 5, 2018.

Following the technical analysis guidelines, you can expect a bit of a correction after this sudden drop, followed by more drops to key support levels on the four-hour chart. With this, a potential trading idea may be to sell at correction or at market price and then to take profit at one or two support levels.

After sudden drops in the markets, sometimes the market corrects itself before dropping more. Often, it corrects itself to key *pivot levels* (levels that are considered trend-changing if the price breaks below or above them), which in this case is the 23 percent Fibonacci retracement level at $7,090. The reward for waiting for a correction is that you may be able to take more profit short-selling at a higher price. The risk with it is that the market may not correct itself, and you may miss out.

TIP

Personally, if I think the market is really going to shift into a bearish sentiment, I sell some at market price and set a sell-limit order at the key pivot level just in case the market corrects itself before further drops. This way, you can distribute your risk. A sell-limit order is a type of trading order you can set on your broker's platform, which enables you to sell your assets at a specific price in the future.

For short-term profit-taking, I consider setting buy-limit orders at both key support levels at 38 percent and 50 percent Fibonacci retracement levels. In this example, I aim to take partial profit at around $6,890, and then exit the trade completely at $6,720. Again, this approach may limit my gains if the market continues to drop, but it also limits my risk if the price doesn't fall as low as the second key support, so it gives me a proportionate risk/reward ratio. Figure 11-7 shows how the market actually performed.

© TradingView, Inc.

FIGURE 11-7: BTC/USD four-hour chart strategy performance.

The BTC/USD price did correct a little bit, but it didn't go as high as the 23 percent Fibonacci retracement level. So, if you had only waited for a correction to sell, you would've missed out on the trading opportunity. The market did drop to both key support levels at 38 percent and 50 percent Fibonacci retracement levels. So, if you had sold at market price, you would've taken profit at both key support levels. On the other hand, the price continued to drop beyond the 50 percent Fibonacci retracement level, so that may represent a missed opportunity to maximize your returns.

However, in my opinion, it's always better to be safe than sorry. That's why I always recommend that my students avoid being greedy when it comes to strategy developments.

Using indicators

Another popular technical analysis method is to use indicators such as the relative strength index (RSI), Bollinger Bands (BOL), and Ichimoku Kinko Hyo (ICH). I call such indicators elements of a beauty kit. By adding them to your chart, you make it more beautiful and accent the important features, just as you would by putting makeup on your face!

Indicators are mathematical tools, developed over the years by technical analysts, that can help you predict the future price actions in the market. You can use these indicators in addition to chart patterns to get a higher analysis accuracy. But in short-term trading, some traders use only one or two indicators without paying attention to chart patterns. In fact, you can create a whole trading strategy by using only one indicator in short-term trading. To find out more about my signature Ichimoku-Fibonacci combo strategy, check out my book *Ichimoku Secrets* (CreateSpace Independent Publishing Platform).

Avoiding illegal pump-and-dump stuff

As a cryptocurrency trader, you need to be aware of what can happen among illegal group activities that manipulate the markets, take profit, and leave others shirtless. A *pump-and-dump scheme* happens when a group of people or an influential individual manipulates the market prices in their own favor.

For example, in an unlikely illegal act, a highly influential person named Joe goes on TV and says, "I think Bitcoin is going to reach $60,000 tomorrow," while he already has an established buy-and-sell strategy to trade a ton of Bitcoin. The moment his speculation hits the news, everyone else who's watching TV gets excited and start buying Bitcoin based on this suggestion. The hype helps Bitcoin's price go up and helps Joe's strategy to go through. But before the rest of the market can catch up, Joe sells (dumps) his Bitcoins, taking a ton of profit but sending Bitcoin's price crashing down.

Managing Short-Term Trading Risk

Managing your risk when short-term trading can be quite different from that of medium- and long-term investing. To avoid a major account meltdown trading short term, you must balance your risk and return more actively. Some short-term traders like using a stop-loss order, one method to consider.

A *stop-loss order* is a price at which you tell your broker to "stop your losses" and get you out of your position. For example, say you think Bitcoin is going to go up from $6,000 to $6,100 in the next hour, so you enter a buy position. But instead, Bitcoin starts dropping below $6,000, putting you in a losing position. To avoid losing too much money, you can set a stop-loss order at $5,950. You can set a risk/reward ratio at any number that makes sense to your risk tolerance.

I famously don't use stop-losses when investing long term. In fact, I believe stop-losses are a scam promoted by brokers. Why? Because it gives you a false feeling of safety while 90 percent of traders end up losing all their money to the stop-loss. Guess who makes money when you lose? The broker.

WARNING

In medium- to long-term trading, using a stop-loss can be riskier than not using it, especially if you're not a full-time trader. Make sure you have a complete understanding of your trading objectives and risk tolerance before using a stop-loss in crypto trading.

TIP

One easy way to calculate your risk/reward ratio is to divide your estimated net profit (the reward) by the price of the maximum risk you're willing to take. For example, if you want to have a 1:2 risk/reward ratio, that means you're willing to make double the amount of what you're willing to risk. But before you understand how much risk you can take, you must calculate your risk tolerance, which I discuss in Chapter 3.

Chapter **12**

Long-Term Crypto-Investing Strategies

D o you know how long the first Bitcoin investors waited to see any type of return? Around seven years. Some Bitcoin miners and early investors actually forgot about their crypto assets and had to go on a treasure hunt to find their Bitcoin wallets during the 2017 bubble.

The point is that just like many other markets, time and patience can be your best friends. But you still need to have a plan based on your risk tolerance and financial goals in order to profit long term. In this chapter, I go over the basics of long-term investing in cryptocurrencies.

On Time: Getting Started with Long-Term Investing

When I talk about long-term investment strategies, I'm basically treating cryptocurrencies as assets. And just like any other type of financial investment, you need to create a portfolio that goes along with your risk tolerance and financial goals. To do so, you can begin by examining the criteria for constructing your crypto portfolio (such as risk management, discussed in Chapter 3) and then use them to develop a plan for allocating different types of crypto assets in the various categories I explore in Chapter 8.

In the following sections, I dig into a couple of things to keep in mind when getting started with your portfolio management.

Your personal goals and current situation

REMEMBER

You should consider a wide variety of issues when managing your portfolio long term. Factors like risk and return are some of the obvious ones that I cover in Chapter 3. But when it comes to long-term investment in risky assets like cryptocurrencies, you need to take it a step further. Here are some questions you should answer:

>> What's your income size now, and where can it go in the future?

>> Are you likely to change your job in the future? Is your current job secure?

>> What's your marital status now? Do you have any children? Where do you see yourself on this front in five years?

>> What's your investment experience?

>> Do you have any other investments in assets such as equities or real estate? How diversified is your overall portfolio?

These questions may sound cliché, and you may already have the answers in your head. But investing long term is a logical process, and actually writing down the most basic elements of your personal goals and characteristics always pays off. When you've assessed your own financial situation and goals, you can have a better understanding of how to move forward with your crypto portfolio. Your needs may even determine the avenue you choose.

For example, if you're retired and your income depends on your portfolio, long-term cryptocurrency investing may not be suitable for you. You may want to consider a lower-risk, current-income-oriented approach. If you're young and willing to take the risk in the hope of getting high returns, you may even consider the short-term trading strategies I cover in Chapter 11.

Personally, as a mom and the owner of a multi-million-dollar business (Invest Diva), I allocated 15 percent of my portfolio to cryptocurrencies in 2017 and gradually increased it as the markets fell. By the 2022 market crash, I increased my crypto allocation to 25 percent of my overall investment portfolio. For my parents, on the other hand, I chose a different approach. They're retired and they need current income to survive. That's why I recommended that they allocate only 5 percent of their savings to cryptocurrencies in 2018 with the goal of capital gains in the next few years. We sold half of their crypto as the markets gained in 2021. I'm repeating this process for them at the time of writing this book.

REMEMBER

To sum it up, build your portfolio around your needs depending on the following variables:

>> Your current income

>> Your age

>> The size of your family

>> Your risk preferences

TIP

For more on risk management and calculating your risk tolerance, check out Chapter 3 and my most popular free Masterclass: https://investdiva.com/masterclass.

Your portfolio's objectives

REMEMBER

Assessing your personal goals and life situation brings you one step closer to creating your own portfolio (see the preceding section). When creating a long-term portfolio, you generally want to consider these objectives:

>> **Generating current income:** These investments can generate a regular payment, which can be at odds with high capital appreciations.

>> **Preserving capital:** This low-risk, conservative investment strategy generates moderate returns.

>> **Growing capital:** Focusing on capital growth requires you to increase your risk tolerance and reduce your need for a current-income-based investment strategy.

>> **Reducing taxes:** If you're in a high tax bracket, you may consider a portfolio that generates capital gains. If you're in a lower tax bracket, you have lower incentive to defer taxes

and earn high investment returns, so a portfolio with higher-current-income assets may be suitable for you.

>> **Managing risk:** You should always consider the risk–return trade-off in all investment decisions.

These objectives get tied together with your personal goals and other investments. For example, current income and capital preservation are good objectives for someone with a low risk tolerance who has a conservative personality. If you have medium risk tolerance and don't need to depend on your investment for current income as much, you can select capital growth as your portfolio objective. In many countries, including the United States, taxes also play a major role in your investment goals. For example, if you're in a high tax bracket, focusing on capital gains may be a better option for you because you can defer taxes. Last but not least, you should consider your risk–return trade-off in all your investment decisions, whether long term or not.

TIME AND CRYPTOS: THE FAMOUS PIZZAS

To truly understand the significance of time in holding your assets, consider this true story: On May 22, 2010, a Bitcoin miner named Laszlo Hanyecz spent 10,000 Bitcoins to buy (hold your breath) two large pizzas from Papa John's. At the time, the 10,000 Bitcoins were worth about $30. This transaction is widely believed to be the first time anyone used Bitcoins to buy something tangible. He even posted about his purchase on a popular Bitcoin forum at the time, BitcoinTalk, as you can see here: https://bitcointalk.org/index.php?topic=137.0.

On May 22, 2022, 12 years later, and even though Bitcoin's price had already dropped from the all-time high levels of above $68,000, the amount he paid in Bitcoin for the two pizzas was the equivalent of $300 million. That's about $150 million per pie. Now May 22 is known as Bitcoin Pizza Day.

What's the moral of this story? Every time you get impatient with your long-term crypto investments, remember poor Laszlo kicking himself on Bitcoin Pizza Day, knowing he could've been a millionaire had he just sat on his Bitcoins for a few years instead of getting the instant gratification those two pizzas brought him.

Creating Long-Term Strategies

Any type of investment can be summed up in four words: Buy low, sell high. But of course no one can get it perfectly right every time. With cryptocurrencies in particular, the market is still testing out new psychological levels, so predicting the highs and lows can be that much more difficult. The following sections introduce some methods I've been using to expand my long-term cryptocurrency portfolio.

Observing psychological levels

If you were to take a guess, who do you think moves the prices of assets in the markets up and down? It's the market participants. It's us. And the bigger our trading position and our influence, the bigger our impact on the markets.

As time goes by, key psychological support and resistance levels start to develop in online financial markets. The same has now happened for most major cryptocurrencies. Of course, the older the crypto, the more historical data we have to study. I've found Fibonacci retracement levels very helpful in identifying key psychological levels even in the newer cryptocurrencies. In my Premium Investing Group (PIG), my students and I are often blown away by how many times Fibonacci predicts the key psychological levels.

The reason psychological levels are already appearing in the crypto market may be that many crypto investors are using traditional technical analysis methods for their cryptocurrency investment strategies. With that, you can expect the crypto crowd psychology to form similar chart patterns to those of other markets, such as equities and the foreign exchange (forex) market, in longer time frames like weekly and monthly charts. Crowd psychology is the constant battle between the sellers (the bears) and the buyers (the bulls) in the market that leads to price movements in an asset. Psychological levels are those that the prices have difficulty breaking, due to the strength or weakness of the bears and bulls in the market.

TIP

You can find a great deal about investing crowd psychology in plain (and funny) videos in the "Forex Coffee Break" portion of my signature Make Your Money Work For You PowerCourse. You can learn more about it by attending my Masterclass: https://investdiva.com/masterclass.

After you identify the psychological levels, you can use them to develop different types of strategies based on your current portfolio, your risk tolerance, and your financial goals. Here are some examples:

>> Buy at a key support level and sell at a key resistance level.

>> Buy at current market price and sell at a key resistance level.

>> Wait for a pullback when the price reaches a key resistance level and buy lower. Then sell at the next key resistance level.

>> Buy at a key support level and hold long term.

Selling when you reach your goal

A cryptocurrency's price may continue going higher after it reaches a key resistance level. But how long do you wait? Which resistance level do you choose? Does using resistance levels even make sense for your financial goals? One realistic way to approach your investment strategy is to sell when you've reached your investment goal. (You can use a sell-limit order, which I talk about later in this chapter, to do this.) The key here is that you shouldn't look back and regret your decision after you've made the sale, even if the price continues going up after you sell. You achieved your goal, so instead of regretting, consider patting yourself on the back and celebrating your win!

REMEMBER Markets may continue to go up after you sell. Don't let your emotions take over your logical decision to sell. If you need the money and have already achieved your investment goal, you have no reason to regret an early sale. If anything, you can always get back in the market with a brand-new investment strategy.

Keeping tax consequences in mind

TIP Tax laws change all the time, and they vary in different countries. However, in most cases, taxes affect nearly all investment actions. As of 2022, in the United States, a maximum of $3,000 of capital losses in excess of capital gains can be written off against other income in any one year. If you have a loss position in an investment and you've concluded that selling it is wise, the best time to sell is when you have a capital gain against which you can apply the loss.

Before starting to invest, you must understand the basics of taxes in your country. Turn to Chapter 14 for an overview of how you should consider taxes before making investment decisions.

Considering Limit Orders and Stop-Loss Orders

Cryptocurrency exchanges and brokers alike allow you to use various types of orders to buy and sell altcoins. Most active traders use market orders to buy or sell at the best available price, but long-term investors can use other types of orders such as limit orders and stop-loss orders.

Long-term investors can also use market orders in abnormal circumstances if they need to make a quick investment decision. Market orders are normally filled quickly at a price close to the current market price.

WARNING

Using market orders can sometimes involve risks, especially in volatile markets such as cryptocurrencies. Sometimes the price of cryptocurrencies drops or skyrockets in a matter of seconds. If you happen to use a market order on those occasions, you may get blindsided by the actual price at which your order is executed. That's why using a limit order is always safer than using a market order.

Limit orders

A *limit order* is a type of transaction order that allows you to buy or sell at your preferred price. For example, if the current Bitcoin market price is at $15,748, you can set a *buy-limit order* to buy at $15,000 or even below that level if you think the price has the potential to drop.

Then you can set a *sell-limit order* to take profit when you reach your investment goal (say, at $16,000). I love using limit orders because they allow me to go about my life without worrying about prices too much while the markets do their usual movements.

WARNING

Always double-check your limit orders before putting them through. Make sure your buy-limit order isn't above the current market price and your sell-limit order isn't below the current market price. Traditional brokers often send you a warning if you make a mistake in setting limit orders, but at the time of writing, most crypto exchanges don't offer such courtesies. I've been the victim of setting a careless buy-limit order that was way above the current market price, and it immediately went through without a warning from my exchange.

Just as in other markets, cryptocurrency limit orders have different options for how long they stay in effect. The most common types are good 'til canceled and fill-or-kill:

>> A *good-'til-canceled* (GTC) *order* normally stays in effect for six months. If it's not executed within that time frame, your broker/exchange may cancel it. If you still want to keep the position in effect, you may need to renew it after six months.

>> A *fill-or-kill order* is canceled if it's not immediately executed. Therefore, it may be a better fit for short-term trading strategies (like those in Chapter 11).

Other types of limit orders offered by your trading platform may include *good 'til time* (your order stays in effect until a specific time you select) and *immediate or cancel* (your order is canceled if it's not immediately fulfilled by your broker). You can set more than one limit order for your cryptocurrencies.

TIP

You can also choose to buy fractions of a cryptocurrency, especially when those like Bitcoin are so expensive. For example, in one account, I've set a buy-limit order for Bitcoin versus the U.S. dollar (BTC/USD) to purchase 0.4 Bitcoins when the price reaches $6,000. On the order form, I've also added a good-'til-canceled buy-limit order to buy 0.2 Bitcoins at $5,851. By having multiple limit orders, I eliminate the risk of missing out and avoid going all in at one price.

Stop-loss orders

You can use *stop-loss orders* to limit the downside loss exposure of your crypto investment. Stop-losses are basically a form of limit orders (see the preceding section), where you ask your broker to close your position and take losses at a specific price. I'm not a big fan of stop-losses. In fact, as the years have gone by, I've become more and more against stop-losses. I believe stop-losses are the biggest trick of all time, helping the brokers make more money.

But for some investors, cutting the losses short in case of a rapid decline in the market may make sense. Just like limit orders, stop-loss orders have different types, like good 'til canceled.

WARNING

Volatile markets such as cryptocurrencies normally bounce back up from the lows as rapidly as they fall. That's why by using a stop-loss order, you may end up getting out of your position prematurely and miss out on potential gains. If you're looking to use a stop-loss order, you must analyze the market carefully and choose an appropriate level for your stop-loss.

TIP

To get the latest cryptocurrency investment strategies and buy/sell-limit order ideas, consider joining Invest Diva's PIG for free at https://investdivapig.com.

Chapter **13**

Minimizing Your Losses and Maximizing Your Gains

D epending on whether you're a short-term trader or a long-term investor, you can manage your portfolio either actively or passively. If you're a long-term investor (see Chapter 12), you may find yourself managing your portfolio passively by buying and holding a well-diversified portfolio over a set amount of time. If you're a short-term trader, you can use the tools I present in Chapter 11 to manage and achieve your desired objectives in a more active way.

I'm a big fan of long-term value investing, but that doesn't mean I'm against active portfolio management. In fact, I've seen over and over again that you can get better returns, whether they're long term or short term, by actively managing your portfolio. Now, by *active*, I don't mean sticking to your screen all the time and covertly checking your investment apps throughout the day during conversations and meetings. This chapter explains some management strategies that can help you find a sweet balance to do it all and still maintain an outside life.

Keeping the Losses Down

A phenomenon called *loss aversion* occurs in behavioral finance when investors keep the losing assets in their portfolios while actively selling the "winners." This tendency is why going against the crowd is one way to curtail your losses. In the following sections, I explain some techniques you can use to keep your crypto-investing losses down.

Measuring returns

Managing your cryptocurrency investments can be challenging because your assets may be scattered over different exchanges and cryptocurrency wallets. Additionally, you may have purchased some altcoins by using Bitcoin, some others by using the U.S. dollar (USD), and more by using cryptos such as Ethereum or Litecoin. That's why I recommend you keep a log of your investments and ink any changes you make to your portfolio.

REMEMBER

Here are the three steps in determining your portfolio returns:

1. **Measure the amount you've invested.**

2. **Measure capital gains, which is the profit you make through buying and selling cryptos.**

3. **Measure income, which is the payment you get by holding some cryptos (if applicable).**

To calculate the amount invested, you can create a list similar to the one in Figure 13-1. The table shows numbers of coins, buying date, cost (both total and per coin), and current value.

My Crypto Portfolio as of September 1, 2018

Coin	Full name	Number of coins	Date bought	Total cost (including commission) (USD)	Cost per coin (USD)	Current price per coin (USD)
BTC	Bitcoin	0.5	6/29/2018	2,965	5,900	7,155
ETH	Ethereum	8	8/14/2018	2,250	275	293
XLM	Stellar Lumens	200	8/07/2018	44	0.200	0.2257
EOS	EOS	50	8/16/2018	225	4.45	6.55

© *John Wiley & Sons, Inc.*

FIGURE 13-1: An example of a cryptocurrency investment log.

Now, because you may be purchasing different coins by using either *fiat* (government-backed) currencies, such as the U.S. dollar, or other cryptocurrencies, you may need to convert your investment value to one type of currency to keep it simple and easier to track. In Figure 13-1, I converted all my purchasing value to the U.S. dollar (USD). Another way to track your investment is to create separate logs depending on how you purchased your altcoins. For example, you can have a separate log for your investments with BTC and another one for those you purchased with USD.

You can create such logs on a monthly, quarterly, or annual basis depending on your investing time frame. For example, if you're a short-term trader, you may need a monthly log. If you're a medium- to long-term investor, you can use quarterly and annual logs. You can normally find the return on your investment calculated by your brokerage or exchange services (see Chapter 6 for more on brokerages and exchanges).

Many crypto enthusiasts have given up measuring returns against fiat currencies like the USD altogether. If you believe Bitcoin is king and Ethereum is queen, you may end up buying most of your altcoins by using the king and queen anyway. Converting your crypto purchase to its USD value can be time-consuming. Also, most of the time you can't cash out in fiat currencies on your exchange anyway. USD, Bitcoin, and Ethereum all have fluctuations of their own versus other currencies, so a conversion may give you a false gain or loss impression. By converting to USD, it may look like you've gained profit on your initial investment, while in reality you may be in a losing position versus Bitcoin.

If you purchased your coins on an exchange by using another cryptocurrency such as Bitcoin, you can find the relevant USD value by searching your coin and the date you purchased it on websites such as www.tradingview.com. Many exchanges and brokers also offer charting services.

To measure your capital gains and income, you can simply check your account information with your broker and exchange. With cryptocurrency exchanges, your capital gains information is normally under tabs labeled "Wallet" or "Funds." Most exchanges provide the estimated value of your whole account either in Bitcoin or USD. If you have more than one account, you can add up these estimated numbers in your investment log and monitor them on a regular basis.

Monitoring exchange fees

To buy and sell cryptocurrencies, you need services like crypto exchanges and brokers. These companies mainly make money through transaction fees, as I discuss in Chapter 6. Although I don't recommend choosing an exchange based only on low fees, sometimes fees can become an important decision-making factor, especially for active traders. The fees can get even larger if you're looking to convert a fiat currency to a cryptocurrency like Bitcoin and then send it to another exchange to buy another cryptocurrency by using Bitcoin, and so on. Fees can be the biggest downside to short-term trading strategies for cryptocurrencies.

TIP

Here are some tips for keeping your exchange fees minimal while keeping your investment secure:

>> **Buy your lump-sum major cryptos on more secure exchanges, which may have higher transaction fees.** For example, when I need Bitcoin and Ethereum to trade other cryptocurrencies, I buy a large amount of both on an exchange with higher fees that allows using the U.S. dollar.

>> **For active trading, choose exchanges that offer lower rates for your specific cryptocurrency pair, but make sure to periodically store your profit in a hardware wallet (see Chapter 7 for more on wallets).**

>> **Consider active trading with the exchange's native cryptocurrency.** It may have a lower transaction fee than trading other cross-cryptos. For example, the Binance exchange offers cheaper trading options for its cryptocurrency, Binance Coin (BNB).

>> **Always include the transaction fee when calculating your profit to be on top of your game.** For example, if you buy 1 Ethereum coin for $200, but you pay $1.50 in transaction fees, you've spent $201.50 for your investment. This amount doesn't make a great impact for long-term investments, but active traders can feel the cumulative fees over time.

Understanding the art of getting out

I normally like to stay true to two of Warren Buffett's most famous investing rules:

1. Never lose money.
2. Never forget rule number one.

But no matter how thoroughly you conduct your analysis, at times you may find that getting out of a bad investment is better than holding onto it. The following sections give a few of my general strategies when it comes to getting out of an investment. Check out Chapter 9 for information on my Invest Diva Diamond Analysis (IDDA) system.

Don't be greedy

REMEMBER

If you're using a technical chart pattern, always set your profit-taking limit order at the price level that's consistent with the technique you're using. You may get a feeling that the market will continue going up after your profit target (PT) is triggered, and you may be tempted to readjust your PT prematurely. Sometimes the market will continue to rise. Sometimes it won't. Personally, I prefer to be safe rather than sorry, so I refrain from readjusting the PT orders way too often (unless I have a valid fundamental reason to do so besides just gut feeling).

Take partial profits

I simply love this rule and swear by it! You can call me a hoarder, but I can never let go of all my coins (or any other assets, for that matter) all at once. I set up strategic, partial profit-taking prices depending on my (or my students') investment goals and let the markets handle the rest.

For example, if I buy ten Ethereum coins (ETH) at $200 and I'm looking to take partial profit at key levels, I may sell two of my Ethereum coins at $470, sell two more at $591, and keep the rest long term. This way, I gain some profit along the way but don't let go of all my coins, so I still feel happy when the Ethereum price continues going up after I sell. Of course, calculating those key levels needs thorough analysis.

TIP

I dive deep into different types of investment strategies and partial profit taking in my award-winning Make Your Money Work For You PowerCourse. Learn more here: https://investdiva. com/masterclass.

Let go of bad investments

Every once in a while, you find yourself holding onto a coin that's just not worth it. With worthy long-term investments, I tend to buy more coins as the price drops, but sometimes the cryptocurrency, its community, and its management simply don't have a future. This point is when reexamining your fundamental analysis (see Chapter 9) becomes important. When it becomes evident that this coin just ain't gonna bounce back, you may as well bite the bullet and get out before your losses get bigger. If you're too scared to do so, you can always take losses in parts, using the partial-profit method I talk about in the preceding section.

REMEMBER

By letting go of your bad investments and taking losses, you may receive tax credits you can use to offset the taxes you must pay on your capital gains. Turn to Chapter 14 for more on taxes.

Letting the Profits Rise

I have to deal with two emotions when the markets start to rise. One is regretting not buying more when the prices were down. The other is the temptation to sell and take profit before reaching my carefully analyzed profit target limit order.

What I need to keep reminding myself (and my students and fellow investors alike) is that emotions rarely lead to maximizing profit. At the end of the day, discipline is what makes your bank. The following sections detail some tricks I use to avoid emotional investing.

Buying at the bottom

Being able to purchase at the lowest price every time you invest is highly unlikely. But studying the market psychology and historical price patterns can help you get close. One of my go-to technical analysis tools to identify the bottom is the Ichimoku-Fibonacci combo.

As I explain in my book *Ichimoku Secrets* (CreateSpace Independent Publishing Platform), you can use the Ichimoku-Fibonacci combination to gauge crowd psychology and identify key support and resistance levels. (*Support* is a price level where the market has difficulty breaking below; *resistance* is a price level where the market has difficulty breaking above.)

For longer-term investing, I generally use the daily chart for Ichimoku analysis. As you can see in Figure 13-2, after the price of Ethereum (ETH) dropped below $3,000 on April 27, 2022, it also broke below the daily Ichimoku cloud. Following the Ichimoku Kinko Hyo's guidelines, I had an indication that the price of ETH might drop further toward key Fibonacci retracement and support levels at around $2,512, $1,977, and $1,301. By conducting this analysis, I was able to set a buy-limit order at these levels ahead of time and aim to purchase at lower prices instead of buying immediately. This way you can maximize your profit and lower your net purchasing price.

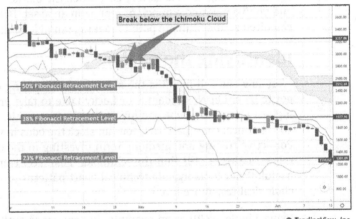

© TradingView, Inc.

FIGURE 13-2: Using the Ichimoku-Fibonacci combo to identify bottoms.

TIP

If you're dealing with new cryptocurrencies, you won't be able to find enough historical data to rely on. In those cases, sometimes the price continues to drop below the all-time-low levels, creating new lows. If you're confident enough in the fundamentals of the cryptocurrency, the new lows can give you an opportunity to buy more at lower prices. You can use Fibonacci's extended levels to identify new lows. To use these levels, you must first identify a trend where the price went either up or down for an extended period of time recently. Then drag the Fibonacci tool on your charting platform from the top to the bottom of the trend (if it's a downtrend) and from the bottom to the top (if it's an uptrend). By doing so, the Fibonacci levels magically appear on your chart.

Knowing that patience is a profitable virtue

"Patience is a profitable virtue" is my main mantra in all the education courses at Invest Diva! My students say repeating this mantra has changed the way they invest and has increased their profit returns by a fair bit. Whenever I feel the adrenaline rushing through my head from looking at a chart, I take a step back. I change the time frame and look at the big picture. I do more fundamental research. If all five points of the IDDA (see Chapter 9) aren't aligned, I simply log off my trading account and go about my day. Getting nervous is very easy when the markets take a dip and you've invested a bunch of money in an asset. Being patient can often be the ultimate path to making tangible returns.

Identifying the peaks

"Buy low and sell high" is the name of the game! Again, you've got to be either Nostradamus or Lucky Luke to take profit at the highest price every time you invest. But if you use historical data and technical chart patterns, you can stack the odds in your favor. For active trading and medium-term investing in the cryptocurrency market, I still find the Ichimoku-Fibonacci combo pretty useful. Other tools include technical chart patterns and key psychological resistance levels.

Using Ripple's XRP as an example, in September 2018, I identified a double-bottom chart pattern in the process of formation on the daily chart, as you can see in Figure 13-3. A *double bottom* is a popular formation on charts, where the price has difficulty breaking below a support level twice, forming two valley-shaped bottoms. When confirmed, it can be interpreted as a bullish reversal pattern, meaning that the prices may start going up.

Following the double-bottom chart pattern guidelines, medium-term investors can expect the market to take profit when the price has moved up from the neckline ($0.3666 in Figure 13-3) the same distance from the bottom to the neckline, or the next available Fibonacci retracement levels (0.4273 and 0.5314). To be safe, I normally recommend taking partial profits at each level to distribute risk.

FIGURE 13-3: A double-bottom chart pattern forming on the XRP/USD daily chart.

As you can see in Figure 13-4, on September 21, XRP reached both levels and then some before dropping back down. A medium-term investor would've taken profit at these levels, while a long-term investor would've stayed in their position.

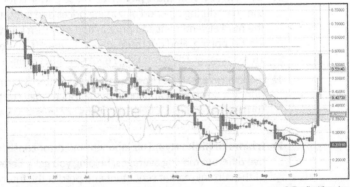

FIGURE 13-4: A double-bottom chart pattern confirms, and XRP reaches profit target levels.

For long-term investors, timing the profit taking can be a bit more challenging. The crypto market is an exciting new investment opportunity that a majority of people are just discovering. Just as with the dot-com bubble, the hype can lead to extreme volatility. You saw the results of the hype in 2017 when Bitcoin's price surged over 1,000 percent and Ripple's XRP gained a whopping 36,018 percent. I personally know investors who sold right at the peak and became millionaires and others who bought at the peak and had to sit on their losses until the next surge. In this case, most investors who were able to sell at the peak are those who went against the hype and against the majority of the crowd.

REMEMBER

Technical chart patterns such as double bottoms, indicators such as Ichimoku, and going against the crowd don't guarantee optimal results. These items are simply tools that increase the probability of identifying the best price to buy and sell. At the end of the day, you must conduct thorough risk management that applies to your personal financial goals and risk tolerance, as I discuss in Chapter 3.

Finding peaks and bottoms with a few trading tools

TIP

Here are some cheat sheets of the trading tools I use to identify peaks and bottoms:

>> **Bearish reversal chart patterns:** These patterns form on the chart during a period of surging prices and indicate that the market sentiment and price action may turn bearish and start dropping. Find out more at www.investdiva.com/investing-guide/bearish-reversal-patterns-list1.

>> **Bullish reversal chart patterns:** These patterns form during a downtrend and indicate that prices may start to turn bullish and rise. Check out https://investdiva.com/bullish-reversal-patterns-list.

>> **Ichimoku Kinko Hyo:** This Japanese indicator consists of five different moving averages, helping you get a better view of the current market sentiment and predict the future price action. See www.investdiva.com/investing-guide/ichimoku-kinko-hyo-explained.

Chapter **14**

Cryptocurrencies and Taxes

Before the 2017 crypto hype, many people who got into cryptocurrencies (whether through mining or investing) probably didn't even think about its tax implications. But as cryptocurrency investing becomes more mainstream, its taxation guidelines have taken center stage, and governments around the world are playing catch-up with people who hold, trade, or use cryptocurrencies, ensuring they pay their fair share of taxes. In this chapter, I review the basics of cryptocurrency taxation.

REMEMBER

Keep in mind that these guidelines are based on the U.S. tax laws as of 2022. Crypto taxes are constantly changing. By the time you read this book, things may have changed. It's critically important that you stay on top of your country's crypto tax code and consult with a professional before tax day to stay safe.

Distinguishing Three Types of Crypto Taxes

The tax setup for cryptos is a big area of enforcement for the U.S. Internal Revenue Service (IRS) at the time of writing. The IRS — alongside the Federal Bureau of Investigation (FBI) — tracks and traces cryptocurrencies such as Bitcoin as part of their criminal investigations, opening the doors for many people to be targeted for an audit or compliance verifications.

The good news is, if you're already familiar with capital gains taxations in other financial instruments (such as stocks), you can treat your crypto-investing activities in a similar manner. That means you pay capital gains taxes on your cryptocurrency investments. In this case, you don't have any tax obligations until you sell your coins for a profit. But what if you got your coins by mining? Or what if your employer pays you in cryptocurrencies?

You're likely to get taxed when being exposed to cryptocurrencies if you are

>> Selling cryptocurrencies for a fiat currency (such as the U.S. dollar)

>> Trading one cryptocurrency for another

>> Using cryptocurrency to buy goods or services

REMEMBER

Buying cryptocurrency is not a taxable event.

To make it simple, I've divided crypto taxation obligations into three likely scenarios in the following sections.

Income taxes

If you've invested in lots of expensive equipment and you're getting crypto-mining rewards as a result, your crypto is considered taxable income. According to https://turbotax.intuit.com, your crypto-mining income can be reported on Form 1099-NEC at the fair market value of the cryptocurrency the day you received it.

TIP

This could mean if you mine cryptocurrencies when their price is lower, not only will you pay less taxes, but you also can enjoy the potential future upside as the value of your crypto asset goes up.

TECHNICAL STUFF

Personally, I was offered to get paid in Bitcoin when I started to report for NewsBTC back in 2016. You know how much I regretted not accepting that offer in 2017 when Bitcoin value surged to $20,000? A lot! But of course, if I had taken it, I would've had to pay the income tax on the Bitcoins I received; if I'd then chosen to trade my Bitcoins for the U.S. dollar (USD) at the 2017 peak, I also would've been subject to capital gains taxes on the profit I made on my transaction. I talk about capital gains taxes in the next section.

If you receive mining or income rewards in crypto worth over $400 in one year, you must report it to the IRS. If you've set up a mining operation at your home, you can report your mining income as self-employment income on Schedule C of your tax return. Personally, though, I've set up my mining activity through my Invest Diva business, which helps me get a more generous tax policy when my net income is high. I talk about minimizing your crypto income tax later in this chapter.

REMEMBER

Always make sure to keep a record of your mining activity and financial statements in case you get audited by the IRS. Also, if you're filing as a business entity, make sure to consult with a tax professional to discover the best options for your particular scenario. Don't worry — you can claim the accountant's fees as a business expense!

REMEMBER

Even as a crypto miner and a business owner, you must understand the basics of cryptocurrency investing. If you sell or trade your cryptocurrencies for other altcoins or any products, then you must pay capital gains taxes as I discuss in the next two sections (depending on whether they're long term or short term). Your mining-activity profits often rely on the market value of the cryptocurrency, as well as the amount of tax you'll be paying on them. To identify the best cryptocurrencies to mine, actively conduct the Invest Diva Diamond Analysis (IDDA) technique I introduce in Chapter 9, and swap to better cryptocurrencies if your mining strategy isn't making sense anymore. One point of IDDA is capital analysis, which includes your tax considerations.

Long-term capital gains taxes

In Chapter 2, I point to capital gains as one of the main reasons people invest in cryptocurrencies. That's how the IRS categorizes cryptocurrencies as well. Just like owning stocks and real estate, you must pay capital gains taxes after you sell your crypto assets for a profit. If you take a loss, you can lower your tax bill. Now, if you hold your crypto assets for over a year, you often get a better tax rate. This rate is called a *long-term capital gains tax*.

TIP

You can calculate your capital gains by doing simple math on the amount you gained or lost after you purchased your cryptos. For example, if you buy one Bitcoin for $5,000 and sell it for $10,000, you've made $5,000 in capital gains minus the amount you paid for transaction fees.

INTRODUCING SOME CRYPTO TAX EXPERTS

The crypto-investing market is a fairly new industry, so many traditional tax folks may not have the necessary knowledge to help you with the best crypto tax decisions. Doing a search within my LinkedIn connections, I found some U.S.-based crypto tax experts who may be able to help you out:

- **Camuso CPA:** Camuso CPA is a certified public accountant (CPA) firm that works with investors, businesses, and individuals nationwide and is a market leader in cryptocurrency tax advisory. In fact, Camuso CPA is the first CPA firm in the country to accept cryptocurrency payments in return for professional services. The firm caters to clients from Camuso CPA's network of investors, miners, and small businesses along with taxpayers who need help dealing with Bitcoin and other cryptocurrencies. My point of contact here is the firm's founder, Patrick Camuso. You can reach him through the firm's website: www.camusocpa.com.

- **Crypto Tax Girl:** My point of contact here is Laura Walter, a CPA specializing in cryptocurrency tax. Her mission is to bring tax clarity to those who currently hold crypto, those who have held crypto in the past, or those who are looking to acquire crypto in the future. You can check her out here: www.cryptotaxgirl.com.

Short-term capital gains taxes

A *short-term capital gains tax* is very similar to the mining and crypto income tax I mention earlier in this chapter. If you sell or trade your cryptos regularly and hold them less than a year, then your profit or losses may be categorized as income, which often has less favorable tax implications. Even if you don't officially cash out your cryptos, you may still be subject to short-term taxes if you use the cryptocurrency to purchase stuff, whether it's tangible products or other cryptocurrencies.

REMEMBER

Active traders who make a few trades every now and then are subject to different tax laws than day-traders who trade cryptos for a living. I discuss the difference in the later section "Reducing your trading tax."

Minimizing Your Crypto Taxes

Whether you've earned your crypto as income or you've seen capital gains on your assets, the following sections show you some ways to cut the amount you owe the IRS.

Lowering your mining income tax

In the United States, you may get a better tax rate if you create a company or a business entity around your mining activities instead of mining as a self-employed individual. By doing so, you can take advantage of the tax breaks business owners get for paying for business-related stuff and get a better tax rate than individuals.

Got that high-end computer to mine Bitcoin? Claim it on your business and lower your taxable income. Got your computer set up with mining equipment like application-specific integrated circuits (ASICs) and expensive graphics processing units (GPUs)? Paying a ton on electricity when mining? Congrats, you can get a tax break on the rewards you got paid through mining.

REMEMBER

That is, of course, if your coins are actually worth something. Even at a personal level, your mining operation can be very profitable, but it also can cost you a ton — way more than its rewards, especially if the crypto market isn't doing very well at the time. At the time of writing, if your overall net income is more than $60,000, filing as an S corporation (or an LLC that's taxed as an S corporation) may help you. Consult a tax professional for guidance.

REMEMBER

You can claim your expenses on your business only if the LLC, C corporation, or S corporation was created prior to earning the income from mining. Anything earned prior to the company formation can't be included under the company for tax purposes.

Reducing your trading tax

Do you consider yourself a day-trader? Then you may be eligible to pay way less in taxes than occasional traders. But first you must pass the IRS day-trading test by being able to answer "yes" to these three questions:

» Do you aim to make profit from the daily price changes in the crypto market instead of holding your positions long term or even overnight?

» Do you spend most of your day trading instead of having a full-time day job?

» Do you have a substantial and regular trading pattern and make a ton of trades on a daily basis?

If you do qualify as a day-trader, you may be able to claim your rewards as a self-employed individual. This designation means you can deduct all your trading-related expenses on Schedule C like any other sole proprietor.

TIP

According to https://finance.zacks.com, your corporation will be taxed based on your profits and losses whether or not it's a one-owner corporation. You can also use the money you make from day-trading to pay for your insurance, health care, and employee benefits, if you have any.

WARNING

Tracking your short-term crypto-trading activities can be incredibly confusing. The industry has a ton of volatility and market fluctuation, and an exploding number of tradable cryptos are available to you 24/7. These situations make monitoring your resources manually almost impossible. Later in this chapter, I introduce some tracking resources you can use for your trading activities.

Bringing down your capital gains taxes

If you can't qualify as a day-trader (see the preceding section), your best bet to reduce your crypto capital gains taxes is to be a long-term investor. That means holding your assets for over a year. Don't sell, trade, or buy anything with your cryptocurrencies within a year of your purchase.

As I mention earlier in this chapter, capital gains taxes on investments held for more than one year (long term) can be much lower than capital gains taxes on investments held for less than one year (short term). In 2022, long-term capital gains are taxed at 0 percent, 15 percent, or 20 percent, depending on your tax bracket. If you're in the high-income tax bracket, for example, your capital gains tax rate may be 20 percent. You can find out more about tax brackets here: www.irs.gov/newsroom/irs-provides-tax-inflation-adjustments-for-tax-year-2022.

REMEMBER

Trading one cryptocurrency for another may put you at risk of paying more taxes. To purchase certain cryptocurrencies at specific crypto exchanges, you have no choice but to convert your cryptos to one another in a shorter time frame, but if you make a huge profit on the initial crypto, you no longer fall into the category of long-term investor. Talk to a tax professional to ensure that you're paying the correct rate.

Checking the rate of your state

In the United States, different states have different state tax laws, and some states have better rates than others for specific groups of people or certain industries. Some states like Florida are considered a "retirement haven" because you don't have to pay individual income and death tax, and you'll also get a ton of asset protection and property tax benefits.

When it comes to cryptocurrency investors, certain states like Wyoming have great tax incentives for crypto companies and investors because cryptocurrencies are exempted from property taxation altogether. In 2018, Wyoming became the first state to define cryptocurrencies as an entirely new asset class. Wyoming officials labeled it as the "utility token bill" and passed it into law in March 2018; it was designed to exempt specific cryptocurrencies from state money transmission laws.

As cryptocurrencies become more popular, you can expect more states to create such laws to incentivize businesses and individuals to bring their crypto talents and money there. That's why it's important that you're in the know with the latest developments in the industry. Websites such as www.coindesk.com can help you get such information in a timely manner.

Evaluating Taxable Income from Crypto Transactions

At the end of the day, reporting your crypto income and capital gains is on you. You must keep track of all your taxable events, which means every time you sell or trade your crypto assets for other stuff. At the time of writing, the IRS doesn't require third-party reporting for cryptocurrencies (meaning the entities you buy the cryptos from don't have to report the sales), which makes the tracking and reporting more complicated.

Here are some tips and points to keep in mind when you're evaluating your crypto activities.

Tracking your crypto activity

The crypto market is expanding, and more monitoring resources are becoming available for traders, investors, and miners alike. Here are a few resources you can check out:

>> **CoinTracker** (www.cointracker.io): CoinTracker automatically syncs your crypto transactions with a growing list of exchanges such as Coinbase, Kraken, KuCoin, and more to generate tax forms. It also has an online support team.

>> **CoinTracking** (https://cointracking.info): CoinTracking analyzes your investment activity and generates a tax report based on your profits and losses.

>> **CoinLedger** (https://coinledger.io): This website connects you to a growing list of exchanges such as Coinbase, Binance, Bittrex, and more, and helps you calculate your crypto taxes in a few minutes. It has great online customer support that answers your questions immediately.

Handling crypto forks

In Chapter 5, I talk about how you can get free coins when a cryptocurrency is *forked* (where a portion of a crypto's community decides to create its own version of the currency).

Of course, nothing is completely free, and you're likely required to pay taxes on the additional cryptos you receive through the fork. For example, if you own Ethereum and it undergoes a hard fork that pays you an equal amount of the new cryptocurrency in addition to your original Ethereum assets, you must pay ordinary taxes on the new free coins as opposed to long-term capital gains tax. You pay these taxes based on the U.S. dollar value of the new cryptocurrency the day you receive it.

The IRS still offers little guidance regarding hard forks and taxation. Make sure you consult with a tax professional and stay ahead of the game by tracking all your crypto records using professional websites such as `https://coinledger.io`.

Reporting international crypto investments

The cryptocurrency market and its rules are constantly evolving. That's why you must remain up-to-date about all your crypto transactions. But even if you invest in cryptocurrencies outside the United States, you must report the activity to the IRS.

At the time of writing, you don't have to report your cryptocurrency on your FBAR. This guideline is based on a 2014 IRS statement that said, "The Financial Crimes Enforcement Network, which issues regulatory guidance pertaining to Reports of Foreign Bank and Financial Accounts (FBARs), is not requiring that digital (or virtual) currency accounts be reported on an FBAR at this time but may consider requiring such accounts to be reported in the future." Make sure you keep up-to-date with the IRS crypto regulations because they're subject to change every year; consult a tax professional. Also, keep in mind that not having to report your cryptos on your FBAR doesn't mean you can hide your foreign cryptocurrency activities from the IRS.

WARNING

It bears repeating: You're responsible for knowing the tax ramifications of your crypto activity. The IRS has been going after cryptocurrency investments inside and outside the United States. It even forced Coinbase to turn over its customer records in 2017 and 2022. People who simply didn't know about the crypto tax implications got into trouble alongside those who were trying to hide their crypto investments.

4

The Part of Tens

Get an overview of what to consider before getting started in the world of cryptocurrencies.

Discover the best things you can do when you're sitting on losses.

Chapter **15**

Ten Considerations Before Getting Started with Cryptos

re you ready to try cryptocurrency investing? In this chapter, I highlight some of the most important things to think about before starting your crypto-investing journey, many of which I explain in detail in earlier chapters.

Don't Get Too Excited

REMEMBER

Starting to explore a whole new world is always exciting. Starting early can also sometimes get you ahead of the crowd. However, just like any type of investment avenue, cryptocurrency investing requires discipline, risk management, and a whole lot of patience. You shouldn't treat crypto investing as a get-rich-quick scheme. Even though your hopes may be up, as we've seen in the many ups and downs in the crypto market in the past decade, the likelihood of seeing such gains in such a short amount of time again is pretty low.

The reason is simple: The crypto market is driven by a whole lot of hype and FOMO (fear of missing out). Investors are becoming more educated about the whole market and making more calculated investment decisions. And so should you!

Measure Your Risk Tolerance

REMEMBER

Is crypto investing right for you? How much of your money should you invest in this market? Can you stomach high volatility? Do you have the patience to wait out potential storms? You can find the answer to all these questions by measuring your risk tolerance. This essential first step to any type of investment includes both your willingness to risk and your ability to risk. Turn to Chapter 3 for an explanation of different risk types and resources on measuring your risk tolerance.

Protect Your Crypto Wallet

A *crypto wallet* is where you store your digital assets like Bitcoin; you have to have one before you buy a cryptocurrency. So many different types of wallets are available, some of which come from the cryptocurrency exchanges that sell you the cryptos. But those aren't the most secure types of wallets, and they've often been the victims of hacking attacks that resulted in the loss of cryptos.

Chapter 7 details different methods you can use to protect your cryptocurrency wallet before you start investing.

Find the Best Crypto Exchange/ Broker for You

Some of the most popular places to get your hands on cryptocurrencies are exchanges and brokers. Some of these marketplaces offer only a few cryptocurrencies, and some carry a wide range. Some have higher transaction fees. Some have better customer service. Some have a better security reputation. With some, you can exchange your *fiat currency* (which is the local currency of your country, such as the U.S. dollar) for cryptocurrencies. With others, you must already have a cryptocurrency, such as Bitcoin, and exchange it for other digital assets, such as Binance exchange's coin (BNB) or Ethereum (ETH).

To find the best crypto exchange or broker, you must go through all these options and see which one fits your crypto needs most. In Chapter 6, I give a more thorough overview of different types of cryptocurrency exchanges and brokers out there.

Sometimes you're better off using multiple exchanges for different purposes. Personally, I use two!

TIP

Determine Whether You Should Invest Short Term or Long Term

The time frame you invest in depends on your risk tolerance, your financial goals, your current financial situation, and the amount of time you have on your hands. For example, if you have a full-time job that requires most of your attention, you don't want to worry about short-term management of your crypto portfolio, or any other asset for that matter. You want to focus your energy on your main job (so you don't get fired) and manage your investment portfolio every few weeks or so to stay on top of things. Investing long term also requires less risk taking.

In Chapter 3, I walk you through calculating your risk tolerance. In Chapters 11 and 12, I explore more about short-term and long-term investing. You can also check out my Make Your Money Work For You PowerCourse by attending this free online Masterclass: https://investdiva.com/masterclass.

TIP

Start Small

If you're just testing the waters and you don't have a solid financial plan, don't dump a whole chunk of money into the market. Start with a few hundred dollars, or whatever you can afford, and slowly grow your portfolio. Also, don't use your money to invest in only one type of crypto. If you're new to investing in anything, don't allocate all your investment funds to cryptos, either. Diversification is key until you find your sweet spot, especially for new investors.

REMEMBER

Personally, my biggest chunk of monthly investments typically goes into myself to learn new skills. The second chunk goes into scaling my business. Having a business is super-important when building wealth, especially because it gives you access to many tax-break techniques that are unavailable to normal people with a regular job. The third chunk goes into online financial markets such as stocks and cryptocurrencies.

REMEMBER

Unless they get super-lucky, most millionaires don't become wealthy just by investing in the online financial markets. There are many avenues for building wealth. In my most popular five-day Build More Wealth challenge, I unveil the five steps I used to go from zero to over a $5 million net worth in ten years:

1. Breaking the wealth mindset you were likely handed down by your parents and society so you're open to receiving more wealth

2. Increasing your income by becoming a business owner

3. Investing your increased income and making your money have babies!

4. Increasing your impact and influence

5. Building a wealth ecosystem where your money makes more money, and the money your money makes also makes more money, to build generational wealth

Join the challenge here: https://buildmorewealth.com!

Follow the Cause

Many cryptocurrencies are based on blockchain applications that aim to solve a specific problem in the world or in society (see Chapter 4 for the scoop on blockchain technology). Blockchain applications can provide a solution to almost any problem that's close to your heart, from banking the underbanked to preventing voter fraud to helping out farmers. By investing in the cryptocurrency of a blockchain application whose cause appeals to you, you support that cause in achieving its goals faster. This sense of accomplishment can make investing more meaningful and more fun for you.

Focusing on causes also helps when you're picking cryptocurrencies out of the hundreds of options available. I talk about different crypto categories in Chapter 8.

Mull Over Mining

Mining is the backbone of many cryptocurrencies like Bitcoin. *Mining* cryptocurrencies refers to solving complex math equations to guess random numbers by using powerful computers; successfully solving the problems earns you a reward in cryptos. Mining is normally considered very expensive because you have to invest in expensive computer gadgets and use up a lot of electricity while you run your computer for mining. But sometimes, especially depending on the cryptocurrency's value, mining may make sense. For example, if your electricity bill for mining is going to be lower than the cost of actually buying that cryptocurrency, you may want to consider mining instead.

TIP

You can check out mining profitability by using mining calculators like the ones at https://investdiva.com/mining-calculator.

Look into Investing in Other Assets First

If you've never invested in anything, you may find the whole cryptocurrency industry a bit overwhelming. Educating yourself about developing investment strategies while also learning about a financial sector you've never had any personal experience with can be difficult. In this case, you may consider starting by investing in things you know, like the stock of a company you're already familiar with. After you become comfortable investing in things you know, you can then expand your portfolio to new vehicles like cryptocurrencies. Turn to Chapter 2 for details on different types of assets.

Get a Support Group

Most people trade alone on their computers or smartphones. That can soon become a very lonely activity, especially if none of your friends are into it. It may become even more dangerous if you're getting all your investing information from Twitter and news media that are fighting for your attention through clickbait. When the markets are going against you, you can get frustrated, and when the markets are doing well, you may get overwhelmed, not knowing when to get out.

Though I explore strategy development methods to identify the best entry and exit points in this book, it always helps to have people who are in the same boat as you. Many cryptocurrencies have channels on the Telegram app or their very own rooms on websites like Reddit and Discord, where you can share information and commiserate with other crypto investors.

Unfortunately, as crypto gains popularity, these public domains are being flooded with bots, scammers, and impersonators. If you ever feel lonely or overwhelmed or simply want to join one of the most authentic investing groups ever, consider joining the Invest Diva Movement. You can discover how you can join us by attending the free Masterclass detailed earlier in this chapter.

Chapter **16**

Ten Potential Moves When Your Crypto Portfolio Is Down

Whether you're a short-term trader or a long-term investor, at times you'll find your crypto portfolio in the red zone with one or more of your holdings moving against you. Before you know it, you can find yourself in a FUD situation (crypto talk for fear, uncertainty, and doubt), which can become incredibly frustrating and contribute to your making an emotional decision rather than executing a well-thought-out strategy. This chapter covers ten potential next steps when the market isn't on your side.

Do Nothing

In most cases, patience is a profitable virtue. If you got into a specific position after doing a thorough analysis from all points of the Invest Diva Diamond Analysis (IDDA; see Chapter 9), chances are, the current dip in the market is temporary. If you give it time, you may find yourself in positive territory again. Even the toughest markets find their way back up again if you wait long enough.

Of course, the cryptocurrency market is very new, and not all crypto assets have shown enough evidence to prove that it follows the sentiment of other markets like the stock market. However, because most investors categorize cryptos as a capital gain asset just like stocks, many of the older cryptocurrencies such as Bitcoin and Ethereum have started following a market psychology similar to traditional assets. *Capital gain assets* are those you invest in expecting a gain in their value to give you a positive return. Of course, waiting for a long time may not be suitable for all traders and investors.

REMEMBER

Depending on where you are in your life and what your financial goals are, you may be able to take advantage of making time your best investing friend. If you're on a ten-year plan to reach a financial goal — buying a house, for example — you shouldn't worry about the minor ups and downs in the markets.

Reevaluate Your Risk Tolerance

As I discuss in Chapter 3, measuring your risk tolerance is the very first step you need to take when you start investing in anything. But as life goes on, circumstances change in ways that may impact your risk tolerance. A down period for your portfolio may be a good time to reassess your risk tolerance to identify the best thing to do next.

For example, if you now have a higher risk tolerance than you did when you entered a position, you may consider adding to your losing position as I discuss later in this chapter. But if your financial situation has impacted your risk tolerance in a negative way and you don't have much time on your hands, you may consider cutting losses (also described later).

REMEMBER

The bottom line, however, is this: Never make a rash decision based only on emotions and the *feeling* that your risk tolerance is high or low. By carefully calculating your tolerance, you may get a surprise to the contrary.

Look at the Bigger Picture

You can evaluate the bigger picture from both technical and fundamental viewpoints:

» On the technical side, you may get a better idea of where the market is going by switching to longer-term time frames. For example, the market may be on a very long-term uptrend, where the price has been going up for quite some time. In that case, the current dip may be a healthy correction, which can even be a good point to buy more of your crypto asset.

» On the fundamental side, you need to go back to the basic reasons you chose to invest in a specific cryptocurrency — things like the cause, the management and community, the technology, and everything else that can contribute to the long-term growth of the cryptocurrency's valuation. Turn to Chapter 9 for more on fundamental analysis.

Research the Fundamental Reasons the Crypto Is Down

When evaluating the bigger picture (as I discuss in the preceding section), you may find that a core fundamental problem is driving the devaluation of your crypto asset. Perhaps the cryptocurrency is no longer backed by giant financial corporations, has gotten involved in a scam, or is running out of money and unable to invest in its technology.

You can use your favorite search engine to look into the fundamental details of any specific cryptocurrency. Simply search the crypto's name online and go through the most recent search results under the "News" category. If the fundamentals have changed for the worse and are the reason the value is down, you may need to reevaluate your position and potentially cut your losses.

TIP

As a crypto enthusiast, I recommend that you keep up-to-date with the most recent crypto news anyway by following websites such as https://cryptobriefing.com, www.coindesk.com, and www.newsbtc.com.

Consider Hedging

Hedging is a common investment practice to manage risk. By *hedging*, you basically go against your current position or industry to offset the risk it involves. There is hedging in derivatives like options and futures, but you can also hedge by diversification (described in the following two sections), as well as by going against your current position.

For example, if you've bought Bitcoin versus another cryptocurrency like Ethereum, and Bitcoin's price is dropping, you can consider selling Bitcoin in a different trade and take advantage of the current downtrend.

TIP

Positional hedging is especially useful when you're trading cryptocurrencies on brokerages that allow short selling. For more on hedging strategies, consider joining Invest Diva's premium group (find out more here: https://investdiva.com/masterclass).

Diversify within Crypto Assets

Adding other crypto assets that are exposed to a different type of risk than your losing cryptocurrency is another form of hedging (see the preceding section) that may help you balance out your portfolio. Identifying such cryptocurrencies can be very difficult, though, because at least at the time of this writing, most crypto assets are exposed to similar types of risk. See Chapter 3 to find out more about risk and Chapter 9 to identify top-performing cryptos.

Diversify across Other Financial Assets

This is the good old "Don't put all your eggs in one basket" thing. If your analysis shows a longer doomsday period in the cryptocurrency market, while other financial instruments like bonds are lucrative, you may consider diversifying away from cryptocurrencies to distribute your risk. This approach is yet again a different form of hedging, which I discuss earlier in this chapter. Turn to Chapters 2 and 10 for more on diversification.

Exchange with a Better Crypto

After redoing the IDDA for your crypto assets that are down (see Chapter 9), you may realize that a particular crypto isn't worth holding onto. Unlike the stock market, where you have no choice but to take losses, in the crypto world you may have the option to exchange with a different, better cryptocurrency.

For example, say you bought a bunch of a crypto called Crappy-Coin at a high price, but its value has been plummeting with no signs of recovery, the founder of the blockchain has gone missing, and their Discord channel is full of bots. At the same time, you hear of a new, cheap cryptocurrency with a bright future, a legit community, and a project that will help humankind. Though you may not be able to buy a ton of the new crypto with your devalued CrappyCoin, you still may benefit from cutting your losses on CrappyCoin early and exchanging with the better crypto.

Think about Adding to
Your Current Position

Warren Buffett is a famous investor who adds on to his losing position — buys more of a falling stock at a cheaper price — when the markets drop. This is also known as *buying the dip*. But, of course, he does so only for assets that have strong fundamentals and are in the midst of a temporary, healthy pullback. He also can handle the risk because, well, he's a gazillionaire (although, at the time of writing, he still hasn't given in to cryptocurrency investing).

The "buy the dip" strategy has the potential to work for cryptos as well. Before you get too excited, keep in mind that the cryptocurrency market may act differently from the stock market (which is what Warren Buffett invests in) and may continue to be unpredictable and volatile in the coming years. That's why you must make sure you can afford a bigger prospective loss for a period of time until the crypto market gets back on track.

WARNING

Avoid using margin and borrowing money from your broker when adding to your losing position. Those approaches increase your investment risk.

By adding on to your losing position, you can bring your average holding price lower and, therefore, profit more when the price eventually goes back up.

Contemplate Cutting Losses

Personally (and famously), I'm not the biggest fan of *stop-losses*, which are market orders you set to cut your losses if the price of an asset like a crypto is going against your investment position. In my time working at brokers on Wall Street, I discovered that stop-losses mainly helped the broker make money while the investor lost. However, sometimes you have no other option for various reasons, including personal risk tolerance and market conditions. In that case, you may want to consider simply getting out of your losing position, calling it quits, and focusing on a different source of profit.

Short-term traders are more likely to use stop-losses (see Chapter 11). Long-term investors (see Chapter 12) are supposed to have made the risk-management calculation ahead of time, making sure they have enough time to wait things out.

Taking losses can be very emotionally draining. If you decide to take a loss, be sure not to beat yourself up too much. I've had students who had given up on investing altogether before joining the Invest Diva Movement, because they had lost money in the markets. There is no success without failure. Your long-term success is only defined by your ability to get back up. Let this be a lesson, and move on to other opportunities!

Index

Numbers

A

B

About the Author

Kiana Danial is an internationally recognized personal investing, entrepreneurship, and wealth creation expert who has been featured in *The Wall Street Journal*, *TIME*, *Forbes*, *Kiplinger*, Business Insider, TheStreet, Nasdaq, Fox Business, CNNi, Yahoo! Finance, and Cheddar.

Kiana is a highly sought-after commentator, professional speaker, and executive coach who has reported on the financial markets directly from the floor of the New York Stock Exchange (NYSE) and Nasdaq; using her Diva Wealth Ecosystem, she built a $6 million-plus net worth within three years.

Kiana's books include *Wall Street Journal* and *USA Today* bestseller *Million Dollar Family Secrets*, *Cryptocurrency Investing For Dummies* (Wiley), and the coauthored bestsellers, *Million Dollar Identity* and *Million Dollar Moms*.

Kiana has also won the 2CC and 2CCX awards from ClickFunnels and has spoken at the same stage as Tony Robbins.

Born and raised in Iran to a Jewish family as a religious minority, Kiana was awarded a scholarship from the Japanese government to study electrical engineering in Japan in 2003, where she obtained two degrees in electrical engineering and researched on quantum physics, being the only female and foreigner in each of her classes. She also became a recurring guest star on the Japanese TV show *Generation Y*. Kiana came to the United States in 2010, securing a job on Wall Street within two weeks of her arrival, and going on to become an adjunct professor of finance at Baruch College in Manhattan.

As the CEO of Invest Diva, Kiana's mission is to empower and educate women to take control of their financial futures by investing in the online financial markets. Kiana provides her Invest Diva students with daily personal finance and investing content via social media, and financial education via Invest Diva's free Masterclass and the "Make Your Money Work For You" Power-Course. Kiana has grown a large social media following thanks to her fun and educational TikTok and YouTube videos on investing and personal finance, as well as her show/podcast *The Invest Diva Movement*, where she features timely financial advice and has interviewed investors such as Guy Spier, Anthony Scaramucci, Nancy Tengler, James McDonald, and Christina Qi; development coaches such as Brian Tracy, Bob Proctor, and Jack Canfield; and financial advisor, author, and podcast host Suze Orman.

Kiana's mission with Invest Diva is to help one million moms take control of their financial futures and build generational wealth so they can change the world and build better futures.

Dedication

To all the Invest Diva students who inspire me to continue leading the Invest Diva movement by sharing their wins daily.

Author's Acknowledgments

I'd like to thank numerous people for their help in making this book a reality. I would like to thank my family and my amazing Invest Diva team who kept my household, our company, and our mission afloat while I dedicated my time to completing this book. In particular, I would like to thank Tristan Craige, as well as Jacqui Short and Arleny Lopez-Cordero, for their continued support.

Publisher's Acknowledgments

Senior Acquisitions Editor:
Tracy Boggier

Senior Managing Editor:
Kristie Pyles

Compilation Editor:
Georgette Beatty

Editor: Elizabeth Kuball

Proofreader: Debbye Butler

Production Editor:
Tamilmani Varadharaj

Cover Design: Wiley

Cover Images:
Frame: © aleksandarvelasevic/
Getty Images
Paper texture: © Dmitrich/
Getty Images
Inset: © 13ree_design/
Adobe Stock